Bibliographical guide to the study of the literature of the U.S.A.

Clarence Gohdes and Sanford E. Marovitz
Bibliographical guide to the study of the
literature of the U.S.A. Fifth edition, completely
revised and enlarged. Duke University Press.   Durham,
N.C.   1984

77660

© 1959, 1963, 1970, 1976, 1984 Duke University Press

All rights reserved

Printed in the United States of America

Library of Congress Cataloging in Publication Data

Gohdes, Clarence Louis Frank, 1901–
    Bibliographical guide to the study of the literature
of the U.S.A.

    Includes indexes.
    1. American literature—Bibliography.   2. Bibliography
—Bibliography—American literature.   3. United States—
Bibliography.   I. Marovitz, Sanford E.   II. Title.
Z1225.G6   1984   016.81   84-1677
[PS88]
ISBN 0-8223-0592-5

With
love and thanks
to
Nora

Contents

Preface

When Professor Clarence Gohdes compiled and published in 1957 the original edition of his *Bibliographical Guide to the Study of the Literature of the U.S.A.*, it was, as he wrote then, "the first of its kind to see print," for it was directed entirely toward facilitating American literary study in particular rather than both English and American with only token respect being paid to the latter. As the first of its kind, it had no competition then, and it has none now. Although the past quarter century has seen a plethora of reference materials on all literary subjects emerging from various specialized publishing houses and university presses, the *Guide* remains unique and true to its original purpose.

Like its four predecessors, the present volume undertakes to provide lists of books and articles that will aid the professional student of the literature of the United States in the acquiring of information and in the techniques of research. It is believed that it will prove useful to teachers of American literature and to reference librarians, as well as to graduate students writing master's theses or doctoral dissertations.

In addition to materials having to do with methods of research and with American literature in its several phases, essential tools are herein listed for the study of such related topics as American history, biography, religion, philosophy, ethnic backgrounds, international relations, and the American language, not only because of the patent need for a cultural context but also because of the special interests of a large number of students or scholars who investigate the literature of the United States in such interdepartmental programs as American Studies or American Civilization. Historians of ideas will find that their favored approach has also been recognized in the selection of titles for this *Guide*. Calculated consideration has, furthermore, been given to American literature as a part of comparative studies, and a special section is devoted to the relationship of the national letters with foreign countries and foreign literatures. The compilers have borne in mind not only the manifest importance of foreign influences upon the belles lettres of the United States but the repercussions, so to speak, of the national literature in foreign countries.

The various headings for the individual sections of the *Guide* will usually provide sufficient direction to the reader, but indexes of subjects and authors, compilers, and editors are appended as additional aids to the locating of information. In some cases the individual items that make up the contents of this book are recorded in "short title" style, but as a rule the subtitle seemed advantageous in calling attention to the contents or purpose of a given work, and it therefore has been printed. Cross-references are supplied at the ends of various sections calling attention to important items classified elsewhere, but the index of subjects will usually provide further aid in locating items dealing in part with a given topic. Very few anthologies have been included, and most of those that do appear are listed because of their special editorial or bibliographical contents.

Despite its comprehensiveness, this *Guide* has been made compact enough to carry easily in a briefcase or bookbag. Its annotations make no attempt to summarize the contents of each item listed but rather to define them concisely and clearly as well as to state in a similar manner the thesis or purpose wherever these are not made explicit by the title or subtitle. It is meant to serve as an interdisciplinary guide, but the focus is distinctly on American literature and American literary scholarship; although it may be possible in some cases that the interdisciplinary listings provide an introductory checklist for those specific areas, their purpose in the present context is to offer a wide-ranging field from which to approach American literary studies.

In revising for the fifth edition, the editors have gone beyond simply updating the previous compilation in order to make the list current. Although the format remains exactly the same as in the earlier editions, certain areas have been expanded, and the subject of one section has been completely changed. Whereas section 19 was originally devoted to "Arts Other than Literature," new reference materials for so vast an area have increased to the extent that covering it other than superficially would have been impossible in only a few pages; consequently, we have deleted it altogether in favor of citing elsewhere in the *Guide* those works that are devoted specifically to literary study in relation to the other arts. In its place, section 19 is now given over entirely to "Women's Studies," a subject that has developed rapidly and received a great deal of attention in the past decade, enough to have acquired its own vast body of reference materials and several journals that focus entirely on that area.

We have also added a subdivision entitled "Computer Aids," which may be found in section 3, "Technical Procedures." The study of popular culture as a discipline expanded markedly during the 1970s also, and therefore it has been given a subheading under section 8, "American Studies." In keeping with the abundant critical attention devoted to literature from a psychological perspective in the past several years, "Psychology" now has its own section (16), and a substantial segment of it deals specifically with the relation of psychology to literature. The subheading "Film and Literature" has been included in section 23, "Drama, Theater, and Film," in an attempt to provide a guide to new resources for the growing number of students and researchers interested in film and its literary antecedents.

Because we hope that this *Guide* will be of service to educators on many levels, we have included in section 26 a special subsection on "Children's Literature," a subject that now warrants a separate division in the Modern Language Association of America. Section 29, "Special Topics and Themes," ends with a subsection on "Science Fiction and Utopian Writings" and another on "Literature of the Sea," subjects that have been receiving increasing scholarly attention in recent years. Also expanded has been section 31, "Racial and Other Minorities"; subdividing that section into separate listings for the different minority groups will make it easier for students of racial, religious, and ethnic studies to use it. Similarly, section 33, "The

American Language," has been enlarged and subdivided into specific areas of linguistic study. All of the subheadings have been included in the table of contents, which should expedite searching when used with the subject and author/editor indexes; together these tools should enable researchers to pinpoint the needed items with a minimum of time and effort.

One of the inevitable problems that occur in attempting to keep a guide of this kind both comprehensive and current, without being superficial in coverage and without relinquishing its compactness, is determining what is significant enough to be added or retained and which items previously listed may be excised without real loss. In the present revision we have eliminated reprints as well as many superseded items in favor of increasing the number of important original and revised editions. Although this modification regarding the listing of reprints may cause some inconvenience, we believe that it will be minimal and of far less consequence than omitting useful original editions and revisions, for reprints are usually easy to identify and locate once the original author, title, and publication data are known. Moreover, to provide greater historical perspective whenever it has been considered useful to do so, we have given publication data for the first edition as well as for the most recent one, though for most items that are revised at regular intervals, we have listed only the current edition. Also for the first time, the names of publishers have been included for all titles listed in this *Guide*.

Another change that time has necessitated pertains to the organization of items within the sections. The increased number of items over the years has led us toward listing entries generally according to an alphabetical arrangement of authors' surnames within sections, subsections, and smaller groups of items where such groups are justified. Because not all sections are equally suitable in content for alphabetizing consistently from beginning to end, some purposeful inconsistency in arranging has been necessary. Nevertheless, we believe that the required items will be easily found under the new system. Two examples to illustrate the value of employing partially different methods of organization among the sections are section 20, "Chief General Bibliographies," and section 32, "Relations with Other Countries"; whereas section 20 is consistently alphabetized throughout because the content is entirely composed of bibliographical listings, section 32 is alphabetized only within the subsections in order that readers may locate more easily reference materials to specific countries. Wherever sectional alphabetizing has been chosen over small clusters of related titles, cross-references both in the annotations and at the end of the section, when used in conjunction with the subject index, will enable researchers to find what they need expeditiously and without the confusion that may be easily generated through the inevitable overlapping that occurs with a proliferation of such small and often interlocking groups. Also, in the sections in which grouping occurs, compiled reference works (e.g., bibliographies, directories, etc.) will normally precede critical and historical studies.

Needless to say, the array of reference materials worthy of being included in a research guide of this kind is very vast indeed, and judicious choices have had to be made. Nevertheless, despite our cautious selectivity, almost nine hundred revised editions and new titles have been added; although most of the new titles are those of recent publication, some identify earlier studies that additional consideration, often upon the advice of other scholars we have consulted, has led us to include in the fifth edition. In selecting titles we of course have assumed the ultimate responsibility for making the final decisions, but we have had the advice of a considerable number of the ablest scholars in a wide variety of special areas.

One of the great pleasures of seeing through publication a work that has been made possible only with the assistance of many willing consultants is that of publicly expressing our immense gratitude for their time and aid. Among colleagues at Kent State University we thank especially Marilyn Apseloff, Robert D. Bamberg, Diana Culbertson, Thomas M. Davis, Donald M. Hassler, Thomas J. Hines, Thomas F. Marshall, Martin K. Nurmi, Sidney W. Reid, and Robert L. Tener, of the English Department; Lawrence S. Kaplan, of the History Department; and Doris J. Turner, of the Department of Romance Languages.

We are also grateful to the following scholars and experts from other institutions: A. Owen Aldridge (Illinois), Martha Banta (California, Los Angeles), Morris Beja (Ohio State), Sacvan Bercovitch (Harvard), Hans Borchers, Siegfried Neuweiler, and Alfred Webber (Tübingen, FRG), Barbara A. Brothers (Youngstown State), Eberhard Brüning (Karl Marx, Leipzig, German Dem. Rep.), Jules Chametzky (Massachusetts), Carol Donley (Hiram), Clayton L. Eichelberger (Texas, Arlington), Everett Emerson (North Carolina), Fred Erisman (Texas Christian), Richard W. Etulain (New Mexico), Warren French (Indiana-Purdue), Martha B. Gibbons (Cleveland Ballet), Arnold Goldman (Keele, Staffordshire, England), Phyllis Gorfain (Oberlin), Giles B. Gunn (North Carolina), Ihab Hassan (Wisconsin, Milwaukee), Wilson Heflin (U.S. Naval Academy), Michael J. Hoffman (California, Davis), Norman N. Holland (SUNY, Buffalo), Karl Keller (San Diego State), Edoardo A. Lebano (Indiana), Mary Jane Lupton (Morgan State), Franciszek Lyra (Warsaw, Poland), Michael T. Marsden (Bowling Green), Jay Martin (Southern California), Raven I. McDavid, Jr. (Chicago), W. Gordon Milne (Lake Forest), Joel Myerson (South Carolina), George Perkins (Eastern Michigan), Olga M. Ragusa (Columbia), Joseph W. Reish (Western Michigan), Kenneth M. Roemer (Texas, Arlington), Wendy Rose (Richmond, Calif.), Bruce A. Rosenberg (Brown), Jane A. Rosenberg (Council on Library Resources, Washington, D.C.), Donald A. Ross (Minnesota), Louis D. Rubin, Jr. (North Carolina), Kenneth Silverman (New York), Vivian Sobchack (California, Santa Cruz), G. Thomas Tanselle (Guggenheim Foundation), Alan Trachtenberg (Yale), Masao Tsunematsu (Shimane; Matsue, Japan), Kermit Vanderbilt (San Diego State), Edward Wagenknecht (Boston), Daniel Walden (Pennsylvania State), Max Westbrook (Texas), and Edwin Wolf, 2d (Library Company, Philadelphia).

The staff of the Kent State University Libraries has been of inestimable aid throughout the process of revising for the fifth edition; we are particularly grateful to Dean H. Keller, Curator of Special Collections, and to Martha G. Goold, of the reference section. Our thanks are due as well to Mary A. Gaylord, Rosemary D. Harrick, Ruth C. Main, and Sara G. Osgood, of the reference staff; their tolerance and patience as well as their knowledge have been a blessing indeed. Joe Rees, of the reference department, Perkins Library, Duke University, also provided valuable assistance.

We also wish to acknowledge with gratitude the assistance and care that Joanne Ferguson, John Menapace, Richard Rowson, and Pam Morrison, of the Duke University Press, have provided in arranging for the publication of this edition. Moreover, we owe a special debt to Philip St. Clair and Eleonora D. Marovitz, who helped with the indexes, and to Paula Reed, student assistant at Kent State, whose thoroughness and sustained good humor were invaluable. Finally, we deeply appreciate the financial assistance granted by Kent State University, which has covered many of the incidental costs that have gone into the preparation of this *Guide*. We wish to share the credit with all the above-mentioned scholars, though we accept, of course, full responsibility for any and all errors or omissions.

September 1983

Clarence Gohdes
Duke University

Sanford E. Marovitz
Kent State University

Bibliographical guide to the study of the literature of the U.S.A.

1. *Aids to information on all subjects*

1.1 **Alexander, Gerard L.   Guide to atlases: world, regional, national, thematic; an international listing of atlases published since 1950.** Metuchen, N.J.: Scarecrow Pr., 1971. Supplement. 1977.

A listing of atlases with comprehensive indexes. The supplement includes atlases published between 1971 and 1975.

1.2 **American Library Association index to general literature.**   2d ed. Boston and Chicago: American Library Assoc., 1901. Supplement. 1914.

A subject guide to books of essays and other collections, including biography, literary and art criticism, history, travel, and reports of historical and literary societies. Predecessor to *Essay and General Literature Index*, 1.20.

1.3 **American reference books annual.**   Ed. Bohdan S. Wynar. Littleton, Colo.: Libraries Unlimited, 1970–.

Generally known as *ARBA*, this series began with coverage of 1969 imprints. Reviews are contributed by professionals, mostly librarians. Cumulative indexes have been issued for 1970–1974 and 1975–1979.

1.4 **American library directory.**   New York: R. R. Bowker, 1923–.

A geographically arranged list of libraries, compiled biennially. Entries include statistical data and names of librarians. Now in 2 vols.

1.5 **Ash, Lee.   Subject collections: a guide to special book collections and subject emphases as reported by university, college, public and special libraries and museums in the U.S. and Canada.** 5th ed. New York: R. R. Bowker, 1978.

A guide to collections, based on Library of Congress subject headings. The work is revised every three to four years, and it records changes in collections that are reported by participating libraries.

1.6 **Baer, Eleanora A.   Titles in series: a handbook for libraries and students.** 3d ed. 4 vols. Metuchen, N.J.: Scarecrow Press, 1978.

See also 1.9.

1.7 **Besterman, Theodore.   A world bibliography of bibliographies and of bibliographical catalogues, calendars, abstracts, digests, indexes, and the like.** 4th ed., rev. and enlarged. 5 vols. Totowa, N.J.: Rowman and Littlefield, 1965–1966.

International in scope, this work lists by subject separately published bibliographies in all fields—from "academic writings" to "zoology." It is the most comprehensive bibliographical guide available, including 117,000 items arranged under 16,000 headings. For a supplement, see Alice F. Toomey, *A World Bibliography of Bibliographies, 1966–1974: A List of*

Works Represented by Library of Congress Printed Catalog Cards, 2 vols., Totowa, N.J.: Rowman and Littlefield, 1977.

1.8 **Bibliographic index: a cumulative bibliography of bibliographies, 1937–.** New York: H. W. Wilson, 1938–.

Issued quarterly and cumulated annually. Separate bibliographies and bibliographies in books as well as periodicals are listed by subject. See also *Bulletin of Bibliography*, Westport, Conn.: Meckler Publ., 1897–; quarterly, with checklists on topics in the humanities and social sciences.

1.9 **Books in series.** [Prepared by R. R. Bowker Company's Dept. of Bibliography.] 3d. ed. 3 vols. New York: R. R. Bowker, 1980.

Covers the period 1950–1980. Popular, scholarly, and professional series; includes originals and reprints; lists books in print and generally provides retrospective coverage. The listing is by series name, with an author, title, and subject index. See 1.6.

1.10 **British Museum. Department of Printed Books. Subject index, 1881–1900–.** London: British Museum, 1902–1903–.

Preceded by Robert Alexander Peddie, *Subject Index of Books Published Before 1880*, 4 vols., London: Grafton, 1933–1948. An alphabetical subject catalog of works added to the library since 1881, the *Subject Index* of the British Museum is supplemented by five-year cumulations. A ten-year cumulation for 1961–1970 is in preparation. No personal names are listed in the subject index; they are listed instead in the British Museum's *General Catalogue of Printed Books*.

1.11 **Buchanan, William W., and Edna M. Kanely. Cumulative subject index to the Monthly Catalog of U.S. Government Publications, 1900–1971.** 15 vols. Washington, D.C.: Carrollton Pr., 1973–1975.

A subject index compiled by merging the *Monthly Catalog* indexes. Variant subject entries and spellings have not been merged, although cross-references are included. For another subject approach, see the *Document Catalog*, Washington, D.C.: GPO, 1896–1945, for the period 1895–1940.

1.12 **Collison, Robert L. Encyclopaedias: their history throughout the ages.** 2d ed. New York: Hafner Publ. Co., 1966.

A guide, with historical notes, on general encyclopedias issued in various countries. For a guide to currently available encyclopedias, see Kenneth F. Kister, *Encyclopedia Buying Guide*, 3d ed., New York: R. R. Bowker, 1981.

1.13 **Comprehensive dissertation index, 1861–1972.** 37 vols. Ann Arbor, Mich.: University Microfilms, 1973. Supplement. 1973.

Attempts to list all dissertations accepted at U. S. and some foreign institutions; supersedes all previous lists. *Five-year Cumulation, 1973–1977*, as above, 1979.

1.14 **Directory of archives and manuscript repositories in the United States.** Washington, D.C.: National Historical Publications and Records Commission, 1978.

Complements the outdated 1961 edition compiled by Philip M. Hamer (and is sometimes still referred to as "Hamer"). The *Directory* provides brief descriptions of major collections in U.S. repositories. The arrangement is by state, with a subject, geographic, and name index.

1.15 **Dissertation abstracts international.** Ann Arbor, Mich.: University Microfilms, 1938–.

Vols. 1–11, 1938–1951, titled *Microfilm Abstracts*; vols. 12–29, 1952–June 1969, called *Dissertation Abstracts*. A monthly compilation of abstracts of dissertations submitted by cooperating institutions to University Microfilms International. Copies of the dissertations are available for purchase. Since vol. 27, issued in two sections: A: Humanities and Social Sciences, and B: Sciences and Engineering. Since July 1969, with vol. 30, no. 1, foreign dissertations have been included.

1.16 **Dodson, Suzanne Cates. Microform research collections: a guide.** Westport, Conn.: Microform Review Inc., 1978.

Lists and describes approximately 200 microform collections, with references to published reviews and bibliographies; well indexed by authors and titles of works and bibliographies.

1.17 **Downs, Robert B., et al. American library resources: a bibliographical guide.** Chicago: American Library Assoc., 1951. Supplements, 1950–1961, 1962; 1961–1970, 1972; 1971–1980, 1981.

A listing of bibliographies, union lists, surveys, checklists, and catalogs of libraries and special collections in the U.S. Indexed by author, subject, and institution.

1.18 **Downs, Robert B., and Frances B. Jenkins, eds. Bibliography: current state and future trends.** Urbana, Ill.: Univ. of Illinois Pr., 1967.

A collection of essays including one on "American Literature Bibliography in the Twentieth Century" (pp. 214–236), by John T. Flanagan. The book was previously published in the January and April 1967 issues of *Library Trends*.

1.19 **Encyclopedia of associations.** 2 vols. in 3. Detroit: Gale Research Co., 1961–.

Revised every two years, this directory provides brief information on U. S. organizations. Associations are grouped by subject category with geographic and executive indexes in vol. 2. Kept up to date by *New Associations and Projects*, Detroit: Gale, 1964–.

1.20 **Essay and general literature index, 1900–.** New York: H. W. Wilson, 1934–.

Kept up to date by regular supplements and cumulated every five years. A detailed index by author and subject to essays and articles that have appeared in book form. Index of works 1900–1969 was published in 1972.

1.21 **Foundation directory.** 8th ed. New York: The Foundation Center, 1981.

The standard guide to information about nongovernmental grant-making foundations in the U.S.

1.22 **Government reference books: a biennial guide to U.S. government publications, 1968/1969–.** Littleton, Colo.: Libraries Unlimited, 1970–.

Edited by Sally Wynkoop as a supplement to her *Subject Guide to Gov-*

ernment Reference Books, same publ., 1972. With the 1978/1979 edition, Walter M. Newsome became the compiler.

1.23   **Guide to microforms in print, 1961–.**   Washington, D.C.: Microcard Editions, 1961–.
A listing of microform publications currently for sale. Recent editions (Westport, Conn.: Microform Review Inc., 1978, 1979) include *International Microforms in Print*. In 1962 an annual *Subject Guide to Microforms in Print* appeared as a companion to the *Guide*.

1.24   **Keller, Helen R. The dictionary of dates.** 2 vols. New York: Macmillan, 1934.
A record from "the earliest times" through 1930 (from the Preface) arranged according to countries. Among other useful dictionaries of dates are Neville Williams, *Chronology of the Modern World, 1763 to the Present Time,* rev. ed., New York: McKay, 1969; Bernard Grun, *The Timetables of History,* rev. ed., New York: Simon and Schuster, 1979; and Robert L. Collison, *Newnes Dictionary of Dates,* 2d ed. rev., London: Newnes, 1966.

1.25   **Koehmstedt, Carol L.   Plot summary index.** Metuchen, N.J.: Scarecrow Pr., 1973.
Covers twenty-six collections, including Frank N. Magill's *Masterplots* series.

1.26   **Library of Congress catalog: a cumulative list of works represented by Library of Congress cards: books: subjects, 1950–.**
The 1950–1954 cumulation was published in Ann Arbor, Mich.; since 1955 the Library of Congress has published the series. The catalog includes listings of post-1945 imprints represented by Library of Congress printed cards. It is arranged alphabetically by Library of Congress subject headings.

1.27   **Masters abstracts.**   Ann Arbor, Mich.: University Microfilms, 1962–.
Published quarterly with selected abstracts.

1.28   **Microform review.**   Westport, Conn.: Microform Review Inc., 1972–.
Especially useful to librarians. Issued quarterly and cumulated every five years.

1.29   **National register of microform masters.**   Washington, D.C.: Library of Congress, 1965–.
Annually lists and locates masters for use in making copies. Holdings of commercial publishers and libraries are represented. A 1965–1975 cumulation has been issued.

1.30   **The national union catalog of manuscript collections, 1959–1961–.**   Ann Arbor, Mich.: J. W. Edwards, 1962–.
Often referred to as *NUCMC,* this catalog is based on reports from American repositories. It is compiled by the Library of Congress, and consists of brief descriptions of the collections reported to LC by participating libraries. Subject, personal, family, corporate, and geographical name indexes in the annual are cumulated every five years beginning with 1970–1974. Previous indexes cumulated every three years.

1.31 **Research centers directory.** Detroit: Gale Research Co., 1960–.

A biennial guide to nonprofit research organizations with continuing programs. A supplement, *New Research Centers*, same publ., 1965–, offers an updating service between editions of the *Directory*.

1.32 **Rogers, A. Robert. The humanities: a selective guide to information sources.** Littleton, Colo.: Libraries Unlimited, 1974. 2d ed. 1979.

A specialized guide intended for library science students and practicing reference librarians. Includes a chapter on computer applications in the humanities and a list of bibliographic data bases.

1.33 **Sheehy, Eugene P. Guide to reference books.** 9th ed. Chicago: American Library Assoc., 1976. 2d supplement. 1982.

The standard guide to reference works in all subject areas. This edition and the supplement may be updated by consulting *ARBA*, ed. Wynar, 1.3.

1.34 **Subject guide to books in print: an index to the Publishers' Trade List Annual, 1957–.** New York: R. R. Bowker, 1957–.

Records the works listed in the catalogs of the major U.S. publishers; arranged by Library of Congress subject headings.

1.35 **Tilton, Eva M. A union list of publications in opaque microforms.** 2d ed. New York: Scarecrow Press, 1964.

Includes both American and European authors. Outdated but still useful.

1.36 **Union list of microfilms.** Rev. ed. Ann Arbor, Mich.: J. W. Edwards, 1951. 1949–1959 cumulation. 2 vols. 1961.

Cooperating libraries reported their microfilm holdings for this compilation; excludes theses and newspapers.

1.37 **Vertical file index.** New York: H. W. Wilson, 1935–.

A monthly selected list of pamphlet material for general libraries, with subject and title indexes.

1.38 **Walford, Albert John, ed. Walford's guide to reference material.** 4th ed. 3 vols. London: Library Assoc., 1980–. Concise ed. 1981.

Similar to Sheehy's *Guide to Reference Books*, the Walford bibliography emphasizes titles published in Great Britain and coverage of current material and bibliographies. Vol. 3 is to include languages, literature, the arts, and general works.

1.39 **White, Carl M., et al. Sources of information in the social sciences: a guide to the literature.** 2d ed. Chicago: American Library Assoc., 1973.

The standard guide to social science literature, consisting of bibliographic essays by specialists and annotated lists of reference works.

1.40 **Young, Margaret L., and Harold C. Young. Directory of special libraries and information centers.** 6th ed. 2 vols. Detroit: Gale Research Co., 1981.

A directory of special and research libraries and data centers maintained by government agencies, businesses, educational institutions, nonprofit organizations and societies. Vol. 1 is an alphabetical listing and subject index; vol. 2 contains geographic and personnel indexes.

1.41 **Zaunmüller, Wolfram. Bibliographisches Handbuch der Sprach-wörterbücher.** Stuttgart: A. Hiersemann, 1958.
An annotated bibliography listing more than 5,600 dictionaries in about 600 languages. See also Annie M. Brewer, *Dictionaries, Encyclopedias and Other Word-Related Books,* 3d ed., Detroit: Gale Research Co., 1982.

See also **9.8, 19.8–9, 20.44, 35.2.**

2. Philosophy and general methodology of literary and historical study

2.1 **Aldridge, A. Owen, ed. Comparative literature: matter and method.** Urbana, Ill.: Univ. of Illinois Pr., 1969.
A collection of articles illustrating the principal methods of comparative literature, accompanied by the editor's explanatory introductions.

2.2 **Altick, Richard D. The art of literary research.** 3d ed., rev. by John A. Fenstermaker. New York: Norton, 1981.
Discusses purposes and methods of literary research on the level of a beginning graduate student. A selected bibliography and a set of exercises point up the fact that it is designed as a textbook.

2.3 **Arrowsmith, William, and Roger Shattuck, eds. The craft and context of translation: a critical symposium.** Garden City, N.Y.: Anchor Books,. 1964.
Most of the papers collected here are the products of experienced translators.

2.4 **Berkhofer, Robert F. A behavioral approach to historical analysis.** New York: Free Press, 1969.

2.5 **Bowers, Fredson. "Textual criticism and the literary critic."** In Textual and literary criticism. Cambridge: Cambridge Univ. Pr., 1959.
Points out the usefulness of textual criticism to aesthetic literary discussion.

2.6 **Brack, O. M., and Warner Barnes, eds. Bibliography and textual criticism: English and American literature, 1700 to the present.** Chicago: Univ. of Chicago Pr., 1969.
Varied essays on aspects of textual methodology followed by a selective bibliography. Many of the illustrations are taken from the American field.

2.7 **Brower, Reuben, ed. On translation.** Cambridge, Mass.: Harvard Univ. Pr., 1959.
Contains a critical bibliography, pp. 271–293. Also see Stallknecht, 2.26.

2.8 **Collingwood, R. G. The idea of history.** Oxford: Oxford Univ. Pr., 1945. Enlarged ed. 1946.
A philosophical attempt to define the special character of historical knowledge.

2.9 **Gibaldi, Joseph, ed. Introduction to scholarship in modern languages and literatures.** New York: Modern Language Assoc., 1981.
A distinguished collection of six essays in the format of its two predecessors (1952 and 1963); like them, it is "aimed primarily at a student audience." Although the six chapters differ widely in subject matter, as a collection they demonstrate "interdependence between literary and linguistic scholars and their diverse fields of study." The volume covers linguistics, textual and historical scholarship, literary criticism, literary theory, and the role of the scholar in society. See also 25.1.

2.10 **Greenlaw, Edwin. The province of literary history.** Baltimore: Johns Hopkins Univ. Pr., 1931.

2.11 **Historical abstracts.** Santa Barbara, Calif.: American Bibliographical Center, 1955– .

2.12 **History and theory: studies in the philosophy of history.** Middletown, Conn.: Wesleyan Univ. Pr., 1960– .

2.13 **Hockett, Homer C. The critical method in historical research and writing.** New York: Macmillan, 1955.
An historical, methodological, and bibliographical introduction; revision of Hockett's *Introduction to Research in American History* (1931).

2.14 **Howe, George Frederick, et al., eds. [The American Historical Association's] Guide to historical literature.** New York: Macmillan, 1961. First published in 1931.

2.15 **Iggers, George G. New directions in European historiography.** Middletown, Conn.: Wesleyan Univ. Pr., 1975.
Attempts to find a common denominator among the more recent West German scholars, the Marxists, and the French historians associated with the review *Annales* in the pursuit of "total history." (The Johns Hopkins Press has published examples of the *Annales* writers.)

2.16 **Jones, Howard Mumford. The theory of American literature.** Ithaca, N.Y.: Cornell Univ. Pr., 1948. Reissued with a new concluding chapter and a revised bibliography in 1966.
Attitudes pervading scholarship on American literature from colonial times to mid-century are briefly surveyed.

2.17 **Langlois, Charles V., and Charles Seignobos. Introduction to the study of history.** Trans. G. G. Berry. New York: Henry Holt, 1898.

2.18 **McDermott, John F., ed. Research opportunities in American cultural history.** Lexington: Univ. of Kentucky Pr., 1961.
Papers by various authorities on such topics as "Travel Literature" (Thomas D. Clark), "Folklore and Cultural History" (Richard Dorson),

"Middlewestern Regional Literature" (John T. Flanagan), and "The Book Trade and Publishing History" (David Kaser).

2.19 **Morize, André. Problems and methods of literary history, with special reference to modern French literature: a guide for graduate students.** New York: Ginn and Co., 1922.

2.20 **New literary history: a journal of theory and interpretation.** Baltimore: Johns Hopkins Univ. Pr., 1969–.
Each issue "examines a theoretical problem which, while specifically literary, has ramifications or analogues in other disciplines."

2.21 **O'Neill, William L., ed. Insights and parallels: problems and issues of American social history.** Minneapolis: Burgess Publ. Co., 1973.
An anthology that illustrates a variety of methods.

2.22 **Poletta, Gregory T., ed. Issues in contemporary literary criticism.** Boston: Little, Brown, 1973.
An anthology that reflects many of the more recent "issues" from abroad. See also, for phenomenology and structuralism, another anthology, more philosophical: *European Literary Theory and Practice,* ed. Vernon W. Gras, New York: Dell Publ. Co., 1973.

2.23 **Richards, Ivor A. Practical criticism: a study of literary judgment.** New York: Harcourt, Brace & World, 1929.
This work is the grandfather, if not the father, of a considerable element in the method of the analytical study of poetry that reached its zenith in the middle of the century.

2.24 **Sanders, Chauncey. An introduction to research in English literary history.** New York: Macmillan, 1952.
Many of the illustrations of problems in editing, source study, etc., are taken from the American field. Part 4, "Suggestions on Thesis-writing," is elementary but clear-cut. Includes a chapter on folklore by Stith Thompson.

2.25 **The social sciences in historical study: a report [of the Committee on Historiography].** Social Science Research Council Bulletin, No. 64. New York: Social Science Research Council, 1954.

2.26 **Stallknecht, Newton P., and Horst Frenz, eds. Comparative literature: method and perspective.** Carbondale, Ill.: Southern Illinois Univ. Pr., 1961. Rev. ed. 1971.
Thirteen essays on topics like definition, translation, indebtedness, relations of literature and psychology, literature and the arts, modes of criticism, and Romanticism.

2.27 **Thorpe, James. Literary scholarship: a handbook for advanced students of English and American literature.** Boston: Houghton Mifflin, 1964.
A practical manual that outlines principles and methods and calls attention to a limited number of essential bibliographical aids to research.

2.28 **Thorpe, James. Principles of textual criticism.** San Marino, Calif.: Huntington Library, 1972.

2.29   **Thorpe, James, ed.   Relations of literary study: essays on interdisciplinary contributions.** New York: Modern Language Assoc., 1967.
Seven scholars discuss the relations of literary studies with history, myth, biography, psychology, sociology, religion, and music. See also Gibaldi, 2.9, and 25.1.

2.30   **Van Hoof, Henry.   International bibliography of translation.** Munich: Verlag Dokumentation, 1973.
Coverage to July 1971. The history and theory of written translation form part of the contents. See also 35.30.

2.31   **Wellek, René, and Austin Warren.   Theory of literature.** New York: Harcourt Brace, 1949. 3d ed. 1956.
Describes the theory and study of literature from the perspective of the "New Criticism"; perhaps the most widely read and accepted exposition of this critical point of view.

2.32   **Wetherill, P. M.   The literary text: an examination of critical methods.** Berkeley: Univ. of California Pr., 1974.
"My aim is basically to point to the problems which I think arise when a text is examined closely."

2.33   **Yule, G. Udny.   The statistical study of literary vocabulary.** Cambridge: Cambridge Univ. Pr., 1944.
The pioneer study in its field.

See also 3.1, 8.12–13, 9.21–22, 9.40, 9.51, 15.11, 29.49, 29.54, 30.54, 34.24, 35.12, 35.18, 35.22, 35.27–28, 35.36, 35.38, 35.43, 35.45.

3. *Technical procedures in literary and historical research*

3.1   **Bowers, Fredson.   Principles of bibliographical description.** Princeton, N.J.: Princeton Univ. Pr., 1949.
A standard work on the methods of analyzing a book with a view to making a scientific description of it as a physical entity. Offers expert technical explanations of such matters as edition, impression, issue, state, format. Of special interest is the section on books of the 19th and 20th centuries.

3.2   **Gaskell, Philip.   A new introduction to bibliography.** New York: Oxford Univ. Pr., 1972. Corrected editions. 1974 and 1979.
Based in part on Ronald B. McKerrow, *An Introduction to Bibliography for Literary Students*, Oxford: Oxford Univ. Pr., 1927, this opus incorporates discussions of recent research and updates the selective lists of references.

3.3   **Studies in bibliography: papers of the Bibliographical Society of the University of Virginia, 1947–.** Charlottesville, Va.: Univ. Pr. of Virginia, 1948–.

Issued annually; devoted to bibliographical studies pertaining especially to English and American literature. Regularly includes a selective checklist of bibliographical scholarship published during the preceding year, with emphasis on printing, publishing, and textual studies.

3.4 **Thorpe, James. Principles of textual criticism.** San Marino, Calif.: Huntington Library, 1972.

Offers an alternative to some of the views identified with Greg, Bowers, and the MLA Center for Editions of American Authors, as well as an exposition of sound practices in collecting and editing literary texts.

3.5 **Burnette, O. Lawrence, Jr. Beneath the footnote: a guide to the use and preservation of American historical sources.** Madison: State Historical Society of Wisconsin, 1969.

Fundamentals of the uses of primary sources. Chapters deal also with national, state, and local archives; private collections; and newspapers. Bibliography, pp. 379–437. See also John Cumming, *A Guide for the Writing of Local History*, Lansing: Michigan Bicentennial Commission, 1974, a pamphlet outline.

3.6 **Moss, William W. Oral history program manual.** New York: Praeger, 1974.

Profiting by the Kennedy Library experiences, this volume provides a guide to starting and conducting a project based on the tapes.

3.7 **Parker, Donald. Local history: how to gather it, write it, and publish it.** Rev. and ed. by Bertha E. Josephson. New York: Social Science Research Council, 1944.

Useful for the study of minor authors of regional interest. Cf. Philip D. Jordan, *The Nature and Practice of State and Local History*, Washington, D.C.: Service Center for Teachers/American Historical Assoc., 1958.

3.8 **Perman, Dagmar H., ed. Bibliography and the historian.** Santa Barbara, Calif.: CLIO, 1968.

Anthology of essays dealing with changes in progress in historical bibliography: new technology, new services of the Library of Congress, etc.

3.9 **Clifford, James L., ed. Biography as an art: selected criticism, 1560–1960.** New York: Oxford Univ. Pr., 1962.

The list of works dealing with the problems and materials of biographies adds to the usefulness of this anthology.

3.10 **Garraty, John A. The Nature of biography.** New York: Knopf, 1957.

Discusses the historical development of biography as a genre and contains a section on the methods of preparing a biography. A helpful list of sources is also provided. See also Catherine D. Bowen, *Biography: The Craft and the Calling*, Boston: Little, Brown, 1969.

3.11 **The American genealogical-biographical index to American genealogical, biographical and local history materials.** Middletown, Conn.: Godfrey Memorial Library, 1952–.

The first 123 volumes cover names Aabrey through E. W. Nelson. See also *Biography and Genealogy Master Index*, Detroit: Gale, 1980–, multivolume, with supp. vols.

3.12 **Doane, Gilbert H. Searching for your ancestors.** 5th ed. Minneapolis, Minn.: Univ. of Minnesota Pr., 1980.

A guide to genealogical investigation. Methodology of genealogical research is considered also in George B. Everton, Sr., and Gunnar Rasmuson, *The Handy Book for Genealogists*, 7th ed., Logan, Utah: Everton Publ., 1981; Noel C. Stevenson, *Search and Research*, rev. ed., Salt Lake City, Utah: Deseret Book Co., 1954; and Jacques Barzun and Henry F. Graff, *The Modern Researcher*, 3d ed., New York: Harcourt, Brace, Jovanovich, 1977, which is an excellent general guide to "the arts of research and writing" with a focus on historical scholarship. Lester J. Cappon, *American Genealogical Bibliography with a Chronological Finding-list*, rev. ed., New York: New York Public Library, 1964, is a comprehensive listing of an "exploratory nature." Describes both national and local journals.

3.13 **Gibson, Jeremy. Wills and where to find them.** Baltimore, Md.: Genealogical Publ. Co., 1974.

A British work that may offer suggestions to those seeking to locate authors' papers.

3.14 **Greenwood, Val D. The researcher's guide to American genealogy.** Baltimore, Md.: Genealogical Publ. Co., 1973.

Methods as well as records and sources are considered.

3.15 **Bauer, Andrew. The Hawthorn dictionary of pseudonyms.** New York: Hawthorn Books, 1971.

International in scope, this goes beyond literary works but may add an item to the literary record occasionally.

3.16 **Cushing, William. Anonyms: a dictionary of revealed authorship.** Cambridge, Mass.: W. Cushing, 1889.

A standard work for English and American anonymous titles of the 18th and 19th centuries. (For a list of handbooks dealing with anonymously or pseudonymously published works in various languages, see Adah V. Morris, "Anonyms and Pseudonyms, an Annotated List," *Library Quarterly*, 3 [1933], 354–372; and the bibliography of Archer Taylor and Frederic J. Mosher, *The Bibliographical History of Anonyma and Pseudonyma*, Chicago: Newberry Library/Univ. of Chicago Pr., 1951.)

3.17 **Halkett, Samuel, and John Laing. Dictionary of anonymous and pseudonymous publications in the English language.** 3d ed. Ed. John Horden. Harlow: Longman, 1980.

Many American works are included. A standard compilation for English literature from the earliest times, this *Dictionary* was originally published in Edinburgh in 1882.

3.18 **Center for Editions of American Authors. Statement of editorial principles and procedures: a working manual for editing nineteenth-century American texts.** New York: Modern Language Assoc., 1967. Rev. ed. 1972.

See also CEAA, *Recovering and Preserving the Author's Intention*, Columbia, S.C.: Vogue Press, 1972.

3.19 "The Center for Scholarly Editions: an introductory statement." *PMLA*, 92 (1977), 583–597.

A general introduction to the aims, methods, and values of the Center for Scholarly Editions regarding textual editing of scholarly editions.

3.20 **Collison, Robert L. Abstracts and abstracting services.** Santa Barbara, Calif.: ABC/Clio, 1971.

General practices in making abstracts are set forth as well as advice on editing and publishing them. There is also a hasty sketch of the history of abstract services in the U.S. "Selected Readings" take the place of a full bibliography.

3.21 **Halpenny, Francess G. Editing twentieth century texts: papers given at the Editorial Conference, University of Toronto, November 1969.** Toronto: Univ. of Toronto Pr., 1972.

3.22 **Halsband, Robert. "Editing the letters of letter-writers."** Studies in bibliography, 11 (1958), 25–37.

Practical suggestions for handling problems presented by the editing of collections of letters. (For a splendid example of techniques applied, see *The Letters of Ralph Waldo Emerson*, ed. Ralph L. Rusk, 6 vols., New York: Columbia Univ. Pr., 1939.)

3.23 **Haselden, Reginald B. Scientific aids for the study of manuscripts.** Oxford: Oxford Univ. Pr., 1935.

Contains much material on general procedures involved in studying manuscripts. (Practical advice on handling manuscripts appears also in *Harvard Guide*, 9.36.)

3.24 **Robson, John M. Editing nineteenth century texts: papers given at the Editorial Conference, University of Toronto, November 1966.** Toronto: Univ. of Toronto Pr., 1967.

Selected bibliography by Warner Barnes, pp. [123]–132.

3.25 **Thorpe, James. The use of manuscripts in literary research: problems of access and literary property rights.** New York: Modern Language Assoc., 1974. 2d ed. 1979.

A pamphlet that sets forth the elementary facts.

3.26 **American Library Association. Directory of library photoduplication services in the U. S., Canada, and Mexico.** 2d ed. Chicago: American Library Assoc., 1962.

See also 1.23.

3.27 **Ballou, Hubbard W., ed. Guide to microreproduction equipment.** 5th ed. Silver Spring, Md.: National Microfilm Assoc., 1973–.

Describes, with many illustrations, cameras, hand viewers, processors, contact printers, enlargers, etc. Issued under the auspices of the National Microfilm Assoc., which also publishes an annual volume of proceedings and a bimonthly *National Micro News*.

3.28 **Lewis, Chester M., and William H. Offenhauser, Jr. Microrecording: industrial and library applications.** New York: Interscience Publ., 1956.

Description of various kinds of microrecording and copying devices and methods, including xerography. See also *Library Trends*, January 1960.

3.29 Collison, Robert L. Published library catalogues: an introduction to their contents and use. London: Mansell Information Publ., 1973.

About 600 catalogs or union lists of the English-speaking countries are considered with a particular slant toward resources and collections.

See also **1.28–29, 1.35–36, 9.24.**

Computer aids

3.30 Aitken, A. J., et al., eds. The computer and literary studies. Edinburgh: University Press, 1973.

One of a series of books that give selected papers on many aspects of literary and language study, including stylistic analysis, editing, concordance and dictionary making. This volume reports on an Edinburgh symposium of 1972.

3.31 Bowles, Edmund A. Computers in humanistic research: readings and perspectives. Englewood Cliffs, N.J.: Prentice-Hall, 1967.

Of the twenty-four papers collected here, six deal with language and literature. One of the better anthologies of its sort. (New York University supported an Institute for Computer Research in the Humanities, which issued news of projects in a newsletter published monthly from 1966 through September 1969. Also beginning in 1966 was *Computers and the Humanities*, 3.34, a more formal periodical that offers surveys as well as an annual bibliography. Charles J. Sippl, *Computer Dictionary*, 3d ed., Indianapolis: H. W. Sams, 1980, is designed to help interpret the terminology of data processing, etc.; and *Computer Yearbook and Directory*, Detroit: Computer Yearbook Co., 1966–, provides bibliography, articles on the "state of the art," and a section describing computer systems introduced since 1963. The MLA has computerized its annual bibliography, and Lewis Sawin and his colleagues at the University of Colorado, Boulder, have experimented with the storage of American literature bibliography. Cornell University has a center for the preparation of concordances with the use of computers.)

3.32 The bulletin of the Association for Literary and Linguistic Computing. Stockport, England: Assoc. for Literary and Linguistic Computing, 1973–.

A bulletin issued three times a year that describes work in progress and occasionally runs tutorial articles such as recent ones on Cummings and Fitzgerald.

3.33 Cluett, Robert. Prose style and critical reading. New York: Teachers College Pr., 1976.

Includes a chapter on Hemingway's development and outlines some good strategies for stylistic analysis.

3.34 Computers and the humanities. Amsterdam: North Holland Publ. Co., 1966–.

A quarterly journal on computer studies. It includes annual bibliographies and period surveys of literary studies and methods. Text is in English, French, and German.

3.35 **Lusignan, S., and J. S. North, eds.** **Computing in the humanities.** Waterloo, Ont.: Univ. of Waterloo Pr., 1977.

3.36 **Mitchell, J. L., ed.** **Computers in the humanities.** Minneapolis: Univ. of Minnesota Pr., 1974.
Papers from an International Conference on Computers in the Humanities held at the Univ. of Minnesota in 1973.

3.37 **Oakman, Robert L.** **Computer methods for literary research.** Columbia: Univ. of South Carolina Pr., 1980.
"This book has a double focus, computer fundamentals and literary applications, in order to convey two kinds of information to the humanist with little or no computer experience."

3.38 **Petty, George R., Jr., and William M. Gibson.** **Project occult: the ordered computer collation of unprepared literary text.** New York: New York Univ. Pr., 1970.
Examples are "Bartleby the Scrivener" and *Daisy Miller*.

3.39 **Ross, Donald, Jr.** **"Computer-aided study of literature."** Computer, 11 (1978), 32–39.
General overview of methods for stylistic analysis.

3.40 **Shorter, Edward.** **The historian and the computer: a practical guide.** Englewood Cliffs, N.J.: Prentice-Hall, 1971.
Contains bibliographical footnotes. Cf. the articles in Robert P. Swierenga, ed., *Quantification in American History: Theory and Research*, New York: Atheneum, 1970.

3.41 **Wisbey, R. A., ed.** **The computer in literary and linguistic research.** Cambridge, England: University Press, 1971.
Selected revised papers from a Cambridge University conference that indicate the ways computers are used in dictionary making, editing texts, analyzing styles, etc.

3.42 **Youden, W. W., ed.** **Computer literature bibliography.** Washington, D.C.: U. S. Government Printing Office, 1965.
This "special" publication by the National Bureau of Standards covers the years 1946–1963. It was reprinted in New York by Arno Press in 1970.

4. *Definitions of literary and related terms*

4.1 **Abrams, Meyer H.** **A glossary of literary terms.** 4th ed. New York: Holt, Rinehart, Winston, 1981.
The definitions are accompanied by examples intended for undergraduate use. Lee T. Lemon, *A Glossary for the Study of English*, New York: Oxford Univ. Pr., 1971, is aimed at the same market but is arranged topically, e.g., types, plot, versification, bookmaking, periods, movements, etc.

4.2 **Barnhart, Clarence L., and William D. Halsey, eds.   The new century handbook of English literature.** Rev. ed. New York: Appleton-Century-Crofts, 1967.
  Contains entries on authors, titles, and characters from works of literature, etc.; includes a fair number of clear definitions.

4.3 **Beckson, Karl, and Arthur Ganz.   Literary terms: a dictionary.** New York: Farrar, Straus and Giroux, 1975.

4.4 **The bookman's concise dictionary.**   Comp. Frederick Compton Avis. London: Philosophical Library, 1956.
  Useful for British terms.

4.5 **Bookman's glossary.**   5th ed., rev. Ed. Jean Peters. New York: R. R. Bowker, 1975.
  Guide to terminology "used in the production and distribution of books new and old." A brief list of works on subjects reflected in the glossary appears as an appendix.

4.6 **Bowman, Walter P., and Robert H. Ball.   Theatre language: a dictionary of terms in English of the drama and stage from medieval to modern times.** New York: Theatre Arts Books, 1961.
  Over 3,000 terms and phrases, including recent jargon, cant, and slang.

4.7 **Carter, John.   ABC for book-collectors.** 3d ed. rev. London: Hart-Davis, 1961.
  Definitions, with occasional comment, of such words and phrases as would be likely to puzzle a student facing for the first time a bookseller's or auctioneer's catalog.

4.8 **Cuddon, J. A.   A dictionary of literary terms.** Garden City, N.Y.: Doubleday and Co., 1977.
  Very comprehensive and useful.

4.9 **Deutsch, Babette.   Poetry handbook: a dictionary of terms.** New York: Funk and Wagnall's, 1957. 4th ed. 1974.
  The definitions are elementary and clear. (Works on versification usually aid greatly in defining poetical terms, e.g., George R. Stewart, Jr., *The Technique of English Verse*, New York: H. Holt, 1930; Paull F. Baum, *The Principles of English Versification*, Cambridge, Mass.: Harvard Univ. Pr., 1922. For others, see Shapiro, 22.6.)

4.10 **Fowler, Roger, ed.   A dictionary of modern critical terms.** London and Boston: Routledge and Kegan Paul, 1973.

4.11 **Glaister, Geoffrey A.   An encyclopedia of the book.** Cleveland and New York: World Publ. Co., 1960. 2d ed. London: G. Allen and Unwin, 1979.
  Chiefly an alphabetical glossary of terms, explanations of practices, materials, etc., relating to papermaking, printing, bookbinding, and publishing. Leans heavily on the Swedish *Grafisk Uppslagbok* (1951).

4.12 **Harvey, Paul, ed.   The Oxford companion to English literature.** 4th ed., rev. by Dorothy Eagle. New York: Oxford Univ. Pr., 1967.
  A standard handbook for the study of English literature, *The Oxford Com-*

panion includes much information on the meaning and application of literary terms. It was first published in 1932.

4.13   **Holman, C. Hugh.   A handbook to literature.** Indianapolis, Ind.: Bobbs-Merrill Educ. Publ., 1960. 4th ed. 1980.
An extremely useful compendium for beginners and old hands alike.

4.14   **Malof, Joseph.   A manual of English meters.** Bloomington: Indiana Univ. Pr., 1970.

4.15   **Preminger, Alex, et al., eds.   The Princeton encyclopedia of poetry and poetics.** Princeton, N.J.: Princeton Univ. Pr., 1965. Enlarged ed. 1974.
Originally published under the title of *Encyclopedia of Poetry and Poetics*, this immensely valuable work includes about a thousand entries on "the history, theory, technique, and criticism of poetry from earliest times to the present," with selected bibliographies.

4.16   **Scott, Arthur F.   Current literary terms.** London and New York: St. Martin's Pr., 1965.
Includes also selected foreign words and phrases.

4.17   **Shaw, Harry.   Dictionary of literary terms.** New York: McGraw-Hill Book Co., 1972.
Includes film and TV as well as printed media.

4.18   **Shipley, Joseph T., ed.   Dictionary of world literary terms: criticism, forms, technique.** Rev. ed. Boston: The Writer, Inc., 1970.
An overhauled and sometimes updated edition of a work already revamped in 1953 and again in 1960. Lacks certain definitions of critical terms contained in earlier editions, which were entitled *Dictionary of World Literature*, New York: The Philosophical Library, 1943; revised and reprinted several times.

4.19   **Thompson, Elizabeth H.   A glossary of library terms: with a selection of terms in related fields.** Chicago: American Library Assoc., 1943.

4.20   **Walsh, Donald D.   What's what: a list of useful terms for the teacher of modern languages.** 3d ed. New York: Modern Language Assoc., 1965.
Linguistic and professional terms.

4.21   **Wolf, Martin L.   Dictionary of the arts.** New York: Philosophical Library, 1951.
Briefly describes many terms used in literature, ballet, architecture, music, painting, etc.

See also **35.15.**

5. *Preparation of manuscripts for publication*

5.1   **Bernstein, Theodore M.   The careful writer: a modern guide to English usage.** New York: Atheneum, 1967.

Used by many editors as an everyday guide to good usage; well written, often amusing, full of common sense.

5.2 **The Chicago manual of style.** 13th ed. Chicago: Univ. of Chicago Pr., 1982.
Rules for preparation of copy, suggestions for editing, specimens of type, etc. This excellent work is widely used by magazine and book publishers. Contains a glossary of technical terms. Formerly, *A Manual of Style.* Also see *MLA Handbook,* 5.6.

5.3 **Harmon, Gary L., and Susanna M. Harmon. Scholar's market: an international directory of periodicals publishing literary scholarship.** Columbus: Ohio State Univ. Libraries, 1974.
The essential information is offered, and there are classifications on "American Ethnic Minorities," "Literary Reviews," "Film," "Poetry," etc.

5.4 **Lee, Marshall. Bookmaking: the illustrated guide to design and production.** New York: R. R. Bowker, 1965. 2d ed., rev. 1979.
Provides an easily understood description of the mechanics (composition, engraving, platemaking, printing, etc.) for authors and editors as well as production people.

5.5 **The literary market place.** New York: R. R. Bowker, 1940–.
Annual directory that arranges American publishers by location and by type of books published. It also supplies lists of national associations, literary awards, columnists, radio book programs, magazines and newspapers containing books news, etc. (Literary awards are more extensively considered in *Literary and Library Prizes*, 10th rev. ed., New York: R. R. Bowker, 1980.)

5.6 **MLA handbook for writers of research papers, theses, and dissertations.** New York: Modern Language Assoc., 1977.
One of the standard guides for literary studies, this handbook replaces the earlier *MLA Style Sheet*, 2d ed., 1970. The other major guide is *The Chicago Manual of Style*, 5.2.

5.7 **McNaughton, Harry H. Proofreading and copyediting: a practical guide to style for the 1970's.** New York: Hastings House, 1973.
An elementary compendium useful for a beginner.

5.8 **Nicholson, Margaret. Practical style guide for authors and editors.** New York: Holt, Rinehart and Winston, 1967.

5.9 **One book/five ways: the publishing procedures of five university presses.** [N.p:] American Assoc. of University Presses, 1977.
Shows how five major university presses—Chicago, MIT, North Carolina, Texas, and Toronto—accept, copyedit, prepare for publication, and market an identical, hypothetical manuscript.

5.10 **Skillin, Marjorie E., Robert M. Gay, et al. Words into type: a guide in the preparation of manuscripts for writers, editors, proofreaders and printers.** New York: Appleton-Century-Crofts, 1948. 4th rev. ed. Englewood Cliffs, N.J.: Prentice-Hall, 1980.

Contains many useful points on good usage, in addition to the preparation of the manuscript, production, and typography.

5.11 **Tanselle, G. Thomas. "Some principles for editorial apparatus."** Studies in bibliography, 25 (1972), 41–48.

5.12 **Von Ostermann, Georg F. Manual of foreign languages.** 4th ed., rev. New York: Central Book Co., 1952.

Editorial manual indicating peculiarities of capitalization, accents, abbreviations, numerals, etc., for a large and diverse list of languages.

5.13 **Wittenberg, Philip. The protection of literary property.** Boston: The Writer, 1968. Rev. ed. 1978.

On American laws concerning copyright, libel, permissions for quotations, censorship, etc. See also Norman H. Pearson, "Problems of Literary Executorship," *Studies in Bibliography*, 5 (1952–1953), 3–20. Harry G. Henn, *Copyright Primer*, New York: Practising Law Inst., 1979, provides a scholarly explanation of the 1976 Copyright Act with its ramifications as they affect various media, institutions, and individuals; the *Primer* is thoroughly documented with detailed expositions of specific parts of the law; a helpful but unannotated bibliography is included, pp. 737–751, and information on "fair use" of multiple copies is provided in chapter 18. William S. Strong, *The Copyright Book: A Practical Guide*, Cambridge, Mass.: MIT Pr., 1981, offers a more distilled version of copyright matters with particular reference to the "rights and responsibilities" of all people who may be affected by them; it is clearly written and well organized. Also helpful is Donald F. Johnson, *Copyright Handbook*, New York: R. R. Bowker, 1978, which attempts to make specific information regarding the law and its application quickly accessible. For useful but considerably more elementary guides, see *Librarian's Guide to the New Copyright Law*, Chicago: American Library Assoc., 1976; and Elizabeth Preston, et al., comps., *A Writer's Guide to Copyright*, Boston: The Writer, 1982.

The history of an important phase of copyright is dealt with by Aubert J. Clark in *The Movement for International Copyright in Nineteenth Century America*, Washington, D.C.: Catholic Univ. of America Pr., 1960. Joseph W. Rogers, *U.S. National Bibliography and the Copyright Law*, foreword by Vernon W. Clapp, New York: R. R. Bowker, 1960, is chiefly a review of the history of catalogs of copyright entries since 1891. Still valuable for historical reference but out of date for current matters is Matt Roberts, *Copyright: A Selected Bibliography of Periodical Literature Relating to Literary Property in the United States*, Metuchen, N.J.: Scarecrow Pr., 1971. See also 32.8.

6. *Library of Congress catalogs and chief registers of U.S. publications*

6.1 **American book publishing record.** New York: R. R. Bowker, 1960–.

Cumulates monthly the *Publishers' Weekly* announcements, along with full Library of Congress cataloging. An annual index started for 1962, as above, 1963–.

6.2 **The American catalogue . . . 1876–1910.** 8 vols. in 13. New York: R. R. Bowker, 1876–1910.

Cumulates the *Annual American Catalogue*, from 1886 to 1910; the standard compilation of American books for general sale.

6.3 **Books in print: an author-title-series index to the Publishers' Trade List Annual.** New York: R. R. Bowker, 1948–.

Registers by authors and then by titles all the books listed for sale in the current catalogs of the vast majority of American publishers. (For the corresponding subject index, see *Essay and General Literature Index, 1900–*, 1.20.) *Forthcoming Books* (January 1966–) appears six times per year and now includes books recently printed, prior to the annual edition of *Books in Print*.

6.4 **Cooper, Gayle. A checklist of American imprints for 1820–1830.** 12 vols. Metuchen, N.J.: Scarecrow Pr., 1972–.

6.5 **Cumulative book index: a world list of books in the English language, 1928/1932–.** New York: H. W. Wilson, 1933–.

Index by author, title, and subject. With its predecessor, the *United States Catalog*, 6.19, the *CBI* is a comprehensive record of American publications with entries from other English-speaking countries. Published since 1898; issued monthly except August and cumulated annually.

6.6 **Evans, Charles. American bibliography: a chronological dictionary of all books, pamphlets and periodical publications printed in the U. S. . . . 1639–[1800].** 14 vols. Chicago and Worcester, Mass.: Blakely Pr. and American Antiquarian Soc., 1903–1959. Supplement by Roger P. Bristol. Charlottesville: Univ. Pr. of Virginia, 1971.

Vol. 13, edited by Clifford K. Shipton, was published in Worcester, Mass. Vol. 14, likewise published in Worcester, is an index, prepared by Roger P. Bristol, who is also responsible for *Index of Printers, Publishers, and Booksellers Indicated by Charles Evans in His American Bibliography*, Charlottesville: Univ. Pr. of Virginia, 1961. The earlier volumes were reprinted by Peter Smith, Gloucester, Mass., in 1941. A number of "ghost" titles appear, especially in the earlier volumes. (The American Antiquarian Society has reproduced in microprint all the available works listed in Evans.)

6.7 **Kelly, James. The American catalogue of books (original and reprints) published in the United States from January 1861 to January 1871. . . .** 2 vols. New York: J. Wiley and Sons, 1866–1871; 1938.

Continuation of Roorbach, 6.14, and similarly incomplete. Continued by *The American Catalogue*, 6.2.

6.8 **Molnar, John Edgar. Author-title index to Joseph Sabin's Dictionary of Books Relating to America.** 3 vols. Metuchen, N.J.: Scarecrow Pr., 1974.

6.9 **The national union catalog, 1956 through 1967: a cumulative author list representing Library of Congress printed cards and titles reported by other American libraries.** 125 vols. Totowa, N.J.: Rowman and Littlefield, 1970–1972.

Cumulates the 1958–1962 and the 1963–1967 quinquennial supplements to *The National Union Catalog* and serves as a continuation of *The National Union Catalog, Pre-1956 Imprints*.

6.10 **The national union catalog, pre-1956 imprints: a cumulative author list representing Library of Congress printed cards and titles reported by other American libraries.** 685 vols. London: Mansell, 1968–1980. Supplement vol. 686–. 1980–.

Supersedes the basic Library of Congress *Catalog of Books* and its supplement, 1942–1947; *The Library of Congress Author Catalog, 1948–1952*; *The National Union Catalog, 1952–1955 Imprints*; and *The National Union Catalog . . . 1953–1957*. Volumes listing motion pictures, filmstrips, and phonograph records (in the catalogs covering 1942–1957) have not been included in the new catalog.

6.11 **The national union catalog: a cumulative author list.** Washington, D.C.: Library of Congress, 1956–.

Issued monthly and cumulated quarterly, annually, and quinquennially. See also 6.9, and 6.10.

6.12 **Paperbound books in print.** New York: R. R. Bowker, 1955–.

A semiannual. Indexed by subject, author, and title. In one volume through 1980; in three volumes beginning with 1982, following a single two-volume year. American publishers only.

6.13 **Publishers' weekly, 1872–.** New York: R. R. Bowker, 1872–.

Lists new publications weekly. Books are often announced in advance, in special numbers issued in January (for spring), May (for summer), and September (for fall). In September 1974 the listing of new books was split off into a separate publication entitled *Weekly Record*, also published by Bowker.

6.14 **Roorbach, Orville A. Bibliotheca Americana, 1820–1861.** 4 vols. New York: Roorbach, 1852–1861.

Catalog of publications, including reprints, arranged by authors and titles, giving publisher, date, price. By no means are all American published works of the period listed. See also 6.7.

6.15 **Sabin, Joseph. Bibliotheca Americana: a dictionary of books relating to America, from its discovery. . . .** 29 vols. New York: Sabin, etc., 1868–1936.

A standard reference for books in Americana.

6.16 **Shaw, Ralph R., and Richard H. Shoemaker. American bibliography: a preliminary checklist for 1801–1819.** 22 vols. New York: Scarecrow Pr., 1958–1966.

Continues 6.6; continued by 6.18.

6.17 **Shipton, Clifford K., and James E. Morney, eds. National index of American imprints through 1800: the short-title Evans.** 2 vols. Worcester, Mass.: American Antiquarian Soc., 1969.

A combined alphabetical index to Evans' *American Bibliography* with corrections, and R. Bristol's "not-in-Evans" items. See also 6.6.

6.18 **Shoemaker, Richard H. A checklist of American imprints for 1820–1829.** 10 vols. New York: Scarecrow Pr., 1964–1971.

Checklists of imprints for 1830–1832 were added in 1972 and 1977 (Scarecrow). Continues Shaw-Shoemaker, 6.16, and lists many more titles than Roorbach, 6.14.

6.19 **The United States catalog: books in print.** Minneapolis and New York: H. W. Wilson, 1900–1928.

Succeeded by Wing, 6.20, which has a wider coverage.

6.20 **Wing, Donald. Short-title catalogue of books printed in England, Scotland, Ireland, Wales, and British America and of books printed in other countries, 1641–1700.** 3 vols. New York: Index Soc., 1945–1951. 2d ed. New York: Index Committee of the Modern Language Assoc., 1972.

The principal reference for books printed in the American colonies during this period. Vol. 2 was edited by Timothy J. Crist in 1981 for the second edition.

See also **12.9, 12.23, 13.9, 13.14, 14.1.**

7. *Indexes to contents of magazines*

7.1 **Abstracts of English studies.** Urbana, Ill.: National Council of Teachers of English, 1958–.

Monthly publication abstracting articles in a variety of professional journals of interest to students of English and American literature and the English language.

7.2 **Annual magazine subjects index, 1907–1949.** 43 vols. Boston: F. W. Faxon Co., 1908–1952.

About half of the titles covered relate to history, especially American local history. The forty-three volumes are cumulated in *Cumulated AMSI*, 2 vols., same publ., 1964.

7.3 **The book review digest, 1905–.** New York: H. W. Wilson, 1906–.

Excerpts from the early reviews of selected newly published books. The periodicals covered are largely general organs like weeklies that review books fairly soon after they appear. Helpful in obtaining a cursory view of contents of books and a sampling of the reviewers' reactions to them. See also *Book Review Digest Author/Title Index, 1905–1974*, 4 vols., same publ., 1976. Many books in English, as in other languages, not covered by this *Digest* are included in the reviews appearing in *Bibliographie der deutschen Rezensionen*, 77 vols., Leipzig: Felix Dietrich, 1900–1943.

7.4 **Book review index, 1965–.** Detroit: Gale Research Co., 1965–.

Covers more than 300 English-language publications; primarily fiction, general literature, humanities, and social sciences. Presently a bimonthly, cumulated quarterly and annually.

7.5   **Cushing, Helen G., and Adah V. Morris.   Nineteenth century readers'
       guide to periodical literature, 1890–1899: with supplementary indexing,
       1900–1922.** 2 vols. New York: Morris, 1944.
       Fifty-one British and American magazines are covered for the nineties;
       fourteen are continued beyond 1899. Many anonymous contributors are
       identified.

7.6   **Dramatic index for 1909–1949.** 41 vols. Boston: F. W. Faxon Co.,
       1910–1952.
       An annual subject index to articles about the drama and theater contained
       in English and American periodicals. Issued separately and as Part 2 of the
       Annual Magazine Subject Index, 7.2. *Cumulated Dramatic Index,
       1909–1949* is a cumulation in two quarto volumes of the *Dramatic Index*.

7.7   **Goode, Stephen H.   Index to American little magazines, 1900–1919
       [with additions and corrections to Goode's earlier listings].** Troy, N.Y.:
       Whitston Publ. Co., 1974.
       Goode's indexes to little magazines after 1919 include: *Index to American
       Little Magazines, 1920–1939*, as above, 1969; *Index to Little Magazines,
       1940–1942*, as above, 1967; and *Index to Little Magazines, 1943–1947*,
       Denver: A. Swallow, 1965. See also 7.10.

7.8   **Humanities index.** New York: H. W. Wilson, 1974–.
       A quarterly with annual cumulations; supersedes *International Index to
       Periodicals* (1916–1965) and *Social Sciences and Humanities Index*
       (1965–1974).

7.9   **Index to early American periodical literature, 1728–1870.**   New York:
       Pamphlet Distributing Co., 1941–1942.
       Describes a card index, compiled by the WPA, housed at New York Uni-
       versity, and available for the use of scholars. Includes information on Poe,
       Whitman, Emerson, and other writers as published in early American
       periodicals.

7.10   **Index to little magazines, 1948–.**   Denver and Chicago: A. Swallow,
       1949–.
       Sporadic publication, for the most part annual. Covers primarily literary
       contents of selected "little" magazines that are not indexed in *Readers'
       Guide* or *International Index*. See also 7.7.

7.11   **Index to periodical articles by and about blacks, 1974–.**   Boston: G. K.
       Hall, 1977–.
       An annual formerly entitled *Index to Periodical Articles by and about Ne-
       groes*, which originated in Winston-Salem, N.C., in 1941.

7.12   **Literary writings in America: a bibliography.**   8 vols. Millwood, N.Y.:
       KTO Press, 1977.
       Reproduces a card file listing American writings published in periodicals
       and other sources from 1850 to 1940. The file was compiled as a WPA proj-
       ect at the University of Pennsylvania.

7.13   **Poole's index to periodical literature, 1802–1907.**   Boston: Houghton
       Mifflin, 1892–1908. 7 vols. in 6. New York: Peter Smith, 1938.

The first index to American and British periodicals covering almost 500 titles over more than a hundred years. Subject entries only; no author entries except when the authors themselves are subjects of articles about them.

7.14 **Readers' guide to periodical literature, 1900–.** New York: H. W. Wilson, 1905–.
The standard subject and author index to general interest periodicals.

7.15 **Sader, Marion, ed. Comprehensive index to English-language little magazines, 1890–1970.** 3 vols. New York: Kraus-Thomson Organization, 1976.

7.16 **Social sciences and humanities index: formerly International Index, 1907/1915–1974.** New York: H. W. Wilson, 1916–1974.
See also 7.8.

7.17 **Ulrich's international periodical directory.** New York: R. R. Bowker, 1932–.
Issued biennially; the standard reference guide to periodicals. Categorized according to general subject matter; indexed by title. Since 1983 in 2 vols. For annuals, monographs in series, and government publications, check *Irregular Serials and Annuals: An International Directory*, same pub., 1967–.

See also **19.12, 20.44, 23.20, 23.36, 24.6, 32.54, 32.61–62, 32.99.**

8. *American studies or American civilization*

8.1 **Gerhard, Dietrich, and Egmont Zechlin. Americana in deutschen Sammlungen.** 6 vols. Munich: Deutsche Gesellschaft für Amerikastudien, 1968.

8.2 **Bradbury, Malcolm, and Howard Temperley, eds. Introduction to American studies.** London and New York: Longman, 1981.
Excellent concise introductions to major subjects (e.g.: "The Old South," "The Frontier West," "The Immigrant Experience"); bibliographies for each chapter, pp. 296–316, provide sufficient titles and brief annotations for assistance with further research.

8.3 **Carman, Harry J., and Arthur W. Thompson. A guide to the principal sources for American civilization, 1800–1900, in the city of New York.** 2 vols. Vol. 1. Manuscripts. New York: Columbia Univ. Pr., 1960. Vol. 2. Printed materials. 1962.
Of far greater use than the limitation to one city might suggest. A kind of predecessor is Evarts B. Greene and Richard B. Morris, *A Guide to the Principal Sources for Early American History (1600–1800) in the City of New York*, 2d ed., rev., New York: Columbia Univ. Pr., 1967.

8.4   **Crick, Bernard R., and Miriam Alman, eds.   A guide to manuscripts relating to America in Great Britain and Ireland.** Oxford: Oxford Univ. Pr., 1961. Rev. and ed. by John W. Raimo. Westport, Conn.: Meckler Books, 1979.

Published for the British Assoc. for American Studies. Manuscripts, letters, etc., of authors are also included. See Crick's article, "A Survey of Library Resources in the United Kingdom for the Teaching of American History and Literature in the Universities," *Journal of Documentation*, 14 (1958), 109–118. Addenda to the *Guide* have appeared in *British Association for American Studies Bulletin*, now *Journal of American Studies*, 8.32.

8.5   **Fishwick, Marshall W., ed.   American studies in transition.** Philadelphia: Univ. of Pennsylvania Pr., 1964. Rev. ed. 1968.

General essays of uneven value by more than a dozen scholars, organized under three headings: "On Understanding America," "On Teaching American Studies," and "On Confronting the World."

8.6   **Kwiat, Joseph T., and M. C. Turpie, eds.   Studies in American culture: dominant ideas and images.** Minneapolis: Univ. of Minnesota Pr., 1960.

Essays on methodology that are old but still useful; includes a reprint of H. N. Smith's essay, 8.12.

8.7   **Lubbers, Klaus.   Einführung in das Studium der Amerikanistik.** Tübingen: M. Niemeyer, 1970.

Heavily weighted in the direction of *Sprachwissenschaft* and *Amerikanisches Englisch*, this valuable guide, intended for German students, occasionally helps to call attention to European studies of both the language and the literature of the U.S.

8.8   **Marcell, David, ed.   American studies: a guide to information sources.** Detroit: Gale Research Co., 1982.

A major interdisciplinary guide in three sections: theoretical and pedagogical, various topics, and bibliographies. Well indexed.

8.9   **Mark, Charles, and Paula F. Mark.   Sociology of America: a guide to information sources.** Detroit: Gale Research Co., 1976.

Lists almost 2,000 books in the field published from 1960 to 1974 with the exception of a few older items; 120 relevant journals are also listed. Well organized and annotated.

8.10   **Mugridge, Donald H., and Blanche P. McCrum.   A guide to the study of the United States of America: representative books reflecting the development of American life and thought.** Washington, D.C.: Library of Congress, 1960.

The largest and most diversified annotated list of books concerned with the various aspects of American culture, this excellent compilation was supervised by Roy P. Basler. A supplement by Oliver H. Orr, also compiled under Basler's supervision, was published in 1976.

8.11   **Skard, Sigmund.   American studies in Europe: their history and present organization.** 2 vols. Philadelphia: Univ. of Pennsylvania Pr., 1958.

Describes seminars, institutes, and programs concerned with the U.S. in various European countries to the time of publication. Also contains much information on the reception of American literature in Europe in days gone by. Skard's *The American Myth and the European Mind: American Studies in Europe, 1776–1960*, Philadelphia: Univ. of Pennsylvania Pr., 1961, is a semipopular redaction of the above, which only occasionally comes closer to date. For more recent activities see the *American Studies International*, 8.28.

8.12   **Smith, Henry Nash. "Can 'American studies' develop a method?"** American Quarterly, 9 (1957), 197–208.
Reprinted in Kwiat, 8.6. Also see Robert Sklar, in *American Quarterly*, 27 (1975), 245–262.

8.13   **Tate, Cecil F. The search for a method in American studies.** Minneapolis: Univ. of Minnesota Pr., 1973.

8.14   **Trachtenberg, Alan. The incorporation of America: culture and society, 1865–1893.** New York: Hill and Wang, 1982.
An interdisciplinary study of the impact of incorporation on modern American culture.

8.15   **Welland, Dennis, ed. The United States: a companion to American studies.** London: Methuen, 1974.

8.16   **Wise, Gene. "'Paradigm dramas' in American studies: a cultural and institutional history of the movement."** American Quarterly, 31 (1979), 293–337.

8.17   **Baltzell, E. Digby. Puritan Boston and Quaker Philadelphia: two Protestant ethics and the spirit of class authority and literature.** New York: Free Press, 1979.
Strong social activity of the Boston upper class in contrast to much more limited social activity of the same class in Philadelphia is traced to differing Protestant backgrounds.

8.18   **Drinnon, Richard. Facing west: The metaphysics of Indian-hating and empire-building.** Minneapolis: Univ. of Minnesota Pr., 1980.
The continuing antagonism of white Americans toward Indians is related to imperialist inclinations in the country as seen in the work of selected writers.

8.19   **Ethnic recordings in America: a neglected heritage.** Studies in American Folklife, No. 1. Washington, D.C.: Library of Congress, 1982.
An important collection of essays with a long and substantial "Guide to Resources," pp. 175–250, compiled by Norm Cohen and Paul F. Wells.

8.20   **MacLeod, Anne Scott. A moral tale: children's fiction and American culture, 1820–1860.** Hamden, Conn.: Archon, 1975.
Children's literature is shown to be a moral conditioning element; it also reveals the shift in value from a primary concern with work to an emphasis on aggressive ambition and acquisitiveness but maintains the premium placed on rural over urban life.

8.21   **Namias, June, comp.   First generation: in the words of twentieth-century American immigrants.** Intro. by Robert Coles. Boston: Beacon Pr., 1978.
An interesting overview by way of oral history, but a little goes a long way because of the repetitiveness of many of the accounts.

8.22   **Pearce, Roy Harvey.   The savages of America: a study of the Indian and the idea of civilization.** Baltimore, Md.: Johns Hopkins Univ. Pr., 1953. Rev. ed. 1965. New title: Savagism and Civilization. 1967.

8.23   **Spiller, Robert E., and Eric Larrabee, et al., eds.   American perspectives: the national self-image in the twentieth century.** Cambridge, Mass.: Harvard Univ. Pr., 1961.

8.24   **Walker, Robert H., ed.   American studies abroad.** Westport, Conn.: Greenwood Pr., 1975.
A useful survey by a prominent scholar.

8.25   **Wyld, Lionel D., ed.   American civilization: an introduction to research and bibliography.** Deland, Fla.: Everett/Edwards, 1975.
Comprises nine chapters, each focused on a special area of American Studies, which together offer a useful survey of the scholarship and a brief bibliography. Also see A. N. J. den Hollander and Sigmund Skard, eds., *American Civilisation: An Introduction*, Harlow: Longman, 1967.

8.26   **American quarterly.**   Philadelphia: Univ. of Pennsylvania Pr., 1949–.
Journal of the American Studies Association. An annual bibliography lists recent publications and dissertations, and a quarterly *ASA Newsletter* publishes information on current activities.

8.27   **American studies.**   Lawrence, Kans.: Univ. Pr. of Kansas, 1960–.
Journal of the Midcontinent American Studies Assoc.; formerly *Midcontinent American Studies Journal*.

8.28   **American studies international.**   Washington, D.C.: George Washington Univ. Pr., 1965–.
Published originally by the American Studies Assoc. under the title *American Studies News*, this serial became *American Studies: An International Newsletter* in 1970 and since then has been issued as the international supplement to *American Quarterly* with slight variations in title. It is an independent newsletter for international scholars with an American Studies interest, and it often includes bibliographical résumés, many of which are excellent, of current scholarship. It is now published six times a year—two journals and four newsletters—and it includes a variety of "timely information" on American Studies activities, awards, publications, etc., as well as notes on current research and academic matters. A cumulative index and list of contents by issue appear in vol. 20, no. 4 (Summer 1982), 46–56, 57–65.

8.29   **Amerikastudien/American studies.**   Munich: Wilhelm Fink, 1955–.
Publication of the German Society for American Studies, chiefly devoted to articles, some in English, on literature and history. Originally entitled *Jahrbuch für Amerikastudien*. Also contains reviews, bibliographies, and

lists of dissertations. The German SAS also issued a *Mitteilungsblatt*, which contains bibliography and lists of dissertations, as well as information about the activities of the various institutes and seminars concerned with American Studies.

8.30**Indian journal of American studies.**Hyderabad: American Studies Research Centre, 1969–.
Also see a *Newsletter* published by the ASR Centre in Hyderabad, which includes checklists of studies produced in India, from July 1966 (no. 9).

8.31**Journal of American culture.**Bowling Green, Ohio: Bowling Green State Univ. Popular Pr., 1978–.
Covers all aspects of American culture and overlaps considerably with *Journal of Popular Culture*, also published at Bowling Green.

8.32**Journal of American studies.**Cambridge, England: Cambridge Univ. Pr., 1967–.
Journal for the British Assoc. for American Studies; includes articles of consistently high quality and substantial review-essays in each issue.

8.33**Prospects: an annual journal of American cultural studies.**New York: Burt Franklin & Co., 1975–.
Well edited by Jack Salzman, this annual gives considerable attention to literature, though with an American Studies approach.

8.34**Studi Americani.**Rome: Edizioni di Storia Letterature, 1955–.
Issued irregularly in recent years, this journal includes articles with texts and summaries in English and Italian.

8.35**Zeitschrift für Anglistik und Amerikanistik.**Leipzig: VEB Verlag Enzyklopädie, 1953–.
Solid and well edited; occasionally includes special issues on single topics; articles and reviews in German and English. This is the principal organ for an East European view of British and American life and letters.

See also section 15 passim and 21.19, 26.13, 32.119–22, 32.150, 34.21.

Popular culture

8.36**Austin, James C., and Donald A. Koch, eds. Popular literature in America: a symposium in honor of Lyon H. Richardson.**Bowling Green, Ohio: Bowling Green State Univ. Popular Pr., 1972.

8.37**Bode, Carl. The anatomy of American popular culture, 1840–1861.**Berkeley: Univ. of California Pr., 1959.

8.38**Bragin, Charles. Dime novels: bibliography, 1860–1964.**Brooklyn, N.Y.: [n.p.], 1964.
A revision of the original mimeographed edition of 1938. Also see Jones, 8.47, and Pearson, 8.51.

8.39**Cawelti, John G. Adventure, mystery, and romance: formula stories as art and popular culture.**Chicago: Univ. of Chicago Pr., 1977.

Formula fiction, in which the formula combines "cultural conventions" with universal narrative or archetypal elements, is very revealing of basic American cultural needs and values.

8.40   **Cawelti, John G.   Apostles of the self-made man.** Chicago: Univ. of Chicago Pr., 1965.

Shows that attitudes toward success as illustrated by writers from Franklin to Faulkner are not so uniform as popular myth would indicate.

8.41   **Cawelti, John G.   The six-gun mystique.** Bowling Green, Ohio: Bowling Green State Univ. Popular Pr., [1971].

Analyzing the mythic framework of pulp fiction and the horse opera offers access to the subliminal consciousness of a substantial part of American culture.

8.42   **Hagen, Ordean A.   Who done it?: a guide to detective, mystery, and suspense fiction.** New York: R. R. Bowker, 1969.

Coverage is from 1841–1967, chiefly American novels. "Writings on the Mystery Novel" appears on pp. 605–619.

8.43   **Hart, James D.   The popular book: a history of America's literary taste.** Berkeley: Univ. of California Pr., 1950.

Relates popular taste in reading to the "social pressures." See also 14.19.

8.44   **Haycraft, Howard.   Murder for pleasure: the life and times of the detective story.** New York: Appleton-Century, 1941. Enlarged ed. 1968.

A popular historical survey covering England and the U.S., 1841–1940. See also Ellery Queen, *The Detective Short Story: A Bibliography*, Boston: Little, Brown, 1942.

8.45   **Inge, Thomas M., ed.   Handbook of American popular culture.** 3 vols. Westport, Conn.: Greenwood, 1978–1981.

Essays with bibliographies on a broad variety of subjects loosely categorized as elements of popular culture.

8.46   **Johannsen, Albert.   The house of Beadle and Adams and its dime and nickel novels: the story of a vanished literature.** 2 vols. Norman, Okla.: Univ. of Oklahoma Pr., 1950. Supplement. 1962.

Contains a list of the authors and their novels. The Beadle firm was one of the chief publishers of "dime novels."

8.47   **Jones, Daryl.   The dime novel western.** Bowling Green, Ohio: Popular Press, 1978.

Brief but comprehensive and useful.

8.48   **Landrum, Larry N., Pat Browne, and Ray B. Browne, eds. Dimensions of detective fiction.** Bowling Green, Ohio: Popular Press, 1976.

8.49   **Mundell, E. H., and G. Jay Rausch.   The detective short story: a bibliography and index.** Manhattan, Kans.: Kansas State Univ. Library, 1974.

Chiefly a checklist of volumes of tales by individual authors. Special sections on Sherlockeana and Poeiana, Problems, Puzzles, etc., and a list of sleuths. No title index provided.

8.50   Nye, Russel B.   **The unembarrassed muse: the popular arts in America.** New York: Dial Pr., 1970.

8.51   Pearson, Edmund.   **Dime novels; or, following an old trail in popular literature.** Boston: Little, Brown, 1929.
Old but still useful for broad coverage.

8.52   Vogt, Jochen, ed.   **Der Kriminalroman: zur Theorie und Geschichte einer Gattung.** 2 vols. Munich: Wilhelm Fink, 1971.
Thirty-nine articles by writers of various nationalities on detective fiction, principally British and American. Most of the selections are reprints and date from the 1960s.

8.53   Wilmeth, Don B.   **American and English popular entertainment: a guide to information sources.** Detroit: Gale Research Co., 1980.
Vol. 7 of the Performing Arts Information Guide Series, this compilation comprises annotated entries on all areas of popular entertainment.

8.54   Winks, Robin W.   **"American detective fiction."** American Studies International, 19, No. 1 (1980), [3]–16.
Alleges that detective fiction is worthy of serious study both for its intrinsic interest and its being "a mirror of the culture." The short essay is followed by a substantial selected bibliography of secondary materials.

See also **19.3–4, 23.57, 23.92–93, 24.53.**

9. *American history: general tools*

9.1   Beers, Henry Putney.   **Bibliographies in American history: guide to materials for research.** New York: H. W. Wilson, 1942.
Often outmoded by the *Harvard Guide*, 9.36, but still useful because of its extensive coverage of over 11,000 bibliographies listed in a classified arrangement and its independent index. The American Historical Association's *Guide to Historical Literature*, ed. George F. Howe et al., New York: Macmillan, 1961, 2.14, includes selected works on all aspects of American history, pp. 711–744. Also see the Goldentree Bibliographies in American History, a series edited by Arthur S. Link, Arlington Heights, Ill.: Harlan Davidson, 1969–; each bibliography is compiled by a specialist, and the entries are arranged topically with an author index.

9.2   Billington, Ray Allen.   **A guide to American history manuscript collections in libraries of the United States.** New York: Peter Smith, 1952.
Reprinted from *Mississippi Valley Historical Review*, 38 (1951). Also see Hale, 9.8; the *Harvard Guide*, 9.36; the U.S. National Archives and Records Service *Guide*, 9.18; the *Directory of Archives and Manuscript Repositories*, 1.14; and *NUCMC*, 1.30. Carman and Thompson, 8.3, and Crick and Alman, 8.4, may assist.

9.3 **Carruth, Gorton, et al., eds.** **The encyclopedia of American facts and dates.** 7th ed. New York: Crowell, 1979.

Chronologically arranged, with four topical subdivisions in parallel columns. Includes listings through 1969 with a "Supplement of the 70's" through 1977. Fully indexed; strong in social history.

9.4 **Cirker, Hayward, and Blanche Cirker, eds.** **Dictionary of American portraits: 4,045 pictures of important Americans from the earliest times to the beginning of the twentieth century.** New York: Dover, 1967.

Contains a bibliography listing, selectively, published sources of portraits and an index analyzing the portraits according to the profession or occupation of the subjects.

9.5 **Directory of historical societies and agencies in the United States and Canada.** 12th ed. Nashville, Tenn.: American Assoc. for State and Local History, 1982.

Originated in 1956, this directory provides names, addresses, and titles of officers to whom correspondence should be addressed.

9.6 **Doctoral dissertations in history.** Washington, D.C.: American Historical Assoc., 1976– .

This semiannual list includes dissertations in progress as well as those which have been completed. The series has been published by the AHA since 1909; title, publisher, and frequency vary. See also Kuehl, 9.9.

9.7 **Griffin, Appleton Prentiss Clark.** **Bibliography of American historical societies (the United States and the Dominion of Canada).** Washington, D.C.: Government Printing Office, 1896. Rev. ed. 1907.

An index to American and Canadian historical society publications covering the years to 1905. Continued by *Writings on American History*, 9.20.

9.8 **Hale, Richard.** **Guide to photocopied historical materials in the United States and Canada.** Ithaca, N.Y.: Cornell Univ. Pr., 1961.

Published for the American Historical Association. Most of the entries relate to American history, and many are official records. Private holdings are not listed.

9.9 **Kuehl, Warren F.** **Dissertations in history: an index to dissertations completed in history departments of United States and Canadian universities.** 2 vols. Lexington: Univ. Pr. of Kentucky, 1965–1972.

Lists doctoral dissertations completed to June 1970. A supplement is in progress. See also *Doctoral Dissertations in History*, 9.6.

9.10 **Meckler, Alan M., and Ruth McMullen.** **Oral history collections.** New York: R. R. Bowker, 1975.

A directory of U.S. and foreign oral history centers, with name and subject indexes. See also *NUCMC*, 1.30, for description of oral history collections.

9.11 **Mitterling, Philip I.** **U.S. cultural history: a guide to information sources.** Detroit: Gale Research Co., 1980.

This is vol. 5 of the American Government and History Information Guide Series. It includes more than 2,200 entries on reference tools, general works, and major areas of study such as the arts, literature, religion, science, etc. It also includes published papers of minor authors only.

9.12 Morris, Richard B., ed. Encyclopedia of American history. 6th ed. New York: Harper, 1982.

A basic chronology is followed by a topical outline, plus biographical data on notable Americans. One of the best chronological outlines of American "civilization."

9.13 Paullin, Charles O. Atlas of the historical geography of the United States. Ed. John Kirtland Wright. Washington and New York: Carnegie Inst. of Washington and the American Geographical Soc. of New York, 1932.

Other useful atlases include Clifford L. Lord and Elizabeth H. Lord, *Historical Atlas of the United States*, rev. ed., New York: Holt, 1953; the excellent *Atlas of American History*, ed. Kenneth T. Jackson, rev. ed., New York: Scribner, 1978 (the original 1943 edition was edited by James Truslow Adams); and *The American Heritage Pictorial Atlas of U. S. History*, New York: American Heritage Publ. Co./McGraw-Hill Book Co., 1966.

9.14 Peterson, Clarence S. Consolidated bibliography of county histories in fifty states in 1961, consolidated 1935–1961. Baltimore, Md.: [n.p.,] 1961. 2d ed. Baltimore, Md.: Genealogical Publ. Co., 1963.

Privately reproduced by the compiler, this bibliography aims to list "all county histories of at least 100 pages, with few exceptions." Not always accurate. There is no apparent change in the 2d edition.

9.15 Research catalog of maps of America to 1860 in the William L. Clements Library. 4 vols. Boston: G. K. Hall, 1972.

The library is located at the Univ. of Michigan in Ann Arbor. Arranged by cartographer and map titles, then by geographical region.

9.16 U.S. Bureau of the Census. Historical statistics of the United States, colonial times to 1970. Bicentennial Ed. 2 vols. Washington, D.C.: U.S. Government Printing Office, 1975.

A "convenient reference source" that offers the compilations of data from a multitude of origins together with referential annotations and definitions to make the data more useful. This is a complete revision of the 1960 edition with about 4,500 new time series. For more recent data, consult the Bureau's annual *Statistical Abstract of the United States*, same pub., 1879– .

9.17 U.S. Library of Congress. United States local histories in the Library of Congress: a bibliography. Ed. Marion J. Kaminkow. 4 vols. Baltimore, Md.: Magna Carta Book Co., 1975.

Arrangement by states and localities within states. Includes all titles classified in the local history portion of the LC classification through mid-1972. Arranged by class number, which provides a state-by-state listing.

9.18 U.S. National Archives and Records Service. Guide to the National Archives of the United States. Washington, D.C.: U.S. Government Printing Office, 1974. Rev. ed. 1976.

Published originally in 1948 under the title *Guide to the Records in the*

National Archives. Describes collections added as of June 30, 1970. Arranged by government agency, with a subject index.

9.19   Writings on American history, 1902–1961. Washington, D.C.: U.S. Government Printing Office, 1904–1976.

An invaluable comprehensive bibliography of U.S. and Canadian history to 1935, and from 1936 on, of U.S. history only; published annually, though vols. for 1904–1905 and 1941–1947 never came out. Publisher varies; early volumes were published as part of the *Annual Report* of the American Historical Assoc., and as House Documents in the U.S. Serial Set. See also *Index to the Writings on American History, 1902–1940*, compiled for the AHA, same publ., [1956], which contains references and subject classifications not to be found in the separate indexes of the individual volumes. See also 9.20.

9.20   Writings on American history, 1962–1973. Comp. James J. Dougherty. 4 vols. Washington, D.C. and Millwood, N.Y.: American Historical Assoc., 1976. Supplements. 1973/74–. Millwood, N.Y.: KTO Press, 1974–.

A continuation of the previous item, except that only periodical articles are included. Supplemented beginning in 1973/74 by annual volumes which cumulate the U.S. entries in the American Historical Association's *Recently Published Articles*, Washington, D.C.: American Historical Assoc., 1976–. Before 1976, *RPA* was a section in the *American Historical Review*. There is no detailed subject index to this series. The arrangement is by topic, with an author index.

9.21   Gottschalk, Louis, ed.   Generalization in the writing of history. Chicago: Univ. of Chicago Pr., 1963.

Edited for the Social Science Research Council, Committee on Historical Analysis, this collection focuses on the problems of theoretically based history. Particularly notable are W. O. Aydelotte's "Notes on the Problem of Historical Generalization," and Martin Klein's "Bibliography of Writings on Historiography and the Philosophy of History."

9.22   Higham, John.   Writing American history: essays on modern scholarship. Bloomington: Indiana Univ. Pr., 1970.

This work consists of nine essays, mostly reprinted from other sources, on American historians and trends in historiography. The volume is meant to supplement Higham et al., *History*, Englewood Cliffs, N.J.: Prentice Hall, 1965, a survey of recent historical writing in the U.S. in which the characteristics of American historical scholarship are compared with those of other countries.

9.23   Kiger, Joseph C.   American learned societies. Washington, D.C.: Public Affairs Pr., 1963.

A workmanlike study of sixty learned societies, twenty-nine of which are devoted to the humanities and social sciences.

9.24   Whitehill, Walter M.   Independent historical societies: an enquiry into their research and publication functions and their financial future. Boston and Cambridge: Boston Athenaeum/Harvard Univ. Pr., 1962.

Excellently written; provides historical background, etc., and concludes with general observations on methods, financing, etc., of such organizations. See also Leslie W. Dunlap, *American Historical Societies, 1790–1860*, Madison, Wisc.: [Priv. Pr., Cantwell Printing Co.], 1944; repr., Philadelphia: Porcupine Press, 1974.

9.25 America: history and life. Santa Barbara, Calif.: ABC/Clio Press, 1964– .

Quarterly; abstracts of articles from some 22,000 serials. Originally an abstracting service which included articles dealing with U.S. and Canadian history. Before 1964 it was part of *Historical Abstracts*, a series published by ABC since 1955. Coverage has been expanded now to include books, book reviews, and dissertations as well as serials. Annual and quinquennial cumulative indexes are issued, and a retrospective set, 2 vols., same pub., 1980, ed. Eric H. Boehm, supplements coverage of vols. 1–10, 1964–1973. The printed index is a product of ABC's computerized data base.

9.26 American historical review. Washington, D.C.: American Historical Assoc., 1895– .

Official organ of the AHA; largely devoted to current bibliography and reviews of books, including extensive lists of current books and articles on the history of the U.S. and its various sections.

9.27 Journal of American history. Bloomington, Ind.: Organization of American Historians, 1914– .

Formerly called *Mississippi Valley Historical Review*, this is the chief journal devoted solely to American history; essays, book reviews, bibliographical notices, and checklists of articles, the last not so inclusive as similar lists in *American Historical Review*, 9.26. Index covering 1914–1964, by Thomas D. Clark, 1973.

9.28 Perspectives in American history. Ed. Donald Fleming and Bernard Bailyn. Cambridge, Mass.: Harvard Univ. Pr., 1967– .

An annual journal emanating from the Charles Warren Center for Studies in American History, Harvard University.

9.29 Reviews in American history. Baltimore, Md.: Johns Hopkins Univ. Pr., 1973– .

Published quarterly; provides scholarly reviews of books in American history and related fields.

9.30 Billias, George A., and Gerald N. Grob, eds. American history: retrospect and prospect. New York: Free Press, 1971.

Consists of ten original articles by leading historians. Six of the essays survey traditional chronological periods. The four remaining selections cover economic and business, social, urban, and diplomatic history.

9.31 Boorstin, Daniel J. The Americans. 3 vols. New York: Random House, 1974.

A cultural history; the volumes were originally published separately with subtitles: *The Colonial Experience*, 1958; *The National Experience*, 1967; and *The Democratic Experience*, 1973.

9.32 **Boorstin, Daniel J., ed. Chicago history of American civilization.** Chicago: Univ. of Chicago Pr., 1956–.

A multivolume history of the U.S. comprising both chronological and topical treatments. Each volume is written by an expert on the subject, but the narratives and bibliographies are less exhaustive than those in the New American Nation series, ed. Morris and Commager, 9.45. The *Chicago History* includes such volumes as Boorstin's *The Genius of American Politics*, 1953; Carl W. Condit's *American Building*, 1968; Richard Dorson's *American Folklore*, 1959 and 1977; etc.

9.33 **Cartwright, William H., and Richard L. Watson, Jr., eds. The reinterpretation of American history and culture.** Washington, D.C.: National Council for the Social Studies, 1973.

Essays on trends in historical scholarship during the 1960s.

9.34 **Cunliffe, Marcus and Robin W. Winks, eds. Pastmasters: some essays on American historians.** New York: Harper and Row, 1969.

The subjects range from Parkman to the two Schlesingers and C. Vann Woodward. The names of the contributors, themselves historians, are as noteworthy as the subjects. The volume provides a useful assessment of trends in American historical writing.

9.35 **Goetzmann, William H. "Time's American adventures: American historians and their writing since 1776."** Social Science Quarterly, 57 (1976), 3–48.

This survey, "more than a bibliographical essay . . . is . . . a condensed intellectual history of the United States, told from the point of view of a Pulitzer Prize winning historian." (From the Introduction to a reprint in *American Studies International*, 19, No. 2 [Winter 1981], [5]–47. A sequel, "American Historiography since the Bicentennial," is promised.)

9.36 **Harvard guide to American history.** Rev. ed. Ed. Frank Freidel et al. 2 vols. Cambridge, Mass.: Harvard Univ. Pr., 1974.

A major guide that was first published in 1954, edited by Oscar Handlin. This is the standard bibliographical source for American history in that it contains classified lists of works on all phases of the subject to July 1970. Preliminary chapters deal with the nature of the historian's task and preparation for research and writing. The American Historical Association's *Guide to Historical Literature*, ed. George F. Howe et al., New York: Macmillan, 1961, 2.14, also has a section on American history, pp. 711–744. For a good general pictorial history, see James T. Adams et al., eds., *Album of American History*, 6 vols., New York: Scribner, 1969, with coverage from the colonial period through 1968.

9.37 **Hofstadter, Richard E. The progressive historians: Turner, Beard, Parrington.** New York: Knopf, 1968.

An analysis of the historical views of the three named historians.

9.38 **Hutchinson, William T., ed. The Marcus W. Jernegan essays in American historiography.** Chicago: Univ. of Chicago Pr., 1937.

Essays on twenty-one notable historians.

9.39 **Kammen, Michael, ed.   The past before us: contemporary historical writing in the United States.** Ithaca, N.Y.: Cornell Univ. Pr., 1980.
Prepared for the International Congress of Historical Sciences, Bucharest, August 1980; includes essays by prominent American scholars on current trends in history. Covers methodological advances, rapidly developing fields such as the new social and political history, and recent contributions for specific time periods and geographic areas.

9.40 **Kraus, Michael.   The writing of American history.** Norman: Univ. of Oklahoma Pr., 1953.
A standard work on American historiography.

9.41 **Landes, David S., and Charles Tilly, eds.   History as social science.** Englewood Cliffs, N.J.: Prentice-Hall, 1971.
One of four studies of history as a discipline sponsored by the Social Science Research Council. Several scholars describe the achievements and limitations of social science history as they relate to the teaching and research needs of the profession. This volume constitutes a major evaluation of the use of theory and quantification in history.

9.42 **Levin, David.   History as romantic art: Bancroft, Prescott, Motley, and Parkman.** Stanford, Calif.: Stanford Univ. Pr., 1959.
Levin establishes this group as part of American Romanticism through analysis of representative works by each author.

9.43 **Loewenberg, Bert J.   American history in American thought: Christopher Columbus to Henry Adams.** New York: Simon and Schuster, 1972.
A history of ideas about the writing of history, beginning with the European backgrounds and ending with Henry Adams. The first fifteen chapters were originally published in 1968 under the title *Historical Writing in American Culture*.

9.44 **Morison, Samuel Eliot, Henry S. Commager, and William E. Leuchtenberg.   The growth of the American Republic.** 7th ed. 2 vols. New York: Oxford Univ. Pr., 1980.
A standard history; originally published in 1930. For a superb comprehensive history of the U.S. in one volume, see Morison's *The Oxford History of the American People*, New York: Oxford Univ. Pr., 1965—written with vigor, grace, and an obvious devotion to the subject.

9.45 **Morris, Richard B., and Henry S. Commager, eds.   The new American nation series.** New York: Harper and Row, 1954–.
An extensive historical series covering the whole range of U.S. history from the discovery period to the mid-20th century. Each volume is written by an authority in the field, and each contains a critical bibliography. For a listing of titles, see *Books in Series*, 1.9.

9.46 **The pageant of America: a pictorial history of the U.S.**   Ed. Ralph H. Gabriel et al. 15 vols. New Haven, Conn.: Yale Univ. Pr., 1925–1929. Independence Ed. 5 vols. New York: United States Publishers Assoc., 1970–.
The most extensive pictorial survey of U.S. history. Vol. 11 is *The American Spirit in Letters*, and vol. 14 is *The American Stage*. The Independence Edition is in progress.

9.47   Schlesinger, Arthur M., and Dixon R. Fox, eds. A history of American life. 13 vols. New York: Macmillan, 1927–1948.
   An extensive social history of the U.S. The individual volumes, written by various authors, are uneven in coverage and quality. Each volume contains annotated bibliographies.

9.48   Skotheim, Robert A. American intellectual histories and historians. Princeton, N.J.: Princeton Univ. Pr., 1966.
   Begins with several historians prior to the 20th century, especially M. C. Tyler and Edward Eggleston, but centers on "the Progressive tradition" (Robinson, Beard, Parrington, et al.) and challengers like Morison, Miller, and Gabriel. Since World War II, Commager, Persons, Goldman, Schlesinger, Jr., and Hofstadter are among the historians discussed.

9.49   Sternsher, Bernard. Consensus, conflict, and American historians. Bloomington: Indiana Univ. Pr., 1975.
   Traces the debate among mid-20th century American historians as to whether the U.S. is rooted mainly in the broad democratic ideal (concensus school) or in the social and economic strife constantly generated by individual and group desire for continuing improvement in life ("New Left").

9.50   Van Tassel, David D. Recording America's past: an interpretation of the development of historical studies in America, 1607–1884. Chicago: Univ. of Chicago Pr., 1960.
   A grass-roots approach to causes and trends that throws light upon many lesser-known historians and on the development of several historical societies.

9.51   Wise, Gene. American historical explanations: a strategy for grounded inquiry. Homewood, Ill.: Dorsey Pr., 1973. 2d ed. Minneapolis: Univ. of Minnesota Pr., 1980.
   A history of American history and its structure, forms, and strategies.

9.52   Wish, Harvey. The American historian: a social-intellectual history of the writing of the American past. New York: Oxford Univ. Pr., 1960.
   Attempts to show how the reactions of historians during national crises were influenced by social conditioning. Includes discussion of writers from Jared Sparks to Allen Nevins.

In addition to sections 8 and 15 of this Guide, see 1.22, 3.12, 30.34.

10. *American history: special studies*

10.1   Bernard, Luther L., and Jessie Bernard. Origins of American sociology: the social science movement in the U.S. New York: Thomas Y. Crowell, 1943.
   History of social-science theory in the 19th century. More contemporary

developments are dealt with in *Handbook of Modern Sociology*, ed. Robert E. L. Faris, Chicago: Rand McNally, 1964, a collection of essays by various sociologists, with bibliographies.

10.2   **Burlingame, Roger.   Engines of democracy: inventions and society in mature America.** New York: Scribner, 1940.
A history of inventions in the U.S. since 1865 and the effect of technology on American culture and economics.

10.3   **Burns, Richard Dean, ed.   Guide to the history of U.S. foreign relations since 1700.** Santa Barbara, Calif.: ABC/Clio Pr., 1982.

10.4   **David, Henry, Harold U. Faulkner, et al., eds.   The economic history of the U.S.** 9 vols. New York: Holt, Rinehart, and Winston, 1947.
Various authorities detail economic development from colonial times to 1941. See also T. Orsagh et al., *The Economic History of the U.S. Prior to 1860: An Annotated Bibliography*, new ed., Santa Barbara, Calif.: ABC/Clio Pr., 1975.

10.5   **Gutman, Herbert G. Work, culture and society in industrializing America: essays in American working-class and social history.** New York: Knopf, 1975.
Essays explore the beliefs and behavior of 19th-century workers and address questions of religion, ideology, social mobility, and race.

10.6   **Heald, Morrell, and Lawrence S. Kaplan.   Culture and diplomacy: the American experience.** Westport, Conn.: Greenwood Pr., 1977.
The central role of isolationism in American foreign policy prior to World War II.

10.7   **Jones, Howard Mumford.   The age of energy: varieties of American experience, 1865–1915.** New York: Viking, 1971.
American cultural history, includes discussion of labor, industry, technology, architecture, athletics, etc.

10.8   **Lindeman, Jack.   The conflict of convictions: American writers report the Civil War.** Philadelphia: Chilton Book Co., 1968.
A selection of writings from the journals, articles, and correspondence of major American authors of the time arranged in chapters on assorted Civil War topics and organized chronologically. Provides a composite and literary yet subjective view of the war.

10.9   **May, Ernest R.   American imperialism: a speculative essay.** New York: Atheneum, 1968.
Impact on America of expansionary policies of European nations at the end of the 19th century. See also Tompkins, 10.16.

10.10   **May, Henry F.   The end of American innocence: a study of the first years of our own time, 1912–1917.** New York: Knopf, 1959.

10.11   **Mitchell, Lee Clark.   Witnesses to a vanishing America: the nineteenth-century response.** Princeton, N.J.: Princeton Univ. Pr., 1981.
A study of the 19th-century American response to the devastation of the wilderness and the Indian caused by the westward progress of settlement.

10.12　**Parry, Albert.　Garrets and pretenders: a history of bohemianism in America.** New York: Covici, Friede, 1933. Rev. ed. New York: Dover, 1960.

A popular and readable but necessarily incomplete account. The revision consists of a new chapter, on the Beatniks, by Harry T. Moore.

10.13　**Persons, Stow.　The decline of American gentility.** New York: Columbia Univ. Pr., 1973.

Deals mainly with New England in tracing the loss of social power among the gentry after the Civil War, particularly from 1880 to 1910.

10.14　**Rothchild, Sylvia, ed.　Voices from the Holocaust.** Intro. Elie Wiesel. New York: New American Library, 1981.

In their own words, Jewish survivors of the Nazi camps relate their experiences in detailed and very moving accounts. The book is divided into three sections: "Life before the Holocaust," "Life during the Holocaust," and "Life in America Afterwards." A masterful representation.

10.15　**Taylor, George Rogers, ed.　The Turner thesis concerning the role of the frontier in American history.** Lexington, Mass.: Heath, 1945. 3d ed. 1971, 1972.

Two essays by Frederick Jackson Turner are followed by discussions pro and con, in a volume included in the series *Problems in American Civilization*, edited from Amherst College. (Turner has been a vital influence on historical studies of a wide variety, including literary history. Ray A. Billington, *America's Frontier Heritage*, New York: Holt, Rinehart, and Winston, 1966, reviews recent discussions of the frontier concept and probes origins in *The Genesis of the Frontier Thesis*, San Marino, Calif.: Huntington Library, 1971. Also see Billington, 10.50; Clark, 10.51; and Hazard, 29.15.)

10.16　**Tompkins, E. Berkeley.　Anti-imperialism in the United States: the great debate, 1890–1920.** Philadelphia: Univ. of Pennsylvania Pr., 1970. See also May, 10.9.

10.17　**Tomsich, John.　A genteel endeavor: American culture and politics in the Gilded Age.** Stanford, Calif.: Stanford Univ. Pr., 1971.

10.18　**Weber, David R., ed.　Civil disobedience in America: a documentary history.** Ithaca, N.Y.: Cornell Univ. Pr., 1978.

An anthology covering three centuries of American history.

10.19　**Wiebe, Robert H.　The search for order, 1877–1920.** New York: Hill and Wang, 1967.

Describes the erosion of traditional values of the village and individual and the search for community and order in the Progressive Era.

10.20　**Binkley, Wilfred T.　American political parties: their natural history.** 4th ed. rev. New York: Knopf, 1962.

A standard textbook that includes bibliography. Ranging outside the discussion of political parties and elections is *Politics, Parties, and Pressure Groups*, by Valdimer O. Key, 5th ed., New York: Crowell, 1964.

10.21 **Filler, Louis. Crusaders for American liberalism.** New York: Harcourt, Brace, 1939. Rev. ed. with new title, The Muckrakers. University, Pa.: Pennsylvania State Univ. Pr., 1976.

History of the muckraking movement 1900–1915. See also David M. Chalmers, *The Social and Political Ideas of the Muckrakers*, New York: Citadel, 1964, for magazine journalists involved.

10.22 **Friedman, Lawrence M. A history of American law.** New York: Simon and Schuster, 1973.

A general survey that makes much of law as reflective of social history. The colonial period is skimpily treated and the coverage extends to about 1900, with illustrations drawn largely from state laws.

10.23 **Gilbert, James B. Writers and partisans: a history of literary radicalism in America.** New York: Wiley, 1968.

10.24 **Keller, Morton. Affairs of state: public life in late nineteenth-century America.** Cambridge, Mass.: Harvard Univ. Pr., 1977.

American politics, law, and government from the Civil War to the end of the 19th century.

10.25 **Kelly, Alfred H., and Winfred A. Harbison. The American Constitution: its origins and development.** 5th ed. New York: Norton, 1976.

The Constitution itself, annotated with cases decided by the Supreme Court to June 22, 1964, may be found in 88 Congress, 1 Session, Senate Documents, no. 39, Washington, D.C.: U.S. Government Printing Office, 1964, ed. Norman Small. Dorothy C. Tompkins, *The Supreme Court of the United States*, Berkeley, Calif.: Bureau of Public Administration, Univ. of California, 1959, is an annotated bibliography useful for the history of the court, its modus operandi, and its relationship to the other branches of the government. Edward Dumbauld, *The Constitution of the United States*, Norman, Okla.: Univ. of Oklahoma Pr., 1964, gives origin, evolution, and interpretations, clause by clause. See also Paul L. Rosen, *The Supreme Court and Social Science*, Urbana, Ill.: Univ. of Illinois Pr., 1972.

10.26 **Kolko, Gabriel. The triumph of conservatism: a reinterpretation of American history, 1900–1916.** New York: Free Press, 1963.

The Progressive Era was really the triumph of business control over politics.

10.27 **Schlesinger, Arthur M., Jr., ed. History of U.S. political parties.** 4 vols. New York: Chelsea House Publ., 1973.

Various authorities contributed twenty-six essays; appended to each are selections from source documents.

10.28 **Bowers, David F., ed. Foreign influences in American life: essays and critical bibliographies.** Princeton, N.J.: Princeton Univ. Pr., 1944.

A symposium with a cursory chapter on "The American Literary Expatriate." The bibliographies cover immigration, the pattern of assimilation, and the impact of foreign elements on American economics, politics, art, literature, religion, and philosophy.

10.29   **Curti, Merle.   American philanthropy abroad.** New Brunswick, N.J.: Rutgers Univ. Pr., 1963.
Nongovernmental aid to foreign lands and peoples. The major portion, understandably, deals with the present century.

10.30   **Handlin, Oscar.   The uprooted: the epic story of the great migrations that made the American people.** Boston: Little, Brown, 1951. 2d ed. 1973.
Classic discussion of the meaning of immigration and the consequent disruption in family and social life on European poor who came to the U.S.

10.31   **Hansen, Marcus L.   The Atlantic migration, 1607–1860: a history of the continuing settlement of the United States.** Cambridge, Mass.: Harvard Univ. Pr., 1940.
Deals with immigration from Europe.

10.32   **Higham, John.   Strangers in the land: patterns of American nativism, 1860–1925.** New Brunswick, N.J.: Rutgers Univ. Pr., 1955. Rev. ed. New York: Atheneum, 1963.
Examines immigration restriction, the drive to "Americanize" the immigrants, and the relationship of nationalism and antiradicalism in the development of racist ideology.

10.33   **Howe, Irving.   World of our fathers.** New York: Harcourt, Brace, Jovanovich, 1976.
The best account of Jewish immigration from Europe to the U.S., especially New York, in the closing decades of the 19th century and the early ones of the 20th. See also Irving Howe and Kenneth Libo, *How We Lived: A Documentary History of Immigrant Jews in America, 1880–1930*, New York: Richard Marek Pub., 1979, for a collection of vital firsthand texts beautifully illustrated with photographs and drawings of the period.

10.34   **Myers, Gustavus.   History of bigotry in the United States.** New York: Random House, 1943.
A substantial and vivid account from early settlement to the beginning of World War II.

10.35   **Wittke, Carl.   We who built America: the saga of the immigrant.** Cleveland, Ohio: Western Reserve Univ. Pr., 1939. Rev. ed. 1964.
Broader outlines of the entire history of immigration, plus special sections on various national groups: Irish, Germans, Chinese, Mexicans, etc.

10.36   **Bode, Carl.   The American lyceum: town meeting of the mind.** New York: Oxford Univ. Pr., 1956. Repr. with a new preface. Carbondale, Ill.: Southern Illinois Univ. Pr., 1968.
The best history of the lyceum movement of the early 19th century.

10.37   **Butts, R. Freeman, and Lawrence A. Cremin.   A history of education in American culture.** New York: Holt, 1953.
See also Barbara S. Marks, *The New York University List of Books in Education*, New York: Citation Pr., 1968, which covers history as well as other aspects of the subject.

10.38 **Cordasco, Francesco, and William W. Brickman, eds. A bibliography of American educational history: an annotated and classified guide.** New York: AMS Pr., 1975.

The broader connections of education with history and society are also encompassed. See also Mark Beach, *A Bibliographical Guide to American Colleges and Universities: From Colonial Times to the Present,* Westport, Conn.: Greenwood Pr., 1975.

10.39 **Cremin, Lawrence A. The transformation of the school: progressivism in American education, 1876–1957.** New York: Knopf, 1961.

Puts the progressive movement in the schools in the broader context of the times.

10.40 **Ellis, Joseph J. After the Revolution: profiles of early American culture.** New York: W. W. Norton, 1979.

An exposition of the hopes and eventual disappointment of notable post-revolutionary American figures who assumed that cultural maturity had come with political independence and learned otherwise. Focuses on Charles Wilson Peale, Hugh Henry Brackenridge, William Dunlap, and Noah Webster. A perceptive and rewarding study.

10.41 **Hohenberg, John. The Pulitzer Prizes: a history.** New York: Columbia Univ. Pr., 1974.

The awards in drama, music, and journalism, as well as in the field of books, are listed, along with notes. (The author administered the program for a number of years.)

10.42 **Lingeman, Richard. Small town America: a narrative history, 1620–the present.** New York: G. P. Putnam's Sons, 1980.

This is both a history of small towns in America and a discussion of the manner in which they affected the writing of selected authors, including Clemens, Dreiser, Lewis, and others.

10.43 **Morrison, Theodore. Chautauqua: a center for education, religion, and the arts in America.** Chicago: Univ. of Chicago Pr., 1974.

A popular account primarily of the New York institution founded in 1874, which spread its educative network all over the country and spawned scores of imitators, these last dealt with in one chapter.

10.44 **Mangione, Jerre. The dream and the deal: the Federal Writers' Project, 1935–1943.** Boston: Little, Brown, 1972.

The author worked with the publishers of the State Guide Series and thus his recollections and observations are prime sources. Also see Monty Noam Penkower, *The Federal Writers' Project: A Study in Government Patronage of the Arts,* Urbana: Univ. of Illinois Pr., 1977, a solid and detailed study focusing on the late 1930s.

10.45 **Nye, Russel B. The cultural life of the new nation, 1776–1830.** New York: Harper, 1960.

Compact, with excellent bibliography, this work is especially valuable for the literature student; one chapter deals with "The Quest for a National Literature."

10.46 **Rudolph, Frederick. The American college and university: a history.** New York: Knopf, 1962.

A semipopular history, with excellent footnotes and an annotated bibliography.

10.47 **Veysey, Laurence R. The emergence of the American university.** Chicago: Univ. of Chicago Pr., 1965.

Describes and evaluates the developments in the period 1865–1910.

10.48 **A history of the South.** Ed. Wendell Holmes Stephenson and E. Merton Coulter. 10 vols. [Baton Rouge:] Louisiana State Univ. Pr., 1947–1967.

Various authorities cover the region from 1607 to 1945.

10.49 **Woodward, C. Vann. The origins of the New South.** Baton Rouge: Louisiana State Univ. Pr., 1951. Rev. ed. 1971.

The authoritative discussion of southern history from the end of Reconstruction to the modern South. The 1971 edition includes a critical essay on recent works, by Charles B. Dew, and a bibliography, pp. 482–628.

10.50 **Billington, Ray Allen. Westward expansion: a history of the American frontier.** New York: Macmillan, 1949. 5th ed. 1982.

An excellent, well-written history, strongly supportive of the Turner thesis, which alleges that the frontier was the principal influence in the development of American values and behavior patterns. See also Billington's *The Far Western Frontier: 1830–1860*, New York: Harper & Brothers, 1956; and Taylor, 10.15.

10.51 **Clark, Thomas D. Frontier America: the story of the westward movement.** New York: Scribner, 1959. 2d ed. 1969.

"No attempt is made to adhere to a thesis," though emphasis is on the "social and economic aspects" of the frontier. Clark acknowledges that the frontier undoubtedly had some effect in developing American values and behavior but believes, in contrast to the Turner thesis, that established cultural patterns were far more important. Sharply contrasts with Billington, 10.50.

10.52 **Webb, Walter Prescott. The Great Plains.** Boston: Houghton Mifflin, 1931.

A significant and highly influential study of the history and culture of the Great Plains with particular relation to its geography, natural resources, and climate. A brief chapter on the literature of the Great Plains, though old and dated, is still suggestive and well worth reading.

10.53 **Berkhofer, Robert F., Jr. The white man's Indian: images of the American Indian from Columbus to the present.** New York: Knopf, 1978.

A concise summary of the history of white attitudes toward Native Americans.

10.54 **Encyclopedia of Indians of the Americas: volume 1, conspectus and chronology.** St. Clair Shores, Mich.: Scholarly Pr., 1974.

The South Americans are slighted in this big venture, which promised many future volumes but has been discontinued. See also *Encyclopedia of Indians of Canada*, same publisher, 1977.

10.55   **Marken, Jack W.   The Indians and Eskimos of North America: a bibliography of books in print through 1972.** Vermillion, S.D.: Dakota Pr., 1973.

Many fictional works are omitted.

10.56   **Washburn, Wilcomb E.   The American Indian and the United States: a documentary history.** 4 vols. New York: Random House, 1973.

The selected government records here assembled are competently introduced and will help greatly in tipping the balance in favor of historical accuracy rather than sentimental journalism. A long index expedites use. Washburn's *The Indian in America*, New York: Harper and Row, 1975, is compact, judicious, and useful also for its well-selected bibliography.

10.57   **Abajian, James de T.   Blacks and their contributions to the American West: a bibliography and a union list of library holdings through 1970.** Boston: G. K. Hall, 1974.

Of more value to black studies in general than to black literature in particular.

10.58   **Blassingame, John.   The slave community: plantation life in the antebellum South.** New York: Oxford Univ. Pr., 1972. Rev. ed. 1979.

A study of the culture, family, personality, religion, and African heritage of slaves which emphasizes the relative freedom of thought and action among slaves and the creation of an Afro-American culture.

10.59   **Fogel, William R., and Stanley L. Engerman.   Time on the cross.** 2 vols. Boston: Little, Brown, 1974.

A sensation-making revision of the historical views on the economics of slavery in the U.S., based on computer research. A supplement published the same year provides the evidence and explains the methods of "cliometricians." Bitterly attacked.

10.60   **Fredrickson, George M.   The black image in the white mind: the debate on Afro-American character and destiny, 1817–1914.** New York: Harper and Row, 1971.

Studies the development of pseudoscientific racist theory and ideology, which relate racial doctrines to social and intellectual developments.

10.61   **Genovese, Eugene D.   Roll, Jordan, roll: the world the slaves made.** New York: Pantheon Books, 1974.

A seminal interpretation of slave culture with much new information on the place of religion in the experience of slavery.

See also **29.54, 30.34.**

11. *Biography*

11.1   **Biography index: a cumulative index to biographical material in books and magazines.**   New York: H. W. Wilson, 1946– .

Quarterly index with annual and triennial cumulations. Covers books and about 2,000 periodicals in English, chiefly American; includes obituaries and some fictional treatments.

11.2 The New York Times obituaries index, 1858–1968. New York: New York Times, 1970.

Includes some 350,000 obituaries that appeared in the *Times*.

11.3 O'Neill, Edward H. Biography by Americans, 1658–1936: a subject bibliography. Philadelphia: Univ. of Pennsylvania Pr., 1939.

A checklist of biographies, individual and collective, written by Americans. In the cases of particularly famous men, only the "important books" on them are recorded.

11.4 Riches, Phyllis M. An analytical bibliography of universal collected biography, comprising books published in the English tongue in Great Britain and Ireland, America and the British dominions. London: The Library Assoc., 1934.

11.5 Adams, Oscar F. A dictionary of American authors. 5th ed. Boston: Houghton Mifflin, 1904.

The first edition, also by Adams, was published by Houghton Mifflin under the title *Handbook of American Authors* in 1884.

11.6 Allibone's dictionary of authors. Philadelphia: Lippincott, 1897.

Includes over 46,000 authors from the earliest accounts to the last half of the 19th century with forty subject indexes. The *Supplement*, also 1897, contains over 37,000 authors and 97,000 titles.

11.7 American writers: a collection of literary biographies. Ed. Leonard Unger. 4 vols. New York: Scribner, 1974. Supplement. 2 vols. 1979.

These literary biographies were originally published by the University of Minnesota as a pamphlet series on American writers. Their value is necessarily limited by their brevity, and they vary in quality, but many of them were written by leading scholars on their subjects and are consequently well worth consulting.

11.8 Benét, William Rose, ed. The reader's encyclopedia. New York: Crowell, 1948. 2d ed. 2 vols. 1965.

11.9 Burke, W. J., and Will D. Howe. American authors and books: 1640 to the present day. Rev. and enlarged by Irving Weiss. 3d ed. New York: Crown Publ., 1972.

Brief sketches; gives many minor names which do not appear in *Oxford Companion to Literature*, 21.21.

11.10 Concise dictionary of American biography. Ed. Joseph G. E. Hopkins et al. New York: Scribner, 1964. 3d ed. 1980.

An abridgment of the *DAB*, 11.13, in one volume. The sketches of distinguished authors are not reduced so radically as are those of most of the other subjects. The third edition is complete to 1960.

11.11 Contemporary authors: a bio-bibliographical guide to current authors and their works. Vol. 1–. Detroit: Gale Research Co., 1962–.

The authors—in various fields—are principally Americans.

11.12 **Dargan, Marion. Guide to American biography. Part 1, 1607–1815; part 2, 1815–1933.** Albuquerque: Univ. of New Mexico Pr., 1949–1952.
Selective; arranged by chronological periods, subdivided by geographical regions. A reprint by Greenwood in 1973 includes a foreword by Dumas Malone.

11.13 **Dictionary of American biography.** 20 vols. plus index. New York: Charles Scribner's Sons, 1928–1937. Supplements. 1946, 1958, and 1973.
Each sketch is followed by a list of sources, often including manuscript material. The following sometimes offer sketches of individuals not represented in the *DAB*: *Appleton's Cyclopaedia of American Biography*, 7 vols., New York: D. Appleton, 1887–1900 (vol. 8, 1918, is an index); *Lamb's Biographical Dictionary of the U.S.*, 7 vols., Boston: James H. Lamb, 1900–1903; *The National Cyclopaedia of American Biography*, Clifton, N.J.: J. T. White, 1892–; *White's Conspectus of American Biography*, 3d ed., Clifton, N.J.: J. T. White, 1973 (now renamed *Notable Names in American History*). For series of more specialized biographies, see *Harvard Guide*, 9.36. Cf. Jane Kline, *Biographical Sources for the U.S.*, Washington, D.C.: Library of Congress, 1961. (*National Cyclopaedia* is the most extensive dictionary.)

11.14 **Dictionary of literary biography.** Detroit: Gale Research Co., 1978–.
A multivolume set in progress, each volume focusing on a major literary area and edited by an expert in the field. Even in progress, this is an invaluable resource, particularly for secondary and tertiary figures.

11.15 **A directory of American poets and fiction writers: names and addresses of 4,853 contemporary poets and fiction writers whose work has been published in the United States.** New York: Poets & Writers, 1980.

11.16 **Directory of American scholars: a biographical directory.** Ed. Jaques Cattell Press. 7th ed. 4 vols. New York: R. R. Bowker, 1978.
Historians and scholars in the various fields of literature and the humanities are listed. Scientists are similarly treated in *American Men and Women of Science*, New York: R. R. Bowker, 1906–.

11.17 **Duyckinck, Evert A., and George L. Duyckinck. Cyclopaedia of American literature.** New York: Scribner, 1855. Rev. ed. 2 vols. Philadelphia, Pa.: W. Rutter, 1875.
Useful chiefly for minor early writers.

11.18 **Hyamson, Albert W. A dictionary of universal biography of all ages and of all peoples.** New York: E. P. Dutton, 1916. 2d ed. 1951.
An index of names included in the chief general biographical dictionaries in English and several other European languages. The second edition is completely revised.

11.19 **James, Edward T., et al. Notable American women, 1607–1950: a biographical dictionary.** 3 vols. Cambridge, Mass.: Harvard Univ. Pr., 1971.
A total of 1,359 sketches, modeled after those in the *DAB*, of women who died before 1951. See also 11.23, for 1951–1975.

11.20 **Kunitz, Stanley J., and Howard Haycraft, eds. American authors, 1600–1900.** New York: H. W. Wilson, 1938.
Contains 1,300 biographical sketches and 400 portraits.

11.21 **Kunitz, Stanley J., and Howard Haycraft. Twentieth century authors.** New York: H. W. Wilson, 1942. Supplement. 1955.
Biographical sketches of 1,850 authors of various nationalities, but chiefly American, plus 1,700 portraits. The supplement adds about 700 new authors, usually those who have come into prominence since 1942. See also 35.42.

11.22 **The new century cyclopedia of names.** Ed. Clarence L. Barnhart et al. 3 vols. New York: Appleton-Century-Crofts, 1954.
A standard reference work for names of consequence of various nationalities.

11.23 **Sicherman, Barbara, and Carol Hurd Green, eds. Notable American women, the modern period: a biographical dictionary.** Cambridge, Mass.: Harvard Univ. Pr., 1980.
This is vol. 4 of 11.19; it covers 1951–1975.

11.24 **Sochen, June. Consecrate every day: the public lives of Jewish American women, 1880–1980.** Albany: State Univ. of New York Pr., 1981.
Successful Jewish-American women portrayed individually and in groups; the figures include Emma Goldman, Fanny Brice, Edna Ferber, Sophie Tucker, Bella Abzug, Betty Friedan, and others.

11.25 **Van Doren, Charles, ed. Webster's American biographies.** Springfield, Mass.: C. Merriam Co., 1974.
Includes 3,000 men and women, dead and alive. Artists are weighted more heavily than in John A. Garraty, ed., *Encyclopedia of American Biography*, New York: Harper & Row, 1974 (1,000 entries).

11.26 **Wallace, W. Stewart. A dictionary of North American authors deceased before 1950.** Toronto: Ryerson Pr., 1951.
The authors may be journalists, lawyers, merchants, etc., but many literary figures are listed, by field of interest, with places and dates of birth and death.

11.27 **Who's who in America.** Chicago: Marquis, 1899–.
Biennial publication containing sketches of living individuals, who themselves supply the information. For persons dropped because of death there is a *Who Was Who*. *Who's Who in the East* and other sectional compilations include many additional names. *Who's Who of American Women, 1958–1959–*, began another series. (These titles are published by Marquis also.)

11.28 **Altick, Richard D. Lives and letters: a history of literary biography in England and America.** New York: Knopf, 1965.
"My special intention . . . has been to show how the biographies of writers have been the product of prevailing cultural conditions." Altick also reveals that literary biographies "have both mirrored and affected the critical thought of their times."

11.29 O'Neill, Edward H. **A history of American biography, 1800–1935.** Philadelphia: Univ. of Pennsylvania Pr., 1935.

11.30 Brignano, Russell. **Black Americans in autobiography.** Durham, N.C.: Duke Univ. Pr. 1974. Rev. ed. 1984.

An annotated bibliography of 710 autobiographical writings since the Civil War; includes a checklist of recent printings of antebellum works.

11.31 Kaplan, Louis, et al. **A bibliography of American autobiographies.** Madison: Univ. of Wisconsin Pr., 1961.

Coverage to 1946. A subject index classifies the books according to occupation, place of residence, and connection with historical events associated with the subjects. For each item one library owning a copy is indicated. For a continuation, see Mary Louise Briscoe, ed., *American Autobiography, 1945–1980: A Bibliography*, Madison: Univ. of Wisconsin Pr., 1982. See also Mary S. Carlock, "American Autobiographies, 1840–1870, a Bibliography," *Bulletin of Bibliography*, 23 (1961), 118–120.

11.32 Lillard, Richard G. **American life in autobiography: a descriptive guide.** Stanford, Calif.: Stanford Univ. Pr., 1956.

Selected autobiographies are listed under headings made according to the profession or occupation of the writers, e.g., "Actors and Show People," "Journalists, Newspaper and Magazine Editors."

11.33 Blasing, Mutlu Konuk. **The art of life: studies in American autobiography.** Austin: Univ. of Texas Pr., 1977.

Deals broadly and imaginatively with a wide range of works in which the central figure or consciousness is identifiably the author or a persona, and the relationship between the writing and the historical period it represents is made clear.

11.34 Butterfield, Stephen. **Black autobiography in America.** Amherst, Mass.: Univ. of Massachusetts Pr., 1974.

A useful and scholarly account that is marred, however, by the author's obvious partiality for revolutionary figures and works—especially with respect to writers of the 20th century.

11.35 Cooley, Thomas. **Educated lives: the rise of modern autobiography in America.** Columbus: Ohio State Univ. Pr., 1977.

A solid study focusing on late 19th-century American autobiography and showing how the nature of the genre modified with the developments occurring in the study of psychology.

11.36 Gunn, Janet Varner. **Autobiography: toward a poetics of experience.** Philadelphia: Univ. of Pennsylvania Pr., 1982.

A discussion of the autobiography largely in terms of reader response to a self-portrait that transcends the individual and personal.

11.37 Olney, James, ed. **Autobiography: essays theoretical and critical.** Princeton, N.J.: Princeton Univ. Pr., 1980.

A collection of essays on the genre by distinguished scholars.

11.38 Spengemann, William C. **The forms of autobiography: episodes in the history of a literary genre.** New Haven, Conn.: Yale Univ. Pr., 1980.

Following Augustine's recognition of three basic autobiographical forms, Spengemann discusses a selection of American books as historic, philosophic, or poetic autobiography; a substantial bibliography is included, pp. 170–245.

11.39   **Matthews, William.   American diaries.** Berkeley and Los Angeles: Univ. of California Pr., 1945.
List of published diaries written prior to 1861.

11.40   **Matthews, William.   American diaries in manuscript, 1580–1954: a descriptive bibliography.** Athens, Ga.: Univ. of Georgia Pr., 1974.
Locations of the manuscripts are also provided.

See also 3.9–11.

12. *Magazines*

12.1   **Ditzion, Sidney.   "The history of periodical literature in the U.S.: a bibliography."** Bulletin of Bibliography, 15 (1935), 110, 129–133.

12.2   **Edgar, Neal L.   A history and bibliography of American magazines, 1810–1820.** Metuchen, N.J.: Scarecrow Pr., 1975.
Provides a good beginning for study of the period.

12.3   **Gilmer, Gertrude C.   Checklist of southern periodicals to 1861.** Boston: F. W. Faxon Co., 1934.

12.4   **Hoornstra, Jean, and Trudy Heath, eds.   American periodicals, 1741–1900. An index to the microfilm collections: 18th century; 1800–1850; 1850–1900.** Ann Arbor, Mich.: University Microfilms International, 1979.

12.5   **Kribbs, Jayne K., ed.   An annotated bibliography of American literary periodicals, 1741–1850.** Boston: G. K. Hall, 1977.
Includes summaries of the contents as well as usual publication data of nearly 1,000 journals; well-indexed and very useful compilation.

12.6   **Lewis, Benjamin M.   A register of editors, printers, and publishers of American magazines, 1741–1810.** New York: New York Public Library, 1957.

12.7   **MLA directory of periodicals: a guide to journals and series in languages and literatures, 1980–81–.** Comp. Eileen M. Mackesy and Karen Mateyak. New York: Modern Language Assoc., 1981–.
Prepared biennially, this directory serves as a "companion" to the *MLA International Bibliography*, an annual compilation. It includes information on more than 3,000 journals and series, over 2,000 of which are published abroad.

12.8   **Patterson, Margaret C.   Author newsletters and journals.** Detroit, Mich.: Gale Research Co., 1979.
An annotated bibliography of serials concerned with individual authors.

12.9   **Titus, Edna Brown, ed.   Union list of serials in libraries of the United States and Canada.** 3d ed. 5 vols. New York: H. W. Wilson, 1965.
Includes reference to more than 155,000 titles in nearly 1,000 libraries in the U.S. and Canada; books and serials. For serials begun since 1949, see *New Serial Titles*, Washington, D.C.: Library of Congress, 1953–.

12.10   **Lewis, Benjamin M.   An introduction to American magazines, 1800–1810.** Ann Arbor, Mich.: Univ. of Michigan Pr., 1961.
Covers 130 magazines published during the decade.

12.11   **Mott, Frank Luther.   A history of American magazines.** 5 vols. Cambridge, Mass.: Harvard Univ. Pr., 1968.
Covers the years 1741 to 1930; this is the standard history.

12.12   **Peterson, Theodore.   Magazines in the twentieth century.** Urbana: Univ. of Illinois Pr., 1956. 2d ed. 1964.
Traces the popular magazine from the late 19th century to 1964, including major trends in the magazine industry and the social and economic forces that helped to shape it. Although the extensive bibliography of the first edition has been excised in the second, additional attention has been given to religious and "little magazines."

12.13   **Richardson, Lyon N.   A history of early American magazines, 1741–1789.** New York: Thomas Nelson and Sons, 1931.
Also see Albert H. Smyth, *The Philadelphia Magazines and Their Contributors, 1741–1850*, Philadelphia, Pa.: R. M. Lindsay, 1892.

12.14   **Tebbel, John.   The American magazine: a compact history.** New York: Hawthorn Books, 1969.

12.15   **Chielens, Edward E.   The literary journal in America to 1900.** Detroit, Mich.: Gale Research Co., 1975.
An annotated survey of criticism on individual journals. A volume covering 1900 to 1950 was published by Gale in 1977.

12.16   **Gohdes, Clarence.   The periodicals of American Transcendentalism.** Durham, N.C.: Duke Univ. Pr., 1931.
The only comprehensive study to date on this subject.

12.17   **Janssens, G. A. M.   The American literary review: a critical history, 1920–1950.** The Hague: Mouton, 1968.

12.18   **Noel, Mary.   Villains galore: the heyday of the popular story weekly.** New York: Macmillan, 1954.
An excellent account.

12.19   **Anderson, Elliott, and Mary Kinzie, eds.   The little magazine in America: a modern documentary history.** Yonkers, N.Y.: Pushcart Pr., 1978.
Complements Hoffman et al., *The Little Magazine: A History and Bibliography*, 12.20, with a broad collection of essays and less comprehensive index of "little magazines."

12.20 **Hoffman, Frederick J., Charles Allen, and Carolyn F. Ulrich. The little magazine: a history and bibliography.** Princeton, N.J.: Princeton Univ. Pr., 1946. 2d ed. 1947.

Partially supplemented by J. B. May, *Twigs as Varied Bent*, Corona, N.Y.: Sparrow Magazine, 1954. The listing of scholarship on "little magazines" is supplemented by Charles L. P. Silet in *Bulletin of Bibliography*, 34 (1977), 157ff. See also *The International Directory of Little Magazines, 1982–83*, 18th ed., Paradise, Calif.: Dustbooks, 1982.

12.21 **Rom, Christine C. "Little magazines in special collections and rare book departments."** Credences: A Journal of Twentieth Century Poetry and Poetics, N.S. 1, Nos. 2–3 (Fall/Winter 1981/82), pp. 100–119.

A concise account of how and where to locate "little magazines" with a brief selected bibliography, pp. 115–119.

12.22 **Ulrich, Carolyn F., and Eugenia Patterson. Little magazines: a list.** New York: New York Public Library, 1947.

"Assembled, with additions," from Hoffman et al., *The Little Magazine*, 12.20. Includes the periodicals in the New York Public Library and covers the period 1890–1946.

12.23 **Union list of little magazines.** Chicago: [Center for Research Libraries], 1956.

A list of more than 1,000 "little magazines" in the libraries of five major midwestern universities.

12.24 **Conlin, Joseph R., ed. The American radical press, 1880–1960.** 2 vols. Westport, Conn.: Greenwood Press, 1974.

A hundred essays on 119 periodicals originally conceived as introductions in a reprint series. Bellamy nationalism, anarchism, socialism, the IWW and the theories of Debs, Upton Sinclair, etc., generated the "radicalism" portrayed.

12.25 **Johnson, Abby A., and Ronald M. Johnson. Propaganda and aesthetics: the literary politics of Afro-American magazines in the twentieth century.** Amherst, Mass.: Univ. of Massachusetts Pr., 1979.

12.26 **Wilson, Harold S. McClure's magazine and the muckrakers.** Princeton, N.J.: Princeton Univ. Pr., 1970.

A careful history of McClure's journalistic career and of the place of his magazine in the "muckraking movement." The literary connections are subordinated to the political and economic.

12.27 **Wood, James Playsted. Magazines in the U.S.: their social and economic influence.** New York: Ronald Pr., 1949. 3d ed. 1971.

Suggestive for the period not treated by Mott. The 3d edition lacks the subtitle.

See also **13.1, 13.3, 14.1–2, 23.34, 26.30, 32.99.**

13. *Newspapers*

13.1 **N. W. Ayer & Son's directory of newspapers and periodicals.** Philadelphia, Pa.: N. W. Ayer, 1880–.

Lists annually, by state and city, newspapers and certain other periodicals published in the U.S. and Canada and supplies relevant information, including circulation, political affiliation, etc.

13.2 **Arndt, Karl J. R., and May E. Olson. German language press of the Americas, 1732–1968: history and bibliography.** Vol. 1. 3d rev. ed. Munich: Verlag Dokumentation, 1976. Vol. 2. Munich: Verlag Dokumentation, 1973. Vol. 3. German-American press research from the American Revolution to the bicentennial. Ridgewood, N.J.: K. G. Saur, 1980.

The original title was *German-American Newspapers and Periodicals, 1732–1955: History and Bibliography*, 1961, 1965.

13.3 **Blum, Eleanor. Basic books in the mass media: an annotated, selected booklist covering general communications, book publishing, broadcasting, film, magazines, newspapers, advertising, indexes, and scholarly and professional periodicals.** 2d ed. Urbana: Univ. of Illinois Pr., 1980.

Update of a work which originally appeared with a slightly different title in 1962. The reference books listed are annotated.

13.4 **Brayer, Herbert O. "Preliminary guide to indexed newspapers in the U.S., 1850–1900."** Mississippi Valley Historical Review, 33 (1946), 237–258.

Repositories indicated; very incomplete.

13.5 **Brigham, Clarence Saunders. History and bibliography of American newspapers, 1690–1820.** 2 vols. Worcester, Mass.: American Antiquarian Soc., 1947. 2d ed. Westport, Conn.: Greenwood Press, 1975.

The standard work for its period. Also see "Additions and Corrections to History and Bibliography of American Newspapers, 1690–1820," *Proceedings of the American Antiquarian Society*, 71 (1961), 15–62, included in a reprint of Brigham: Hamden, Conn.: Archon, 1962.

13.6 **Campbell, Georgetta Merritt. Extant collections of early black newspapers: a research guide to the black press, 1880–1915.** Troy, N.Y.: Whitston Publ. Co., 1981.

Identifies and pulls together most known bibliographical information on the accessibility of extant black newspapers of the specified years.

13.7 **Downs, Robert B., et al. American library resources: a bibliographical guide.** Chicago: American Library Assoc., 1951. Supplement, 1950–1961. 1962. Supplement, 1961–1970. 1972.

Lists, among other materials, a limited number of published checklists of local holdings of newspapers and magazines. (There are numerous catalogs of newspapers from various states and localities as well as of holdings in individual libraries. Consult the card catalog of your library under the name of state, locality, or special library.)

13.8   **Editor & publisher international yearbook.** New York: Editor & Publisher Co., 1921–.
  A listing of all daily and weekly newspapers, U.S. and foreign, with abundant data about them, their publication, and their circulation.

13.9   **Gregory, Winifred. American newspapers, 1821–1936: a union list of files available in the U.S. and Canada.** New York: H. W. Wilson, 1937.
  Partially superseded by the numerous union lists covering newspaper files located in various cities, states, and regions.

13.10   **Index to the Christian Science Monitor.** Wooster, Ohio: Bell and Howell, 1960–.
  Annual cumulation of monthly index, Corvallis, Ore.: H. M. Cropsey, 1960–1969; monthly with annual cumulations, Wooster, Ohio: Bell & Howell, 1970–1978.

13.11   **Lathem, Edward C. Chronological tables of American newspapers, 1690–1820: being a tabular guide to holdings of newspapers published in America through the year 1820.** Worcester, Mass.: American Antiquarian Soc., 1972.
  Indicates the availability of the 86 earliest American newspapers; a companion to Brigham, 13.5.

13.12   **The New York Times index.** New York: New York Times Co., 1913–.
  An index to the published news, issued quarterly, 1913–1929; monthly, 1930–1947; and semimonthly, 1948–. Annual cumulations, 1930–. Also available on microfilm.

13.13   **New York Daily Tribune index for 1875–1906.** 32 vols. New York: The Tribune Assoc., 1876–1907.

13.14   **Newspapers in microform, 1948–1972.** Washington, D.C.: Library of Congress, 1974. Annual. 1973–.
  Cumulates all reports of U.S. and foreign newspapers on microfilm (1948–1967) with those received to mid-1972. Lists over 34,000 titles from holdings reported by 843 American libraries. The annuals provide new titles and new locations for earlier ones.

13.15   **Press intelligence directory: a manual of newspaper content, local writers, and syndicated columnists.** Washington, D.C.: [n.p.], 1957.
  Published for Press Intelligence, Inc. Part II is a list of topics—e.g., book news, theater news—followed by selected examples of papers carrying such material and often supplying names of the local writers of it.

13.16   **Price, Warren C. The literature of journalism: an annotated bibliography.** Minneapolis: Univ. of Minnesota Pr., 1959.
  Focuses principally on the U.S. and Canada; lists histories of journalism and of individual newspapers and magazines, biographies, etc. Updated in 1970 with the help of Calder M. Pickett to include items published from 1958–1968.

13.17   **Rowell's American newspaper directory . . . 1869–1908.** Ed. George P. Presbury. 40 vols. in 61. New York: G. P. Rowell & Co., 1869–1908.

An attempt at a complete compilation with publication and distribution data. Absorbed in 1908 by *N. W. Ayer & Son's American Newspaper Annual and Directory*, Philadelphia: N. W. Ayer & Son, 1910–1929; see 13.1.

13.18   **The Wall Street Journal index, 1958–.**   New York: Dow Jones, 1959–. Monthly with semiannual and annual cumulations.

13.19   **JQ [Journalism Quarterly].**   Columbia: Univ. of South Carolina Pr., 1924–.
Since 1930 includes annotated bibliographies on various journalistic subjects. Published under the abbreviated title since 1971.

13.20   **Detweiler, Frederick G.   The Negro press in the United States.** Chicago: Univ. of Chicago Pr., 1922.

13.21   **Emery, Edwin and Henry L. Smith.   The press and America.** New York: Prentice-Hall, 1954. 4th ed. Englewood Cliffs, N.J.: Prentice-Hall, 1978.
The basic text in journalistic history. Annotated chapter bibliographies are very helpful.

13.22   **Halaas, David Fridtjof.   Boom town newspapers: journalism on the Rocky Mountain mining frontier, 1859–1881.** Albuquerque: Univ. of New Mexico Pr., 1981.
The newspapers served as promoters, with questionable effect, for struggling and usually ephemeral mining communities.

13.23   **Mott, Frank Luther.   American journalism: a history, 1690–1960.** 3d ed. New York: Macmillan, 1962.
The standard work on American newspaper history.

13.24   **Rosewater, Victor.   History of cooperative news-gathering in the United States.** New York: D. Appleton and Co., 1930.

13.25   **Schlesinger, Arthur M.   Prelude to independence: the newspaper war on Britain, 1764–1776.** New York: Knopf, 1958.
Very informative; includes an appendix on newspaper circulations at the time.

13.26   **Watson, Elmo S.   A history of newspaper syndicates in the U.S., 1865–1935.** Chicago: [Watson,] 1936.
A brief but competent history that evolved from college and graduate courses of study.

See also **14.12.**

14. *Book trade and publishing*

14.1   **Tanselle, G. Thomas.   Guide to the study of United States imprints.** 2 vols. Cambridge, Mass.: Harvard Univ. Pr., 1971.

Three checklists of materials on printing and publishing, arranged according to region, genre, and author, are followed in the first volume by items dealing with copyright records, catalogs, and book-trade directories. The second volume includes studies of individual printers and publishers, "general studies," and a basic collection of 250 titles on U.S. printing and publishing, plus a full index for the whole.

14.2 **Trienens, Roger J. Pioneer imprints from fifty states.** Washington, D.C.: Library of Congress, 1973.

A chapter on each state describes the Library of Congress holdings of the earliest items printed there, and in the process provides a careful account of what is presently known about the beginnings of printing in that state.

14.3 **Bowker lectures on book publishing.** Collected ed. New York: R. R. Bowker, 1957.

Reprint of the first 17 Bowker Memorial Lectures, 1935–1956. Additional lectures were given 1958–1960, 1964, 1967. A "New Series" of annual lectures began in 1973; each is separately published.

14.4 **Cheney, Orion H. Economic survey of the book industry, 1930–1931.** New York: National Assoc. of Book Publishers, 1931. Supplement. New York: Employing Bookbinders of America, 1932. With 1947–1948 Statistical Report [of the American Book Publishers' Council]. New York: R. R. Bowker, 1949. With new Introduction by Robert W. Frase. New York: R. R. Bowker, 1960.

The "only comprehensive economic study of the American book publishing industry," the "Cheney Report" is still valuable despite its age. The 1960 edition includes new appendixes and an index providing opportunities for comparisons. For more recent information, see Benjamin M. Compaine, *The Book Industry in Transition: An Economic Study of Book Distribution and Marketing*, White Plains, N.Y.: Knowledge Industry Publ., 1978.

14.5 **Dessauer, John P. Book publishing: what it is, what it does.** New York: R. R. Bowker, 1974. 2d ed. 1981.

Chiefly concerned with book manufacturing; includes a chapter on the finances of publishing.

14.6 **Grannis, Chandler B., ed. What happens in book publishing.** New York: Columbia Univ. Pr., 1957. 2d ed. 1967.

A group of specialists explain operations in the American book-publishing business, from securing of manuscripts and copyediting to university presses, book clubs, paperback markets, and distribution of U.S. books abroad. Each chapter has a bibliography appended.

14.7 **Hawes, Gene R. To advance knowledge: a handbook on American university press publishing.** New York: American University Press Services, 1967.

See also Chester Kerr, *A Report on American University Presses*, Washington, D.C.: Assoc. of American University Presses, 1948.

14.8 **Miller, William. The book industry: a report of the public library inquiry.** New York: Columbia Univ. Pr., 1949.

Commercial and editorial aspects of publishing, including relations with public libraries and book clubs.

14.9   **Nemeyer, Carol A.   Scholarly reprint publishing in the United States.** New York: R. R. Bowker, 1972.
A history with an appended directory of reprint publishers.

14.10   **Strauss, Victor.   The printing industry: an introduction to its many branches, processes, and products.** Washington, D.C.: Printing Industries of America, 1967.
An encyclopedic account of printing technology in America.

14.11   **Welter, Rush.   Problems of scholarly publication in the humanities and the social sciences.** New York: American Council of Learned Societies, 1959.
Concise and useful, especially for graduate students; deals with periodicals as well as books.

14.12   **Bailyn, Bernard, and John B. Hench, eds.   The press and the American Revolution.** Worcester, Mass.: American Antiquarian Soc., 1980.
Seven substantial essays on the role of the press between 1760 and 1820, with an emphasis on the Revolutionary years.

14.13   **Blumenthal, Joseph.   The printed book in America.** Boston: D. R. Godine, 1977.
A handsome picture book with excellent material concerning the fine printers from 1880 to the present day, much of the work executed by typographers whom Blumenthal knew. The earlier period is done once-over-quickly.

14.14   **Charvat, William.   Literary publishing in America, 1790–1850.** Philadelphia: Univ. of Pennsylvania Pr., 1959.
A "skimming" and a condensation of materials collected on the subject of the history of the economics of authorship. Of considerable value in explaining the careers of various prominent authors. See also Charvat's *The Profession of Authorship in America, 1800–1870*, ed. Matthew J. Bruccoli, Columbus: Ohio State Univ. Pr., 1968.

14.15   **Franklin, Benjamin, V.   Boston printers, publishers, and booksellers: 1640–1800.** Boston: G. K. Hall, 1980.

14.16   **Hackett, Alice P., and James Henry Burke.   80 years of best sellers, 1895–1975.** New York: R. R. Bowker, 1977.
First published in 1945 as *Fifty Years of Best Sellers* and brought up to date each decade since then. Primarily lists of books; must be used with caution, for authentic sales figures are often not available. Includes a bibliography on "Books and Articles about Best Sellers." See also Charles B. Anderson, ed., *Bookselling in America and the World*, New York: Quadrangle/N.Y. Times Book Co., 1975.

14.17   **Lehmann-Haupt, Hellmut, et al.   The book in America: a history of the making, the selling, and the collecting of books in the United States.** New York: R. R. Bowker, 1939. 2d rev. American ed. 1951.

Revised and enlarged from the original German text published in Leipzig in 1937. Still the standard work on its subject, with sections on 1638–1783 by Lawrence C. Wroth, 1784–1860 by Wroth and Rollo G. Silver, and 1860–1950 by Lehmann-Haupt.

14.18   **McMurtrie, Douglas C.   A history of printing in the U.S.: Middle and South Atlantic states.** 2 vols. New York: R. R. Bowker, 1936.

Covers Pennsylvania, Maryland, New York, New Jersey, Delaware, District of Columbia, Virginia, South Carolina, North Carolina, and Georgia to 1800. (McMurtrie also edited a vast assortment of bibliographies listing the early imprints of various states and sections, many of which are now superseded; for a list of such works, see Tanselle, 14.1.)

14.19   **Mott, Frank Luther.   Golden multitudes: the story of best sellers in the United States.** New York: Macmillan, 1947.

A standard study. See also Hart, 8.43.

14.20   **Schick, Frank L.   The paperbound book in America: the history of paperbacks and their European antecedents.** New York: R. R. Bowker, 1958.

14.21   **Sheehan, Donald.   This was publishing: a chronicle of the book trade in the gilded age.** Bloomington: Indiana Univ. Pr., 1952.

From the Civil War to World War I; largely material on four firms: Holt; Harper; Scribner; and Dodd, Mead. (There are, of course, many individual histories of various publishing companies; see Tanselle, 14.1, for a record of them.)

14.22   **Shove, Raymond H.   Cheap book production in the United States, 1870–1891.** Urbana: Univ. of Illinois Pr., 1937.

Deals chiefly with works brought out in various series or "libraries," which were counterparts of the contemporary paperback series of reprints.

14.23   **Silver, Rollo G.   The American printer, 1787–1825.** Charlottesville: Univ. Pr. of Virginia, 1967.

A careful work carrying the story on from where Wroth (14.29) stops. Nothing more definitive has been written concerning the handpress era of American printing; it covers economics as well as ways and means. Two years earlier, Silver published an equally authoritative study, *Typefounding in America, 1787–1825*, Charlottesville: Univ. Pr. of Virginia, 1965.

14.24   **Smith, Roger H., ed.   The American reading public: what it reads, why it reads.** New York: R. R. Bowker, 1964.

Various aspects of the publishing business, including book reviewing, are discussed by several contributors. Some of the essays appeared earlier in a symposium in *Daedalus*, 92, no. 1 (1963).

14.25   **Stern, Madeleine B.   Imprints on history: book publishers and American frontiers.** Bloomington: Indiana Univ. Pr., 1956.

Chiefly concerned with various regional publishers but contains also a list of 191 firms surviving from the era prior to 1900. (A more recent assemblage of her pieces on publishers appears in *Books and Book People in 19th-Century America*, New York: R. R. Bowker, 1978.) Walter Sutton, *The*

Western Book Trade, Columbus: Ohio Univ. Pr., 1961, views Cincinnati as a publishing and bookselling center during the 19th century. For retrospective directories of publishers in various areas, see Tanselle, 14.1.

14.26 **Stern, Madeleine B., ed. Publishers for mass entertainment in nineteenth century America.** Boston: G. K. Hall, 1980.
Very brief articles by numerous authors on forty-six publishers, each with a few bibliographical references—a useful starting point.

14.27 **Tebbel, John. A history of book publishing in the United States.** 4 vols. New York: R. R. Bowker, 1972–1981.
The first three volumes cover 1630–1940 in a journalistic manner. The work often provides a useful synthesis of secondary sources, but it must be used with caution. Some of the problems are suggested by Gordon B. Neavill's review in *Publishing History*, 6 (1979), 107–11. For other popular general accounts, see Charles A. Madison, *Book Publishing in America*, New York: McGraw-Hill, 1966; and *Irving to Irving: Author-Publisher Relations, 1800–1974*, New York: R. R. Bowker, 1974.

14.28 **Thomas, Isaiah. The history of printing in America.** 2d ed. 2 vols. Albany, N.Y.: J. Munsell, 1874.
The first volume includes an appendix with a history of printing in Spanish America and a list of books printed in Mexico and Peru before 1600. Long out-of-date but contains information still not available elsewhere.

14.29 **Wroth, Lawrence C. The colonial printer.** 2d ed. Portland, Me.: The Southworth-Anthoensen Pr., 1938.
The standard account of colonial typography, printing, and binding; for the postrevolutionary and early romantic periods, see Silver, 14.23.

14.30 **Lehmann-Haupt, Hellmut, et al. Bookbinding in America.** Portland, Me.: The Southworth-Anthoensen Pr., 1941. Repr. with supplements by the authors. New York: R. R. Bowker, 1967.
The standard work on the subject. Includes three essays: "Early American Bookbinding by Hand," by Hannah Dustin French; "The Rise of American Edition Binding," by Joseph W. Rogers; and "On the Rebinding of Old Books," by Hellmut Lehmann-Haupt.

14.31 **Ringwalt, John Luther, ed. American encyclopaedia of printing.** Philadelphia: Menamin & Ringwalt, 1871.
Old-fashioned, out-of-date, but invaluable for history and background of printing in the U.S.; includes details of methods and technology.

14.32 **Smith, David C. History of papermaking in the United States (1691–1969).** New York: Lockwood Publ. Co., 1970.
The most comprehensive volume on the subject.

14.33 **Wells, James M. "Book typography in the United States of America."** Book Typography, 1815–1965, in Europe and the United States of America. Ed. Kenneth Day. Chicago: Univ. of Chicago Pr., 1966. Pp. 325–370.
A concise and authoritative historical survey of American printing and book design.

14.34 **American book-prices current.** New York: R. R. Bowker, 1895–.
Annual list of auction prices drawn for "literary properties" sold in the
U.S. and, after 1958, abroad. Various cumulative indexes of its contents
have been published.

14.35 **Cannon, Carl L. American book collectors and collecting from colonial times to the present.** New York: H. W. Wilson, 1941.

14.36 **McKay, George L. American book auction catalogues, 1713–1934: a
union list.** New York: New York Public Library, 1937. With supplements
from 1946 and 1948. Detroit: Gale Research Co., 1967.
The supplements, which appeared in vols. 50 and 52 of the N.Y. Public
Library *Bulletin*, are included in the Gale edition. (The libraries of the Gro-
lier Club, N.Y., and the American Antiquarian Soc., Worcester, Mass.,
contain two of the largest collections of American book dealers' and auction
catalogs.)

See also **5.4, 5.9, 13.3, 21.34, 30.6, 32.8, 32.34.**

15. *Selected histories of ideas in the U.S.*

15.1 **Beard, Charles A., and Mary R. Beard. The American spirit: a study
of the idea of civilization in the United States.** New York: Macmillan,
1942.
This is vol. 4 of a work entitled *The Rise of American Civilization.*

15.2 **Commager, Henry S. The American mind: an interpretation of American thought and character since the 1880's.** New Haven, Conn.: Yale
Univ. Pr., 1950.

15.3 **Curti, Merle. The growth of American thought.** 3d ed. New York: Harper and Row, 1964.
A standard work on the history of ideas in the U.S. Special attention
should be directed to its bibliography, which is both chronologically and
topically arranged. See also Robert A. Skotheim, *American Intellectual Histories and Historians*, Princeton, N.J.: Princeton Univ. Pr., 1966.

15.4 **Curti, Merle. Human nature in human thought: a history.** Madison:
Univ. of Wisconsin Pr., 1980.
A history of the changing concept of human nature in American culture
with special attention to major 19th-century authors, including Hawthorne
and the Transcendentalists. Based on a lecture series originally published in
1968.

15.5 **Degler, Carl N. Out of our past: The forces that shaped modern
America.** New York: Harper, 1959. Rev. ed. 1970.
An idealistic if somewhat arbitrary examination of the American present
by way of the history through which it evolved.

15.6   **Hartz, Louis. The liberal tradition in America: an interpretation of American political thought since the Revolution.** New York: Harcourt, Brace, 1955.

A highly reductive description of American development on the foundation of Lockeian liberalism, which generated uniformity through the freedom from artificial restraints.

15.7   **Jones, Howard Mumford. Ideas in America.** Cambridge, Mass.: Harvard Univ. Pr., 1944.

Fugitive essays collected under three headings: "The Need for Literary History," "Studies in the History of Ideas in America," and "The Responsibilities of Contemporary American Literature."

15.8   **Lerner, Max. America as a civilization: life and thought in the United States today.** New York: Simon and Schuster, 1957.

An attempt to grasp "the pattern and inner meaning of contemporary American civilization and its relation to the world of today." The bibliography adds many relatively recent works to the record.

15.9   **Miller, Perry. The New England mind: the seventeenth century.** Cambridge, Mass.: Harvard Univ. Pr., 1939.

The first volume of a three-volume intellectual history of America from the early 17th century to the Civil War. It was followed by Miller's *The New England Mind: From Colony to Province*, same pub., 1953, and the posthumously published *The Life of the Mind in America: From the Revolution to the Civil War*, New York: Harcourt, Brace, 1965.

15.10   **Persons, Stow. American minds: a history of ideas.** New York: Holt, 1958.

An interesting but too selective and rigid categorization of American thought; identifies five "social minds" in the country's history, from "colonial religious" to contemporary "neodemocratic."

15.11   **Welter, Rush. The mind of America: 1820–1860.** New York: Columbia Univ. Pr., 1975.

An intellectual history that centers on economic issues, the emergence of Jacksonian and Whig political ideas, and the development of free "institutions," i.e., religion, education, and land. An introductory chapter offers various suggestions for the student of methodology.

15.12   **Horton, Rod W., and Herbert W. Edwards. Backgrounds of American literary thought.** New York: Appleton-Century-Crofts, 1952. 3d ed. 1974.

Elementary historical treatments of Puritanism, the Enlightenment, Transcendentalism, evolution and Pragmatism, gentility and revolt, imperialism, Naturalism, Freudianism, southern sectionalism, and existentialism.

15.13   **Lewis, R[ichard] W. B. The American Adam: innocence, tragedy, and tradition in the nineteenth century.** Chicago: Univ. of Chicago Pr., 1955.

An important study of which the central idea and title have become mainstays in the criticism of American literature.

15.14   **Lynn, Kenneth S.   The dream of success: a study of the modern American imagination.** Boston: Little, Brown, 1955.

Dreiser, London, Phillips, Norris, and Herrick as affected by the "success myth." There is a chapter on Horatio Alger. Occasionally suggestive. See also Richard Weiss, *The American Myth of Success*, New York: Basic Books, 1969, which runs over the theme from the early colonial writings to Norman Vincent Peale.

15.15   **Marx, Leo.   The machine in the garden: technology and the pastoral ideal in America.** New York: Oxford Univ. Pr., 1964.

A landmark study of the conflict between industrial and pastoral motifs frequently illustrated in literary works.

15.16   **Parrington, Vernon Louis.   Main currents in American thought: an interpretation of American literature from the beginnings to 1920.** 3 vols. New York: Harcourt, Brace, 1927–1930, 1954.

Survey of the political and social philosophy of American authors from colonial times to about 1860. The third volume, which takes the history from the Civil War to 1920, was left incomplete at the author's death, but the fragments were salvaged and later published. (Parrington's study is often mistaken for a history of literature.)

15.17   **Beitzinger, A. J.   A history of American political thought.** New York: Dodd, Mead, 1972.

A textbook survey, with two-thirds of the space devoted to the theories pervasive in the era from colonial times to the Civil War.

15.18   **Bercovitch, Sacvan.   The American jeremiad.** Madison: Univ. of Wisconsin Pr., 1978.

Shows how the shift from Puritan sermons and typology to 19th century political addresses and symbolism both reflected the old and helped produce a new American identity.

15.19   **Burns, Edward M.   The American idea of mission: concepts of national purpose and destiny.** New Brunswick, N.J.: Rutgers Univ. Pr., 1957.

15.20   **Burns, Rex.   Success in America: the yeoman dream and the industrial revolution.** Amherst: Univ. of Massachusetts Pr., 1976.

Maintains that success in America before the middle of the 19th century was dependent more upon respect, independence, and material comfort than upon the acquisition of great wealth. Sources are varied, but Hawthorne's fiction, given chief attention, is treated more in relation to economy than to literature.

15.21   **Dorfman, Joseph.   The economic mind in American civilization.** 5 vols. New York: Viking Pr., 1946–1959.

History of economic ideas, popular and technical, from 1606 to 1933.

15.22   **Fredrickson, George M.   The inner Civil War: northern intellectuals and the crisis of the union.** New York: Harper and Row, 1965.

Intellectual reactions to the Civil War and the development of science, the professions, and the ideology of a "strenuous life."

15.23 **Gabriel, Ralph Henry. The course of American democratic thought: an intellectual history since 1815.** New York: Ronald Pr., 1940. 2d ed. 1956.
Literature is included among other elements of social and intellectual history.

15.24 **Hofstadter, Richard. The American political tradition and the men who made it.** New York: Knopf, 1948.

15.25 **Potter, David M. People of plenty: economic abundance and the American character.** Chicago: Univ. of Chicago Pr., 1954.

15.26 **Purcell, Edward A., Jr. The crisis of democratic theory: scientific naturalism and the problem of value.** Lexington: Univ. Pr. of Kentucky, 1973.
Explores the 20th-century conflict between those who hold to the permanent ethical and ideal foundation of democracy and those who perceive democracy as simply another of many expendable and transient political systems.

15.27 **Sanford, Charles L. The quest for paradise: Europe and the American moral imagination.** Urbana: Univ. of Illinois Pr., 1961.
The impact of the Edenic myth on the evolution of American culture. See also Lewis, 15.13.

15.28 **Berthoff, Rowland. An unsettled people: social order and disorder in American history.** New York: Harper and Row, 1971.
An extensive excursion in social history that interprets the balance between the social order and stability achieved in the colonial period as upset in the 19th century by the forces of individualism and economic progress. An epilogue looks forward to a new epoch, which holds a reasonable possibility for restoring the balance.

15.29 **Boyer, Paul S. Urban masses and moral order in America, 1820–1920.** Cambridge, Mass.: Harvard Univ. Pr., 1978.
Examines the continuities in the moral response to the city and the search for an urban community that replicated the order and values of the village. Includes discussion of tract societies, the American Sunday School Union, Children's Aid Society, YMCA, and the City Beautiful Movement.

15.30 **Hofstadter, Richard. Social Darwinism in American thought.** Philadelphia: Univ. of Pennsylvania Pr., 1944. Rev. ed. Boston: Beacon Pr., 1955.
A highly perceptive and influential analysis.

15.31 **Persons, Stow, ed. Evolutionary thought in America.** New Haven, Conn.: Yale Univ. Pr., 1950.
A symposium and bibliography.

15.32 **White, Morton G. Social thought in America: the revolt against formalism.** New York: Viking, 1949. Repr. with new preface and epilogue by the author. Boston: Beacon Pr., 1957. Repr. with a "Foreword for 1976." New York: Oxford Univ. Pr., 1976.
An effort to trace "the development of the leading ideas" of Charles A.

Beard, John Dewey, Oliver Wendell Holmes, Jr., James H. Robinson, and Thorstein Veblen.

15.33 **Wish, Harvey. Society and thought in America.** 2 vols. New York: Longmans, Green, 1950–1952. Vol. 2 revised. New York: D. McKay, 1963–1964.

An intellectual history that stresses the social conditioning of American ideas. See also Alice F. Tyler, *Freedom's Ferment: Phases of American Social History to 1860*, Minneapolis: Univ. of Minnesota Pr., 1944.

15.34 **Egbert, Donald D., and Stow Persons, eds. Socialism and American life.** 2 vols. Princeton, N.J.: Princeton Univ. Pr., 1952.

Vol. 1 is a symposium, including outlines of European backgrounds; Vol. 2 is an uneven bibliography.

15.35 **Lasch, Christopher. The new radicalism in America: the intellectual as a social type.** New York: Knopf, 1966.

Describes modern radicalism and the creation of an intellectual class in biographical essays on Jane Addams, Randolph Bourne, Mabel Dodge Luhan, and Lincoln Steffens, among others.

15.36 **Pells, Richard H. Radical visions and American dreams: culture and social thought in the depression years.** New York: Harper and Row, 1973.

15.37 **Unger, Irwin. The movement: a history of the American New Left, 1959–1972.** New York: Harper and Row, 1974.

A brief and popular but nevertheless useful account.

15.38 **Williams, William Appleman. The great evasion: an essay on the contemporary relevance of Karl Marx and on the wisdom of admitting the heretic into the dialogue about America's future.** Chicago: Quadrangle Books, 1964.

Analyzes the relevance of Marx in America and the U.S. manipulation of nature to avoid the challenge of building a genuine community.

15.39 **Diggins, John P. Up from communism: conservative odysseys in American intellectual history.** New York: Harper and Row, 1975.

This intellectual history of the roots of the Cold War includes studies of Max Eastman, John Dos Passos, John Burnham, and William F. Buckley, Jr.

15.40 **Guttmann, Allen. The conservative tradition in America.** New York: Oxford Univ. Pr., 1967.

A thoughtful study that uses literature to great advantage, arguing that American conservatism historically has been basically literary rather than political.

15.41 **Haney, Robert W. Comstockery in America: patterns of censorship and control.** Boston: Beacon Pr., 1960.

Sketchy, but contains a useful bibliography. Cf. James C. N. Paul and Murray L. Schwartz, *Federal Censorship: Obscenity in the Mail.* [New York:] Free Press of Glencoe, 1961; Paul S. Boyer, *Purity in Print: The*

Vice-Society Movement and Book Censorship in America, New York: Scribner, 1968; Ralph E. McCoy, *Freedom of the Press: An Annotated Bibliography*, Carbondale: Southern Illinois Univ. Pr., 1968, which was supplemented by his *Freedom of the Press: A Bibliocyclopedia—Ten-Year Supplement (1967–1977)*, foreword by Robert B. Downs, same pub., 1979. Also see Felice Flanery Lewis, *Literature, Obscenity, & Law*, Carbondale: Southern Illinois Univ. Pr., 1976; and Charles H. Busha, ed., *An Intellectual Freedom Primer*, Littleton, Colo.: Libraries Unlimited, 1977.

15.42 **Rossiter, Clinton L. Conservatism in America.** New York: Knopf, 1955. 2d ed. 1962.
Includes a discussion of contemporary "New Conservatism."

15.43 **Genovese, Eugene D. The world the slaveholders made: two essays in interpretation.** New York: Pantheon Books, 1969.
Essays on the social thought of proslavery writer George Fitzhugh and on comparative world slave systems offer a Marxist interpretation of history and connect slavery to the development of social class.

15.44 **Gossett, Thomas F. Race: the history of an idea in America.** Dallas, Tex.: Southern Methodist Univ. Pr., 1963.
Explores racism in social and scientific theories and literature from colonial times to the present.

15.45 **Jordan, Winthrop D. White over black: American attitudes toward the Negro, 1550–1812.** Chapel Hill: Univ. of North Carolina Pr., 1968.
Traces conscious and unconscious attitudes toward blacks in discussion of religion, interracial sex, economic issues, and social thought.

15.46 **Slotkin, Richard. Regeneration through violence: the mythology of the American frontier, 1600–1860.** Middletown, Conn.: Wesleyan Univ. Pr., 1973.
The myth of the heroic hunter struggling with the forces of raw nature and the Indian to gain the land is seen as the basis of a fundamental pattern of American life and values. This is a highly controversial point of view, as may be seen in John Seelye's sharp critique, "Ugh!," *Seventeenth-Century News*, 34 (1977), 37–41.

15.47 **Smith, Henry Nash. Virgin land: the American West as symbol and myth.** Cambridge, Mass.: Harvard Univ. Pr., 1950.
A history of the West as a popular and literary concept in America from Crèvecoeur to the end of the 19th century; a germinal and highly influential study not likely to be superseded in the foreseeable future.

15.48 **Taylor, William R. Cavalier and Yankee: the Old South and American national character.** New York: G. Braziller, 1961.
Effectively traces the conditions from which the conflicting archetypal symbols of the antebellum American South and North emerged—the agrarian cavalier and the mercantile Yankee.

See also 10.26, 18.30, 19.14, 25.36, 27.3, 27.27, 29.19, 29.30, 29.33, 35.36.

16. *Psychology*

16.1 **Boring, Edwin G. A history of experimental psychology.** 2d ed. New York: Prentice-Hall, 1957.

A standard work containing special chapters on the establishment of "modern psychology" in America.

16.2 **Davies, John D. Phrenology, fad, and science: a 19th-century American crusade.** New Haven, Conn.: Yale Univ. Pr., 1953.

Useful for study of Poe, Whitman, and other writers of their day who were greatly influenced by phrenology. See also Kerr, 29.21, and Madeleine B. Stern, *Heads & Headlines: The Phrenological Fowlers*, Norman: Univ. of Oklahoma Pr., 1971.

16.3 **Fay, Jay W. American psychology before William James.** New Brunswick, N.J.: Rutgers Univ. Pr., 1939.

16.4 **Hale, Nathan G., Jr. Freud and the Americans: the beginnings of psychoanalysis in the United States, 1876–1917.** New York: Oxford Univ. Pr., 1971.

This detailed study is the first volume in a series on Freud in America.

16.5 **Hearst, Eliot, ed. The first century of experimental psychology.** Hillsdale, N.J.: L. Earlbaum Assoc., 1979.

16.6 **Heidbreder, Edna. Seven psychologies.** New York: Appleton-Century, 1933.

Heidbreder specifically treats American psychology, though she acknowledges the importation of three of the seven systems—structuralism, Gestalt psychology, and psychoanalysis—from Europe. The remaining four systems include that of William James, the University of Chicago's functionalism and behaviorism, and Columbia University's dynamic psychology. A chapter is devoted to each.

16.7 **Herrnstein, Richard J., and Edwin G. Boring. A sourcebook in the history of psychology.** Cambridge, Mass.: Harvard Univ. Pr., 1965.

See also Raymond E. Fancher, *Pioneers of Psychology*, New York: Norton, 1979.

16.8 **A history of psychology in autobiography.** 7 vols. Vols. 1–3, ed. Carl A. Murchison; vols. 4–5, ed. Edwin Boring; vols. 6–7, ed. Gardner Lindzey. New York: Russell and Russell, etc., 1952–1974.

16.9 **Jung, Carl G., et al., eds. and intro. Man and his symbols.** London: Aldus Books, 1964.

Jung and four professional associates he selected have collaborated on this illustrated "examination of man's relation to his own unconscious"—an extraordinarily rich and rewarding exposition of Jungian psychology, especially in relation to myth and the visual arts.

16.10 **Leahey, Thomas Hardy. A history of psychology: main currents in psychological thought.** Englewood Cliffs, N.J.: Prentice-Hall, 1980.

16.11 **Mazlish, Bruce, ed. Psychoanalysis and history.** Englewood Cliffs, N.J.: Prentice-Hall, 1963. Rev. ed. New York: Grosset & Dunlap, 1971.

16.12 **Neumann, Erich. The origins and history of consciousness.** Trans. R. F. C. Hull. Bollingen Series No. 42. Princeton, N.J.: Princeton Univ. Pr., 1954.
Traces the fundamental correspondence between the development of individual and universal consciousness through several mythic stages revealed in archetypal symbolism.

16.13 **Nordby, Vernon J., and Calvin S. Hall. A guide to psychologists and their concepts.** San Francisco, Calif.: W. H. Freeman, 1974.

16.14 **Oberndorf, Clarence P. A history of psychoanalysis in America.** New York: Grune & Stratton, 1953.

16.15 **Quen, Jacques, and Eric T. Carlson, eds. American psychoanalysis: origins and development.** The Adolf Meyer Seminars. New York: Brunner/Mazel, 1978.

16.16 **Roazen, Paul. Freud and his followers.** New York: Knopf, 1974, 1975.

16.17 **Roback, A[braham] A. History of American psychology.** New York: Library Publ., 1952. Rev. ed. New York: Collier Books, 1964.
Uneven and sometimes biased.

16.18 **Robinson, Daniel N. An intellectual history of psychology.** New York: Macmillan, 1976. Rev. ed. 1981.

16.19 **Sahakian, William S., ed. History of psychology: a sourcebook in systematic psychology.** Itasca, Ill.: F. E. Peacock Publ., 1968. Rev. ed. 1981.

Psychology and literature

16.20 **Bickman, Martin. The unsounded centre: Jungian studies in American Romanticism.** Chapel Hill: Univ. of North Carolina Pr., 1980.
Illuminating Jungian interpretations of selected major American authors of the Romantic period with the concept of individuation as central; focuses on Poe, Emerson, Whitman, and Dickinson.

16.21 **Bloom, Harold. The anxiety of influence: a theory of poetry.** New York: Oxford Univ. Pr., 1973.
Bloom exposes the struggle of a poet to escape and react against the hold of his or her major literary antecedents—a rewarding, controversial study.

16.22 **Fraiberg, Louis. Psychoanalysis & American literary criticism.** Detroit, Mich.: Wayne State Univ. Pr., 1960.
Following expositions of the views on art and creativity held by Freud, Jones, Hans Sachs, and Ernst Kris, the author analyzes the application and often misapplication of those views in the literary criticism of V. W. Brooks, J. W. Krutch, L. Lewisohn, E. Wilson, K. Burke, and L. Trilling, the last of whom he believes used them with the greatest understanding.

16.23 **Greenberg, Harvey R.** **The movies on your mind.** New York: Saturday Review Pr., 1975.

A psychoanalytic discussion of seven classic films, including *The Wizard of Oz*, *The Treasure of Sierra Madre*, etc.

16.24 **Hoffman, Frederick J.** **Freudianism and the literary mind.** Baton Rouge: Louisiana State Univ. Pr., 1945. 2d ed. 1957.

After four theoretical chapters delineating Freudian concepts and their influence, Hoffman analyzes the work of several major authors from a psychoanalytical perspective. S. Anderson, W. Frank, and F. S. Fitzgerald receive extended attention in chapter 8; C. Aiken, L. Lewisohn, and H. Miller are treated more cursorily in chapter 9. "Psychology and Literature," a paper read by the author at the English Institute (9/56), constitutes an appendix; the "Selected Bibliography" for the volume is now too dated to be of much value.

16.25 **Holland, Norman N.** **The dynamics of literary response.** New York: Oxford Univ. Pr., 1968.

A psychological approach to literature in terms of reader response by one of the foremost proponents of the theory.

16.26 **Holland, Norman N.** **5 readers reading.** New Haven, Conn.: Yale Univ. Pr., 1975.

The reader's response to a work of literature is determined by one's total personality including the psychological defense mechanisms.

16.27 **Holland, Norman N.** **Poems in persons: an introduction to the psychoanalysis of literature.** New York: Norton, 1973.

An introduction to the manner in which people respond to poetry according to their own preconceptions and experience, thus generating individualized understandings of what the poem "says" and "means."

16.28 **Jung, C[arl] G.** **"On the relation of analytical psychology to poetry"** and **"Psychology and literature."** In The Spirit in Man, Art, and Literature. Trans. R. F. C. Hull. Bollingen Series No. 20. Princeton, N.J.: Princeton Univ. Pr., 1966. Pp. 65–83, 84–105.

Invaluable for gaining a firsthand understanding of Jung's highly influential views on the subject. See 16.9.

16.29 **Kaplan, Morton, and Robert Kloss.** **The unspoken motive: a guide to psychoanalytic literary criticism.** New York: Free Press, 1973.

Treats the development and practice of psychoanalytic literary criticism. Especially useful as an introductory text with brief accounts of major background figures and examples of application.

16.30 **Kiell, Norman, ed.** **Psychoanalysis, psychology, and literature: a bibliography.** 2d ed. 2 vols. Metuchen, N.J.: Scarecrow Pr., 1982.

A compilation of more than 20,000 unannotated entries indexed precisely as well as generally under three main headings (author, title, and subject). Vol. 1 is the bibliography, and vol. 2 is the index.

16.31 **Kris, Ernst.** **Psychoanalytic explorations in art.** New York: International Universities Pr., 1952.

Previously published essays by Kris are collected to reveal the complex relation between psychoanalytic theory and creativity. The five sections are: (1) "Introduction: Approaches to Art and The Image of the Artist," (2) "The Art of the Insane," (3) "The Comic," (4) "Problems of Literary Criticism," and (5) "Psychology and the Creative Processes." Illustrations are included as well as a detailed index and a substantial bibliography, pp. 321–341.

16.32   **Lesser, Simon O.   Fiction and the unconscious.** Preface by Ernest Jones. Boston: Beacon Pr., 1957.

An attempt to provide a comprehensive account of man's psychological attraction to storytelling.

16.33   **Malin, Irving Y., ed.   Psychoanalysis and American fiction.** New York: Dutton, 1965.

16.34   **Morrison, Claudia C.   Freud and the critic: the early use of depth psychology in literary criticism.** Chapel Hill: Univ. of North Carolina Pr., 1968.

Traces the introduction and early application of Freudian theory to literature, focusing on certain critics of the first quarter of the 20th century, including Conrad Aiken, Van Wyck Brooks, Joseph Wood Krutch, etc., to exemplify its use and mishandling in the beginning stage.

16.35   **Murphy, Gardner.   "The current impact of Freud on American psychology."** In Freud and the Twentieth Century. Ed. Benjamin Nelson. Cleveland: World Publ. Co./Meridian Books, 1957. Pp. 101–122.

16.36   **Sievers, W. David.   Freud on Broadway: a history of psychoanalysis and the American drama.** New York: Hermitage House, 1955.

Gives separate chapters to O'Neill and Philip Barry only.

16.37   **Skura, Meredith Anne.   The literary use of the psychoanalytic process.** New Haven: Yale University Pr., 1981.

A psychoanalytical approach to literature in which examples are taken from the work of several major authors (e.g., Chaucer, Shakespeare, Henry James) to show how the clinical practice of identifying the four aspects of discourse—content, psychic function, mode of representation, and rhetorical strategy—may be applied to critical reading.

16.38   **Stone, Albert E.   "Psychoanalysis and American literary culture."** American Quarterly, 28 (1976), 309–323.

A call for further exploration in developing a sound psychoanalytic theory for the critical reading of literature, one based on specific cases and on general laws.

16.39   **Suleiman, Susan, and Inge Crosman, eds.   The reader in the text: essays on audience and interpretation.** Princeton, N.J.: Princeton Univ. Pr., 1980.

16.40   **Tennenhouse, Leonard, ed.   The practice of psychoanalytic criticism.** Detroit, Mich.: Wayne State Univ. Pr., 1976.

Fourteen essays previously published in *American Imago* and *Criticism*, the first, a journal devoted to psychoanalytical criticism, and the second, a

critical journal published at Wayne State; the fourteen essays apply a variety
of psychoanalytic approaches to specific and general literary subjects.

16.41   **Weissman, Philip. Creativity in the theater: a psychoanalytic study.**
New York: Basic Books, 1965.
A psychoanalyst's approach to theater from a psychological perspective in
terms of creativity and development with specific attention given to selected
figures associated with the stage and to heroines of numerous plays, including certain ones of Williams and O'Neill.

See also **19.44, 25.30–31, 25.38–43.**

17. *Philosophy*

17.1   **Guerry, Herbert. A bibliography of philosophical bibliographies.**
Westport, Conn.: Greenwood Pr., 1977.
Over 2,350 entries compiled according to individual philosophers and
subjects, both general and specific; includes references to works from 1450
to 1974.

17.2   **Passmore, John. "Philosophical scholarship in the United States,
1930–1960."** In Philosophy. By Roderick M. Chisolm et al. Englewood
Cliffs, N.J.: Prentice-Hall, 1964. Pp. 3–124.
Occasionally suggestive.

17.3   **Adams, George P., and William P. Montague, eds. Contemporary
American philosophy: personal statements.** 2 vols. New York: Mac-
millan, 1930.
Statements of belief by thirty-four philosophers.

17.4   **Anderson, Paul Russell, and Max Harold Fisch, eds. Philosophy in
America from the Puritans to James, with representative selections.**
New York: D. Appleton, 1939.
Has useful bibliographies.

17.5   **Ayer, A[lfred] J. The origins of Pragmatism: studies in the philosophy
of Charles Sanders Peirce and William James.** San Francisco, Calif.:
Freeman, Cooper, 1968.
Selected topics are treated without reference to other studies.

17.6   **Boller, Paul F., Jr. Freedom and fate in American thought: from Edwards to Dewey.** Dallas, Tex.: Southern Methodist Univ. Pr., 1978.
Individual chapters on Edwards, Paine, Emerson, Calhoun, Douglass,
Bellamy, W. James, Clemens, and Dewey constitute a valuable introduction
to American intellectual history from the mid-18th century to the 20th
century.

17.7   **Fadiman, Clifton, ed.   I believe: the personal philosophies of certain eminent men and women of our time.** New York: Simon and Schuster, 1939.
Contains statements of belief by Pearl Buck, Ellen Glasgow, George Santayana, and James Thurber as well as revised statements by Dreiser, Mencken, and other Americans, Europeans, and Asians. Several volumes in this series appeared with different writers in each one.

17.8   **Fisch, Max H., ed.   Classic American philosophers.** New York: Appleton-Century-Crofts, 1951. Rev. 5th printing. 1966.
Scholarly anthology representing Peirce, James, Royce, Santayana, Dewey, and Whitehead.

17.9   **Flower, Elizabeth, and Murray G. Murphey.   A history of philosophy in America.** 2 vols. New York: Putnam, 1977.
Scholarly and detailed with respect to the relations between American and European philosophies and to the thought of the individual philosophers themselves.

17.10   **Hook, Sidney, ed.   American philosophers at work: the philosophic scene in the United States.** New York: Criterion Books, 1956.

17.11   **Kallen, Horace M., and Sidney Hook, eds.   American philosophy today and tomorrow.** New York: L. Furman, 1935.
Statements of belief by twenty-five thinkers.

17.12   **Kuklick, Bruce.   The rise of American philosophy: Cambridge, Massachusetts, 1860–1930.** New Haven, Conn.: Yale Univ. Pr., 1977.
A substantial study of the most influential Harvard philosophers of the period.

17.13   **Moore, Edward C.   American Pragmatism: Peirce, James, and Dewey.** New York: Columbia Univ. Pr., 1961.
A study of underlying doctrines.

17.14   **Perry, Ralph Barton.   The thought and character of William James.** 2 vols. Boston: Little, Brown, 1935.
Provides the best means of gaining the background for American philosophy in its most creative period.

17.15   **Philosophy and literature.** Baltimore, Md.: Johns Hopkins Univ. Pr., 1976–.
A semiannual that covers all aspects of the relations of philosophy to literature.

17.16   **Reck, Andrew J.   The new American philosophers: an exploration of thought since World War II.** Baton Rouge: Louisiana State Univ. Pr., 1968.
A sequel to 17.17, with discussion of Blanshard, Buchler, Feibleman, Hartshorne, Hook, Lewis, Nagel, Northrop, Pepper, Randall, Weiss, and Wild. Archie J. Bahm, *Directory of American Philosophers, 1980–81*, Bowling Green, Ohio: Philosophy Documentation Center/Bowling Green

State Univ. Pr., 1980, lists members of philosophy departments, periodicals in the field, etc.

17.17 **Reck, Andrew J. Recent American philosophy: studies of ten representative thinkers.** New York: Pantheon Books, 1964.

"To furnish a fair sample of philosophical thinking for the period from the turn of the century to World War II," ten philosophers are discussed: Perry, Hocking, Mead, Boodin, Urban, Parker, Sellars, Lovejoy, Jordan, and Sheffield.

17.18 **Riley, I. Woodbridge. American philosophy: the early schools.** New York: Dodd, Mead, 1907.

Out of date but contains material not available elsewhere.

17.19 **Riley, I. Woodbridge. American thought from Puritanism to Pragmatism and beyond.** New York: H. Holt, 1915. 2d ed. 1923.

17.20 **Sandeen, Ernest R., and Frederick Hale. American religion and philosophy: a guide to information sources.** Detroit, Mich.: Gale Research Co., 1978.

Over 1600 entries in twenty-one chapters arranged chronologically; emphasis is on work published since 1961; well indexed and annotated.

17.21 **Scheffler, Israel. Four Pragmatists: a critical introduction to Peirce, James, Mead, and Dewey.** New York: Humanities Pr., 1974.

Includes bibliographical references.

17.22 **Schneider, Herbert W. A history of American philosophy.** New York: Columbia Univ. Pr., 1946. 2d ed. 1963.

17.23 **Thayer, Horace S. Meaning and action: a critical history of Pragmatism.** Indianapolis, Ind.: Bobbs-Merrill, 1968. 2d ed. 1981.

A comprehensive and scholarly treatment of Pragmatism.

17.24 **Townsend, Harvey G. Philosophical ideas in the United States.** New York: American Book Co., 1934.

Better on the later movements than the earlier; the account is slightly Hegelian.

17.25 **Werkmeister, William H. A history of philosophical ideas in America.** New York: Ronald Press, 1949.

Contains a fairly full account of the period 1867–1939. Chapters 17 ("New Realism") and 18 ("Critical Realism") are the most valuable portions.

17.26 **White, Morton [G]. Science and sentiment in American philosophical thought from Jonathan Edwards to John Dewey.** New York: Oxford Univ. Pr., 1972.

A philosophers' survey; includes bibliographical references. White has also edited, with commentary, a sourcebook entitled *Documents in the History of American Philosophy: From Jonathan Edwards to John Dewey*, New York: Oxford Univ. Pr., 1972.

See also **24.18, 25.5, 32.29, 32.57, 32.76, 32.101, 32.184.**

Transcendentalism

17.27 **Albanese, Catherine L. Corresponding motion: Transcendental religion and the new America.** Philadelphia: Temple Univ. Pr., 1977.
A predominantly religious approach to Transcendentalism in New England.

17.28 **Ando, Shoei. Zen and American Transcendentalism—an investigation of one's self.** Tokyo: Hokuseido, 1970.
Includes three substantial chapters (1, "Zen"; 2, "Transcendentalism"; 3, "Zen and Transcendentalism") followed by an appendix on Zen and Christianity.

17.29 **Barbour, Brian M., ed. American Transcendentalism: an anthology of criticism.** Notre Dame, Ind.: Univ. of Notre Dame Pr., 1973.
An excellent selection of essays, both general and particular.

17.30 **Boller, Paul F., Jr. American Transcendentalism, 1830–1860: an intellectual inquiry.** New York: G. P. Putnam's Sons, 1974.
A useful overall history and account of the Transcendentalists but leaves much still to be said.

17.31 **Buell, Lawrence. Literary Transcendentalism: style and vision in the American renaissance.** Ithaca, N.Y.: Cornell Univ. Pr., 1973.
An effort to produce new evaluations based in part on the "ways in which the demands of vision and the demands of expression reinforce and qualify each other in Transcendentalist writing," and in part on the relation of the Transcendentalist authors to the literary traditions from which they drew.

17.32 **Christy, Arthur. The Orient in American Transcendentalism: a study of Emerson, Thoreau, and Alcott.** New York: Columbia Univ. Pr., 1932.
An important work not yet superseded by any single study.

17.33 **Cooke, George Willis, ed. The poets of Transcendentalism.** Boston: Houghton, Mifflin, 1903.
An anthology with a general introduction and biographical notes; includes many rather obscure figures associated with the group.

17.34 **ESQ: a journal of the American renaissance.** Pullman: Washington State Univ. Pr., 1955– .
Covers all aspects of 19th-century American literary study; see also *ATQ* [*American Transcendental Quarterly*], Kingston: Univ. of Rhode Island, 1969– , for 19th-century New England writers and culture.

17.35 **[Ellis, Charles Mayo.] An essay on Transcendentalism.** Ed. Walter Harding. Gainesville, Fla.: Scholars' Facsimiles and Reprints, 1954.
Originally published anonymously in 1842, this is one of the better attempts to systematize what cannot be systematized.

17.36 **Frothingham, Octavius Brooks. Transcendentalism in New England: a history.** New York: G. P. Putnam's Sons, 1876. New ed. with Intro. by Sydney E. Ahlstrom. New York: Harper, 1959.
An old but invaluable contribution by a participant.

17.37   **Goddard, Harold Clarke.   Studies in New England Transcendentalism.** New York: Columbia Univ. Pr., 1908.
An early but still valuable account.

17.38   **Hochfield, George, ed.   Selected writings of the American Transcendentalists.** New York: New American Library, 1966.
An excellent introduction precedes this remarkably comprehensive anthology, which includes many important selections by minor authors; this volume complements rather than overlaps any other collection of writings in the area. Brief biographical notes are appended. See also 17.44.

17.39   **Hutchison, William R.   The Transcendentalist ministers: church reform in the New England renaissance.** New Haven, Conn.: Yale Univ. Pr., 1959.
A well-rounded account of Transcendentalism in its chief manifestation. The bibliography is one of the most adequate on the subject.

17.40   **Kaplan, Nathaniel, and Thomas Katsaros.   Origins of American Transcendentalism in philosophy and mysticism.** New Haven, Conn.: College and University Pr., 1975.
Necessarily limited in depth by the immensity of its subject, this account nevertheless offers a useful introduction to sources for students developing an interest in the area.

17.41   **Kern, Alexander.   "The rise of Transcendentalism."** In Transitions in American Literary History. Ed. Harry Hayden Clark. Durham, N.C.: Duke Univ. Pr., 1954. Pp. 245–314.

17.42   **Koster, Donald N.   Transcendentalism in America.** Boston: Twayne, 1975.
The brevity of this account limits its value considerably, even as a general introduction for undergraduates.

17.43   **Leighton, Walter L.   French philosophers and New-England Transcendentalism.** Charlottesville: Univ. Pr. of Virginia, 1908.
Deals with the important influence of Victor Cousin and other French thinkers.

17.44   **Miller, Perry, ed.   The Transcendentalists: an anthology.** Cambridge, Mass.: Harvard Univ. Pr., 1950.
One of the best collections of Transcendentalist writings. Miller avoided anthologizing the easily found items in favor of providing a comprehensive view by both major and minor figures associated with the Transcendentalist group. See also his shorter collection, *The American Transcendentalists*, which is a complement to the larger volume rather than an abridgment; published for many years by Doubleday, it is now being issued by Johns Hopkins. Both volumes include useful bio-bibliographical and historical data. See also Hochfield, 17.38.

17.45   **Myerson, Joel, and Philip F. Gura, eds.   Critical essays on American Transcendentalism.** New York: G. K. Hall, 1982.
Includes more than fifty statements and articles on Transcendentalism by 19th- and 20th-century authors from England as well as the U.S. See also

The Transcendentalists: A Review of Research and Criticism, ed. Joel Myerson, New York: Modern Language Assoc., 1983.

17.46   **Myerson, Joel.   Brook Farm: an annotated bibliography and resources guide.** New York: Garland, 1978.
The principal bibliography on the subject; well annotated and indexed, this guide is divided into seven sections: "Members," "Visitors," "Contemporaries," "Histories," "*The Harbinger*," "Ana," and "Manuscripts" (including letters on and off microfilm, copies of which may be ordered from various libraries).

17.47   **Myerson, Joel.   The New England Transcendentalists and *The Dial*: a history of the magazine and its contributors.** Rutherford, N.J.: Fairleigh Dickinson Univ. Pr., 1980.
An invaluable resource for those interested in the Transcendentalists in general as well as for scholars giving particular attention to *The Dial*.

17.48   **Persons, Stow.   Free religion: an American faith.** New Haven, Conn.: Yale Univ. Pr., 1947.
Free religion eventually absorbed many of the later Transcendentalists.

17.49   **Pochmann, Henry A.   New England Transcendentalism and St. Louis Hegelianism: phases in the history of American idealism.** Philadelphia, Pa.: Carl Schurz Memorial Foundation, 1948.

17.50   **Simon, Myron, and Thornton H. Parsons, eds.   Transcendentalism and its legacy.** Ann Arbor: Univ. of Michigan Pr., 1966.
Ten essays on Emerson, Thoreau, Emily Dickinson, and later authors.

17.51   **Vogel, Stanley M.   German literary influences on the American Transcendentalists.** New Haven, Conn.: Yale Univ. Pr., 1955.
On this important topic, see also the extensive treatments in 17.49, 32.101 (in which conclusions are more authoritative), and René Wellek, *Confrontations*, Princeton, N.J.: Princeton Univ. Pr., 1965, on 19th-century cultural relations among Germany, England, and the U.S.

17.52   **Wells, Ronald V.   Three Christian Transcendentalists: James Marsh, Caleb Sprague Henry, Frederic Henry Hedge.** New York: Columbia Univ. Pr., 1943. Repr. with new manuscript material and new Intro. by the author. New York: Octagon Books, 1971.

See also **12.16, 18.44–47, 30.10–12, 32.25, 32.184.**

18. *Religion in the U.S.*

18.1   **Burr, Nelson R.   A critical bibliography of religion in America.** 2 vols. Princeton, N.J.: Princeton Univ. Pr., 1961.
The most extensive bibliography of the subject. The first volume surveys

guides, general histories, etc., and then turns to individual denominations and sects. The second volume treats religion in American life and culture, including the arts, literature, and intellectual history.

18.2   **Hills, Margaret T., ed. The English Bible in America: a bibliography of editions of the Bible and the New Testament published in America, 1777–1957.** New York: American Bible Soc., 1961. Rev. ed. 1962.

18.3   **Wallace, Dewey D., Jr. "Recent publications on American religious history: a bibliographical essay and review."** American Studies International, 19, Nos. 3/4 (Spr./Sum. 1981), [15]–42.

A substantial and clearly written résumé of scholarship of the 1970s arranged according to general topics, e.g., "Puritanism and Its English Background," "Unitarianism," "New Religious Groups."

18.4   **Burr, Nelson R. Religion in American life.** New York: Appleton-Century-Crofts, 1971.

May be used to locate many of the publications that have appeared since 1960.

18.5   **Hudson, Winthrop S. Religion in America.** New York: Scribner, 1965. 3d ed. 1981.

The best general survey for students and laymen.

18.6   **Hutchison, William R. The modernist impulse in American Protestantism.** Cambridge, Mass.: Harvard Univ. Pr., 1976.

A thorough study of the impact of liberalism on American Protestantism.

18.7   **Mead, Frank S. Handbook of denominations in the United States.** 7th ed. Nashville, Tenn.: Abingdon, 1980.

Brief sketches of 200-odd sects or denominations. (Annual statistics appear in *Yearbook of the Churches*, published by the National Council of the Churches of Christ in the U.S.A.) First published in 1951 by Abingdon-Cokesbury Pr., N.Y.

18.8   **Morgan, Richard E. The Supreme Court and religion.** New York: Free Press, 1972.

A brief, up-to-date analysis of scholarly discussions of the subject plus views of the authors on various court opinions and practices.

18.9   **Mulder, John M., and John F. Wilson, eds. Religion in American history.** Englewood Cliffs, N.J.: Prentice-Hall, 1978.

An excellent collection of essays.

18.10 **Niebuhr, H. Richard. The kingdom of God in America.** Chicago: Willett, Clark and Co., 1937.

A classic study of eschatological thinking in America written from a neo-orthodox theological perspective.

18.11 **Smith, James Ward, and A. Leland Jameson, eds. Religion in American life.** 4 vols. Princeton, N.J.: Princeton Univ. Pr., 1961.

A somewhat loosely organized symposium of papers centered on "The Shaping of American Religion" and "Religious Perspectives in American Culture."

18.12 **Strout, Cushing. The new heavens and new earth: political religion in America.** New York: Harper & Row, 1973, 1974.

A "Tocquevillian" interpretation of the relation between religious movements and political issues such as liberty, equality, community, and justice.

18.13 **Tuveson, Ernest L. Redeemer nation: the idea of America's millennial role.** Chicago: Univ. of Chicago Pr., 1968.

A careful treatment of millennial thinking in America and about America.

18.14 **Wilson, John F. Public religion in American culture.** Philadelphia, Pa.: Temple Univ. Pr., 1979.

A careful attempt to assess and redirect the debate about "civil religion in America" initiated by Robert Bellah's 1967 essay by that title.

18.15 **Ahlstrom, Sydney E. A religious history of the American people.** New Haven, Conn.: Yale Univ. Pr., 1972.

An exhaustive history of American religion with ample notes and bibliography; updates the prevailing histories but does not altogether supplant them.

18.16 **Bowden, Henry Ward. American Indians and Christian missions: studies in cultural conflict.** Chicago: Univ. of Chicago Pr., 1981.

An account of the cultural conflict between Christianity and Native American religious beliefs that evolved with the attempts of missionaries to convert the Indians from the 16th century on.

18.17 **Clebsch, William A. American religious thought: a history.** Chicago: Univ. of Chicago Pr., 1973.

Focuses on Edwards, Emerson, and William James. One of the volumes in the University of Chicago's History of American Religion series, ed. Martin E. Marty.

18.18 **Gaustad, Edwin Scott. Dissent in American religion.** Chicago: Univ. of Chicago Pr., 1973.

A quick survey over the whole period from the colonial era to the present. A volume in the University of Chicago's History of American Religion series, ed. Martin E. Marty.

18.19 **Gaustad, Edwin Scott. Historical atlas of religion in America.** New York: Harper & Row, 1962. Rev. ed. 1976.

An excellent pictorial representation of the distribution of the sects at various times in the past; equipped with bibliographical and statistical information.

18.20 **Gaustad, Edwin Scott. Religious history of America.** New York: Harper & Row, 1966.

Describes "the role of religion" in various aspects of the national history, with a selective annotated list of "further readings."

18.21 **Gunn, Giles, ed. New World metaphysics: readings on the religious meaning of the American experience.** New York: Oxford Univ. Pr., 1981.

A useful collection of source documents from the Renaissance to the present that deal with the cultural as well as religious attempt to define an American "idea of order."

18.22 **Koch, G. Adolf. Republican religion: the American Revolution and the cult of reason.** New York: H. Holt, 1933.
Deism and the reaction against it. A reprint is entitled *Religion of the American Enlightenment*, 1968.

18.23 **May, Henry F. The enlightenment in America.** New York: Oxford Univ. Pr., 1976.
A careful and detailed study of the American enlightenment "as religion" by a major American intellectual historian.

18.24 **McLaughlin, William G. Revivals, awakenings, and reform: an essay on religion and social change in America, 1607–1977.** Chicago: Univ. of Chicago Pr., 1978.
An excellent study of evangelical renewal in American Christianity, published in the Univ. of Chicago's History of American Religion series.

18.25 **Mead, Sidney. The lively experiment: the shaping of Christianity in America.** New York: Harper & Row, 1963.
An important monograph which places emphasis on the role of voluntarism in the structure of American religious life.

18.26 **Smith, H. Shelton, et al., eds. American Christianity: an historical interpretation with representative documents.** 2 vols. New York: Scribner, 1960–1963.
An anthology of Catholic and Protestant documents with historical introductions and extensive bibliographies classified according to various periods and movements.

18.27 **Smith, James Ward, and A. Leland Jameson, eds. The shaping of American religion.** Princeton, N.J.: Princeton Univ. Pr., 1961.
Essays by various authorities, including "Theology in America," by Sydney E. Ahlstrom, an important article.

18.28 **Mathews, Donald G. Religion in the Old South.** Chicago: Univ. of Chicago Pr., 1977.
An excellent interpretation of the ideology of southern evangelicalism in the antebellum period, with a brilliant chapter on black religion in the South.

18.29 **Raboteau, Albert J. Slave religion: the "invisible institution" in the antebellum South.** New York: Oxford Univ. Pr., 1978.
The first book-length treatment of the religion of American slaves with important implications for understanding the legacy of slave religion to the wider life of American culture.

18.30 **Brumm, Ursula. American thought and religious typology.** New Brunswick, N.J.: Rutgers Univ. Pr., 1970.
A significant study of the Puritan roots of typological thinking in America. See also Sacvan Bercovitch, ed., *Typology and Early American Literature*, Amherst: Univ. of Massachusetts, 1972, which includes his annotated bibliography on the subject, pp. [249]–337, previously published in more compact form in *Early American Literature*, 5 (1970).

18.31　**Hall, David D.　The faithful shepherd: a history of the New England ministry in the seventeenth century.** Chapel Hill, N.C.: Univ. of North Carolina Pr., 1972.

A detailed study; bibliographical essay appended.

18.32　**Jones, Phyllis M., and Nicholas R. Jones, eds.　Salvation in New England: selections from the sermons of the first preachers.** Austin: Univ. of Texas Pr., 1977.

An illustrated collection of important sermons by major first-generation ministers of New England; includes a sound introduction and appended brief biographies, list of early editions, and recommended readings. See also Levy, 27.22.

18.33　**McGiffert, Michael, ed.　Puritanism and the American experience.** Reading, Mass.: Addison-Wesley, 1969.

An excellent anthology of primary and secondary materials on Puritanism in its wider cultural implications.

18.34　**Pope, Robert G.　The Half-Way Covenant: church membership in Puritan New England.** Princeton, N.J.: Princeton Univ. Pr., 1969.

An analysis of the background for, and the circumstances attendant upon, the adoption of the Half-Way Covenant in Massachusetts and Connecticut in the later 17th century.

18.35　**Rosenmeier, Jesper.　The language of Canaan.** Medford, Mass.: Rosenmeier, 1976.

A highly useful collection of primary source materials on the innovations in religious language achieved by the Puritans. See also Mason I. Lowance, Jr.'s *The Language of Canaan*, 27.23.

18.36　**Simpson, Alan.　Puritanism in Old and New England.** Chicago: Univ. of Chicago Pr., 1955.

Balanced and intelligent introduction to Puritanism and its legacy of feeling.

18.37　**Stoever, William K. B.　A faire and easie way to heaven: covenant theology and Antinomianism in early Massachusetts.** Middletown, Conn.: Wesleyan Univ. Pr., 1978.

A clear and intelligent treatment of the Antinomian crisis in New England.

18.38　**Billington, Ray Allen.　The Protestant crusade, 1800–1860: a study of the origins of American nativism.** New York: Macmillan, 1938.

Treats the opposition to Catholicism, which was part of the Know-Nothing movement.

18.39　**Hopkins, Charles H.　The rise of the social gospel in American Protestantism, 1865–1915.** New Haven, Conn.: Yale Univ. Pr., 1940.

Deals with the "progressive" theology and sociological tendencies resulting from the impact of industrial society and scientific theories.

18.40　**Marty, Martin E.　Righteous empire: the Protestant experience in America.** New York: Dial Pr., 1970.

A significant interpretation of the imperial character of American Protestantism from the 17th century to the present.

18.41   **Meyer, Donald B.   The Protestant search for political realism.** Berkeley: Univ. of California Pr., 1960.

The best study of the neo-orthodox movement in modern American religious thought.

18.42   **Sandeen, Ernest R.   The roots of Fundamentalism.** Chicago: Univ. of Chicago Pr., 1970. Rev. ed. Grand Rapids, Mich.: Baker Book House, 1978.

Considers the roots in Britain and the U.S.; includes the millenarians. Covers the period 1800–1930.

18.43   **Smith, Timothy L.   Revivalism and social reform: American Protestantism on the eve of the Civil War.** Baltimore, Md.: Johns Hopkins Univ. Pr., 1980.

A landmark study that challenges the association of religious evangelicalism and social conservatism. Originally published in 1957 under the title *Revivalism and Social Reform in Mid-nineteenth Century America*, the 1980 edition has a new Afterword by the author.

18.44   **Cooke, George W.   Unitarianism in America: a history of its origin and development.** Boston: American Unitarian Assoc., 1902.

An excellent account of 19th-century developments, with a special chapter on "Unitarianism and Literature." Provides a neat history of the emergence of Transcendentalism. See also Daniel W. Howe, *The Unitarian Conscience*, Cambridge, Mass.: Harvard Univ. Pr., 1970.

18.45   **Wilbur, Earl M.   A history of Unitarianism in Transylvania, England, and America.** 2 vols. Cambridge, Mass.: Harvard Univ. Pr., 1952.

18.46   **Wright, Conrad.   The beginnings of Unitarianism in America.** Boston: Starr King Pr., 1955.

Carefully traces the development of Unitarianism from 1735 to 1805 with special emphasis on the Arminian background.

18.47   **Wright, Conrad, ed.   A stream of light: a sesquicentennial history of American Unitarianism.** Boston: American Unitarian Assoc., 1975.

18.48   **Ellis, John Tracy.   American Catholicism.** 2d ed., rev. Chicago: Univ. of Chicago Pr., 1969.

Standard short treatment in the University of Chicago's History of American Civilization series.

18.49   **Blau, Joseph L.   Judaism in America: from curiosity to third faith.** Chicago: Univ. of Chicago Pr., 1976.

Competent treatment of the assimilation of Judaism in America.

18.50   **Glazer, Nathan.   American Judaism.** Chicago: Univ. of Chicago Pr., 1957. 2d ed. 1972.

A compact account that may be fortified by documentary materials included in Joseph L. Blau and Salo W. Baron, eds., *The Jews in the United*

States, 1790–1840, 3 vols., New York: Columbia Univ. Pr., 1963; and Blau's *Judaism in America*, 18.49.

18.51 **Fairchild, Hoxie N. Religious trends in English poetry.** 6 vols. New York: Columbia Univ. Pr., 1939–1968.
The last two volumes include discussion of some of the American poets.

18.52 **Frederick, John T. The darkened sky: nineteenth-century novelists and religion.** Notre Dame, Ind.: Univ. of Notre Dame Pr., 1969.
Religion as bearing on the lives and works of Cooper, Hawthorne, Melville, Clemens, Howells, and James.

18.53 **Gunn, Giles B. The interpretation of otherness: literature, religion, and the American imagination.** New York: Oxford Univ. Pr., 1979.
Interpretive essays on the religious meaning of American writing as well as the religious meaning of literature as such.

18.54 **Gura, Philip F. The wisdom of words: language, theology, and literature in the New England renaissance.** Middletown, Conn.: Wesleyan Univ. Pr., 1981.
The theological controversies of the early 19th-century U.S. are seen as a matrix for studies of the language and symbolism in the literature of that time.

18.55 **Jones, Howard Mumford. Belief and disbelief in American literature.** Chicago: Univ. of Chicago Pr., 1967.
Six readable but somewhat introductory lectures on American writers, sponsored by the Frank L. Weil Institute for Studies in Religion and the Humanities; subjects extend from Paine to Frost, though heavy emphasis is on the 19th century.

18.56 **Reynolds, David S. Faith in fiction.** Cambridge, Mass.: Harvard Univ. Pr., 1981.
A comprehensive survey of popular religious fiction from before the Revolution to the period following the Civil War.

18.57 **Shurr, William H. Rappaccini's children: American writers in a Calvinist world.** Lexington: Univ. Pr. of Kentucky, 1981.
The Calvinist legacy is traced through American literary history; comprehensive but compact, this is a very rewarding study.

See also section 27 passim of this Guide and **10.33, 15.27, 17.20, 17.39, 17.48, 17.52, 31.49, 32.43.**

19. *Women's studies in the U.S.*

19.1 **Catalogs of the Sophia Smith Collection: women's history archive.** Boston: G. K. Hall, 1975.

The oldest archive of women's history, from 1795; emphasizes the history of women in the U.S.

19.2   Davis, Lenwood G.   The black woman in American society: a selected annotated bibliography. Boston: G. K. Hall, 1975.

19.3   Friedman, Leslie J.   Sex roles stereotyping in the mass media: an annotated bibliography. New York: Garland, 1977.
Lists books about the image of women in television, advertising, film, comics, and other areas of popular culture.

19.4   Haber, Barbara.   Women in America: a guide to books, 1903–1975. Boston: G. K. Hall, 1978. 2d ed. Urbana: Univ. of Illinois Pr., 1981.
Comprises a selective list of books under a wide range of subject headings, such as abortion, black women and Native American women, crime and punishment, education, feminism, health, history, biography, anthologies, law and politics, life-styles, literature, the fine arts, popular culture, etc. Annotations clearly summarize the significance of each book to the new feminism. Omits "fiction, poetry, drama and juvenile literature; highly technical studies; . . . reference books; nonbook materials; reprints and books about women which do not relate to American life." The 1981 edition includes an appendix on books, 1976–1979.

19.5   Harrison, Cynthia E.   Women in American history: a bibliography. Santa Barbara, Calif.: ABC/Clio Pr., 1979.
Abstracts (3395) from *America: History and Life* (vols. 1–14, 1963–1976) of articles in some 550 periodicals and 5 collections that are of value to a historian of women in the U.S. and Canada. Categories include not only women's organizations, woman suffrage, sex roles, religion, employment and social problems, etc., but also works by and about individual women and "articles about women novelists and fiction that dealt markedly with the subject of women's lives."

19.6   Hinding, Andrea, et al., eds.   Women's history sources: a guide to archive and manuscript collections in the United States. 2 vols. New York: R. R. Bowker, 1979. Vol. 2. Index. Ed. Suzanna Moody.
Over 18,000 annotated entries arranged alphabetically by locations within states; a particularly valuable resource.

19.7   Ritchie, Maureen.   Women's studies: a checklist of bibliographies. London: Mansell, 1980.
A useful but unannotated compilation with name and keyword indexes.

19.8   Stineman, Esther.   Women's studies: a recommended core bibliography. Littleton, Colo.: Libraries Unlimited, 1979.
The best bibliography to date in women's studies. Provides summaries of an extensive list of books that illuminate women's experiences and contributions to society under such subject headings as anthropology, autobiography, biography, literature, psychology, sociology, women's movement, and feminist theory. Also includes a list of "women-related periodicals," each of which is evaluated and described.

19.9   **Terris, Virginia R. Woman in America: a guide to information sources.** Detroit, Mich.: Gale Research Co., 1980.
An extensive reference tool with brief but useful annotations.

19.10   **Williamson, Jane. New feminist scholarship: a guide to bibliographies.** Old Westbury, N.Y.: Feminist Press, 1979.
Annotated list of 391 bibliographies, resource lists, and literary reviews on women; a comprehensive guide to women's studies, it includes thirty subject headings but does not include bibliographies of individuals.

19.11   **Feminist studies.** College Park: Univ. of Maryland Pr., 1972–.
Originally a quarterly, now issued three times per year. Focuses on women's experience and feminist views.

19.12   **Women's studies abstracts.** Rush, N.Y.: Rush Publ. Co., 1972–.
The only abstracting and indexing service that searches the scholarly literature on women. Includes bibliographic essays. Special issues of journals and reports and special publications are identified and annotated. Provides and cites book reviews for major titles of interest to scholars in women's studies. Published quarterly with an annual index.

19.13   **Women's studies newsletter.** Old Westbury, N.Y.: Feminist Pr., 1972–.
Clearinghouse for information pertaining to the scholarly study of women, including bibliographic essays on available resources; since 1977 the official publication of the National Women's Studies Assoc.

19.14   **Douglas, Ann. The feminization of American culture.** New York: Knopf, 1977.
Shows how the Victorian middle class produced through women and the clergy a sentimental society that was the precursor of modern mass culture.

19.15   **Heilbrun, Carolyn G. Reinventing womanhood.** New York: Norton, 1979.
Draws on literature, history, and the author's own life to analyze the failure of women to imagine themselves as autonomous.

19.16   **Hoch-Smith, Judith, and Anita Spring, eds. Women in ritual and symbolic roles.** New York: Plenum Pr., 1978.
Thirteen essays by anthropologists present a "cross-cultural perspective on women and religion," showing the origins of many literary images of women (as witches, nurturers, prostitutes, etc.).

19.17   **Chafe, William Henry. The American woman: her changing social, economic, and political roles, 1920–1970.** New York: Oxford Univ. Pr., 1972.
An analysis of the changing roles of women that emphasizes the impact of World War II.

19.18   **Chafe, William H. Women and equality: changing patterns in American culture.** New York: Oxford Univ. Pr., 1977.
A reflective essay on analytical problems confronting the history of women, such as the relationship of sex and race.

19.19   **Cott, Nancy F. The bonds of womanhood: "women's sphere" in New England, 1780–1835.** New Haven, Conn.: Yale Univ. Pr., 1977.

Using women's diaries and letters, Cott examines how women's working lives, education, religion, and consciousness were affected by the transformation to an industrial economy. She reveals how women created networks and maintained a sense of power in their lives despite constrictions placed upon them by early 19th-century New England.

19.20 **Degler, Carl. At odds: women and the family in America from the Revolution to the present.** New York: Oxford Univ. Pr., 1980.
A comprehensive work attempting to combine the fields of woman's history and family history, alleging that the roles of autonomous woman and family woman are "at odds."

19.21 **Flexner, Eleanor. Century of struggle: the woman's rights movement in the United States.** Cambridge, Mass.: Harvard Univ. Pr., 1959. Rev. ed. 1975.
A readable, scholarly, and comprehensive account.

19.22 **Kessler-Harris, Alice. Out to work: a history of wage-earning women in the United States.** New York: Oxford Univ. Pr., 1982.
A comprehensive examination of the experience of wage-earning women from colonial times to the present.

19.23 **Lerner, Gerda, ed. The female experience: an American documentary.** Indianapolis, Ind.: Bobbs-Merrill Educational Publ., 1977.
A compilation of primary source material organized by life cycle and an introductory essay on Lerner's historiographical approach.

19.24 **Lerner, Gerda. The majority finds its past: placing women in history.** New York: Oxford Univ. Pr., 1979.
Essays on women's history and methodology by a pioneer in the field.

19.25 **Marzolf, Marion. Up from the footnote: a history of women journalists.** New York: Hastings House, 1977.
Includes a survey of the news media's treatment of women and of the development of women's publications.

19.26 **Norton, Mary Beth. Liberty's daughters: the revolutionary experience of American women, 1750–1800.** Boston: Little, Brown, 1980.
A challenge to the "golden age" theory about women in colonial America and a revaluation of the impact of the American Revolution on women.

19.27 **Rossi, Alice, ed. The feminist papers: from Adams to de Beauvoir.** New York: Columbia Univ. Pr., 1973.
A compilation of works from advocates of woman's rights, preceded by thoughtful historical essays.

19.28 **Lerner, Gerda. Black women in White America: a documentary history.** New York: Pantheon Books, 1972.
Documents of the history of black women in the 19th- and 20th-century U.S. See also 19.2

19.29 **Notable American women: a biographical dictionary.** Ed. Edward T. James, Janet Wilson James, and Paul S. Boyer. 3 vols. Cambridge, Mass.: Harvard Univ. Pr., 1971.

Important source of information about women who lived in America from 1607 to 1950; lists primary and secondary sources for each entry. For women who lived after 1950, see 11.23, which covers 1951–1975.

Women and literature in the U.S.

19.30 **Batchelder, Eleanor. Plays by women: a bibliography.** New York: Womanbooks, 1977.
Lists 150 women playwrights.

19.31 **Bergstrom, Len V., and Marie B. Rosenberg, eds. Women and society: a critical review of literature with a selected annotated bibliography.** 2 vols. Beverly Hills, Calif.: Sage Publ., 1975, 1978.
Comprehensive bibliography. Particularly useful to those in literary studies are the sections "Women in Literature and the Arts" and "Women in Biography, Autobiography, and Memoirs," though the selection of literature was apparently random.

19.32 **Fairbanks, Carol. More women in literature: criticism of the seventies.** Metuchen, N.J.: Scarecrow Pr., 1979.
A bibliography of criticism for 1970–1977 on women writers, female characters, and feminist approaches to literature. Lists interviews and selected reviews. This volume is an enlargement of Carol Fairbanks Myers's *Women in Literature: Criticism of the Seventies*, Berkeley, Calif.: Women's Concerns Group/University Section Club, 1976. More than 1,000 writers are listed.

19.33 **Reardon, Joan, and Kristine A. Thorsen, eds. Poetry by American women, 1900–1975: a bibliography.** Metuchen, N.J.: Scarecrow Pr., 1979.
Lists 5,500 separately published volumes of poetry by women who are U.S. citizens. Includes a bibliography of secondary sources.

19.34 **Resnick, Margery, ed. Women writers in translation: an annotated bibliography, 1945–1980.** New York: Garland, 1981.
A compilation of women's writings published originally in languages other than English, including French, German, Japanese, Portuguese, Russian, and Spanish.

19.35 **Schwartz, Narda Lacey. Articles on women writers, 1960–1975: a bibliography.** Santa Barbara, Calif.: ABC-Clio Pr., 1977.
Over 600 writers are listed in this unannotated compilation, including many Americans.

19.36 **White, Barbara Anne, ed. American women writers: an annotated bibliography of criticism.** New York: Garland, 1977.
Identifies background works for the study of women in literature and criticism in which they are treated as a "distinct" group. Includes 413 entries annotated and cross-referenced. Among the bibliographical subheadings are feminist literary criticism, including definition, discriminatory treatment of female writers, feminine sensibility, and biography.

19.37   **Women and literature: an annotated bibliography of women writers.** 3d ed. Ed. Iris Biblowitz. Cambridge, Mass.: Women and Literature Collective, 1976.

An expansion of the 1973 bibliography produced by the Sense and Sensibility Collective, the earliest bibliography on women and literature to receive wide distribution in the women's movement. Also see the annual bibliography in 19.38 and *American Women Writers: Bibliographical Essays*, ed. Maurice Duke et al., Westport, Conn.: Greenwood Pr., 1983.

19.38   **Women and literature.** New York: Holmes & Meier, 1974–.

In the fall of 1975 appeared the first annual bibliography of articles on British and American women writers from 1660 to 1900, compiled by Florence Boos, indexing 200 scholarly journals. In 1976 the bibliography was expanded to include women writers in all English-speaking countries from the years 600 to 1960 and in 1977 the title was changed to "Bibliography of Literature in English by and about Women, 600–1960." Reviews as well as articles are included. The journal is issued quarterly with the bibliography in the fall number.

19.39   **Allen, Mary. Necessary blankness: women in major American fiction of the sixties.** Urbana: Univ. of Illinois Pr., 1976.

A view of female characters as presented by male (Barth, Roth, Updike, etc.) and female (Plath and Oates) authors. For an earlier, more feminist treatment of women in fiction, see *Images of Women in Fiction: Feminist Perspectives*, ed. Susan Koppleman Cornillon, Bowling Green, Ohio: Bowling Green Univ. Popular Pr., 1973, bibliography, pp. 355–91. Allen's bibliography is also worth consulting, pp. 187–222.

19.40   **Auerbach, Nina. Communities of women: an idea in fiction.** Cambridge, Mass.: Harvard Univ. Pr., 1978.

An important and well-written study. After giving a historical overview of how society has viewed communities of women, she examines the portrayal of sisterhood in British and American literature. Includes chapters on *Little Women* and *The Bostonians*.

19.41   **Baym, Nina. Women's fiction: a guide to novels by and about women in America, 1820–1870.** Ithaca, N.Y.: Cornell Univ. Pr., 1978.

The thesis of this complete and detailed historical literary study is that women's literature from 1820 to 1870 is distinct from that produced by women earlier and later in the century in presenting a "range of self-assertive and aggressive behavior, including the undomestic," as "consistent" with "true womanhood." Extremely useful chronological bibliography of novels by women from 1822 to 1869 as well as a valuable annotated bibliographical note on secondary material are included.

19.42   **Brown, Cheryl L., and Karen Olsen, eds. Feminist criticism: essays on theory, poetry, and prose.** Metuchen, N.J.: Scarecrow Pr., 1978.

In addition to theoretical essays on feminist literary criticism by Margaret Andersen, Annis Pratt, Lillian S. Robinson, and Annette Kolodny, there are essays applying a feminist perspective to Emily Dickinson, H.D., Sylvia Plath, Anne Sexton, Alta and Adrienne Rich, Cynthia MacDonald, Constance Fenimore Woolson, Zora Neale Hurston, Anaïs Nin, and other American women authors after the Civil War, though the emphasis is on contemporary writers; one essay is included on recent women's poetry.

19.43 **Christian, Barbara.   Black women novelists: the development of a tradition, 1892–1976.** Westport, Conn.: Greenwood Pr., 1980.

Traces the historical forces that shaped the images of black women in the U.S. and the effect of those images on the fiction of black women writers from 1892 to the present. Includes chapters on Paule Marshall, Toni Morrison, and Alice Walker.

19.44 **Davidson, Cathryn N., and E. M. Broner, eds.   The lost tradition: mothers and daughters in literature.** New York: F. Ungar Publ. Co., 1980.

Twenty-four essays covering literature from 2300 B.C. to our own century; includes a wide range of approaches from Jungian archetypal criticism to formalist and historical, and a useful bibliography of primary and secondary sources.

19.45 **Diamond, Arlyn, and Lee R. Edwards, eds.   The authority of experience: essays in feminist criticism.** Amherst: Univ. of Massachusetts Pr., 1977.

Three theoretical essays on feminist criticism, including material on Kate Chopin and Katherine Anne Porter.

19.46 **Donovan, Josephine, ed.   Feminist literary criticism: explorations in theory.** Lexington: Univ. Pr. of Kentucky, 1975.

Included among the six essays are a dialogue written by Carolyn Heilbrun and Catherine Stimpson to define "two distinct approaches to the feminist critical process" and a bibliographical introduction.

19.47 **Erens, Patricia, ed.   Sexual stratagems: the world of women in film.** New York: Horizon Pr., 1979.

Essays treat images of women in film and women film makers. Included are filmographies of women directors and an extensive bibliography on the image of women in film and on individual directors. See also Rosemary Ribich Kowalski, *Women and Film: A Bibliography*, Metuchen, N.J.: Scarecrow Pr., 1976.

19.48 **Fetterly, Judith.   The resisting reader: a feminist approach to American fiction.** Bloomington: Indiana Univ. Pr., 1978.

Rereads many of the "classic" male masterpieces of American fiction to illustrate how their presentation of women has been an attack on women and a false rendering of women's actual lives. Her examination of how the form of their works shapes our perceptions of women makes this analysis much more than merely a study of images of women in male literature.

19.49 **Fryer, Judith.   The faces of Eve: women in the nineteenth century American novel.** New York: Oxford Univ. Pr., 1976.

Discusses the images of women that such writers as Hawthorne, Melville, Holmes, Frederic, James, Howells, and Chopin project in their fiction.

19.50   **Gilbert, Sandra M., and Susan Gubar. Madwoman in the attic: the woman writer and the nineteenth-century literary imagination.** New Haven, Conn.: Yale Univ. Pr., 1979.

The authors draw on the methodology of psychological and phenomenological literary critics to construct a convincing feminist poetics—"the anxiety of authorship." Detailed analyses of the works of women writers from Jane Austen to Emily Dickinson demonstrate their theory's effectiveness as a paradigm for reading; moreover, the theory establishes a coherent interpretation of the literary tradition of women.

19.51   **Gilbert, Sandra M., and Susan Gubar, eds. Shakespeare's sisters: feminist essays on women poets.** Bloomington: Indiana Univ. Pr., 1979.

Twenty scholarly and critical essays written especially for this volume consider British and American women poets. Includes an introductory theoretical essay on gender and creativity, an essay that surveys Afro-American women poets, and another that focuses on the language of the American woman poet. A fourteen-page bibliography of feminist criticism accompanies the essays.

19.52   **Hoffmann, Leonore, and Deborah Rosenfelt, eds. Teaching women's literature from a regional perspective.** New York: Modern Language Assoc., 1982.

The first of the two sections of essays composing this volume discuss the literary importance of women's letters and diaries with respect to the region in which they were written; the second section explores pedagogical strategies for employing them with special attention to their value in feminist studies.

19.53   **Jacobus, Mary, ed. Women writing and writing about women.** New York: Barnes & Noble, 1979.

Includes essays by Elaine Showalter on feminist poetics, Laura Mulvey on "Feminism, Film and the Avant-garde," and others.

19.54   **Janeway, Elizabeth. "Women's literature."** In Harvard Guide to Contemporary American Writing. Ed. Daniel Hoffman. Cambridge, Mass.: Harvard Univ. Pr., 1979.

An excellent feminist overview of women writers, including feminist critics, from 1940 on. Janeway discusses the problem of defining women's literature, states several ways to address them, and within this context discerningly examines particular novels and poems. She also looks briefly at the social context from which the new feminism emerged.

19.55   **Jelinek, Estelle C., ed. Women's autobiography: essays in criticism.** Bloomington: Indiana Univ. Pr., 1980.

Fourteen critical essays about the theory and practice of women's autobiography and how they differ from those of men's autobiography. Includes essays on Lillian Hellman, Gertrude Stein, Maya Angelou, Anaïs Nin, and others.

19.56   **Lee, L. L., and Merrill Lewis, eds. Women, women writers, and the West.** Troy, N.Y.: Whitston Publ. Co., 1979.

Essays on Willa Cather, Dorothy Scarborough, Caroline Gordon, et al., and on images of men and women in the literature of the West, including diaries and other written materials that reflect the Western experience from a woman's perspective.

19.57 **Mainiero, Lina, ed.   American women writers: a critical reference guide from colonial times to the present.** 4 vols. New York: Ungar, 1979–1982.
Entries provide a critical assessment of the author's works as well as basic biographical data and primary and secondary bibliographies. Includes women scholars as well as creative writers.

19.58 **Moers, Ellen.   Literary women: the great writers.** Garden City, N.Y.: Doubleday, 1976.
An excellent survey of the history and tradition of women's literature, which emphasizes its variety and innovations. Offers considerable insight into the lives of individual women writers and their work.

19.59 **Springer, Marlene, ed.   What manner of woman: essays on English and American life and literature.** New York: New York Univ. Pr., 1977.
A useful collection of thirteen original critical essays that provide a historical overview of women as they have been portrayed in literature, setting those portraits against the realities of women's lives during various periods. Includes an essay by E. A. Schultz on "The Image of the Black Woman in Black American Fiction."

19.60 **Tulsa studies in women's literature.** Tulsa, Okla.: Univ. of Tulsa, 1982–.
Semiannual journal of the Tulsa Center for the Study of Women's Literature; devoted chiefly to the study of female writers and focusing entirely "on women and their work."

19.61 **Watts, Emily Stipes.   The poetry of American women from 1632 to 1945.** Austin: Univ. of Texas Pr., 1977.
An important and well-written study defining the poetic tradition of American women. Primary and secondary bibliographies included.

19.62 **Welter, Barbara.   Dimity convictions: the American woman in the nineteenth century.** Athens: Ohio Univ. Pr., 1976.
A social history that examines literature as one of the sources for changing attitudes toward women; chapters on Margaret Fuller, "Women Novelists of Religious Controversy," and "The Mystery Novels of Anna Katharine Green" are included.

19.63 **Westbrook, Arlen Runzler, and Perry D. Westbrook, eds.   The writing women of New England, 1630–1900: an anthology.** Metuchen, N.J.: Scarecrow Pr., 1982.

See also **11.19, 11.23–24, 22.26, 23.50, 24.31, 29.8, 30.11, 30.31, 31.2, 31.29, 31.50, 31.62, 31.99, 31.104–05, 32.133.**

20. *Chief general bibliographies of American literature*

20.1   **Altick, Richard D., and Andrew Wright. Selective bibliography for the study of English and American literature.** 6th ed. New York: Macmillan, 1979.
   A compact and helpful guide to the general reference materials.

20.2   **"American bibliography for 1921–."** PMLA, 37–. New York: Modern Language Assoc., 1922–.
   Annual listing of books and articles on various modern European languages and literature; until 1957 largely limited to works by Americans. Carries regularly a special section on American literature. In 1963 title was changed to *MLA International Bibliography*, and it was published separately in hard covers. It is now issued in several volumes, which include listings on British and American literatures, foreign-language literatures, English pedagogy, folklore, linguistics, and interdisciplinary topics.

20.3   **American literary manuscripts: a checklist. . . .**   Ed. J. Albert Robbins. 2d ed. Athens: Univ. of Georgia Pr., 1977.
   Identifies and locates literary manuscripts in libraries and archives.

20.4   **American literary Realism, 1870–1910.**   Arlington: Univ. of Texas at Arlington, 1967–.
   Originally a quarterly, *ALR* is now issued semiannually; it long specialized in "comprehensive annotated bibliographies of secondary comment" on the authors of American Realism, but in recent years it has been devoting much of its attention to literary history and criticism.

20.5   **American writers series.**   General editor, Harry Hayden Clark. New York: American Book Co., 1934–1950.
   A series of textbooks, most of which are devoted to individual authors, from Edwards and Franklin to Harte and James; in addition to the anthologized *Representative Selections* are long and especially valuable introductions, selective bibliographies, and notes. Each volume was edited by a specialist on the literary figure or group of authors, such as the Knickerbockers and early southern prose writers. To the date of their publication, the bibliographies are exceptionally well selected. Several of the books have been reprinted with substantially revised bibliographies as part of the American Century series of Hill and Wang.

20.6   **Baker, Nancy L. A research guide for undergraduate students: English and American literature.** New York: Modern Language Assoc., 1982.
   A useful forty-page introductory guide to library research material.

20.7   **Blanck, Jacob. Bibliography of American literature.** New Haven, Conn.: Yale Univ. Pr., 1955–.
   Descriptive bibliographies of all first editions and various other separates; about 35,000 items on some 300 authors who died before 1931. A most accurate work with invaluable lists. Locates copies in selected libraries. Vol.

7, the most recently published, covers James Kirke Paulding to Frank Richard Stockton.

20.8 **Boston Public Library.** **American literary manuscripts in the Boston Public Library: a checklist.** Boston: The Library, 1973.

20.9 **Bryer, Jackson R., ed.** **Sixteen modern American authors: a survey of research and criticism.** Durham, N.C.: Duke Univ. Pr., 1973.
Capable scholars provide a chapter each on Anderson, Cather, H. Crane, Dreiser, Eliot, Faulkner, Fitzgerald, Frost, Hemingway, O'Neill, Pound, Robinson, Steinbeck, Stevens, Williams, and Wolfe.

20.10 **Burkholder, Robert E.** **"Books Received."** Studies in the American Renaissance, 1977–. Ed. Joel Myerson. Boston: G. K. Hall, 1978–1982. Charlottesville: University Press of Virginia, 1983–.
Each item listed includes a brief descriptive annotation.

20.11 **The Cambridge history of American literature.** Ed. William P. Trent et al. 4 vols. New York: G. P. Putnam's Sons, 1917–1921.
Bibliographies, arranged by chapters, appear at the end of vols. 1, 2, and 4. Both text and bibliographies are often, but not always, outmoded, especially as they concern major figures. In 1931 Macmillan took over the publication of this history, and in 1944 the three vols. were reprinted in one, without the bibliographies.

20.12 **First printings of American authors: contributions toward descriptive checklists.** Ed. Matthew Bruccoli, C. E. Frazer Clark, Jr., Richard Layman, and Benjamin Franklin, V. 4 vols. Detroit: Gale Research Co., 1977–1979.
A useful compilation that is heavily weighted toward the 20th century; the selection of authors is at times arbitrary and surprisingly omissive.

20.13 **Foley, Patrick K.** **American authors, 1795–1895: a bibliography of first and notable editions chronologically arranged with notes.** Boston: The Publishers' Printing Co., 1897.
Still useful for works by certain minor authors.

20.14 **Gohdes, Clarence.** **Literature and theater of the states and regions of the U.S.A.: an historical bibliography.** Durham, N.C.: Duke Univ. Pr., 1967.
A checklist with more than 6,000 items covering books and articles on local belles lettres and drama. Unpublished dissertations are not included. Lists materials on New York and other cities and cites items published in books of local history as well as magazine articles. Appendixes list works on "western" writing and regionalism. Stratman, 23.35, is fuller on children's and collegiate theaters.

20.15 **Havlice, Patricia P.** **Index to American author bibliographies.** Metuchen, N.J.: Scarecrow Pr., 1971.
The intention is to gather under one cover "as many American author bibliographies as possible which have been published in periodicals." Supplements Nilon, 20.27, though its coverage is limited to twenty-eight periodicals.

20.16 **Heard, J. Norman, et al. Bookman's guide to Americana.** 7th ed. Metuchen, N.J.: Scarecrow Pr., 1981.

First published in 1953, this alphabetically arranged compilation lists out-of-print Americana and the prices asked; the data have been drawn from a few scores of dealers' catalogs.

20.17 **Johnson, Merle D. Merle Johnson's American first editions.** 4th ed. Rev. and enlarged by Jacob Blanck. New York: R. R. Bowker, 1942.

Lists the chief first editions of 194 American authors of the 19th and 20th centuries. The 1936 edition contained 24 authors omitted from this one, including Ray S. Baker, Zona Gale, Mary N. Murfree, David G. Phillips, and Upton Sinclair.

20.18 **Kennedy, Arthur G., et al. A concise bibliography for students of English.** Stanford, Calif.: Stanford Univ. Pr., 1940. 5th ed. Rev. by William E. Colburn. 1972.

W. E. Colburn's revision of this standard tool for students in English departments gives additional weight to the element dealing with American literature. It is accurate, though at times confusing because of the lack of editorial comment.

20.19 **Kolb, Harold H., Jr. A field guide to the study of American literature.** Charlottesville: Univ. Pr. of Virginia, 1976.

A well-annotated compilation that lists anthologies as well as bibliographies and other general reference tools.

20.20 **Koster, Donald N. American literature and language: a guide to information sources.** Detroit: Gale Research Co., 1982.

A selective but well-annotated bibliography of secondary material mostly from recent decades and largely comprising books on individual authors.

20.21 **Leary, Lewis, and John Auchard. American literature: a study and research guide.** New York: St. Martin's, 1976.

A handbook that should be of particular value to students with a serious interest in the field.

20.22 **Leary, Lewis G., et al. Articles on American literature, 1900–1950.** Durham, N.C.: Duke Univ. Pr., 1954. 1951–1967, 1970. 1968–1975, 1979.

Published articles listed by primary author.

20.23 **Lepper, Gary M. A bibliographical introduction to seventy-five modern American authors.** Berkeley, Calif.: Serendipity Books, 1976.

Basic nondescriptive listing of primary materials of writers "who have achieved literary prominence since 1945."

20.24 **Literary history of the United States.** Ed. Robert E. Spiller et al. 3 vols. New York: Macmillan, 1948. 4th ed., rev. 2 vols. 1974.

The second volume is the most extensive bibliography of the subject, containing both a general section and special lists on many individual authors. It originally appeared as vol. 3 of *LHUS* in 1948 and was prepared by Thomas H. Johnson. In 1959 and 1972 Richard M. Ludwig added supplements. Although it is still worth consulting, it is rapidly going out of date, and the index is insufficient. See also 21.29.

20.25   **Literary writings in America: a bibliography.**   8 vols. Millwood, N.Y.: KTO Pr., 1977.

Writings by and about more than 600 authors, 1850–1942, which were published in more than 2,000 magazines and over 600 volumes, are accounted for in this photo-offset reproduction of 250,000 cards arranged alphabetically; includes reviews. Very valuable for assistance in locating obscure references and previously "lost" items by minor and major authors.

20.26   **Marshall, Thomas F.   An analytical index to American Literature.** Vols. 1–30 (March, 1929–January, 1959). Durham, N.C.: Duke Univ. Pr., 1963.

Indexes by author and subject the articles published in the journal *American Literature* and the chief books reviewed in it.

20.27   **Nilon, Charles H.   Bibliography of bibliographies in American literature.** New York: R. R. Bowker, 1970.

Conflates items in the regular sources and provides a generous index to subjects as well as authors. For bibliographies on American authors published as separates, see especially the bibliographies cited in Woodress, *American Literary Scholarship, 1963–*, 20.41, and works like Wynar, *American Reference Books Annual*, 1.3.

20.28   **Northup, Clark Sutherland.   A register of bibliographies of the English language and literature.** New Haven, Conn.: Yale Univ. Pr., 1925.

Includes various American authors and topics, such as local literature, printing, and publishing.

20.29   **Pownall, David E., comp.   Articles on twentieth century literature: an annotated bibliography, 1954–1970.** 7 vols. New York: Kraus-Thomson Org., 1973–1980.

An alphabetized cumulation of the approximately 12,000 entries in the bibliographies of *Twentieth Century Literature* from 1954 to 1970 with the addition of some 10,000 more items. Extremely valuable for thoroughness and useful annotations. The index, to constitute vol. 8, is forthcoming.

20.30   **Proof: the yearbook of American bibliographical and textual studies.**   Columbia: Univ. of South Carolina Pr., 1971–1980.

Bibliography and texts connected with American literature are the province of this serial edited by Joseph Katz. A "Registry of Current Publications" in the field is also a feature.

20.31   **Quinn, Arthur Hobson, ed.   The literature of the American people: an historical and critical survey.** New York: Appleton-Century-Crofts, 1951.

Contains a 120-page bibliography with critical comments, prepared by the four authors of the volume. Now out of date but still useful for its selection.

20.32   **Rees, Robert A., and Earl N. Harbert, eds.   Fifteen American writers before 1900.** Madison: Univ. of Wisconsin Pr., 1971.

Substantial bibliographical essays on J. Adams, Bryant, Cooper, Crane, Dickinson, Edwards, Franklin, Holmes, Howells, Irving, Longfellow, Lowell, Norris, E. Taylor, and Whittier, plus two on the literature of the South. See also Woodress, *Eight American Authors*, 20.43.

20.33   **Roach, Helen.   Spoken records.** New York: Scarecrow Pr., 1963. 3d ed. Metuchen, N.J.: Scarecrow Pr., 1970.

Each chapter includes an informative commentary preceding a discography; chapters are arranged according to genre and reader (whether read by the author or someone else). A name and title index follows a substantial appendix on historical backgrounds of recording and collecting literary readings.

20.34 **Resources for American literary study.** College Park: Univ. of Maryland Pr., 1971–.
A semiannual that specializes in checklists, evaluative bibliographical essays, descriptions of collections of research materials, edited documents, etc. Carries a short section of book reviews.

20.35 **The Serif series: bibliographies and checklists.** Kent, Ohio: Kent State Univ. Pr., 1967–.
American authors dominate this helpful series; among them are writers of popular fiction as well as such literary figures as E. A. Robinson, John Gould Fletcher, and Gertrude Stein.

20.36 **Somer, John, and Barbara E. Cooper, comps. American & British literature, 1945–1975: an annotated bibliography.** Lawrence: Regents Press of Kansas, 1980.
An annotated bibliography of books only, arranged principally according to genre and "General Studies."

20.37 **Spear, Dorothea N. Bibliography of American directories through 1860.** Worcester, Mass.: American Antiquarian Soc., 1961.
Contains 1,647 items, of which the American Antiquarian Soc. holds 1,110.

20.38 **20th century American literature.** Intro. Warren French. New York: St. Martin's Press, 1980.
A volume in the Great Writers Student Library.

20.39 **Van Patten, Nathan. An index to bibliographies and bibliographical contributions relating to the work of American and British authors, 1923–1932.** Stanford, Calif.: Stanford Univ. Pr., 1934.
A few of the works listed were published in 1933, though most fall within the period cited.

20.40 **Woodress, James. American fiction, 1900–1950: a guide to information sources.** Detroit: Gale Research Co., 1974.
An excellent beginner's bibliography that gives the outstanding information on the subject in general and then proceeds to treat forty-four writers, from Sherwood Anderson to Richard Wright. Similar guides are in progress or already available on such topics as literary journals, Transcendentalism, black literature, etc.

20.41 **Woodress, James, et al. American literary scholarship: an annual/1963–.** Durham, N.C.: Duke Univ. Pr., 1965–.
The first volume covers books and articles on selected topics and authors published in 1963 (indexed in the 1964 volume). More than a dozen collaborators treat such general topics as "Literature to 1800," "Poetry: 1900 to the 1930s," "Drama," "Fiction: The 1930s to the Present," along with the work

done on major authors such as Emerson, Thoreau, Hawthorne, James, Faulkner, and Hemingway. A chapter on folklore began to appear in the third annual volume. For editions and secondary material published in American literature from 1963 on, *ALS* should be the first general reference source to check for data and assessments; it is thorough, dependable, and exhaustive.

20.42 **Woodress, James. Dissertations in American literature, 1891–1966.** Durham, N.C.: Duke Univ. Pr., 1968.
A classified list of doctoral dissertations from about 100 universities. A new edition is promised shortly. See also 21.39.

20.43 **Woodress, James, ed. Eight American authors: a review of research and criticism.** Rev. ed. New York: Norton, 1971.
Poe, Emerson, Hawthorne, Thoreau, Melville, Whitman, Clemens, and James are treated by well-known scholars, among them five who contributed to the first edition in 1956, edited by Floyd Stovall and published by the MLA.

20.44 **Wortman, William A. A guide to serial bibliographies for modern literatures.** New York: Modern Language Assoc., 1982.
In addition to literature, this compilation includes tangential areas that may be of interest to literary scholars.

See also **14.1, 16.30, 17.1, 18.1, 19.4, 19.7–8, 19.10, 27.32, 34.1–3, 35.1–2.**

21. *Chief general histories and selected critical discussions of American literature*

21.1 **Aaron, Daniel. The unwritten war: American writers and the Civil War.** New York: Oxford Univ. Pr., 1973.
From Emerson to Crane, the reaction of the authors to the war.

21.2 **American literature.** Durham, N.C.: Duke Univ. Pr., 1929–.
The chief journal in its field, published quarterly by the Duke University Press, with the cooperation of the American Literature Section of the MLA. Contains articles of a historical, critical, or bibliographical sort, and book reviews.

21.3 **Andrews, William L., ed. Literary Romanticism in America.** Baton Rouge: Louisiana State Univ. Pr., 1981.
Essays on major authors under a broad definition of Romanticism.

21.4 **Arnavon, Cyrille. Histoire littéraire des États-Unis.** Paris: Hachette, 1953.
The best general history of the subject written by a French scholar. The

standard history in Italian is Carlo Izzo, *Storia della letteratura nord-americana*, Milan: Nuova Academia Editrice, 1957; published in 1967 under the title: *La letteratura nord-americana*. See also Borges, 21.6.

21.5 **Berthoff, Warner. The ferment of Realism: American literature, 1884–1919.** New York: Free Press, 1965.

Described by Robert E. Spiller as a "thoroughly provocative book of impressionistic and analytical criticism in a loosely historical context." Commentators on the social scene, such as Veblen, Lloyd, and Henry George, are discussed as well as major literary figures of the period such as James, Howells, Dreiser, and Robinson.

21.6 **Borges, Jorge Luis. Introduction to American literature.** Ed. and trans. Robert O. Evans and L. Clark Keating. Lexington: Univ. Pr. of Kentucky, 1971.

21.7 **Bradbury, Malcolm, et al., eds. The Penguin companion to American literature.** New York: McGraw-Hill, 1971.

Chiefly biographical sketches of authors. The final third of the volume covers Latin American literature.

21.8 **Brooks, Van Wyck. Makers and finders: a history of the writer in America, 1800–1925.** New York: E. P. Dutton, 1937–1952.

A series of five volumes containing a well-written, impressionistic history in which many minor writers are interwoven. The scholar usually finds the treatment of the minor authors more rewarding factually than the discussion of the major figures. As a venture in criticism in the broader sense, the series is the most extensive as well as the most engagingly written survey of its subject ever produced by a single author. The five volumes in the order of coverage are: *The World of Washington Irving* (1944); *The Flowering of New England, 1815–1865*, new and rev. ed. (1937); *The Times of Melville and Whitman* (1947); *New England: Indian Summer, 1865–1915* (1940); *The Confident Years: 1885–1915* (1952).

21.9 **Browne, Ray B., and Donald Pizer, eds. Themes and directions in American literature: essays in honor of Leon Howard.** Lafayette, Ind.: Purdue Univ. Pr., 1969.

A distinguished collection of essays on subjects ranging from Puritan devotion to Randall Jarrell's poetry.

21.10 **Brownell, William C. American prose masters.** New York: C. Scribner's Sons, 1909.

Discriminating essays on Cooper, Hawthorne, Emerson, Poe, Lowell, and Henry James. An edition edited by Howard Mumford Jones was published by the Harvard Univ. Pr. in 1963.

21.11 **Bruccoli, Matthew J., ed. The chief glory of every people: essays on classic American writers.** Carbondale, Ill.: Southern Illinois Univ. Pr., 1973.

A group of essays on authors represented in the editions sponsored by the Center for Editions of American Authors.

21.12 **Clark, Harry Hayden, ed. Transitions in American literary history.** Durham, N.C.: Duke Univ. Pr., 1953.

A symposium of seven exploratory essays by various scholars: "The Decline of Puritanism," "The Late Eighteenth Century," "The Decline of Neoclassicism," "The Rise of Romanticism," "The Rise of Transcendentalism," "The Decline of Romantic Idealism," and "The Rise of Realism, 1871–1891."

21.13 **Cunliffe, Marcus. The literature of the United States.** 3d ed. Baltimore, Md.: Penguin Books, 1976.
A brief account originally published in 1954; useful for occasional criticisms.

21.14 **Deakin, Motley, and Peter Lisca, eds. From Irving to Steinbeck: studies in American literature in honor of Harry Warfel.** Gainesville: Univ. of Florida Pr., 1972.
A miscellaneous collection of considerable value.

21.15 **DeMott, Robert J., and Sanford E. Marovitz, eds. Artful thunder: versions of the Romantic tradition in American literature in honor of Howard P. Vincent.** Kent, Ohio: Kent State Univ. Pr., 1975.
A collection of essays on romanticism in American literature from Charles Brockden Brown through Wallace Stevens and Howard Nemerov; five deal with Melville.

21.16 **Falk, Robert, ed. Literature and ideas in America: essays in memory of Harry Hayden Clark.** Athens: Ohio Univ. Pr., 1975.
An outstanding collection of critical essays on major American authors with heavy emphasis on the 19th century.

21.17 **Foerster, Norman, ed. The reinterpretation of American literature.** New York: Harcourt, Brace, 1928.
Contains essays on the influence of Puritanism, the frontier, etc. This work was very influential on the academic study of American literature during the second quarter of the century and for some years after.

21.18 **Garland, Hamlin. Roadside meetings.** New York: Macmillan, 1930. **Companions on the trail.** 1931. **My friendly contemporaries.** 1932. **Afternoon neighbors.** 1934.
A series of recollections of authors and literary history covering "the purely literary side" of Garland's experiences during the period 1885–1930. See also *Hamlin Garland's Diaries*, ed. Donald Pizer, San Marino, Calif.: Huntington Library, 1968.

21.19 **Gohdes, Clarence, ed. Essays on American literature in honor of Jay B. Hubbell.** Durham, N.C.: Duke Univ. Pr., 1967.
Twenty-three essays by eminent scholars on subjects or authors ranging from the 17th century to the present, including several "neglected" writers like Harriet Beecher Stowe, Kate Chopin, Lafcadio Hearn, Jack London, O. Henry, and Thornton Wilder. Also contains an important article on American studies by Howard Mumford Jones.

21.20 **Gross, Theodore L. The heroic ideal in American literature.** New York: Free Press, 1971.
This dissertation considers "some of the representative heroes of American literature and their struggle with a conflict central to the moral life of

our country—the conflict between idealism and authority." Begins with Emerson and Melville and tops off with Mailer. The southern hero, as well as the black, comes in for a chapter.

21.21 **Hart, James D. The Oxford companion to American literature.** New York: Oxford Univ. Pr., 1941. 5th ed. 1982.

The standard handbook; includes sketches of authors and magazines, outlines of plots, explanations of movements, and terminology.

21.22 **Herzberg, Max J., et al., eds. The reader's encyclopedia of American literature.** New York: Crowell, 1962.

An exceedingly uneven collection of entries, chiefly biographical, a few by capable authorities. Many of the authors listed have little or nothing to do with belles lettres. Occasionally useful in supplementing Hart's *Oxford Companion*, 21.21; see also Burke, 11.9.

21.23 **Howard, Leon. Literature and the American tradition.** Garden City, N.Y.: Doubleday, 1960.

A short comprehensive history that in part undertakes to "seek out those attitudes of mind which controlled the creative imagination and helped shape the country's literature toward a recognizable national character."

21.24 **Howells, William Dean. Literary friends and acquaintance: a personal retrospect of American authorship.** New York: Harper & Brothers, 1900. Ed. David F. Hiatt and Edwin H. Cady. Bloomington: Indiana Univ. Pr., 1968.

Contains much firsthand material on Boston and New York as literary centers, 1860–1900, and presents invaluable portraits of Holmes, Longfellow, and Lowell in old age.

21.25 **Hubbell, Jay B. Who are the major American writers? a study of the changing literary canon.** Durham, N.C.: Duke Univ. Pr., 1972.

A splendid account of the shifting of literary reputations, based on polls, anthologies, prizes, etc., as well as on the ranking by historians and critics.

21.26 **Knight, Grant C. The critical period in American literature.** Chapel Hill: Univ. of North Carolina Pr., 1951.

Literary history of the decade 1890–1900; for later decades see Fishman, 28.17.

21.27 **Link, Franz H., ed. Amerika, Vision und Wirklichkeit.** Frankfurt a. M., Bonn: Athenäum-Verlag, 1968.

Sturdy essays by German authorities on aspects of the literature from Franklin to Tennessee Williams.

21.28 **Link, Franz H. Amerikanische Literatur-geschichts-schreibung.** Stuttgart: Metzler, 1963.

A survey of the historiography of American literature treating both American and European historians of the subject.

21.29 **Literary history of the United States.** Ed. Robert E. Spiller et al. 4th ed. rev. 2 vols. New York: Macmillan, 1974.

Usually referred to as *LHUS*. Fifty-five authors contributed one or more chapters, which vary in quality but make up the most extensive academic history of the subject. The second volume is exclusively devoted to bibliography, for which see 20.24. Originally published in 1948 in three volumes. A one-volume edition with a very limited bibliography has been published from time to time.

21.30   **Lüdeke, Henry.   Geschichte der amerikanischen Literatur.** Bern: A. Francke, 1952. 2d ed. 1963.
Especially useful for its references to German backgrounds.

21.31   **Macy, John, ed.   American writers on American literature.** New York: H. Liveright, 1931.
Thirty-seven writers contributed a chapter each on an important author or topic like colonial historians or contemporary poetry. One of the better ventures of the sort.

21.32   **Martin, Jay.   Harvests of change: American literature, 1865–1914.** Englewood Cliffs, N.J.: Prentice-Hall, 1967.
The most comprehensive and perceptive book-length survey of the period comprising American Realism and Naturalism—clear, detailed, and substantial.

21.33   **Matthiessen, F[rancis] O.   American renaissance: art and expression in the age of Emerson and Whitman.** New York: Oxford Univ. Pr., 1941.
A brilliant interdisciplinary critical study concerned with Emerson, Hawthorne, Melville, Thoreau, and Whitman; ties with such later writers as James and Eliot are also suggested. Indispensable.

21.34   **Miller, Perry.   The raven and the whale: The war of words and wits in the era of Poe and Melville.** New York: Harcourt, Brace, 1956.
An outstanding account of the tribulations of authors and publishers in the heyday of American Romanticism.

21.35   **Myerson, Joel, ed.   The American renaissance in New England.** Detroit: Gale Research Co., 1978.
The first volume of Gale's *Dictionary of Literary Biography* series, comprising bio-bibliographies of major and minor figures in American literature; a particularly valuable resource.

21.36   **Nye, Russel B.   American literary history: 1607–1830.** New York: Knopf, 1970.
A short but excellent survey.

21.37   **Pattee, Fred Lewis.   A history of American literature since 1870.** New York: Century, 1915.
Still very helpful, though it must be used with the author's later study, 21.38; obviously dated.

21.38   **Pattee, Fred Lewis.   The new American literature, 1890–1930.** New York: Century, 1930.
A vigorous critical and historical account that in part reassesses authors and works published prior to 1890.

21.39 **Polk, Noel, ed.** **"Guide to dissertations on American literary figures, 1870–1910."** American Literary Realism, 1870–1910, 8 (1975), 177–280, 291–348.

Descriptions and critiques of dissertations on authors of the Realist/Naturalist period in the U.S. are provided by a multitude of contributors in two issues of *ALR*.

21.40 **Quinn, Arthur Hobson, ed.** **The literature of the American people: an historical and critical survey.** New York: Appleton-Century-Crofts, 1951.

Written by four scholars—Kenneth B. Murdock, "Colonial and Revolutionary Periods"; Arthur Hobson Quinn, "Late 18th Century and Romantic Periods"; Clarence Gohdes, "Late 19th Century"; and George F. Whicher, "20th Century"—this is still in method the most scholarly narrative of the literature of the U.S. in English, and it remains valuable for its comprehensiveness and insight.

21.41 **Spiller, Robert E., ed.** **The American literary revolution, 1783–1837.** New York: New York Univ. Pr., 1967.

A substantial anthology of writings from the period that encapsulates the desire for American cultural independence.

21.42 **Spiller, Robert E.** **The cycle of American literature: an essay in historical criticism.** New York: Macmillan, 1955.

A useful short history, along with a partial elaboration of a dubious theory of cycles.

21.43 **Studies in the American renaissance, 1977–.** Ed. Joel Myerson. Boston: G. K. Hall, 1978–1982. Charlottesville: University Press of Virginia, 1983–.

An annual comprising biographical, historical, and bibliographical articles on the literature and general culture of the U.S. from 1830 to 1860; includes a list of recent "Books Received" with brief descriptive annotations.

21.44 **Sundquist, Eric J., ed.** **American Realism: new essays.** Baltimore, Md.: Johns Hopkins Univ. Pr., 1982.

Fourteen essays, mostly devoted to studies of individual novels by the major authors of the period, follow an editorial introduction.

21.45 **Taylor, Walter F.** **The story of American letters.** Chicago: H. Regnery Co., 1956.

Revised edition of a historical survey originally (1936) entitled *A History of American Letters*. Uses the colonial period as a point of departure and ends with authors established at the time of World War II.

21.46 **Twayne's United States authors series.** Boston: G. K. Hall, 1961–.

Initiated in New York, this series now includes several hundred volumes, each of about 125–200 pages, largely critical and interpretive, and equipped with notes and selective bibliography. The quality varies considerably; Steinbeck, Welty, and K. Patchen appear as subjects side by side with Franklin, Cooper, Hawthorne, and Howells. Works on general topics or genres are also included.

21.47 **Vinson, James, ed.** **Great writers of the English language.** 3 vols. New York: St. Martin's Pr., 1979.

An alphabetical listing of authors in English, with bio-bibliographical and critical summaries for each. Vol. 1, *Poets*; vol. 2, *Novelists and Prose Writers*; vol. 3, *Dramatists*.

21.48 **Wilson, Edmund. Patriotic gore: studies in the literature of the American Civil War.** New York: Oxford Univ. Pr., 1962.

A thorough and important study of a long-neglected area of literary history. For ideology emanating from the war, see also Robert Penn Warren, *The Legacy of the Civil War: Meditations on the Centennial*, New York: Random House, 1961.

21.49 **Wilson, Edmund, ed. The shock of recognition: the development of literature in the United States recorded by the men who made it.** 2 vols. Garden City, N.Y.: Doubleday, Doran, 1955.

A collection of literary documents by distinguished American authors commenting on other authors. Vol. 1, 1845–1900; vol. 2, the 20th century.

21.50 **Ziff, Larzer. The American 1890s: life and times of a lost generation.** New York: Viking, 1966.

Correlates political, social, and other trends with the productions of the chief authors and a number of the minor ones.

See also **2.10, 2.20.**

22. *Poetry*

22.1 **A directory of American poets: including names and addresses of 1500.** . . . New York: Poets & Writers, 1974. Supplement. 1976.

The poets and poetasters are listed, with addresses, by state. There are also a list of organizations sponsoring verse and a miscellaneous welter of anthologies, films, tapes, little magazines, and awards.

22.2 **Gershator, Phillis. A bibliographic guide to the literature of contemporary American poetry, 1970–1975.** Metuchen, N.J.: Scarecrow Pr., 1976.

A guide to criticism, biography, and anthologies with a very useful bibliographical introduction.

22.3 **Granger's index to poetry.** 7th ed. New York: Columbia Univ. Pr., 1982–.

An old work with inception in 1904 is revamped and enlarged to the point of covering hundreds of anthologies. The new editors are William J. Smith and William F. Bernhardt.

22.4 **Lemay, J. A. Leo. A calendar of American poetry in the colonial newspapers and magazines and in the major English magazines through 1765.** Worcester, Mass.: American Antiquarian Soc., 1970.

Notes on the authors are among the features of this valuable tool.

22.5 **Literary recordings: a checklist of the archives of recorded poetry and literature of the Library of Congress.** Rev. ed. Comp. Jennifer Wittington. Washington, D.C.: Library of Congress, 1981.
This list brings the inventory up to date through May 1975.

22.6 **Shapiro, Karl. A bibliography of modern prosody.** Baltimore, Md.: Johns Hopkins Univ. Pr., 1948.
English and American books and articles are listed with brief comments on their contents. Only a few items are earlier than the 20th century.

22.7 **Wegelin, Oscar. Early American poetry.** . . . 2d ed. rev. and enlarged. 2 vols. New York: Peter Smith, 1930.
Incomplete list of volumes of verse, 1650–1820, first published in an edition of 150 copies, New York: The Compiler, 1903–1907.

22.8 **Zulauf, Sander W., and Irwin H. Weiser. Index of American periodical verse: 1971–.** Metuchen, N.J.: Scarecrow Pr., 1973–.
The periodicals selected for coverage range from the academic through the popular to the weird.

22.9 **Pearce, Roy Harvey. The continuity of American poetry.** Princeton, N.J.: Princeton Univ. Pr., 1961.
A purposefully unhistorical discussion of the tradition of American poetry in relation to the national culture.

22.10 **Stauffer, Donald Barlow. A short history of American poetry.** New York: Dutton, 1974.
An objective survey of the poets, Bryant to Williams, with a minimum of deference to the "isms."

22.11 **Waggoner, Hyatt H. American visionary poetry.** Baton Rouge: Louisiana State Univ. Pr., 1982.
Includes discussion of Whitman, H. Crane, Williams, and others.

22.12 **Wells, Henry W. The American way of poetry.** New York: Columbia Univ. Pr., 1943.
Uneven survey of the "indigenous and unique," with good critical chapters on Freneau, Whitman, Emerson, Dickinson, et al. For an informative recent survey, see Bernard Duffey, *Expression and Its Values in the Times of Bryant, Whitman, and Pound,* Durham, N.C.: Duke Univ. Pr., 1978.

22.13 **Arms, George Warren. The fields were green: a new view of Bryant, Whittier, Holmes, Lowell, and Longfellow, with a selection of their poems.** Stanford, Calif.: Stanford Univ. Pr., 1953.

22.14 **Kindilien, Carlin T. American poetry in the eighteen nineties.** Providence, R.I.: Brown Univ. Pr., 1956.
Based on the Harris Collection at Brown University, which is one of the largest special collections of poetry in the U.S.

22.15 **Loving, Jerome. Emerson, Whitman, and the American muse.** Chapel Hill: Univ. of North Carolina Pr., 1982.
Relates the poetic development and art of Emerson and Whitman.

22.16 **Stedman, Edmund C. Poets of America.** Boston: Houghton Mifflin, 1885.
Old but still useful, both as history and commentary, especially on Bryant, Whittier, Emerson, Longfellow, Poe, Holmes, Lowell, Whitman, and Bayard Taylor.

22.17 **Walker, Robert H. The poet and the Gilded Age: social themes in late nineteenth century American verse.** Philadelphia: Univ. of Pennsylvania Pr., 1963.
Covers poets of the period 1876–1901.

22.18 **Bogan, Louise. Achievement in American poetry, 1900–1950.** Chicago: H. Regnery Co., 1951.
A sketch padded out with selections from the poets.

22.19 **Braithwaite, William S. B., ed. Anthology of magazine verse for 1913–1929, and yearbook of American poetry.** New York: G. Sully, [1913]–1929.
More than a dozen additional anthologies were edited by Braithwaite in the following years, and in 1959 Margaret Haley Carpenter edited an anthology from them: *Anthology of Magazine Verse for 1958*, New York: Schulte Publ. Co., 1959.

22.20 **Coffman, Stanley K. Imagism: a chapter for the history of modern poetry.** Norman: Univ. of Oklahoma Pr., 1951.

22.21 **Cook, Bruce. The Beat generation.** New York: Scribner, 1971.
An account of the radical and influential Beat writers of the 1950s—Ginsberg, Ferlinghetti, et al.—centered in San Francisco.

22.22 **Dembo, L. S. Conceptions of reality in modern American poetry.** Berkeley and Los Angeles: Univ. of California Pr., 1966.
Principally Fletcher, H.D., Amy Lowell, W. C. Williams, Stevens, Marianne Moore, Cummings, H. Crane, Pound, and Eliot.

22.23 **Gregory, Horace, and Marya Zaturenska. A history of American poetry, 1900–1940.** New York: Harcourt, Brace, 1946. Repr. with new Intro. by the authors. 1969.
Written by poets, not scholars.

22.24 **Hughes, Glenn. Imagism and the imagists: a study in modern poetry.** Stanford, Calif.: Stanford Univ. Pr., 1931.

22.25 **Irish, Wynot R. The modern American muse . . . 1900–1925.** Syracuse, N.Y.: Syracuse Univ. Pr., 1950.
Lists chronologically by year of publication 6,906 books of verse.

22.26 **Juhasz, Suzanne. Naked and fiery forms: modern American poetry by women—a new tradition.** New York: Harper and Row, 1977.
The contemporary woman poet is a union of masculine strength and feminine caution; an analysis of the work of many poets is provided, including Levertov, Plath, Sexton, and Brooks, among others.

22.27 **Kenner, Hugh. The Pound era.** Berkeley and Los Angeles: Univ. of California Pr., 1971.

Eliot, Williams, and Marianne Moore are brought into the Pound vortex and the critical insights of the influential figure.

22.28 **Kuntz, Joseph M., and Nancy C. Martinez. Poetry explication: a checklist of interpretation since 1925 of British and American poems past and present.** Boston: G. K. Hall, 1980.

The best checklist to date, generally through 1977. A periodical entitled the *Explicator*, Washington, D.C.: Heldref Publ., 1941–, is especially devoted to explication; many of the poems treated are American. The June issues contain an annual checklist of explication. The material is reassembled in *Explicator Cyclopedia*, Chicago: Quadrangle Books, 1966–.

22.29 **Lowell, Amy. Tendencies in modern American poetry.** Boston and New York: Houghton Mifflin and Macmillan, 1917.

Robinson, Frost, Masters, Sandburg, H.D., and Fletcher.

22.30 **Malkoff, Karl. Crowell's handbook of contemporary American poetry.** New York: Crowell, 1973.

A concise but rapid survey of American verse since 1940 is followed by material on seventy poets, plus various schools and movements.

22.31 **Miller, James E., Jr. The American quest for a supreme fiction: Whitman's legacy in the personal epic.** Chicago: Univ. of Chicago Pr., 1979.

A study of the importance of Whitman's influence on the development of the long poem in 20th-century America, with particular reference to Robert Lowell, Berryman, Olson, and Ginsberg.

22.32 **Murphy, Rosalie, ed. Contemporary poets of the English language.** Preface by C. Day Lewis. Chicago: St. James Pr., 1970. 3d ed. Edited by James Vinson and D. L. Kirkpatrick. New Title: Contemporary Poets. New York: St. Martin's Pr., 1980.

Bio-bibliographies.

22.33 **Perkins, David. A history of modern poetry: from the 1890s to the high modernist mode.** Cambridge, Mass.: Harvard Univ. Pr., 1976. Vol. I.

The first volume carries Perkins' history of the modern period to the mid-1920s; a promised second volume will complete his study of the age. It is not simply a survey.

22.34 **Rexroth, Kenneth. American poetry in the twentieth century.** New York: Herder and Herder, 1971.

An unsatisfactory summary, of value only for individual glimpses based on the author's own participation in the turmoils of American verse since the 1920s.

22.35 **Rittenhouse, Jessie B. The younger American poets.** Boston: Little, Brown, 1904.

A turn-of-the-century anthology with portraits of a few memorable poets and many forgettable ones.

22.36 **Rosenthal, M. L. The new poets: American and British poetry since World War II.** New York: Oxford Univ. Pr., 1967.

Focuses primarily on the Americans. The attempt to find general themes results in a loss of perspective, but many neglected poets are included.

22.37   **Stepanchev, Stephen.   American poetry since 1945: a critical survey.** New York: Harper & Row, 1965.
Elementary but clearheaded.

22.38   **Sutton, Walter.   American free verse: the modern revolution in poetry.** New York: New Directions, 1973.
A compressed survey of practitioners from Emerson and Whitman as precursors through Pound, Williams, et al.

22.39   **Tate, Allen.   Sixty American poets, 1896–1944.** Rev. ed. Washington, D.C.: [n.p.], 1954.
Lists selected books by and about the poets; includes "A Preliminary Check List," by Frances Cheney.

22.40   **Untermeyer, Louis.   American poetry since 1900.** New York: Henry Holt and Co., 1923.

22.41   **Wells, Henry W.   New poets from old: a study in literary genetics.** New York: Columbia Univ. Pr., 1940.
The relationship of 20th-century poets, chiefly American, with older traditions in English verse.

22.42   **Allen, Gay Wilson.   American prosody.** New York: American Book Co., 1935.
Versification of eleven poets, from Freneau to Dickinson.

22.43   **Conner, Frederick W.   Cosmic optimism: a study of the interpretation of evolution by American poets from Emerson to Robinson.** Gainesville: Univ. of Florida Pr., 1949.

22.44   **Lenhart, Charmenz S.   Musical influence on American poetry.** Athens: Univ. of Georgia Pr., 1956.
See also Nancy Anne Cluck, ed., *Literature and Music: Essays on Form,* Provo, Utah: Brigham Young Univ. Pr., 1981; 11 of the 19 essays, including 6 on Eliot, are devoted to American authors; all were previously published.

22.45   **Waggoner, Hyatt H.   The heel of Elohim: science and values in modern American poetry.** Norman: Univ. of Oklahoma Pr., 1950.
Attention is given largely to thematic discussion and to the following poets: Robinson, Frost, Eliot, Jeffers, MacLeish, and H. Crane. Waggoner sees poets as largely reacting against science.

22.46   **Winn, James Anderson.   Unsuspected eloquence: a history of the relations between poetry and music.** New Haven, Conn.: Yale Univ. Pr., 1981.
A history and survey of the relations between the two disciplines in the Western hemisphere from archaic Greece to the 20th century.

See also **4.14–16, 11.15, 16.27, 17.33, 18.51, 19.33, 19.51, 19.61, 25.25, 25.38, 26.38, 27.39–42, 29.45, 29.91, 31.10–11, 31.22, 31.24, 31.47–50, 32.68, 32.135, 34.18.**

23. *Drama, theater, and film*

23.1 Adelman, Irving, and Rita Dworkin. **Modern drama: a checklist of critical literature on 20th century plays.** Metuchen, N.J.: Scarecrow Pr., 1967.

23.2 Baker, Blanch M. **Theatre and allied arts: a guide to books dealing with the history, criticism, and technic of the drama and theatre and related arts and crafts.** New York: H. W. Wilson, 1952.
Entries are annotated; treats U.S. and Canada on pp. 163–190 and includes regional studies as well as works on individual actors and playwrights.

23.3 **Bibliographic guide to theatre arts: 1975–.** Boston: G. K. Hall, 1974–.
Includes "all materials catalogued during the past year by the New York Public Library Theatre and Drama Collections, with additional entries" from the Library of Congress. Annually supplements *Catalogue of the Theatre and Drama Collections* of the New York Public Library, 1967, 23.8.

23.4 Bonin, Jane F. **Prize-winning American drama: a bibliographical & descriptive guide.** Metuchen, N.J.: Scarecrow Pr., 1973.
Pulitzer, Critics' Circle, and other awards, 1917–1971, with a summary of each play and an account of its stage history and critical reception.

23.5 Breed, Paul, and Florence M. Sniderman. **Dramatic criticism index.** Detroit: Gale Research Co., 1972.
A history of "commentaries on playwrights from Ibsen to the avant-garde."

23.6 **The Burns Mantle yearbook.** Ed. Otis L. Guernsey, Jr. New York: Dodd, Mead, 1920–.
Annual compendium of statistics pertaining to the American stage; includes a directory of professional theaters located throughout the country and a record of productions.

23.7 Carpenter, Charles A. **"Modern drama studies: an annual bibliography."** Modern Drama, 17 (1974)–.
An extension and "regeneration" of Robert G. Shedd's "Modern Drama: A Selective Bibliography of Works Published in English in [1959–1968]," which appeared in *Modern Drama*, Univ. of Toronto, 1960–1969. For a sound, compact survey of critical books on American drama, see also Carpenter's "American Drama: A Bibliographical Essay," *American Studies International*, 26, No. 5 (1983), 3–52, which includes an unannotated checklist, pp. 40–52; few studies published before 1950 are mentioned, and the focus is specifically on drama, not theater.

23.8 **Catalogue of the theatre and drama collections.** Comp. Research Libraries of the New York Public Library. Boston: G. K. Hall, 1967. Supplement. 1974.

Annually supplemented by *Bibliographic Guide to Theatre Arts*, 1975–, 23.3.

23.9 **Connor, John M., and Billie M. Connor. Ottemiller's index to plays in collections.** 6th ed. Metuchen, N.J.: Scarecrow Pr., 1976.

23.10 **Dramatic compositions copyrighted in the United States, 1870–1916.** 2 vols. Washington, D.C.: U.S. Government Printing Office, 1918.
    About 60,000 plays registered for copyright. (For titles of plays, etc., copyrighted since 1916, see U.S. Copyright Office catalog of copyright entries.)

23.11 **Eddleman, Floyd Eugene. American drama criticism: interpretations, 1890–1977.** 2d ed. Hamden, Conn.: Shoe String Pr., 1979.
    Locates reviews and articles on all produced plays by American playwrights. The first edition, by H. H. Palmer, was published in 1967.

23.12 **Fidell, Estelle A. Play index, 1976–1977.** New York: H. W. Wilson, 1978.
    Earlier indexes by the same editor have been published since 1949.

23.13 **Firkins, Ina T. E. Index to plays, 1800–1926.** New York: H. W. Wilson, 1927. Supplement, 1927–1934. 1935.
    Lists published plays written chiefly by British and American authors. (*Play Index: 1949–1952*, comp. Dorothy H. West and Dorothy M. Peake, New York: H. W. Wilson, 1953, is a kind of sequel.) See also Fidell, 23.12.

23.14 **Harris, Richard H., ed. Modern drama in America and England, 1950–1970: a guide to information sources.** Detroit: Gale Research Co., 1982.
    A list of plays and criticism.

23.15 **Hartnoll, Phyllis, ed. The Oxford companion to the theatre.** London: Oxford Univ. Pr., 1951. 4th ed. 1983.
    Contains many entries on American theaters, playwrights, producers, etc.

23.16 **Hatch, James V. Black image on the American stage: a bibliography of plays and musicals, 1770–1970.** New York: DBS Publ., 1970.
    An unannotated compilation with an index.

23.17 **Hewitt, Barnard. Theatre U.S.A., 1665–1957.** New York: McGraw-Hill, 1959.
    Surveys the professional theater primarily through contemporary accounts. Most of the book is source material, chiefly reviews of plays.

23.18 **Hill, Frank Pierce. American plays printed 1714–1830: a bibliographical record.** Stanford, Calif.: Stanford Univ. Pr., 1934.

23.19 **Kaye, Phyllis Johnson, ed. National playwrights directory.** 2d ed. Waterford, Conn.: O'Neill Theater Center, 1981.
    Biographical data and playlists for approximately 500 American playwrights.

23.20   **Keller, Dean H.   Index to plays in periodicals.** Metuchen, N.J.: Scarecrow Pr., 1971. Rev. ed. 1979.
Over 9,000 citations from 267 magazines; translations are also registered.

23.21   **King, Kimball.   Ten modern American playwrights: an annotated bibliography.** New York: Garland, 1981.
Includes lists of plays and secondary material for Albee, Shepard, and other contemporary American dramatists.

23.22   **Larson, Carl F. W.   American regional theatre history to 1900: a bibliography.** Metuchen, N.J.: Scarecrow Pr., 1979.

23.23   **Lewis, Allan.   American plays and playwrights of the contemporary theatre.** New York: Crown, 1965. Rev. ed. 1970.
Brief comments on most playwrights after 1957.

23.24   **Litto, Frederic M.   American dissertations on the drama and the theatre: a bibliography.** Kent, Ohio: Kent State Univ. Pr., 1969.
Products of foreign language as well as English, speech, history, and music departments, to the number of approximately 4,500, are computerized.

23.25   **Meserve, Walter J.   American drama to 1900: a guide to information sources.** Detroit: Gale Research Co., 1980.

23.26   **Palmer, Helen H., and Anne J. Dyson.   American drama criticism: interpretations, 1890–1965 inclusive.** Hamden, Conn.: Shoe String Pr., 1967. 2d ed. Ed. Floyd Eddleman. 1979.
Bibliography of selected critical reactions to American plays and playwrights beginning with the 18th century. Books and periodicals, including scholarly journals, are covered. More comprehensive than Salem, 23.31.

23.27   **Performing arts resources.**   New York: Drama Book Specialists, 1974– .
Provides "documentation for theatre, film, television, and popular entertainments" but not music and dance.

23.28   **Rigdon, Walter.   The biographical encyclopaedia & who's who of the American theatre.** New York: J. H. Heineman, 1965, 1966.
In addition to biographical sketches, this contains a list of New York City productions from Jan. 1, 1900 to May 31, 1964; complete playbills of same, 1959–1964, as well as accounts of theater groups and buildings. A list of biographies and autobiographies of leading persons in the theater, living and dead, appears on pp. 983–993.

23.29   **Roden, Robert F.   Later American plays, 1831–1900.** New York: Dunlap Soc., 1900.
Very incomplete compilation of American plays published and performed in America during the years cited; see Wegelin, 23.39.

23.30   **Ryan, Pat M.   American drama bibliography: a checklist of publications in English.** Fort Wayne, Ind.: Fort Wayne Public Library, 1969.
Covers colonial times to date. The first section, "History and Reference," offers 60 items; the second section deals with general background. The third section offers selective items on almost 200 individual dramatists. Drama, rather than theater, is the fundamental criterion.

23.31 **Salem, James M.   A guide to critical reviews.** New York: Scarecrow Pr., 1966.
  The first installment covers American drama from O'Neill to Albee, with indexes of reviews of plays and musicals from 1909 to date.

23.32 **Samples, Gordon.   How to locate reviews of plays and films: a bibliography of criticism from the beginnings to the present.** Metuchen, N.J.: Scarecrow Pr., 1976.

23.33 **Santaniello, A. E.   Theatre books in print.** New York: Drama Book Shop, 1963. 2d ed. 1966.
  An annotated guide to books on drama, theater, movies, television, and radio available in the U.S. and their prices. U.S. theater is covered on pp. 120–28. See also *Chicorel Theater Index to Drama Literature*, New York: Chicorel Library Publ. Corp., 1975.

23.34 **Stratman, Carl J.   American theatrical periodicals, 1798–1967: a bibliographical guide.** Durham, N.C.: Duke Univ. Pr., 1970.
  Almost 700 periodicals are listed, 85 of which have never been located in any library.

23.35 **Stratman, Carl J.   Bibliography of the American theatre: excluding New York City.** Chicago: Loyola Univ. Pr., 1965.
  Arranged by state and city, this listing covers college and school dramatics along with professional activities. Includes a limited number of unpublished theses as well as published articles but does not include chapters or sections of local histories. Complements Gohdes, 20.14.

23.36 **Theatre magazine.**   53 vols. New York: Theatre Magazine Co., 1900–1931.
  There is *A Selective Index to Theatre Magazine*, by Stan Cornyn, New York: Scarecrow Pr., 1964.

23.37 **Veinstein, André, et al.   Performing arts collections: an international handbook.** Paris: Centre National de la Recherche Scientifique, 1960.
  Lists the chief collections, libraries, etc., in various countries, including the U.S. (The card catalog of the New York Public Library's theater collection has been printed in offset by G. K. Hall, 23.3 and 23.8.)

23.38 **Vinson, James, and D. L. Kirkpatrick, eds.   Contemporary dramatists.** New York: St. Martin's Pr., 1973. 2d ed. 1977.
  A compilation of bio-bibliographies.

23.39 **Wegelin, Oscar.   Early American plays, 1714–1830.** 2d rev. ed. New York: The Literary Collector Press, 1905.
  A list of titles of plays and dramatic poems. Supplemented by Roden, 23.29.

23.40 **Weingarten, Joseph A.   Modern American playwrights, 1918–1945: a bibliography.** 2 vols. New York: [n.p.], 1946–1947.
  A list of plays, arranged alphabetically by authors, plus occasional information on publication or availability of scripts.

23.41   **Wilmeth, Don B.   The American stage to World War I: a guide to information sources.** Detroit: Gale Research Co., 1978.
A comprehensive guide to writings of the past two centuries on American theater except for literary matters.

23.42   **Young, William C.   American theatrical arts: a guide to manuscripts and special collections in the United States and Canada.** Chicago: American Library Assoc., 1971.
Primary source materials on persons, playbills, theatrical histories, posters, etc. The contents of the special collections of 138 institutions, many not previously listed, are covered.

23.43   **Baumol, William J., and William G. Bowen.   Performing arts: the economic dilemma: a study of problems common to theater, opera, music, and dance.** New York: Twentieth Century Fund, 1966.
A careful analysis covering theater, opera, concert music, and dance that points out the losing battle against the "income gap."

23.44   **Broussard, Louis.   American drama: contemporary allegory from Eugene O'Neill to Tennessee Williams.** Norman: Univ. of Oklahoma Pr., 1962.

23.45   **Cohn, Ruby.   Dialogue in American drama.** Bloomington: Indiana Univ. Pr., 1971.
Particularly good in the chapters on O'Neill, Miller, Williams, and Albee.

23.46   **Herron, Ima Honaker.   The small town in American drama.** Dallas, Tex.: Southern Methodist Univ. Pr., 1969.

23.47   **Moore, Thomas G.   The economics of the American theater.** Durham, N.C.: Duke Univ. Pr., 1968.
A professional economist concentrates on the producers and the playwrights. A final chapter offers remedies and suggestions.

23.48   **Nathan, George Jean.   The theatre book of the year: a record and an interpretation, 1942–1950.** 9 vols. New York: Knopf, 1943–1951.
Comments on various plays by a popular journalist and critic. Somewhat similar commentary for the seasons 1952–1956 may be found in Eric Bentley, *The Dramatic Event: An American Chronicle*, New York: Horizon Pr., 1954; and *What Is Theatre: A Query in Chronicle Form*, New York: Horizon Pr., 1956. See also John Gassner, *Theatre at the Crossroads: Plays and Playwrights on the Mid-century American Stage*, New York: Holt, Rinehart, and Winston, 1960.

23.49   **Novick, Julius.   Beyond Broadway: the quest for permanent theatres.** New York: Hill and Wang, 1968.
Helpful for theaters outside of New York City, but not a scholarly production.

23.50   **Olauson, Judith.   The American woman playwright: a view of criticism and characterization.** Troy, N.Y.: Whitston Publ. Co., 1981.
Focuses on the plays of selected American women dramatists from 1930 to 1970; Zoe Atkins, Lorraine Hansberry, Lillian Hellman, and Carson McCullers are among the seventeen playwrights considered.

23.51   **Poland, Albert, and Bruce Mailman.   The off off Broadway book: the plays, people, theatre.** Indianapolis, Ind.: Bobbs-Merrill, 1972.

23.52   **Price, Julia S.   The off-Broadway theater.** New York: Scarecrow Pr., 1962.
     Covers the 1920s to 1960; loaded with lists.

23.53   **Reed, Perley I.   The realistic presentation of American characters in native American plays prior to 1870.** Columbus: Ohio State Univ. Pr., 1918.

23.54   **Theatre arts monthly: a magazine of the world theatre.**   New York: Theatre Publ., 1916–1964.

23.55   **America's lost plays.** 20 vols. Princeton, N.J.: Princeton Univ. Pr., 1940–1942.
     A series of previously unpublished plays by a variety of authors. Reissued by Indiana Univ. Pr., 1963–1969, and compressed into eleven vols. from twenty-one in 1980, the series is being extended by Indiana, 1969– .

23.56   **Brockett, Oscar G., and Robert R. Findlay.   Century of innovation: a history of European and American theater and drama since 1870.** Englewood Cliffs, N.J.: Prentice-Hall, 1973.
     A reference manual rather than a history; illustrated.

23.57   **DiMeglio, John.   Vaudeville U.S.A.** Bowling Green, Ohio: Bowling Green Univ. Popular Pr., 1973.

23.58   **Dormon, James H., Jr.   Theater in the antebellum South: 1815–1861.** Chapel Hill: Univ. of North Carolina Pr., 1967.
     The best treatment of the topic; foci for the history are the theaters in Richmond, Charleston, New Orleans, and St. Louis. The bibliography is noteworthy.

23.59   **Downer, Alan Seymour.   Fifty years of American drama, 1900–1950.** Chicago: Regnery, 1951.
     A brief survey that covers the earlier years in a rather selective manner.

23.60   **The drama.** 21 vols. Chicago: Dramatic Publ. Co., 1911–1931.
     Issued quarterly until May 1919 when it became a monthly.

23.61   **Felheim, Marvin.   The theater of Augustin Daly: an account of the late nineteenth century American stage.** Cambridge, Mass.: Harvard Univ. Pr., 1956.
     Daly was a key figure in his day.

23.62   **Gagey, Edmond M.   Revolution in American drama.** New York: Columbia Univ. Pr., 1947.
     A kind of descriptive catalog covering the thirty years prior to publication.

23.63   **Gagey, Edmond M.   The San Francisco stage: a history.** New York: Columbia Univ. Pr., 1950.

23.64   **Goldstein, Malcolm.   The political stage: American drama and theater of the Great Depression.** New York: Oxford Univ. Pr., 1974.
     Adds to previous accounts a discussion of the amateur leftist groups.

23.65 **Graham, Philip. Showboats: the history of an American institution.** Austin: Univ. of Texas Pr., 1951.

23.66 **Grimsted, David.   Melodrama unveiled: American theater and American culture, 1800–1850.** Chicago: Univ. of Chicago Pr., 1968.
The melodrama of the period is yoked to intellectual history. Based on primary sources. The bibliography includes unpublished theses and is one of the best available for the theater of the period.

23.67 **Havens, Daniel F.   The Columbian muse of comedy: the development of a native tradition in early American social comedy, 1787–1845.** Carbondale: Southern Illinois Univ. Pr., 1973.
Fourteen plays are discussed.

23.68 **Himelstein, Morgan Y.   Drama was a weapon: the left-wing theatre in New York, 1929–1941.** New Brunswick, N.J.: Rutgers Univ. Pr., 1963.
See also Caspar H. Nannes, *Politics in the American Drama: Broadway Plays, 1890–1959*, Washington, D.C.: Catholic Univ. of America Pr., 1960, on plays with a dominant political theme.

23.69 **Rabkin, Gerald.   Drama and commitment: politics in the American theatre of the thirties.** Bloomington: Indiana Univ. Pr., 1964.
Deals with organizations like the Theatre Union, the Group Theatre, and the Federal Theatre; then turns to a survey and criticism of the works of Lawson, Odets, Behrman, Rice, and Anderson.

23.70 **Hornblow, Arthur.   A history of the theatre in America from its beginnings to the present time.** 2 vols. Philadelphia, Pa.: Lippincott, 1919.
Contains some material not in Quinn, 23.87–88.

23.71 **Hughes, Glenn.   A history of the American theatre, 1700–1950.** New York: S. French, 1951.
A satisfactory general account with occasional minor inaccuracies.

23.72 **James, Reese D.   Old Drury of Philadelphia: a history of the Philadelphia stage, 1800–1835.** Philadelphia: Univ. of Pennsylvania Pr., 1932.

23.73 **Kinne, Wisner P.   George Pierce Baker and the American theatre.** Cambridge, Mass.: Harvard Univ. Pr., 1954.
Much detailed information on the background of theatrical history, 1900–1940.

23.74 **Knox, George A., and Herbert M. Stahl.   Dos Passos and "the revolting playwrights."** Uppsala: Lundequistska Bokhandeln, 1964.
A carefully documented account of the attempt to establish a workers' theater. Several American reprints since 1965 have made the book more readily accessible in the U.S.

23.75 **Laufe, Abe.   Broadway's greatest musicals.** New York: Funk and Wagnalls, 1969. Rev. ed. 1977.
Deals with 101 musicals that had a run of at least 500 performances as of May 1972. The most stellar, like *Show Boat* and *Oklahoma!*, are given separate chapters.

23.76 Macgowan, Kenneth. Footlights across America: towards a national theater. New York: Harcourt, Brace, 1929.
Discusses the "little theater" movement.

23.77 Mathews, Jane D. The Federal Theatre, 1935–1939: plays, relief, and politics. Princeton, N.J.: Princeton Univ. Pr., 1967.
Supplants the previous study by Hallie Flanagan, *Arena*, New York: Duell, Sloan and Pearce, 1940.

23.78 McNamara, Brooks. The American playhouse in the eighteenth century. Cambridge, Mass.: Harvard Univ. Pr., 1969.
An architectural account; see also Young, 23.100.

23.79 Meserve, Walter J. An emerging entertainment: the drama of the American people to 1828. Bloomington: Indiana Univ. Pr., 1977.
A solid history of American drama from the earliest colonial work to 1828. Other volumes covering the more recent periods are promised. See also Quinn, 23.87.

23.80 Moody, Richard. America takes the stage: Romanticism in American drama and theatre, 1750–1900. Bloomington: Indiana Univ. Pr., 1955.
Contains a treatment of native themes and characters and attempts to relate stage material to contemporary painting, architecture, etc.

23.81 Moody, Richard, ed. Dramas from the American theatre, 1762–1909. Boston: Houghton Mifflin, 1966.
An anthology that contains excellent selective bibliographies not only on the individual plays and authors represented but on basic sources of historical or critical value, etc.

23.82 Mordden, Ethan. The American theatre. New York: Oxford Univ. Pr., 1981.
A sound history of the New York stage with particular emphasis on the past half century.

23.83 O'Connor, John, and Lorraine Brown, eds. Free, adult, uncensored: the living history of the Federal Theatre Project. Washington, D.C.: New Republic Books, 1978.
Based on a selection of unpublished materials stored at Johns Hopkins Univ., this volume provides accounts of performances of the Federal Theatre from 1935 to 1939.

23.84 Odell, George C. D. Annals of the New York stage. 15 vols. New York: Columbia Univ. Pr., 1927–1949.
Covers greater New York City plays, operas, etc., from the beginnings through the season of 1894: first performances, original casts, criticisms. (Since many of these plays went on the road, Odell is valuable also for theatrical history outside the New York area.) The N.Y. Public Library has in scrapbooks a dramatic index covering new plays and important revivals produced in the city between August 20, 1896, and January 1, 1923.

23.85 Poggi, Jack. Theater in America: the impact of economic forces, 1870–1967. Ithaca, N.Y.: Cornell Univ. Pr., 1968.

23.86 **Pollock, Thomas Clark. The Philadelphia theatre in the eighteenth century together with the day book of the same period.** Philadelphia: Univ. of Pennsylvania Pr., 1933.

23.87 **Quinn, Arthur Hobson. A history of American drama from the beginning to the Civil War.** New York: Harper & Brothers, 1923. 2d ed. New York: F. S. Crofts, 1943.
This, with 23.88, is the standard work in the field.

23.88 **Quinn, Arthur Hobson. A history of the American drama from the Civil War to the present day.** 2 vols. New York: Harper & Brothers, 1927. Rev. ed. New York: Appleton-Century-Crofts, 1936.
The revision includes an updated bibliography and play list in addition to a new chapter on the decade 1927–1936.

23.89 **Rankin, Hugh F. The theater in colonial America.** Chapel Hill: Univ. of North Carolina Pr., 1965.
Based largely on newspaper sources, this study offers full-scale treatment to 1764.

23.90 **The Revels history of drama in English.** Vol. 8, **American Drama.** By Travis Bogard et al. New York: Methuen, 1978.
Comprises three long sections on: (1) the history of the American theater with several cultural foci, (2) the people associated with the American theater, and (3) American playwrights and their plays.

23.91 **Seilhamer, George O. History of the American theatre.** 3 vols. Philadelphia, Pa.: Globe Printing House, 1888–1891.
Covers the period 1749–1797.

23.92 **Slout, William L. Theatre in a tent: the development of a provincial entertainment.** Bowling Green, Ohio: Bowling Green Univ. Popular Pr., 1972.
A survey of the history of the tent show in the U.S.

23.93 **Smith, Cecil, and Glenn Litton, eds. Musical comedy in America.** New York: Theatre Arts Books, 1950. 2d ed. 1981.
The first section is edited by Smith and the second, dealing with more recent plays, by Litton.

23.94 **Toohey, John L. A history of the Pulitzer Prize plays.** New York: Citadel Pr., 1967.
Casts and other details are supplied.

23.95 **Weales, Gerald. American drama since World War II.** New York: Harcourt, Brace, and World, 1962.
More recent dramatists are discussed by Weales in *The Jumping-Off Place: American Drama in the 1960s,* New York: Macmillan, 1969.

23.96 **Wilson, Arthur Herman. A history of the Philadelphia theatre: 1835–1855.** Philadelphia: Univ. of Pennsylvania Pr., 1935.

23.97 **Wilson, Garff B. A history of American acting.** Bloomington: Indiana Univ. Pr., 1966.
A pioneer study climaxed by a whole chapter on Minnie Maddern Fiske.

23.98 Wilson, Garff B. **Three hundred years of American drama and theatre: from** *Ye Bare and Ye Cubb* **to** *Hair.* Englewood Cliffs, N.J.: Prentice-Hall, 1973. 2d ed. 1982.

A well-illustrated introduction for the beginning drama student and the general reader only.

23.99 Wittke, Carl F. **Tambo and bones: a history of the American minstrel stage.** Durham, N.C.: Duke Univ. Pr., 1930.

A useful history with a helpful index that includes names and song titles as well as more general references. See also a more recent account by Robert C. Toll, *Blacking Up: The Minstrel Show in Nineteenth-Century America*, New York: Oxford Univ. Pr., 1974.

23.100 Young, William C. **Famous actors and actresses on the American stage.** New York: R. R. Bowker, 1975.

Contemporary assessments of actors and actresses together with observations on their approaches to their art. See also Young's *Famous American Playhouses*, 2 vols., Chicago: American Library Assoc., 1973, which covers 1716–1899 in vol. 1 and 1900–1971 in vol. 2.

See also **7.6, 16.36, 16.41, 19.30, 20.14, 21.41, 31.9, 31.13, 31.51–53, 32.9, 32.28, 32.32–33, 32.51, 32.60, 32.64, 32.69, 32.73, 32.88, 32.91, 32.153, 32.155, 32.158, 32.169, 35.25.**

Film and literature

23.101 Batty, Linda. **Retrospective index to film periodicals: 1930–1971.** New York: R. R. Bowker, 1975.

23.102 Enser, A. G. S. **Filmed books and plays: a list of books and plays from which films have been made, 1928–1974.** London: Deutsch, 1975.

Adaptations indexed by authors and the titles of both source and film.

23.103 Film literature index. Albany: New York State Univ. Pr., 1973–.

Quarterly index to international film periodicals.

23.104 Gerlach, John C., and Lana Gerlach. **The critical index: a bibliography of articles on film in English, 1946–1973, arranged by names and topics.** New York: Teachers College Pr., 1974.

23.105 Gottesman, Ronald, and Harry M. Geduld, eds. **Guidebook to film: an eleven-in-one reference.** New York: Holt, Rinehart, and Winston, 1972.

Bibliographies add to the usefulness of this work covering varied aspects of the study of film.

23.106 MacCann, Richard Dyer, and Edward S. Perry. **The new film index: a bibliography of magazine articles in English, 1930–1970.** New York: Dutton, 1975.

23.107 Welch, Jeffrey Egan. **Literature and film: an annotated bibliography, 1900–1977.** New York: Garland, 1981.

Covers major books on the interdisciplinary relation as well as interviews, pedagogical articles, and criticism. The appendix identifies authors and playwrights with films based on their works; also identified are the director, producer, screenplay writer, and studio for each film.

23.108 Beja, Morris. Film and literature. New York: Longman, 1979.
Part 1 provides a theoretical discussion of various relations between films and literature; part 2 is an extensively annotated filmography of twenty-five films, including several produced in the U.S.

23.109 Bluestone, George. Novels into film. Berkeley: Univ. of California Pr., 1968.
The classic work in its field, somewhat dated but essential. Contains a theoretical introduction and an analysis of six adaptations.

23.110 Harrington, John. Film and/as literature. Englewood Cliffs, N.J.: Prentice-Hall, 1977.
Anthology with essays arranged under chapter headings: "Adaptation"; "Film and Theater"; "Film and Novel"; "Film and Poetry"; "Message, Medium, and Literary Art"; and "Film's Literary Resources."

23.111 Hurt, James, ed. Focus on film and theatre. Englewood Cliffs, N.J.: Prentice-Hall, 1974.
Compact collection of excerpts from theoretical and critical essays and interviews with actors, directors, and playwrights. Includes a selected filmography and bibliography.

23.112 Katz, John Stuart. Perspectives on the study of film. Boston: Little, Brown, 1971.
A collection of essays that focuses on film study and education, film as an art and one of the humanities, and film as communication, environment, and politics.

23.113 Marcus, Fred H. Film and literature: contrasts in media. Scranton, Pa.: Chandler Publ. Co., 1971.
Anthology of theoretical and critical articles with appendices of film distributors and a selected filmography.

23.114 Marcus, Fred H. Short story/short film. Englewood Cliffs, N.J.: Prentice-Hall, 1977.
Short prose fiction and continuity scripts of their adaptations. Treats ten stories and mentions others. Includes a useful glossary of film terms, a list of film distributors, and a bibliography.

23.115 Peary, Gerald, and Roger Shatzkin, eds. The classic American novel and the movies. New York: Ungar, 1977.
Brief essays on, and photos from, films on American classics from *The Last of the Mohicans* to *The Sound and the Fury*, arranged chronologically according to publication date of the fiction. Includes filmography, pp. 321–36, and bibliography, pp. 337–44.

23.116 Peary, Gerald, and Roger Shatzkin, eds. The modern American novel and the movies. New York: Ungar, 1978.

A collection of critical essays on thirty-two adaptations ranging from the works of Caldwell to Dickey. Includes extensive filmography, pp. 349–428, and bibliography, pp. 429–43.

See also **8.41, 16.23, 19.47, 23.27, 25.1, 26.15, 31.107.**

24. *Fiction*

24.1 **Adelman, Irving, and Rita Dworkin. The contemporary novel: a checklist of critical literature on the British and American novel since 1945.** Metuchen, N.J.: Scarecrow Pr., 1972.

Items are derived from certain scholarly journals, principally from 1950 to 1970. Works of novelists who wrote before 1945 are considered if they continued to produce after that date.

24.2 **Aldridge, John W. After the lost generation: a critical study of the writers of two wars.** New York: McGraw-Hill, 1951.

A somewhat personal treatment of changes in taste and fashion during the 1940s, plus discussion of novelists like Mailer, Shaw, Vidal, Capote, et al.

24.3 **Coan, Otis W., and Richard G. Lillard. America in fiction: an annotated list of novels that interpret aspects of life in the United States.** Stanford, Calif.: Stanford Univ. Pr., 1941. 5th ed. 1967.

24.4 **Cotton, Gerald B., et al. Fiction index.** London: Assoc. of Assistant Librarians, 1953–.

Covers novels, short story collections, anthologies, etc., mainly available since 1945, arranged under numerous subject headings.

24.5 **Dickinson's American historical fiction.** 4th ed. Ed. Virginia Brokaw Gerhardstein. Metuchen, N.J.: Scarecrow, 1981.

A well-indexed and briefly annotated compilation of historical novels organized both geographically and chronologically.

24.6 **Eichelberger, Clayton L. A guide to critical reviews of U.S. fiction, 1870–1910.** 2 vols. Metuchen, N.J.: Scarecrow Pr., 1971–1974.

Thirty British or American periodicals are covered; arrangement is by author. Volume 2 adds ten more to the coverage.

24.7 **Fiction catalog.** Ed. Estelle A. Fidell. New York: H. W. Wilson, 1908–.

An annotated list of novels chiefly; covers works in the English language only. The 10th ed., 1981, includes well over 4,000 titles selected by staffs of public libraries. The annotations are helpful in determining plot outlines. A supplement to the 10th ed. was published in 1982.

24.8 **Gerstenberger, Donna, and George Hendrick. The American novel, 1789–1959: a checklist of twentieth-century criticism.** Denver, Colo.: Swallow Pr., 1961. 2d ed. Vol. 1, 1789–1959. Vol. 2, 1960–1968. Chicago: Swallow Pr., 1970.

Lists materials in books and articles on about 230 individual novelists from all periods and follows with a checklist of general studies of the American novel. Dated but still useful.

24.9   **Griswold, William M.   Descriptive list of novels and tales dealing with history of North America.** Cambridge, Mass.: W. M. Griswold, 1895.
Separate compilations list fiction on American country life and city life.

24.10   **Kirby, David K.   American fiction to 1900: a guide to information sources.** Detroit: Gale Research Co., 1975.
A selective companion bibliography to Woodress, its sequel, 20.40.

24.11   **VanDerhoof, Jack.   A bibliography of novels related to American frontier and colonial history.** Troy, N.Y.: Whitston Publ. Co., 1971.
About 6,500 novels, from colonial times up to 1790. The frontier ranges to the present. The listing is by author only.

24.12   **Vinson, James, ed.   Contemporary novelists.** Pref. by Walter Allen. New York: St. Martin's Pr., 1972. 3d ed. Pref. by Jerome Klinkowitz. 1982.
An alphabetical listing of writers in English, with bio-bibliographical and critical summaries for each.

24.13   **Warfel, Harry R.   American novelists of today.** New York: American Book Co., 1951.
Sketches of 575 writers "who have published one or more serious novels, one of them in the last ten years."

24.14   **Wright, Lyle H.   American fiction, 1774–1850: a contribution toward a bibliography.** Rev. ed. San Marino, Calif.: Huntington Library, 1969. 1851–1875. Rev. ed. 1965. 1876–1900. 1966.
Books listed in these three volumes are available on microcards: Louisville, Ky.: Lost Cause Pr., 1970; an index for the microfilm edition of *American Fiction* may be obtained from New Haven, Conn.: Research Publ., 1969.

24.15   **Blake, Fay M.   The strike in the American novel.** Metuchen, N.J.: Scarecrow Pr., 1972.
About 250 novels, 1855–1945, are considered. The annotated bibliography is a redeeming feature.

24.16   **Chase, Richard.   The American novel and its tradition.** Garden City, N.Y.: Doubleday, 1952.
Views poetic elements and romance as central to the development of American fiction; an influential if sometimes controversial study.

24.17   **Fiedler, Leslie A.   Love and death in the American novel.** New York: Criterion Books, 1960. Rev. ed. 1966.
A comprehensive study marked by lively, imaginative insights.

24.18   **Gérard, Albert.   Les Tambours du néant: le problème existentiel dans le roman américain.** Brussels: La Renaissance du Livre, 1969.
Tracks the American novelists' consciousness of "antimonies fondamental de la condition humaine." James, Melville, Wright, and on to the present.

24.19 **Hoffman, Daniel G.   Form and fable in American fiction.** New York: Oxford Univ. Pr., 1961.
A thematic treatment of ten works by Irving, Hawthorne, Melville, and Clemens.

24.20 **The journal of narrative technique.** Ypsilanti: Eastern Michigan Dept. of English, 1971–.
Issued three times a year; criticism on "narrative literature in English."

24.21 **Leisy, Ernest E.   The American historical novel.** Norman: Univ. of Oklahoma Pr., 1950.
Covers the history to the end of the 19th century. A valuable appendix lists additional historical novels beyond those discussed in the text, pp. 219–59.

24.22 **Lyons, John O.   The college novel in America.** Carbondale: Southern Illinois Univ. Pr., 1962.
Begins with Hawthorne but is chiefly concerned with 20th-century novels dealing with college or university life. See also 29.23.

24.23 **Messenger, Christian K.   Sport and the spirit of play in American fiction: Hawthorne to Faulkner.** New York: Columbia Univ. Pr., 1981.
A serious and rewarding study of the relation between competitive play and American fiction through reference to different types of hero figures as envisioned by Americans and represented by authors.

24.24 **Millgate, Michael.   American social fiction: James to Cozzens.** New York: Barnes & Noble, 1964.

24.25 **Miller, Wayne C.   An armed America: its face in fiction.** New York: New York Univ. Pr., 1970.
A survey of military novels from *The Spy* to *Dr. Strangelove*. Of lesser amplitude are such studies as Stanley Cooperman, *World War I and the American Novel*, Baltimore, Md.: Johns Hopkins Univ. Pr., 1967; and Joseph J. Waldmeir, *American Novels of the Second World War*, The Hague and Paris: Mouton, 1968.

24.26 **Milne, Gordon.   The American political novel.** Norman: Univ. of Oklahoma Pr., 1966.
A general study, readable and informative, with a limited number of novels listed as primary sources and a useful roster of secondary works.

24.27 **Milne, Gordon.   The sense of society: a history of the American novel of manners.** Rutherford, N.J.: Fairleigh Dickinson Univ. Pr., 1977.
Brings up to date current scholarship on the major authors associated with the novel of manners. See also 24.38.

24.28 **Morris, Wright.   Earthly delights, unearthly adornments: American writers as image-makers.** New York: Harper & Row, 1978.
Brief essays on imagery in American writers, from Melville to Carson McCullers.

24.29 **Nagel, James, ed.   American fiction: historical and critical essays.** Boston: Northeastern Univ. Pr./Twayne, 1977.

An excellent collection of critical essays on specific areas in American fiction by first-rate scholars, including Milton R. Stern ("American Values and Romantic Fiction"), Ronald Sukenick ("Fiction in the Seventies"), Daniel Aaron ("The Occasional Novel"), and Viola Hopkins Winner ("The Pictorial Vision").

24.30 Oriard, Michael. Dreaming of heroes: American sports fiction, 1868–1980. Chicago: Nelson-Hall Publ., 1982.

In the 20th century, sports satisfy America's craving for religious ritual and pageantry as well as providing opportunity for hero worship and reenactment in competitive play of the frontier experience. Includes a "Checklist of American Sports Fiction," pp. 263–330, and a bibliography, pp. 357–72. See also Messenger, 24.23.

24.31 Papashvily, Helen Waite.   All the happy endings: a study of the domestic novel in America, the women who wrote it, the women who read it, in the nineteenth century. New York: Harper, 1956.

A popular study that helps to fill the gap following Brown, 24.42.

24.32 Perkins, George, ed.   The theory of the American novel. New York: Holt, Rinehart, and Winston, 1970.

An intelligently conceived anthology that gathers specimens of the novelists' comments on their own craft, from Brackenridge and Brown to Bellow and Nabokov.

24.33 Quinn, Arthur Hobson.   American fiction: an historical and critical survey. New York: Appleton-Century Co., 1936.

Discusses also the short stories by the chief authors. Factually very reliable; bibliography, pp. 725–772.

24.34 Smith, Herbert F.   The popular American novel: 1865–1920. Boston: Twayne/G. K. Hall, 1980.

A rapid and necessarily superficial survey of chief value for its gathering of relatively unfamiliar and often forgotten authors and titles.

24.35 Stineback, David C.   Shifting world: social change and nostalgia in the American novel. Lewisburg, Pa.: Bucknell Univ. Pr., 1976.

More useful for pulling things together than for providing new insights or information.

24.36 Stuckey, William J.   The Pulitzer Prize novels: a critical backward look. Norman: Univ. of Oklahoma Pr., 1966.

Critical is the key word in the title.

24.37 Studies in American fiction.   Boston: Northeastern Univ. Pr., 1973–.

Critical essays, notes, and reviews. A semiannual.

24.38 Tuttleton, James.   The novel of manners in America. Chapel Hill: Univ. of North Carolina Pr., 1972.

A major study of the genre from Cooper through Marquand, Cozzens, and other 20th-century authors. See also 24.27.

24.39 Van Doren, Carl.   The American novel, 1789–1939. 2d ed. New York: Macmillan, 1940.

Originally published in 1921, this study is largely outmoded by Quinn and Cowie but is still valuable for its illuminating criticism.

24.40   **Wagenknecht, Edward.   Cavalcade of the American novel.** New York: Holt, 1952.
From the beginnings to 1940; heavily weighted with 20th-century novelists.

24.41   **Åhnebrink, Lars.   The beginnings of Naturalism in American fiction: a study of the works of Hamlin Garland, Stephen Crane, and Frank Norris with special reference to some European influences, 1891–1903.** Uppsala and Cambridge, Mass.: Harvard Univ. Pr., 1950.

24.42   **Brown, Herbert R.   The sentimental novel in America, 1789–1860.** Durham, N.C.: Duke Univ. Pr., 1940.

24.43   **Cady, Edwin H.   The light of common day.** Bloomington: Indiana Univ. Pr., 1971.
Ten essays on Realism in American fiction; the first two chapters—"'Realism': Toward a Definition" and "Three Sensibilities: Romance, Realist, Naturalist"— are especially noteworthy.

24.44   **Cowie, Alexander.   The rise of the American novel.** New York: American Book Co., 1948.
An intelligent historical treatment ending in the 1890s.

24.45   **Dunlap, George A.   The city in the American novel, 1789–1900: a study of American novels portraying contemporary conditions in New York, Philadelphia, and Boston.** New York: Russell and Russell, 1962.
The original for this volume was a doctoral dissertation, Univ. of Pennsylvania, 1934.

24.46   **Falk, Robert.   The Victorian mode in American fiction, 1865–1885.** East Lansing: Michigan State Univ. Pr., 1965.
Treats the novelists, chiefly DeForest, Howells, James, and Clemens, as seeking an "equilibrium of conflicting forces."

24.47   **Jones, Arthur E.   Darwinism and its relationship to Realism and Naturalism in American fiction, 1860–1900.** [Madison, N.J.]: Drew Univ. Pr., 1950.
An issue of the *Drew University Bulletin*, vol. 38, no. 4.

24.48   **Kaul, A. N.   The American vision: actual and ideal society in nineteenth-century fiction.** New Haven, Conn.: Yale Univ. Pr., 1963.
The conflict between actual and ideal democracy in America as presented by American authors is effectively traced through the fiction.

24.49   **Lawrence, D. H.   Studies in classic American literature.** New York: T. Seltzer, 1923.
An important but highly idiosyncratic and controversial reading of major American writers, including Franklin, Hawthorne, Melville, Whitman, Clemens, and others; the comments on Cooper and Melville are particularly striking.

24.50   **Lively, Robert A.   Fiction fights the Civil War: an unfinished chapter in the literary history of the American people.** Chapel Hill: Univ. of North Carolina Pr., 1957.

Contains a list of about 500 novels on the war. (Cf. a catalog of "chief novels and short stories" by Americans, 1861–1899, which deal with the war or its effects, by Rebecca W. Smith, *Bulletin of Bibliography*, 16–17 [1939–1941], 193–94; 10–12, 33–35, 53–55, 72–75.)

24.51   **Petter, Henri.   The early American novel.** Columbus: Ohio State Univ. Pr., 1971.

Some ninety novels are examined and discussed in detail. Synopses of sixty in an appendix and an excellent bibliography enhance the value of this survey.

24.52   **Porte, Joel.   The romance in America: studies in Cooper, Poe, Hawthorne, Melville, and James.** Middletown, Conn.: Wesleyan Univ. Pr., 1969.

Thoughtful and comprehensive chapters on each of these major authors.

24.53   **Smith, Henry Nash.   Democracy and the novel: popular resistance to classic American writers.** New York: Oxford Univ. Pr., 1978.

Hawthorne, Melville, Henry Ward Beecher, Howells, Clemens, and James are seen in relation to the popular audience of their time.

24.54   **Taylor, Walter F.   The economic novel in America.** Chapel Hill: Univ. of North Carolina Pr., 1942.

Period covered is 1865–1900. The bibliography is considerably amplified by Lisle A. Rose, "A Bibliographical Survey of Economic and Political Writings, 1865–1900," *American Literature*, 15 (1944), 381–410.

24.55   **Baumbach, Jonathan.   The landscape of nightmare: studies in the contemporary novel.** New York: New York Univ. Pr., 1965.

The writers discussed include Bellow, Ellison, Malamud, Morris, O'Connor, Salinger, Styron, Wallant, and Warren; a chapter is given to one major novel of each.

24.56   **Beach, Joseph Warren.   American fiction, 1920–1940.** New York: Macmillan, 1941.

Caldwell, Dos Passos, Farrell, Faulkner, Hemingway, Marquand, Steinbeck, and Wolfe are discussed.

24.57   **Beja, Morris.   Epiphany in the modern novel.** Seattle: Univ. of Washington Pr., 1971.

On the moment of vision and revelation in 20th-century fiction, with separate chapters on Wolfe and Faulkner.

24.58   **Bellamy, Joe David.   The new fiction: interviews with innovative American writers.** Urbana: Univ. of Illinois Pr., 1975.

The writers are Barth, Barthelme, Gass, Gardner, Hawkes, Kosinski, Oates, Reed, Sontag, Sukenick, Vonnegut, and Wolfe.

24.59   **Blotner, Joseph.   The modern American political novel: 1900–1960.** Austin: Univ. of Texas Pr., 1966.

An attempt to "discover the image of American politics" as seen in the novels. Critical assessments are limited. See also 24.26.

24.60 **Bradbury, Malcolm, and David Palmer, eds. The American novel and the nineteen twenties.** New York: Crane, Russak, 1971.

24.61 **Bryant, Jerry H. The open decision: the contemporary American novel and its intellectual background.** New York: Free Press, 1970.
A wide-ranging study that seeks to demonstrate that our fiction since World War II is largely existentialist. War novels, business novels, and the "Beat" variety of Kerouac and Burroughs form aspects of the examination, along with Barth, Bellow, Updike, Malamud, Vonnegut, and Mailer.

24.62 **Eisinger, Chester E. Fiction of the forties.** Chicago: Univ. of Chicago Pr., 1963.
Discusses selected works under headings such as "The War Novel," "Naturalism," and "The Conservative Imagination."

24.63 **Federman, Raymond, ed. Surfiction: fiction now and tomorrow.** Chicago: Swallow, 1975. Rev. ed. 1981.
A collection of criticism on contemporary fiction.

24.64 **Frohock, Wilbur M. The novel of violence in America.** Dallas: Southern Methodist Univ. Pr., 1950. 2d ed. 1957.
Chiefly Dos Passos, Wolfe, Farrell, Warren, Caldwell, Steinbeck, Faulkner, Hemingway, Agee. The first edition announces the limits of coverage as 1920–1950. Louise Y. Gossett, *Violence in Recent Southern Fiction*, Durham, N.C.: Duke Univ. Pr., 1965, treats Warren, O'Connor, Welty, Styron, Capote, McCullers, and Grau.

24.65 **Galloway, David D. The absurd hero in American fiction: Updike, Styron, Bellow, and Salinger.** Austin: Univ. of Texas Pr., 1966. 2d ed. 1981.

24.66 **Geismar, Maxwell. American moderns: from rebellion to conformity.** New York: Hill and Wang, 1958.
The central focus is on the "transitional decade" from World War II to the 1950s.

24.67 **Geismar, Maxwell. The last of the provincials: the American novel, 1915–1925.** Boston: Houghton Mifflin, 1947.
Mencken, Lewis, Cather, Anderson, Fitzgerald.

24.68 **Geismar, Maxwell. Rebels and ancestors: the American novel, 1890–1915.** Boston: Houghton Mifflin, 1953.
Norris, Crane, London, Glasgow, Dreiser.

24.69 **Geismar, Maxwell. Writers in crisis: the American novel between two wars.** Boston: Houghton Mifflin, 1942.
Lardner, Hemingway, Dos Passos, Faulkner, Wolfe, Steinbeck.

24.70 **Gelfant, Blanche H. The American city novel.** Norman: Univ. of Oklahoma Pr., 1954. 2d ed. 1970.
Dreiser, Anderson, Wharton, Wolfe, Dos Passos, Farrell, Algren, Betty Smith. See also 24.45 and 29.27.

24.71 **Hartwick, Harry. The foreground of American fiction.** New York: American Book Co., 1934.
The novel from 1890 to 1930 is treated from a New Humanist point of view.

24.72 **Hassan, Ihab. Radical innocence: studies in the contemporary American novel.** Princeton, N.J.: Princeton Univ. Pr., 1961.
McCullers, Capote, Salinger, and Bellow are treated substantially though several other authors are given some critical attention as well.

24.73 **Hoffman, Frederick J. The modern novel in America, 1900–1950.** Chicago: Regnery, 1951. Rev. ed. 1963.
Criticism rather than history.

24.74 **Klein, Marcus. After alienation: American novels in mid-century.** Cleveland: World, 1964.
Critical interpretations of Bellow, Ellison, Baldwin, Morris, and Malamud. The subtitle was added after the first edition.

24.75 **Klinkowitz, Jerome. Literary disruptions: the making of a post-contemporary American fiction.** Urbana: Univ. of Illinois Pr., 1975. 2d ed. 1980.
The "post-contemporaries" are Vonnegut, Barthelme, LeRoi Jones, Sukenick, Federman, and Sorrentino. Bibliographies are included.

24.76 **MacConnell, Frank. Four postwar American novelists: Bellow, Mailer, Barth, and Pynchon.** Chicago: Univ. of Chicago Pr., 1977.

24.77 **Malin, Irving. New American gothic.** Carbondale: Southern Illinois Univ. Pr., 1962.
A consideration of "gothic" elements in Capote, McCullers, O'Connor, Purdy, and Salinger.

24.78 **Mellard, James M. The exploded form: the modernist novel in America.** Urbana: Univ. of Illinois Pr., 1980.
An argument supporting traditional modes in fiction and opposing the notion of "postmodernist" theories in which words and complex verbal structures are said to have meanings in themselves without external referents. Also holding this view is Sanford Pinsker, *Between Two Worlds: The American Novel in the 1960s.* Troy, N.Y.: Whitston, 1980.

24.79 **Olderman, Raymond M. Beyond the wasteland: a study of the American novel in the 1960s.** New Haven, Conn.: Yale Univ. Pr., 1972.
In and out of the Wasteland with novels by Kesey, Elkin, Barth, Heller, Pynchon, Hawkes, Vonnegut.

24.80 **Rideout, Walter B. The radical novel in the United States, 1900–1954: some interrelations of literature and society.** Cambridge, Mass.: Harvard Univ. Pr., 1956.
"Radical" here means socially or politically radical. Cf. *Proletarian Writers of the Thirties*, ed. David Madden, Carbondale: Southern Illinois Univ. Pr., 1968.

24.81   **Sale, Roger.**   **On not being good enough: writings of a working critic.** New York: Oxford Univ. Pr., 1979.

A gathering of reviews and essays from 1966–1978, mostly on contemporary novelists and critics.

24.82   **Tanner, Tony.**   **City of words: American fiction, 1950–1970.** New York: Harper & Row, 1971.

A study of individual novels especially in terms of idiosyncratic language and style.

24.83   **Best American short stories of 1915–, and the yearbook of the American short story.** Ed. Edward J. O'Brien (1915–1941) and Martha Foley (1942–1977). Boston: Houghton Mifflin, 1915–.

Annual compilation containing texts of selected short stories plus other bibliographical material.

24.84   **Cook, Dorothy E., et al.**   **Short story index.** New York: H. W. Wilson, 1953–.

Stories in English or translated into English are listed by author, title, and, often, subject. Supersedes a similar index compiled by Ina T. E. Firkins, 1923 plus supplements.

24.85   **Smith, Frank R.**   **"Periodical articles on the American short story: a selected, annotated bibliography."** Bulletin of Bibliography, 23 (1960, 1961), 9–13, 46–48, 69–72, 95–96.

Deals with the short story in general, not with individual authors or stories.

24.86   **Weixlmann, Joe.**   **American short-fiction criticism and scholarship, 1959–1977: a checklist.** Chicago: Swallow Pr., 1982.

Covers secondary material on the short fiction of more than 500 authors; includes material compiled from approximately 5,000 books and over 300 serials.

24.87   **Freese, Peter.**   **Die amerikanische Kurzgeschichte nach 1945.** Frankfurt a. M.: Athenäum, 1974.

Salinger, Malamud, Baldwin, Purdy, and Barth.

24.88   **Pattee, Fred Lewis.**   **The development of the American short story: an historical survey.** New York: Harper, 1923.

Though out of date, still an occasionally useful survey as a general history.

24.89   **Peden, William.**   **The American short story: continuity and change, 1940–1975.** 2d ed. Boston: Houghton Mifflin, 1975.

Primarily historical and bibliographical treatment. Contains as an appendix a checklist of "notable" authors. The first edition, published in 1964, had for its subtitle: *Front Line in the National Defense of Literature.*

24.90   **Voss, Arthur.**   **The American short story: a critical survey.** Norman: Univ. of Oklahoma Pr., 1973.

Ranges over the entire history, topping off with Roth and Updike. The balance is good, and the plot summaries, though numerous, are often useful for readers not already somewhat familiar with the genre.

24.91 Walker, Warren S. Twentieth-century short story explication: interpretations, 1900–1966, inclusive of short fiction since 1800. 3d ed. Hamden, Conn.: Shoe String Pr., 1977. Supplement. 1980.

Few items included were published before 1920, and most are representative of the "New Criticism." Many of the authors included are Americans.

24.92 West, Ray B., Jr. The short story in America, 1900–1950. Chicago: Regnery, 1952.

A survey tempered by analytical criticism rather than historical perspective and centered on the 1940s.

24.93 Wright, Austin M. The American short story in the twenties. Chicago: Univ. of Chicago Pr., 1961.

Especially Anderson, Fitzgerald, Hemingway, Faulkner, and Katherine Anne Porter; more analytical than critical.

24.94 Hellmann, John. Fables of fact: the New Journalism as new fiction. Urbana: Univ. of Illinois Pr., 1981.

Focuses on the "non-fiction novel[s]" of Norman Mailer, Tom Wolfe, Hunter S. Thompson, and Michael Herr.

24.95 Hollowell, John. Fact and fiction: the New Journalism and the nonfiction novel. Chapel Hill: Univ. of North Carolina Pr., 1977.

General chapters describing and characterizing the genre are followed by individualized chapters on Capote, Mailer, and Thomas Wolfe.

See also 1.25, 3.33, 8.38–54, 12.18, 14.16, 16.33, 18.52, 18.56, 19.41, 19.43, 19.49, 28.21, 28.35, 31.14–15, 31.44–46, 32.65, 32.77–78, 32.109, 35.37.

25. Criticism

25.1 Barricelli, Jean-Pierre, and Joseph Gibaldi, eds. Interrelations of literature. New York: Modern Language Assoc., 1982.

An exemplary collection of thirteen interdisciplinary essays by specialists for nonspecialists, each of which is followed by a brief bibliography. The subjects include literature in relation to linguistics, philosophy, religion, myth, folklore, sociology, politics, law, science, psychology, music, the visual arts, and film. A glossary and name index follow the essays. See also Gibaldi, 2.9, and Thorpe, 2.29.

25.2 Webster, Grant. "American literary criticism: a bibliographical essay." American Studies International, 20, No. 1 (1981), 3–44.

A comprehensive résumé of criticism with heavy emphasis on work of the 1960s and 1970s, this essay is organized according to four major headings—Traditional, Myth, Counter-Culture, and Influence from European Theories—and several subheadings under each.

25.3   **Zabel, Morton D., ed.   Literary opinion in America.** New York: Harper & Brothers, 1937. 2d ed. 1951. 3d ed. 2 vols. 1962.
Copious selections, historical outline, lists of recent works in criticism, collections, and names of chief magazines publishing critical articles. Good bibliography of 20th-century American criticism to about 1962.

25.4   **Baym, Max I.   A history of literary aesthetics in America.** New York: Ungar, 1973.
From Jonathan Edwards to Wallace Stevens, this opus surveys the subject, or relatives of the subject, by summarizing the theories of eighty-odd individuals.

25.5   **Charvat, William.   The origins of American critical thought, 1810–1835.** Philadelphia: Univ. of Pennsylvania Pr., 1936.
Particularly valuable for its treatment of the influence of the Scottish philosophers and critics.

25.6   **Foerster, Norman.   American criticism.** Boston: Houghton Mifflin, 1928.
Poe, Emerson, Lowell, Whitman; one chapter on the 20th century.

25.7   **Goldsmith, Arnold.   American literary criticism.** Vol. 1, 1800–1860. Vol. 2, 1860–1905. Vol. 3, 1905–1965. Boston: G. K. Hall, 1979.
Vol. 3 is the best of the three volumes; comprehensive. See also 25.13.

25.8   **Lang, Hans-Joachim.   Studien zur Entstehung der neueren amerikanischen Literaturkritik.** Hamburg: Cram, De Gruyter, 1961.
A comprehensive analysis of the period from 1880 to about 1940. Occasionally critics are discussed who are seldom treated elsewhere.

25.9   **O'Connor, William Van.   An age of criticism, 1900–1950.** Chicago: Regnery, 1952.
Well planned but uneven in treatment as a survey of prevailing critical trends in the first half of the century.

25.10   **Parks, Edd Winfield.   Ante-bellum southern literary critics.** Athens: Univ. of Georgia Pr., 1962.
Covers the field 1785–1861 but omits Poe.

25.11   **Pritchard, John P.   Criticism in America: an account of the development of critical techniques from the early period of the Republic to the middle years of the twentieth century.** Norman: Univ. of Oklahoma Pr., 1956.
A historical survey through the "New Critics" and the "Chicago School"; bibliographical notes, pp. 287–316.

25.12   **Pritchard, John P.   Literary wise men of Gotham: criticism in New York, 1815–1860.** Baton Rouge: Louisiana State Univ. Pr., 1963.

25.13   **Rathbun, John W.   American literary criticism.** Vol. 1, 1800–1860. Vol. 2, 1860–1905, with Harry H. Clark. Boston: G. K. Hall, 1979.
Comprehensive but uneven. See also 25.7.

25.14   **Ruland, Richard.   The rediscovery of American literature: premises of critical taste, 1900–1940.** Cambridge, Mass.: Harvard Univ. Pr., 1967.

Treats especially Mencken, Matthiessen through Brooks, the New Humanists, the Southern Agrarians, the Marxists, and others.

25.15 **Santayana, George. The genteel tradition at bay.** New York: Scribner's, 1931.

Contains unfavorable criticism of the New Humanism. This work was in part responsible for the vogue of the expression "genteel tradition." Reprinted in *The Genteel Tradition: Nine Essays by George Santayana,* ed. Douglas L. Wilson, Cambridge, Mass.: Harvard Univ. Pr., 1967.

25.16 **Stovall, Floyd, ed. The development of American literary criticism.** Chapel Hill: Univ. of North Carolina Pr., 1955.

Five professors discuss five different aspects of the subject, 1800–1950.

25.17 **Wellek, René. A history of modern criticism: 1750–1950.** 4 vols. New Haven, Conn.: Yale Univ. Pr., 1955.

Attention is given to "pure aesthetics" on the one hand and impressionistic or unsubstantiated opinion on the other, with particular concern for "the principles and theory of literature" in terms of "its nature, its creation, its function, its effects, its relations to the other activities of man, its kinds, devices, and techniques, its origins and history." Vols. 1–2 treat the British Isles, France, Germany, and Italy; vols. 3–4 add Russia, Spain, and the U.S. to the discussion.

25.18 **Wimsatt, William K., Jr., and Cleanth Brooks. Literary criticism: a short history.** New York: Knopf, 1957.

A history of criticism in which three focal ideas are discussed in relation to poetry and the poetic principle, which itself is based heavily on metaphor. Ultimately the poetic theory to which the authors subscribe, one that provides a prevailing point of view throughout this history, must assert "the special character of . . . poetry as a tensional union of *making* with *seeing* and *saying*" (editors' emphasis for clarity).

25.19 **Booth, Wayne. Critical understanding: the powers and limits of pluralism.** Chicago: Univ. of Chicago Pr., 1979.

Booth compares and analyzes three different types of American criticism as represented by Ronald Crane, M. H. Abrams, and Kenneth Burke, using his observations to support his own pluralistic approach.

25.20 **Fish, Stanley E. Is there a text in this class?: the authority of interpretive communities.** Cambridge, Mass.: Harvard Univ. Pr., 1980.

Fish's essays of the 1970s manifest the development of his critical views from partial to almost pure reader response.

25.21 **Frye, Northrop. Anatomy of criticism: four essays.** Princeton, N.J.: Princeton Univ. Pr., 1957.

A brilliant attempt to formulate a coherent "synoptic view of the scope, theory, principles, and techniques of literary criticism" in which the association is confirmed between "creation and knowledge, art and science, myth and concept." The four essays of the subtitle are: "Historical Criticism: Theory of Modes," "Ethical Criticism: Theory of Symbols," "Archetypal Criticism: Theory of Myths," and "Rhetorical Criticism: Theory of Genres." This text has been a provocative and influential force in the shaping and practice of literary criticism during the past twenty-five years.

25.22 **Graff, Gerald. Literature against itself: literary ideas in modern society.** Chicago: Univ. of Chicago Pr., 1979.
An uneven but lively polemic against the "deconstructionist" school of criticism.

25.23 **Hartman, Geoffrey H. Criticism in the wilderness: the study of literature today.** New Haven, Conn.: Yale Univ. Pr., 1980.
To the "wilderness" of critical points of view Hartman adds his own peculiar one—that literary criticism is primary rather than secondary in relation to fiction, poetry, and drama.

25.24 **Hyman, Stanley Edgar. The armed vision: a study in the methods of modern literary criticism.** New York: Knopf, 1948. Abridged ed. 1955.
Conveys a fair amount of information, with considerable bias, on Wilson, Brooks, Winters, Eliot, Blackmur, Burke, and other American and British critics.

25.25 **Krieger, Murray. The new apologists for poetry.** Minneapolis: Univ. of Minnesota Pr., 1956.
A perceptive analysis and assessment of "representative modern critics" of poetry—the "New Critics"—in part to clarify and distinguish them as individual theorists and in part to indicate the value of each in defining a contemporary aesthetic for poetry.

25.26 **Lentricchia, Frank. After the New Criticism.** Chicago: Univ. of Chicago Pr., 1980.
An analytical overview of five critical methodologies that have become predominant in the past two decades—archetypal criticism, existentialism, phenomenology, structuralism, and poststructuralism—followed by individual chapters on four leading literary theorists of today: Murray Krieger, E. D. Hirsch, Paul de Man, and Harold Bloom. An outstanding comprehensive study. An innovative exploration of contemporary critical approaches with an ultimate resolution in favor of pluralism may be found in James Phelan, *Worlds from Words: A Theory of Language in Fiction,* Chicago: Univ. of Chicago Pr., 1981.

25.27 **McKean, Keith F. The moral measure of literature.** Denver: Swallow Pr., 1961.
Contains chapters on Babbitt, More, and Winters. See also John Gardner, *On Moral Fiction,* New York: Basic Books, 1978, for an acid attack on the current tendency to subordinate literature to literary theory and to disregard its essential moral center.

25.28 **Morris, Wesley. Toward a new historicism.** Princeton, N.J.: Princeton Univ. Pr., 1972.
A dissertation that very selectively offers bright ideas on Parrington, Marxist criticism in the U.S., Van Wyck Brooks, Ransom, and a scattering of more recent critics, especially Krieger.

25.29   **Sutton, Walter.   Modern American criticism.** Englewood Cliffs, N.J.: Prentice-Hall, 1963.
Repeats material in various works listed elsewhere in this section and offers helpful summaries of books and articles.

25.30   **Tompkins, Jane P.   Reader-response criticism: from formalism to post-structuralism.** Baltimore, Md.: Johns Hopkins Univ. Pr., 1980.

25.31   **Trilling, Lionel.   The liberal imagination: essays on literature and society.** New York: Viking, 1950.
A good antidote to a surfeit of overtheorizing in recent years that has divorced literature from social and moral worth.

25.32   **Webster, Grant.   The republic of letters: a history of postwar American literary opinion.** Baltimore, Md.: Johns Hopkins Univ. Pr., 1979.
An uneven but valuable assessment of the "New Critics" and the "New York Intellectuals."

25.33   **Weimann, Robert.   "New Criticism" und die Entwicklung bürgerlicher Literaturwissenschaft.** Halle: M. Niemeyer, 1962. 2d ed. Munich: C. H. Beck, 1974.
A systematic treatment, both historical and critical, not confined to Americans altogether and touched by socialist realism.

25.34   **Wellek, René.   The attack on literature and other essays.** Chapel Hill: Univ. of North Carolina Pr., 1982.
An assessment of contemporary literary theories. See also Wellek's *History of Modern Criticism,* 25.17.

25.35   **Wellek, René.   Concepts of criticism.** Ed. Stephen G. Nichols, Jr. New Haven, Conn.: Yale Univ. Pr., 1963.
Specific attention is given to methods of studying literature; provides a good overview of terms such as romanticism, realism, positivism in scholarship, etc.

25.36   **Wiener, Philip P., ed.   Dictionary of the history of ideas: studies of selected pivotal ideas.** 4 vols. New York: Scribner, 1973–1974.
Literature, criticism, and aesthetic theory loom large in the materials herein. Bibliographies follow each of the articles, about 300 in all. The fourth volume is an index, which needs to be used.

25.37   **Wimsatt, William K., Jr., ed.   Literary criticism: idea and act.** Berkeley and Los Angeles: Univ. of California Pr., 1974.
A judicious selection of essays from the English Institute, 1939–1974.

25.38   **Bush, Douglas.   Mythology and the Romantic tradition in English poetry.** Cambridge, Mass.: Harvard Univ. Pr., 1937.
Chap. 15 surveys American poets such as Longfellow, Lowell, H.D., Pound, and Eliot; a list of American poems connected with classical mythology appears on pp. 577–92.

25.39   **Campbell, Joseph.   The hero with a thousand faces.** New York: Pantheon, 1949. 2d ed. Princeton, N.J.: Princeton Univ. Pr., 1968.
The hero Campbell presents is a composite of mythic and divine figures,

the archetypal hero, through which universal human truths have been revealed symbolically in a multitude of ways. Because these symbols are "spontaneous productions of the psyche" rather than conscious creations, the key that Campbell employs to reveal the truths behind them is the language of psychoanalysis.

25.40 **Cassirer, Ernst. Language and myth.** Trans. Susanne K. Langer. New York: Harper, 1953.
A useful investigation of approaches to the study of myth criticism.

Cassirer reveals that basic truths lie in spontaneously generated, as opposed to consciously created, symbols and that a study of symbols—particularly those of language and myth—provides a key to understanding the primal forms of mental conception.

25.41 **Ostendorf, Bernhard. Der Mythos in der neuen Welt: eine Untersuchung zum amerikanischen Myth Criticism.** Frankfurt a. M: Thesen Verlag, 1971.
A useful investigation of approaches to the study of myth criticism.

25.42 **Richardson, Robert D., Jr. Myth and literature of the American renaissance.** Bloomington: Indiana Univ. Pr., 1978.
Presents the conflicting attitudes toward myth as insight into truth among writers of the period and explains these attitudes in relation to their work.

25.43 **Vickery, John B., ed. Myth and literature: contemporary theory and practice.** Lincoln: Univ. of Nebraska Pr., 1966.
A valuable collection of essays on the theoretical relation of myth to literature with individual chapters treating its application to specific literary works.

25.44 **Brown, Clarence A., ed. The achievement of American criticism: representative selections from three hundred years of American criticism.** New York: Ronald Press, 1954.
A substantial and very useful collection for both reading and reference. Valuable bibliography, pp. 678–724.

25.45 **Bryfonski, Dedria, and Sharon K. Hall, eds. Twentieth century literary criticism: excerpts from the works of poets, playwrights, short story writers, and other creative writers, 1900–1960.** Detroit: Gale Research Co., 1978.

25.46 **Leary, Lewis. American literary essays.** New York: Crowell, 1960.
A comprehensive and judicious selection of literary critical essays by American authors from Crèvecoeur to Faulkner, with a valuable introduction by the editor.

25.47 **Ruland, Richard, ed. The native muse: theories of American literature.** Vol. 1. New York: Dutton, 1972. Vol. 2. 1976.
An anthology, with thoughtful comments, of selections from writers ranging in time from the colonials to Whitman that deal with the debate over the "existence of native literature." The second volume, *The Storied Land,* takes the selections from Whitman to Edmund Wilson.

25.48 **Stallman, Robert W. The critic's note book.** Minneapolis: Univ. of Minnesota Pr., 1950.

Three hundred quotations from British and American critics from 1920 to 1950 are organized into eight chapters "dealing systematically with central concepts and problems of modern criticism." An extensive bibliography consists of checklists of books and articles topically arranged and includes a section on "Scholarship and Literary Criticism."

25.49 **Stallman, Robert W., ed. Critiques and essays in criticism, 1920–1948: representing the achievement of modern British and American critics.** New York: Ronald Press, 1949.
A collection of material drawn largely from out-of-print sources.

See also 2.5–6, 2.16, 2.22, 2.28, 2.31–32, 3.33, 16.12, 16.20–41, 19.42, 19.44–45, 24.81, 35.32, 35.36, 35.43, 35.45.

26. *Humor, essay, and other special genres*

26.1 **Anderson, John Q., ed. With the bark on: popular humor of the Old South.** Nashville, Tenn.: Vanderbilt Univ. Pr., 1967.

26.2 **Bier, Jesse. The rise and fall of American humor.** New York: Holt, Rinehart, and Winston, 1968. Repr. with new Afterword. New York: Octagon, 1981.
A critical study, described by the author as "selective" but covering humorists from the time of Franklin to that of Faulkner. An extensive but incomplete bibliography is appended. Valuable chiefly in that it complements earlier studies, especially for the period following 1920. Attention is also given to local colorists.

26.3 **Blair, Walter. Horse sense in American humor, from Benjamin Franklin to Ogden Nash.** Chicago: Univ. of Chicago Pr., 1942.
An excellent history of certain aspects of American humor.

26.4 **Blair, Walter, ed. Native American humor.** 2d ed. San Francisco: Chandler, 1960.
The selections cover the 19th century, but the introduction and very useful bibliography venture closer to date.

26.5 **Blair, Walter, and Raven I. McDavid, Jr. The mirth of a nation: America's great dialect humor.** Minneapolis: Univ. of Minnesota Pr., 1982.
A collection of "vintage humor" edited by a leading scholar in the genre and a foremost dialectician. The selections are "outrageous stories about ordinary American life" by rustic Yankees, frontier storytellers, funny fellows, and local colorists—plus Mark Twain—in "carefully modernized texts" to facilitate reading without loss of the original "wit [and] grit."

26.6   **Blair, Walter, and Franklin J. Meine, eds.   Half-horse, half-alligator: the growth of the Mike Fink legend.** Chicago: Univ. of Chicago Pr., 1956.
A selection of Mike Fink anecdotes and tales with valuable commentary and illustrations.

26.7   **Cohen, Hennig, and William B. Dillingham, eds.   Humor of the old Southwest.** 2d ed. Athens: Univ. of Georgia Pr., 1975.
Originally published in 1964, this outstanding collection of antebellum humor—from Georgia and the Carolinas across what is now the Deep South to the states along the western shore of the Mississippi River from Missouri down—has been reissued with the original introduction and commentaries but with a new preface and a substantially enlarged bibliography.

26.8   **Falk, Robert P., ed.   American literature in parody: a collection of parody, satire, and literary burlesque of American writers past and present.** New York: Twayne, 1955.
Selections deal with major and minor authors from Franklin through Hemingway, Wolfe, and Faulkner.

26.9   **Hall, Wade.   The smiling phoenix: southern humor from 1865 to 1914.** Gainesville: Univ. of Florida Pr., 1965.
A dissertation with an extensive bibliography of primary sources, more or less mechanically arranged.

26.10   **Inge, M. Thomas, ed.   The frontier humorists: critical views.** Hamden, Conn.: Archon, 1975.
Critical reactions to the work of the Old Southwest humorists are anthologized. There is also a critical checklist by C. E. Davis and M. B. Hudson.

26.11   **Kenney, W. Howland, ed.   Laughter in the wilderness: early American humor to 1783.** Kent, Ohio: Kent State Univ. Pr., 1976.
A judicious selection of primary material with a valuable introduction and useful commentaries on the authors but lacking a bibliography.

26.12   **Levin, Harry, ed.   Veins of humor.** Cambridge, Mass.: Harvard Univ. Pr., 1972.
Seven English Institute essays by various authors deal briefly and intelligently with the American product.

26.13   **Rourke, Constance.   American humor: a study of the national character.** New York: Harcourt, Brace, 1931.
Popular work that often goes beyond its title; see 32.15–16.

26.14   **Rubin, Louis D., Jr., ed.   The comic imagination in American literature.** New Brunswick, N.J.: Rutgers Univ. Pr., 1973.
A collection of essays by distinguished scholars on American humor from the colonial period to the present. The thirty-two pieces are brief but useful; originally designed for broadcasting over the Voice of America, they constitute a sound, comprehensive survey of the genre.

26.15   **Schecter, William.   The history of Negro humor in America.** New York: Fleet Pr., 1970.

A superficial survey that centers chiefly on the stage and screen, and ranges from minstrel shows to the Flip Wilson TV serial.

26.16. **Studies in American humor.** San Marcos: Southwest Texas State Univ. Pr., 1974–.
A "major outlet" for recent scholarship in its field.

26.17 **Tandy, Jennette. Crackerbox philosophers in American humor and satire.** New York: Columbia Univ. Pr., 1925.

26.18 **Williams, Kenny J., and Bernard Duffey, eds. Chicago's public wits: a chapter in the American comic spirit.** Baton Rouge: Louisiana State Univ. Pr., 1983.

26.19 **Yates, Norris W. The American humorist: conscience of the twentieth century.** Ames: Iowa State Univ. Pr., 1964.
Begins with the era of J. K. Bangs and Mr. Dooley and tops off with Cuppy, Perelman, Thurber, and their contemporaries. A substantial and very useful study.

26.20 **Yates, Norris W. William T. Porter and the *Spirit of the Times:* a study of the big bear school of humor.** Baton Rouge: Louisiana State Univ. Pr., 1957.
For a generation following 1830, Porter and the *Spirit* shaped the course of the mainstream of journalistic humor.

26.21 **Auer, J. Jeffery. An introduction to research in speech.** New York: Harper, 1959.
A handbook on methodology of research in the various areas included in speech and a bibliographical guide to professional writing in these fields.

26.22 **Baskerville, Barnet. The people's voice: the orator in American society.** Lexington: Univ. Pr. of Kentucky, 1979.
Public speaking reflects prevailing culture. See also Bercovitch, *The American Jeremiad*, 15.18.

26.23 **Braden, Waldo W., ed. Oratory in the Old South, 1828–1860.** Baton Rouge: Louisiana State Univ. Pr., 1970.
A collection of essays, mostly by professors of speech, on various political-historical subjects from the perspective of oratory and rhetoric. See also Braden's collection, *Oratory in the New South,* same publ., 1979, which is less political in content than broadly cultural. Cf. Gaines, 26.27.

26.24 **Brigance, William N., and Marie K. Hochmuth, eds. A history and criticism of American public address.** 3 vols. New York: McGraw-Hill, 1943–1955.
On American oratory. Contains also a chapter on rhetoric as taught in colleges in the earlier 19th century. Sponsored by the Speech Assoc. of America.

26.25 **Cleary, James W., and Frederick W. Haberman. Rhetoric and public address: a bibliography, 1947–1961.** Madison: Univ. of Wisconsin Pr., 1964.
The checklists published serially in the *Quarterly Journal of Speech,*

1947–1951, and since then in *Speech Monographs,* are here assembled. The coverage is international. See also 26.26.

26.26   **Communications monographs.** Falls Church, Va.: Speech Communication Assoc., 1934–.
Formerly *Speech Monographs;* title changed in 1976. Includes bibliographies and an annual record of graduate theses in speech.

26.27   **Gaines, Francis Pendleton.   Southern oratory: a study in idealism.** University: Univ. of Alabama Pr., 1946.

26.28   **Kitzhaber, Albert R.   A bibliography on rhetoric in American colleges, 1850–1900.** Denver, Colo.: Denver Public Library, 1954.

26.29   **Christadler, Martin.   Der amerikanische Essay, 1720–1820.** Heidelberg: C. Winter, 1968.
A comprehensive survey. A long-promised second volume covering 1820–1860 has not yet appeared.

26.30   **Cox, Edward G.   A reference guide to the literature of travel.** 3 vols. Seattle: Univ. of Washington Pr., 1935–1949.
The three volumes deal with the Old World, the New World, and Great Britain.

26.31   **Granger, Bruce.   American essay serials from Franklin to Irving.** Knoxville: Univ. of Tennessee Pr., 1978.
An analysis of the serials; not an anthology.

26.32   **Hicks, Philip Marshall.   The development of the natural history essay in American literature.** Philadelphia: Univ. of Pennsylvania Pr., 1924.

26.33   **Kirkham, E. Bruce, and John W. Fink, eds.   Indices to American literature annuals and gift books, 1825–1865.** New Haven, Conn.: Research Publ., 1975.
An extensive compilation that provides a guide to more than 450 annuals and gift books; a valuable listing indexed according to author, title, publisher, illustration, and other data.

26.34   **Thompson, Ralph.   American literary annuals and gift books, 1825–1865.** [New York]: H. W. Wilson, 1936.
Supplemented by forty-six new titles in Alan E. James, "Literary Annuals and Gift Books," *Journal of the Rutgers University Library,* 1 (1938), 14–21. Works listed in Thompson are microfilmed by Research Publications, Inc., New Haven, Conn.

26.35   **O'Neal, David L.   Early American almanacs: the Phelps Collection, 1679–1900.** Peterborough, N.H.: David L. O'Neal/Antiquarian Booksellers, 1979.
A catalog with index and bibliography.

26.36   **Stowell, Marion Barber.   Early American almanacs: the colonial weekday Bible.** New York: B. Franklin, 1977.

26.37   **Foote, Henry W.   Three centuries of American hymnody.** Cambridge, Mass.: Harvard Univ. Pr., 1940.

Traces the story of hymns and their writers from colonial times. Supplemented by the same author's pamphlet, *Recent American Hymnody,* New York: Hymn Soc. of America, 1952.

See also **11.39–40, 19.52, 27.14, 27.43–44, 29.93–94, 30.24, 31.92, 32.15, 32.40.**

Children's literature

26.38 **Haviland, Virginia, and William Jay Smith. Children and poetry: a selective annotated bibliography.** Washington, D.C.: Library of Congress, 1969. 2d ed. 1979.

26.39 **Rahn, Suzanne. Children's literature: an annotated bibliography of the history and criticism.** New York: Garland, 1981.
A wide-ranging bibliography, including poetry, drama, and light nonfiction as well as fiction; mostly works in English but some non-English classics are included.

26.40 **Townsend, John Rowe. Written for children: an outline of English-language children's literature.** Boston: Horn Book, 1974. 2d ed. Philadelphia: Lippincott, 1975.
Separate chapters on American Realism and American picture books. Selected bibliographies included. Also see Elva S. Smith, *The History of Children's Literature: A Syllabus with Selected Bibliographies,* rev. ed., Chicago: American Library Assoc., 1980; and Jacob Blanck, ed., *Peter Parley to Penrod,* New York: R. R. Bowker, 1978.

26.41 **Welch, d'Alté Aldridge. A bibliography of American children's books printed prior to 1821.** Worcester, Mass.: American Antiquarian Soc., 1972.
A chronological history of 18th-century American children's books is given in the introduction; important institutional and private collections are noted.

26.42 **Bader, Barbara. American picturebooks from Noah's ark to the beast within.** New York: Macmillan, 1976.

26.43 **Cameron, Eleanor. The green and burning tree: on the writing and enjoyment of children's books.** Boston: Atlantic-Little, Brown, 1962.
A writer and critic's appreciation; selected bibliography of sources included.

26.44 **Cech, John, ed. American writers for children.** Detroit: Gale Research Co., 1981, 1982.
Critical biographies of more than 150 writers from the 18th through the 20th centuries. Helpful also is D. L. Kirkpatrick, ed., *Twentieth-Century Children's Writers,* New York: St. Martin's, 1978.

26.45 **Children's literature: an annual journal of the MLA Division on Children's Literature and the Children's Literature Association.** New Haven, Conn.: Yale Univ. Pr., 1972–.

26.46 Fraser, James H., ed. Society & children's literature. Boston: David R. Godine, 1978.

A sound collection of essays on a variety of subjects related to children's literature, including "Regionalism in American Children's Literature," by Fred Erisman, pp. 55–75. Also see Erisman's "American Regional Juvenile Literature, 1870–1910: An Annotated Bibliography," *American Literary Realism,* 6 (1973), 109–122.

26.47 Haviland, Virginia, ed. Children and literature: views and reviews. Glenview, Ill.: Scott, Foresman, 1973.

Essays on children's literature from its beginnings to the modern scene, primarily British and American. Many by prominent children's authors and illustrators. Chapters on criticism, reviewing, and awards are included. Helpful also is Sheila Egoff, et al., *Only Connect: Readings on Children's Literature,* 2d ed., New York: Oxford Univ. Pr., 1980.

26.48 Haviland, Virginia, and Margaret Coughlan. Yankee Doodle's literary sampler of prose, poetry, & pictures. New York: Crowell, 1974.

An anthology of works published for children before 1900, with introductions to each section. Extensively illustrated; selected bibliography included. Comprises selections from the Rare Book Collections of the Library of Congress.

26.49 Jordan, Alice. From Rollo to Tom Sawyer and other papers. Boston: Horn Book, 1948.

Twelve essays on 19th-century American children's books and magazines.

26.50 Meigs, Cornelia, et al. A critical history of children's literature. New York: Macmillan, 1953. Rev. ed. 1969.

Surveys English and American writers. See also Monica Kiefer, *American Children through Their Books, 1700–1835,* Philadelphia: Univ. of Pennsylvania Pr., 1948.

26.51 Sutherland, Zena, et al. Children and books. 6th ed. Glenview, Ill.: Scott, Foresman, 1981.

A general textbook with selected but extensive annotated bibliographies. Helpful also is Francelia Butler, *Sharing Literature with Children.* New York: David McKay, 1977.

See also **8.20, 31.87–88.**

27. *Studies of the 17th and 18th centuries*

27.1 Andrews, Charles M. The colonial period of American history. 4 vols. New Haven, Conn.: Yale Univ. Pr., 1934–1938. Rev. ed. 1964.

27.2   **Bercovitch, Sacvan, ed.   The American Puritan imagination: essays in revaluation.** New York and London: Cambridge Univ. Pr., 1974.

A notable collection of essays on major themes and writers identified with American Puritanism written by American and other scholars. A selected bibliography is included, pp. 241–58.

27.3   **Bercovitch, Sacvan.   The Puritan origins of the American self.** New Haven, Conn.: Yale Univ. Pr., 1975.

A perceptive exploration of the development of the American "identity"; ranges over a broad panorama of the Puritan cultural context with documentary support for all points. See also Bercovitch, *The American Jeremiad*, 15.18.

27.4   **Clark, Harry Hayden.   "The influence of science on American ideas, from 1775–1809."** Transactions of the Wisconsin Academy of Sciences, Arts, and Letters, 35 (1943), 305–49.

27.5   **Cremin, Lawrence A.   American education: the colonial experience, 1607–1783.** New York: Harper and Row, 1970.

The first of three projected volumes on the history of American education; the second volume, with the subtitle *The National Experience*, was published in 1980.

27.6   **Davis, Richard Beale.   Intellectual life in Jefferson's Virginia, 1790–1830.** Chapel Hill: Univ. of North Carolina Pr., 1964.

Considers such topics as education, reading and libraries, arts, literature, oratory, religion, and social theory.

27.7   **Davis, Richard Beale.   Intellectual life in the colonial South.** 3 vols. Knoxville, Tenn.: Univ. of Tennessee Pr., 1978.

A respected work on the grand scale written by an expert.

27.8   **Demos, John.   A little commonwealth: family life in Plymouth colony.** New York: Oxford Univ. Pr., 1970.

An important and somewhat revisionary approach to colonial history, which has traditionally emphasized the intellectual roots.

27.9   **Early American literature.**   Chapel Hill: Univ. of North Carolina Pr., 1966–.

A triquarterly journal devoted to American literature of the 17th and 18th centuries; the principal journal in the field.

27.10   **Emerson, Everett.   Puritanism in America: 1620–1750.**   Boston: Twayne/G. K. Hall, 1977.

A concise, readable, and sound introduction that covers the major points and figures of the period; written by one of the leading scholars in the field.

27.11   **Emerson, Everett, ed.   American literature, 1764–1789.** Madison: Univ. of Wisconsin Pr., 1977.

Essays by various colonialists on Jefferson, Crèvecoeur, the drama, and Afro-American writers, among others.

27.12   **Emerson, Everett, ed.   Major writers of early American literature.** Madison: Univ. of Wisconsin Pr., 1972.

Substantial essays on Bradford, Bradstreet, Taylor, Cotton Mather, Edwards, Byrd, Franklin, Freneau, and C. B. Brown by distinguished scholars of early American writing.

27.13 **Gilmore, Michael T., ed. Early American literature: a collection of critical essays.** Englewood Cliffs, N.J.: Prentice-Hall, 1980.
A collection, in the Spectrum series, of previously published critical essays.

27.14 **Granger, Bruce I. Political satire in the American Revolution.** Ithaca, N.Y.: Cornell Univ. Pr., 1960.
A survey and analysis, 1763–1783.

27.15 **Gummere, Richard M. The American colonial mind and the classical tradition: essays in comparative culture.** Cambridge, Mass.: Harvard Univ. Pr., 1963.
Deals with the general aspects of the subject as well as with the specific indebtedness of writers like Byrd, Sewall, and Logan.

27.16 **Hornberger, Theodore. Scientific thought in the American colleges, 1638–1800.** Austin: Univ. of Texas Pr., 1946.

27.17 **Howard, Leon. The Connecticut Wits.** Chicago: Univ. of Chicago Pr., 1943.
Trumbull, Dwight, Humphreys, and Barlow; a standard study of an area of literary history now often neglected.

27.18 **Israel, Calvin, ed. Discoveries & considerations: essays on early American literature & aesthetics presented to Harold Jantz.** Albany: State Univ. of New York Pr., 1976.
A diverse and rewarding collection of essays on individual writers and broader topics by many contemporary critics in colonial literary studies.

27.19 **Jones, Howard Mumford. The literature of Virginia in the seventeenth century.** Boston: [American Academy of Arts and Sciences], 1946. 2d ed. Charlottesville: Univ. Press of Virginia, 1968.

27.20 **Leary, Lewis. Soundings: some early American writers.** Athens: Univ. of Georgia Pr., 1975.
Attractively written and authoritative essays, chiefly on 18th-century authors, but with a chapter each on Irving and Cooper.

27.21 **Lemay, J. A. Leo. Men of letters in colonial Maryland.** Knoxville: Univ. of Tennessee Pr., 1972.
A sound pioneering study of belletrists in early Maryland.

27.22 **Levy, Babette M. Preaching in the first half century of New England history.** Hartford, Conn.: American Soc. of Church History, 1945.
See also A. W. Plumstead, ed., *The Wall and the Garden: Selected Massachusetts Election Sermons, 1670–1775,* Minneapolis: Univ. of Minnesota Pr., 1968; and Jones and Jones, eds., 18.32.

27.23 **Lowance, Mason L., Jr. The language of Canaan: metaphor and symbol in New England from the Puritans to the Transcendentalists.** Cambridge, Mass.: Harvard Univ. Pr., 1980.

A perceptive exposition of the way that the "prophetic and metaphorical language" as derived from the Bible and employed by the Puritans strongly affected and reappeared in the writings of later American authors, including Emerson and Thoreau. See also Bercovitch, *The American Jeremiad*, 15.18.

27.24   **Middlekauff, Robert.   The Mathers: three generations of Puritan intellectuals, 1596–1728.** New York: Oxford Univ. Pr., 1971.

A solid survey of the main intellectual interests of Richard, Increase, and Cotton Mather.

27.25   **Miller, Perry, and Thomas H. Johnson, eds.   The Puritans.** New York, etc.: American Book Co., 1938. Rev. ed. 2 vols. New York: Harper & Row, 1963.

A particularly rich anthology containing important critical material by the editors on the intellectual background of 17th-century writing in New England.

27.26   **Morgan, Edmund S.   The birth of the Republic, 1763–1789.** Chicago: Univ. of Chicago Pr., 1956. Rev. ed. 1977.

A history of the revolutionary period and the manner in which the principles of the Constitution grew out of the needs and experience of 18th-century Americans.

27.27   **Morgan, Edmund S.   Visible saints: the history of a Puritan idea.** New York: New York Univ. Pr., 1963.

The genesis, flowering, and decline of the Puritan idea of a church of the elect in New England from the 1630s to 1700.

27.28   **Murdock, Kenneth B.   Literature and theology in colonial New England.** Cambridge, Mass.: Harvard Univ. Pr., 1949.

Strikes a happy balance between "erudition and popular interpretation," largely because it originated as "a course of lectures" for the Lowell Institute in Boston (March and April 1944) as one of its annual series on "Current Topics in Theology."

27.29   **Raesly, Ellis L.   Portrait of New Netherland.** New York: Columbia Univ. Pr., 1945.

Discusses, among other matters, the literary productions of the Dutch settlers.

27.30   **Silverman, Kenneth.   A cultural history of the American Revolution: painting, music, literature, and the theatre in the colonies and the United States from the Treaty of Paris to the inauguration of George Washington, 1763–1789.** New York: Thomas Y. Crowell, 1976.

A detailed, illustrated, and rewarding history of the period that provides a corrective to doubts over the rich cultural life that existed during the revolutionary years.

27.31   **Stearns, Raymond P.   Science in the British colonies of America.** Urbana: Univ. of Illinois Pr., 1970.

Natural history of the colonists is admirably treated.

27.32   **Stillwell, Margaret Bingham.   Incunabula and Americana, 1450–1800.** New York: Columbia Univ. Pr., 1931.

Lists on pp. 341–440 about 550 bibliographies of, and monographs on, Americana before 1800.

27.33 **Tolles, Frederick B. Quakers and the Atlantic culture.** New York: Macmillan, 1960.
The role of the Quakers in the 17th and 18th centuries; includes chapters on "The Quaker Ethic" and "The Culture of Early Pennsylvania."

27.34 **Tyler, Moses Coit. A history of American literature during the colonial time.** Rev. ed. 2 vols. New York: G. P. Putnam's Sons, 1897. Abridged ed. Ed. Archie H. Jones. Chicago: Univ. of Chicago Pr., 1967.
Covers 1607–1765; despite its age, it remains indispensable.

27.35 **Tyler, Moses Coit. The literary history of the American Revolution, 1763–1783.** 2 vols. New York: G. P. Putnam's Sons, 1897.
Still the standard work on the subject, though Silverman, 27.30, provides a rich source for additional information and insight. See also 27.11.

27.36 **Wood, Gordon S. The creation of the American Republic, 1776–1787.** Chapel Hill: Univ. of North Carolina Pr., 1969.
An interpretation of the Revolution and formation of the Constitution; emphasizes the creation of a distinctly American political culture.

27.37 **Wright, Louis B. The cultural life of the American colonies, 1607–1763.** New York: Harper, 1957.
A social history that establishes close connections with the literature of the period.

27.38 **Yannella, Donald J., and John H. Roch, comps. American prose to 1820: a guide to information sources.** Detroit: Gale Research Co., 1979.
A thoroughly annotated and indexed compilation of nearly 3,000 entries itemizing American nonfiction prose written before 1820, with a generous selection of mostly 20th-century secondary material relating to it and its authors. A clearly arranged and very substantial listing of obscure items as well as the more commonly known ones. For additional authors and background material, see also *American Writers before 1800: A Biographical and Critical Reference Guide,* ed. James A. Levernier and Douglas M. Wilmes, 3 vols., Westport, Conn.: Greenwood Pr., 1983.

27.39 **Scheick, William J., and JoElla Doggett, comps. Seventeenth-century American poetry: a reference guide.** Boston: G. K. Hall, 1977.
A good bibliography with which to begin a study of the subject.

27.40 **Daly, Robert. God's altar: the world and the flesh in Puritan poetry.** Berkeley: Univ. of California Pr., 1978.
A corrective to the prevailing view that American Puritans were hostile to poetry, and a reading of the major poets of the period. Provides good intellectual background.

27.41 **Jantz, Harold S. The first century of New England verse.** Worcester, Mass.: The [American Antiquarian] Soc., 1944.

27.42 **Lewalski, Barbara Kiefer. Protestant poetics and the seventeenth-century religious lyric.** Princeton, N.J.: Princeton Univ. Pr., 1979.

An important study that relates in detail scriptural to poetic language and the imaginative impulse toward lyric creativity.

27.43 **Forbes, Harriette. New England diaries, 1602–1800: a descriptive catalogue of diaries, orderly books, and sea journals.** [Topsfield, Mass.: Privately printed], 1923. Repr. New York: Russell & Russell, 1967.

27.44 **Kagle, Steven E. American diary literature: 1620–1799.** Boston: Twayne, 1979.
A surprisingly full account for so limited a format; consequently, a very useful starting point for further investigation in the area.

See also 12.13, 14.29, 15.9, 15.18, 18.30–37, 19.26, 22.4, 22.7, 23.78–81, 23.86–87, 23.89, 23.91, 24.11, 26.31, 30.11, 30.26, 32.1, 32.45, 32.79.

28. *Studies of 20th-century literature*

28.1 **The American year book, 1910–1950.** New York and London: D. Appleton and Co., 1911–1951.
Annual surveys of accomplishments and events; the arts and literature are included.

28.2 **Jones, Howard Mumford, and Richard M. Ludwig. Guide to American literature and its backgrounds since 1890.** 4th ed., rev. and enlarged. Cambridge, Mass.: Harvard Univ. Pr., 1972.
This outline, accompanied by lists of books, is both a bibliography and an attempt to impose order upon the literature as well as the backgrounds. The first edition, 1953, was compiled by Jones alone.

28.3 **Literature and language bibliographies from the American Year Book, 1910–1919.** Ann Arbor, Mich.: Pierian Press, 1970.
E. E. Hale and A. H. Quinn survey the field of American literature year by year. Their work, along with that of others, is reprinted.

28.4 **Millett, Fred B. Contemporary American authors: a critical survey and 219 bio-bibliographies.** New York: Harcourt, Brace, 1940.
A bibliographical handbook, out-of-date but still helpful.

28.5 **Aaron, Daniel. Writers on the left: episodes in American literary communism.** New York: Harcourt, Brace, and World, 1961.
"A social chronicle of the Left Wing writer" from 1912 to the early 1940s. Part of a series called "Communism in American Life," with Clinton L. Rossiter as the general editor.

28.6 **Allen, Frederick L. Only yesterday: an informal history of the nineteen-twenties.** New York: Harper and Brothers, 1931.
Very useful for its portrayal of fashions and attitudes of the intellectuals.

28.7   **Allen, Frederick L.   Since yesterday: the nineteen-thirties in America.**
New York: Harper and Row, 1940.
Not as consequential as Allen's earlier volume on the 1920s, 28.6.

28.8   **Berthoff, Warner.   A literature without qualities: American writing since 1965.** Berkeley: Univ. of California Pr., 1979.
Brief mention of many writers, emphasis on few, including Henry Miller and Wallace Stevens.

28.9   **Bogardus, Ralph F., and Fred Hobson, eds.   Literature of the barricades: the American writer in the 1930s.** University: Univ. of Alabama Pr., 1982.
Essays by Irving Howe, James T. Farrell, and others, mostly presented at the Fifth Alabama Symposium on English and American Literature, Tuscaloosa, Oct. 19–21, 1978.

28.10   **Brooks, Van Wyck.   Opinions of Oliver Allston.** New York: E. P. Dutton, 1941.
A vigorous arraignment of much of the literature, criticism, and ideology of the period 1915–1940; the essays are dated but are nevertheless worth consulting because of Brooks's stature as a popular critical voice of that era.

28.11   **Christadler, Martin.   Amerikanische Literatur der Gegenwart in Einzeldarstellung.** Stuttgart: Kröner, 1973.
Various scholars survey a number of contemporary fiction writers, dramatists, and poets.

28.12   **Cowley, Malcolm, ed.   After the genteel tradition.** New York: W. W. Norton, 1937. With a preface by Harry T. Moore. Carbondale: Southern Illinois Univ. Pr., 1965.
Various critics discuss a variety of authors or topics treating the period 1910–1930.

28.13   **Cowley, Malcolm.   Exile's return: a narrative of ideas.** New York: W. W. Norton, 1934. New ed. New York: Viking, 1951.
Deals with "ideas that dominated the literary world of the 1920's."

28.14   **Cowley, Malcolm.   The literary situation.** New York: Viking, 1954.
"A social history of literature in our times"—war novels, paperback books, how authors earn a living, etc.

28.15   **Cowley, Malcolm.   A second flowering: works and days of the lost generation.** New York: Viking, 1973.
With much warmed-over material the comments center mainly on Fitzgerald, Hemingway, Dos Passos, Cummings, Wilder, Faulkner, Wolfe, and H. Crane.

28.16   **Duffey, Bernard.   The Chicago renaissance in American letters: a critical history.** East Lansing: Michigan State Univ. Pr., 1954.
Covers the period 1890–1930. See also Kramer, 28.27, and Kenny J. Williams, *Prairie Voices: A Literary History of Chicago from the Frontier to 1893*, Nashville, Tenn.: Townsend, 1980, for a careful history and lists of relevant publications.

28.17   **Fishman, Solomon.   The disinherited of art: writer and background.**
Berkeley: Univ. of California Pr., 1953.
Speculation on the "impact of culture" on 20th-century American literature: alienation of writers in the 1920s, Naturalism, Marxism, and Agrarianism in the 1930s, the rise of the "New Criticism," attitudes toward Europe,
etc.

28.18   **Ford, Hugh.   Published in Paris: American and British writers, painters, and publishers in Paris, 1920–1939.** New York: Macmillan, 1975.
This solid, readable, and well-documented account emphasizes the important support given to the authors by their publishers.

28.19   **French, Warren, ed.   The thirties: fiction, poetry, drama.** Deland, Fla.:
E. Edwards, 1967. 2d ed. 1976.
A useful and coherent collection of essays, historical and critical, by various collaborators; Jackson R. Bryer provides a bibliography that is briefly
annotated. Also edited by French and brought out by the same publisher are
The Forties, 1969; *The Fifties,* 1971; and *The Twenties,* 1975; all have a
similar format.

28.20   **Hassan, Ihab.   Contemporary American literature, 1945–1972: an introduction.** New York: Ungar Publ. Co., 1973.
An introductory survey.

28.21   **Hicks, Jack.   In the singer's temple: prose fictions of Barthelme,
Gaines, Brautigan, Percy, Kesey, and Kosinski.** Chapel Hill: Univ. of
North Carolina Pr., 1981.

28.22   **Hoffman, Daniel, ed.   Harvard guide to contemporary American writing.** Cambridge, Mass.: Harvard Univ. Pr., 1979.
A useful volume but oddly selective.

28.23   **Hoffman, Frederick J.   The twenties: American writing in the postwar
decade.** New York: Viking, 1955. Rev. ed. New York: Collier, 1962.
A systematic study centered on eight themes or trends, with accompanying analyses of eight illustrative literary texts.

28.24   **Kazin, Alfred.   On native grounds.** New York: Harcourt, Brace, 1942.
Abridged ed. Garden City, N.Y.: Doubleday, 1956.
Criticism of prose writers from Howells to the authors of the 1930s in
their historical context. After the first edition a subtitle, *An Interpretation of
American Prose Literature,* was added.

28.25   **Kenner, Hugh.   A homemade world: the American modernist writers.**
New York: Knopf, 1974.
Faulkner, Fitzgerald, Hemingway, M. Moore, Stevens, and Williams are
scrutinized by a critic of considerable experience.

28.26   **Knight, Grant C.   The strenuous age in American literature.** Chapel
Hill: Univ. of North Carolina Pr., 1954.
The literature of 1900–1910 is discussed in relation to the political and
social climate of the decade. Knight's *The Critical Period in American Literature,* same publ., 1951, deals similarly with the preceding decade.

28.27   **Kramer, Dale. Chicago renaissance: the literary life in the Midwest, 1900–1930.** New York: Appleton-Century, 1966.
Often supplements Duffey, 28.16.

28.28   **Krutch, Joseph Wood. The modern temper: a study and a confession.** New York: Harcourt, 1929.
Tendencies in thought in the 1920s and the mood induced by those tendencies.

28.29   **Rood, Karen Lane, ed. American writers in Paris, 1920–1939.** Dictionary of Literary Biography. Vol. 4. Detroit: Gale Research Co., 1980.

28.30   **Spiller, Robert E., ed. A time of harvest: American literature, 1910–1960.** New York: Hill and Wang, 1962.
A series of historical or critical essays by various hands, apparently originally conceived for broadcasting in Europe, which treat briefly criticism, poetry, drama, fiction, humor, and folklore. Has a special chapter on the "New Criticism," by David Daiches.

28.31   **Stevenson, Elisabeth. Babbitts and bohemians: the American 1920s.** New York: Macmillan, 1967.
A popular work, like Allen, 28.6, which it often supplements.

28.32   **Straumann, Heinrich. American literature in the twentieth century.** London: Hutchinson's Universal Library, 1951. 3d rev. ed. New York: Harper and Row, 1965.
A systematic survey by a Swiss professor.

28.33   **Thorp, Willard. American writing in the twentieth century.** Cambridge, Mass.: Harvard Univ. Pr., 1960.
A useful brief survey prepared for the Library of Congress series on American studies; selective bibliography, pp. 325–32.

28.34   **Tytell, John. Naked angels: the lives and literature of the Beat generation.** New York: McGraw-Hill, 1976.
A sound comprehensive study of the Beat writers and their "philosophy."

28.35   **Weinberg, Helen. The new novel in America: the Kafkan mode in contemporary fiction.** Ithaca, N.Y.: Cornell Univ. Pr., 1970.

28.36   **Whipple, T. K. Spokesmen: modern writers and American life.** New York and London: D. Appleton and Co., 1928.
Adams, Robinson, Dreiser, Frost, Anderson, Cather, Sandburg, Lindsay, Lewis, O'Neill. A contemporary appraisal that still has considerable value because of its critical insights.

28.37   **Writers at work: the Paris Review interviews.** Ed. Malcolm Cowley. New York: Viking, 1958.
A collection of discriminating interviews with sixteen contemporary authors, chiefly Americans, including Dorothy Parker, Thurber, Wilder, Faulkner, R. P. Warren, Algren, Styron, and Capote. A second series, 1963, carries on, with an introduction by Van Wyck Brooks. A third series, 1967, is introduced by Alfred Kazin.

In addition to numerous related items in sections 22–25 and 30–32 of this Guide, see also 12.12, 12.17, 12.19–26, 20.29, 20.40, 35.5, 35.19.

29. *Special topics and themes in American literature*

29.1   **Banta, Martha. Failure & success in America: a literary debate.** Princeton, N.J.: Princeton Univ. Pr., 1978.

This solid and comprehensive study shows the way that the language and attitudes of Americans reflect the struggle to come out ahead. Primary attention is given to imaginative literature, with support from other disciplines.

29.2   **Basler, Roy Prentice. The Lincoln legend: a study in changing conceptions.** Boston: Houghton Mifflin, 1935.

Abraham Lincoln in poetry, fiction, drama, etc.

29.3   **Bell, Michael Davitt. The development of American romance: the sacrifice of relation.** Chicago: Univ. of Chicago Pr., 1980.

A study of the organic relation between the American romance and the early 19th-century culture that generated it, with emphasis on Poe, Hawthorne, and Melville.

29.4   **Bode, Carl. The young rebel in American literature.** New York: Praeger, 1959.

29.5   **Cady, Edwin H. The gentleman in America: a literary study in American culture.** Syracuse, N.Y.: Syracuse Univ. Pr., 1949.

The concept of the "gentleman" as reflected in American literature.

29.6   **Carter, Everett. The American idea: the literary response to American optimism.** Chapel Hill: Univ. of North Carolina Pr., 1977.

Traces the idea of optimism and progress through American literary history.

29.7   **Clough, Wilson D. The necessary earth: nature and solitude in American literature.** Austin: Univ. of Texas Pr., 1964.

Focuses on the impact of nature on man as presented in American literature.

29.8   **Eakin, Paul John. The New England girl: cultural ideals in Hawthorne, Stowe, Howells, and James.** Athens: Univ. of Georgia Pr., 1976.

29.9   **Earnest, Ernest. Expatriates and patriots: American artists, scholars, and writers in Europe.** Durham, N.C.: Duke Univ. Pr., 1968.

A useful study in its comprehensiveness but with a decidedly chauvinistic bias. Also see a worthwhile account of ten 19th- and 20th-century American authors by Harold T. McCarthy, *The Expatriate Perspective*, Rutherford, N.J.: Fairleigh Dickinson Univ. Pr., 1974.

29.10   **Feidelson, Charles, Jr. Symbolism and American literature.** Chicago: Univ. of Chicago Pr., 1953. Abridged ed. 1959.

Suggests that "the concept of symbolism" is not only a key to Hawthorne, Whitman, Melville, and Poe but also "a link between their literature and our own." A substantial discussion of American symbolism.

29.11 **Foerster, Norman.** **Nature in American literature.** New York: Macmillan, 1923.
Chiefly concerned with the 19th century.

29.12 **Franklin, H. Bruce.** **The victim as criminal and artist: literature from the American prison.** New York: Oxford Univ. Pr., 1978.

29.13 **Fussell, Edwin.** **Frontier: American literature and the American West.** Princeton, N.J.: Princeton Univ. Pr., 1965.
A controversial study that brings much more traditional American literature within the range of the frontier than is usually suspected. See also Leslie A. Fiedler, *The Return of the Vanishing American,* New York: Stein and Day, 1968.

29.14 **Girgus, Sam B.** **The law of the heart: individualism and the modern self in American literature.** Austin: Univ. of Texas Pr., 1979.

29.15 **Hazard, Lucy L.** **The frontier in American literature.** New York: Crowell, 1927.
Exhibits the excess with which the frontier hypothesis was applied.

29.16 **Hicks, Granville.** **The great tradition: an interpretation of American literature since the Civil War.** New York: Macmillan, 1933. Rev. ed. 1935.
Undertakes to show the approximations to Marxism in the literature of the period; strongly Marxist in its criticism.

29.17 **Hilfer, Anthony C.** **The revolt from the village, 1915–1930.** Chapel Hill: Univ. of North Carolina Pr., 1969.
Begins with Eggleston, Frederic, and Clemens; includes a chapter on the 1930s and after.

29.18 **Johnson, Timothy W., and Julia Johnson, eds.** **Crime fiction criticism: an annotated bibliography.** New York: Garland, 1981.
More than 2,000 entries on American, British, and European mystery and detective fiction, from Poe's tales through 1980.

29.19 **Kaplan, Harold.** **Democratic humanism and American literature.** Chicago: Univ. of Chicago Pr., 1972.
An intelligent effort to point out a major theme underlying the work of Emerson, Thoreau, Melville, Hawthorne, Whitman, Clemens, and James.

29.20 **Kernan, Alvin B.** **The imaginary library: an essay on literature and society.** Princeton, N.J.: Princeton Univ. Pr., 1982.
An important and timely essay exposing the natural effects that take place between society and literature, with particular emphasis on the manner in which destructive or otherwise harmful elements in contemporary society are reflected in works dealing specifically with writing or language as their subject.

29.21 **Kerr, Howard.** **Mediums, and spirit-rappers, and roaring radicals: spiritualism in American literature, 1850–1900.** Urbana: Univ. of Illinois Pr., 1972.
A witty survey of the impact of the extrasensory phenomena that engaged

the interest of Hawthorne, Lowell, Clemens, Howells, and James, among others.

29.22   **Kolodny, Annette.   The lay of the land: metaphor as experience and history.** Chapel Hill: Univ. of North Carolina Pr., 1975.
A study of the way that land and natural resources have been exploited as represented in American literature from the earliest writings; Kolodny discloses how authors have characteristically described the exploitation in sexist terms—masculine subjugating feminine.

29.23   **Kramer, John E., Jr.   The American college novel: an annotated bibliography.** New York: Garland, 1981.
Provides information on 425 novels written between 1828 and 1979. See also 24.22.

29.24   **Lindberg, Gary.   The confidence man in American literature.** New York: Oxford Univ. Pr., 1982.
A fascinating study of this archetypal American figure, from Franklin to Barth.

29.25   **Lynen, John F.   The design of the present: essays on time and form in American literature.** New Haven, Conn.: Yale Univ. Pr., 1969.

29.26   **MacMillan, Duane J., ed.   The stoic strain in American literature.** Toronto: Univ. of Toronto Pr., 1979.
Generally solid essays on nine authors of the 19th and 20th centuries follow an introduction by Peter Buitenhuis.

29.27   **Siegel, Adrienne.   The image of the American city in popular literature, 1820–1870.** Port Washington, N.Y.: Kennikat, 1981.
An analysis and survey of urban fiction from the middle decades of the 19th century; probably more useful as a reference source for the more than 300 novels brought together than for critical or historical insight. See also 24.70.

29.28   **Spencer, Benjamin T.   The quest for nationality: an American literary campaign.** Syracuse, N.Y.: Syracuse Univ. Pr., 1957.
A history of the nationalistic element in American literature from colonial times to 1892, with emphasis on the period 1830–1860, and with individual chapters on Whitman, Transcendentalism, and local-color fiction.

29.29   **Stafford, John.   The literary criticism of "Young America": a study in the relationship of politics and literature, 1837–1850.** Berkeley: Univ. of California Pr., 1952.
A clear, concise, and readable account.

29.30   **Stovall, Floyd.   American idealism.** Norman: Univ. of Oklahoma Pr., 1943.
Illustrates the rise and fall of idealism in American literature from the colonial period to the 1940s.

29.31   **Tanner, Tony.   The reign of wonder.** Cambridge, England: University Press, 1965.
Traces the sense of wonder in American literature from the Transcendentalists to the mid-20th century.

29.32 Thompson, G. R., and Virgil L. Lokke, eds. **Ruined Eden of the present—Hawthorne, Melville, and Poe: critical essays in honor of Darrell Abel.** Lafayette, Ind.: Purdue Univ. Pr., 1981.

An outstanding collection of essays by many of the major scholars in the field of American Romanticism.

29.33 Tichi, Cecilia. **New world, new earth: environmental reform in American literature from the Puritans through Whitman.** New Haven, Conn.: Yale Univ. Pr., 1979.

What the author presents as "reform" environmentalists call destruction and exploitation, no matter how the changes in the American landscape may be explained and perhaps justified with recourse to the religious idealism of the Puritans and those who followed them.

29.34 Turner, Lorenzo D. **Anti-slavery sentiment in American literature prior to 1865.** Washington, D.C.: The Assoc. for the Study of Negro Life and History, 1929.

29.35 Wasserstrom, William. **Heiress of all the ages: sex and sentiment in the genteel tradition.** Minneapolis: Univ. of Minnesota Pr., 1959.

An account that "undertakes to study the genteel tradition, its place in American social history, its effect on literature," especially the novel.

29.36 Fried, Lewis, and Yoshinobu Hakutani, eds. **American literary Naturalism: a reassessment.** Heidelberg: Carl Winter, 1975.

Essays on ten American authors from Howe to Algren written by major literary scholars in the field. Other authors treated include Crane, Norris, Adams, Wright, Dreiser, Steinbeck, et al.

29.37 Krause, Sydney J., ed. **Essays on determinism in American literature.** Kent, Ohio: Kent State Univ. Pr., 1964.

A useful introduction by the editor precedes seven essays on assorted American authors from Melville to Faulkner written by major critics with the naturalistic motif in mind.

29.38 Pizer, Donald. **Realism and Naturalism in 19th-century American literature.** Carbondale: Southern Illinois Univ. Pr., 1966.

A reprint of articles, but the notes are updated; this is a compact but substantial volume by a leading critic in the area.

29.39 Walcutt, Charles Child. **American literary Naturalism, a divided stream.** Minneapolis: Univ. of Minnesota Pr., 1956.

The unity of nature and spirit in American Transcendentalism split toward the end of the 19th century and generated the "divided stream" of American Naturalism, in which two opposing approaches to attaining truth conflicted—scientific investigation and intuitive idealism. This thesis is developed and applied in relation to several major novelists, from Frederic and Garland to Steinbeck, Hemingway, and Dos Passos.

29.40 Aichinger, Peter. **The American soldier in fiction, 1880–1963: a history of attitudes toward warfare and the military establishment.** Ames: Iowa State Univ. Pr., 1975.

Useful for its comprehensiveness, this account somewhat sketchily covers war in American literature in the past century and a half.

29.41 Jones, Peter G.   War and the novelist: appraising the American war novel. Columbia: Univ. of Missouri Pr., 1976.

29.42 Miller, Wayne Charles.   An armed America, its face in fiction: a history of the American military novel. New York: New York Univ. Pr., 1970.

A comprehensive survey of American war fiction from Cooper to Heller. More useful as a resource for reference to often unfamiliar fiction than as criticism, its principal value is in its extensive coverage of the genre.

29.43 A bibliography on the relations of literature and the other arts, 1952–1967.   New York: AMS Press, 1969.

Published for the General Topics IX Group of the Modern Language Assoc.

29.44 Callow, James T.   Kindred spirits: Knickerbocker writers and American artists, 1807–1855. Chapel Hill: Univ. of North Carolina Pr., 1967.

Major and minor Knickerbockers are studied for the close relationship between literary authors and the visual arts; included are detailed expositions of personal and professional relations, similarities in techniques, publication data, etc. Valuable bibliographical appendixes, pp. 231–250; bibliography, pp. 253–273.

29.45 Huddleston, Eugene L., and Douglas A. Noverr.   The relationship of painting and literature. Detroit: Gale Research Co., 1978.

A well-indexed compilation in which poetry dominates the literature discussed.

29.46 Novak, Barbara.   Nature and culture: American landscape painting, 1825–1875. New York: Oxford Univ. Pr., 1980.

Relates major Transcendentalist ideas, especially the envisioning of God in nature, to the landscape painting of the period and indicates the changes effected in the relations by the Civil War, Darwinism, and technology. A substantial and important study; well illustrated. See also Stein, 29.95.

29.47 Ringe, Donald A.   The pictorial mode: space & time in the art of Bryant, Irving & Cooper. Lexington: Univ. Pr. of Kentucky, 1971.

Points out parallels between the literature and the landscape painting of the early Romantics.

29.48 Steiner, Wendy.   The colors of rhetoric: problems in the relation between modern literature and painting. Chicago: Univ. of Chicago Pr., 1982.

29.49 CLIO: a journal of literature, history, and the philosophy of history.   Indianapolis, Ind.: Western Newspaper Publ. Co., 1971–.

Published by the Division of Literature and Science of the Modern Language Assoc.; includes an annual bibliography of more than 200 entries on relations between literature and science. Issued three times a year.

29.50 Himmelfarb, Gertrude.   Darwin and the Darwinian revolution. Garden City, N.Y.: Doubleday, 1959.

One of the best studies of the period. A bibliography was added in 1962.

29.51 **Kuhn, Thomas S.   The structure of scientific revolutions.** Chicago: Univ. of Chicago Pr., 1962. 2d ed. 1970.
Influential in the study of the philosophy of science, this volume has had an important impact on literary criticism.

29.52 **Martin, Ronald E.   American literature and the universe of force.** Durham, N.C.: Duke Univ. Pr., 1981.
The concept of "force" in 19th-century scientific and social thought as manifested in American Naturalism is central in this study. See also 29.36–39.

29.53 **Purdy, Strother B.   The hole in the fabric: science, contemporary literature, and Henry James.** Pittsburgh, Pa.: Univ. of Pittsburgh Pr., 1977.
Looks at James in relation to modern science and to certain innovative writers of the present.

29.54 **Reingold, Nathan, ed.   The sciences in the American context: new perspectives.** Washington, D.C.: Smithsonian Institution Pr., 1979.
Papers delivered at a conference of the American Assoc. for the Advancement of Science, Boston, Feb. 1976, which collectively evince both the increased attention given to studying the history of the sciences in the U.S. and the relation of that study to a broader understanding of American history in general.

29.55 **Science, technology, and human values.**   Boston: MIT Pr., 1972– .
STHV is a quarterly review that includes bibliographies on science and society in each issue; some are relevant to literary relations to science.

29.56 **Spencer, Sharon.   Space, time, and structure in the modern novel.** New York: New York Univ. Pr., 1971.
A scientific approach to several contemporary writers that is both fresh and significant.

See also **8.18, 16.20–41, 17.50, 18.51–57, 19.14, 19.39–63, 22.43–46, 25.42, 26.20, 28.35, 30.33, 30.56, 31.57, 31.93–94, 32.32, 32.35.**

Science fiction and utopian writings

29.57 **Clareson, Thomas.   Science fiction criticism: an annotated checklist.** Kent, Ohio: Kent State Univ. Pr., 1972.

29.58 **Currey, L. W., and R. Reginald.   Science fiction & fantasy reference guide: an annotated list of critical, bibliographical, and biographical works.** San Bernardino, Calif.: Borgo Press, 1980.

29.59 **Day, Donald B.   Index to the science fiction magazines, 1926–1950.** Portland, Ore.: Perri Press, 1952. 2d ed. Boston: G. K. Hall, 1982.
The second edition "incorporates several hundred corrections."

29.60 **Hall, Halbert W.   Science fiction book review index: 1923–1973.** Detroit: Gale Research Co., 1975. 1974–1979. 1981.
Lists all books reviewed in science fiction magazines for the specified pe-

riods. 1970–1973 reviews of science fiction books in selected non-science fiction magazines are also included. Very well indexed. Annual supplementary indexes are being published by Texas A & M Univ. Library, Bryan, Texas.

29.61 **Magill, Frank N., ed.** **Survey of science fiction literature.** 5 vols. Englewood Cliffs, N.J.: Salem Press, 1979.
Comprises 500 essay-reviews of famous science fiction novels and 2,500 bibliographical references.

29.62 **N.E.S.F.A. index: science fiction magazines and anthologies.** Cambridge, Mass.: New England Science Fiction Assoc., Inc., 1966–.
Formerly, 1966–1970, *Index to the Science Fiction Magazines;* now an annual listing. See also earlier compilations by Day, 29.59, and Strauss, 29.65.

29.63 **Reginald, R.** **Science fiction and fantasy literature: a checklist, 1700–1974.** 2 vols. Detroit: Gale Research Co., 1979.
Includes information on contemporary science fiction authors.

29.64 **Siemon, Frederick.** **Science fiction story index, 1950–1968.** Chicago: American Library Assoc., 1971. 2d ed. By Marilyn P. Fletcher. 1950–1979. 1981.
The stories are listed from anthologies.

29.65 **Strauss, Erwin S.** **The MIT Science Fiction Society's index to the science fiction magazines, 1951–1965.** Cambridge, Mass.: MIT Science Fiction Soc., 1966.
See also 29.59 and 29.62.

29.66 **Tymn, Marshall B., and Roger C. Schlobin.** **The year's scholarship in science fiction and fantasy: 1972–1975.** Kent, Ohio: Kent State Univ. Pr., 1979.

29.67 **Tymn, Marshall B., Roger C. Schlobin, and L. W. Currey.** **A research guide to science fiction studies: an annotated checklist. . . .** New York: Garland, 1977.

29.68 **Attebery, Brian.** **The fantasy tradition in American literature: from Irving to Le Guin.** Bloomington: Indiana Univ. Pr., 1980.
Defines "fantasy" and relates it to authors in various genres, including many writers not usually associated with science fiction and the fantastic.

29.69 **Barron, Neil, ed.** **Anatomy of wonder: science fiction.** 2d ed. New York: R. R. Bowker, 1981.
A critical collection with bibliography.

29.70 **del Rey, Lester.** **The world of science fiction, 1926–1976: the history of a subculture.** New York: Ballantine Books, 1979.

29.71 **Extrapolation: the newsletter of the MLA Conference on Science Fiction.** Wooster, Ohio: Wooster College, 1959–1979. Kent, Ohio: Kent State Univ. Pr., 1979–.

29.72 **Nicholls, Peter, ed. The science fiction encyclopedia.** Garden City, N.Y.: Doubleday, 1979.

A useful tool; also see the larger and quite comprehensive work by Donald H. Tuck, *The Encyclopedia of Science Fiction and Fantasy through 1968: A Bibliographic Survey,* 3 vols., Chicago: Advent Publ., 1974–1982, which comprises bio-bibliographies of individual authors and a checklist of publications in the field.

29.73 **Olander, Joseph D., and Martin Harry Greenberg, eds. Writers of the 21st century.** New York: Taplinger, 1977–.

A continuing series with each volume comprising essays on individual authors, thus far including Isaac Asimov, Ray Bradbury, Arthur C. Clarke, Robert Heinlein, Ursula Le Guin, et al.

29.74 **Sargent, Lyman Tower. British and American utopian literature, 1516–1975: an annotated bibliography.** Boston: G. K. Hall, 1979.

Includes the most complete published listing of American utopias with brief annotations and library locations as well as an extensive list of secondary sources. Both primary and secondary lists will be updated in supplements and in "News Center" in *Alternative Futures: The Journal of Utopian Studies,* Troy, N.Y.: Rensselaer Polytechnic Inst., Human Dimensions Center, 1968–. For an international bibliography containing many American entries and library locations, see Glenn Negley, *Utopian Literature: A Bibliography with a Supplementary Listing of Works Influential in Utopian Thought,* Lawrence: Regents Press of Kansas, 1977.

29.75 **Parrington, Vernon Louis, Jr. American dreams: a study of American utopias.** Providence, R.I.: Brown Univ. Pr., 1947. 2d ed., enl. New York: Russell and Russell, 1964.

An early study that offers a chronological, book-by-book survey from 1659 through 1868, then continues to 1946 (1963 in the postscript to the 2d edition) with discussions of individual books and themes. A partially annotated bibliography lists eighty-six utopias through 1946.

29.76 **Roemer, Kenneth M., ed. America as utopia: collected essays.** New York: Burt Franklin, 1981.

Includes a general introduction and four sections with brief introductory comments for each: essays by utopian authors; case studies; thematic studies; and chronological, bibliographical, and historical surveys covering pre-European discovery attitudes to contemporary science fiction. Epilogue by Ursula Le Guin; bibliographies list over 700 utopias; includes a 2,000-item index.

29.77 **Roemer, Kenneth M. The obsolete necessity: America in utopian writings, 1888–1900.** Kent, Ohio: Kent State Univ. Pr., 1976.

A solid, well-researched survey of a brief but very fertile period for utopian works. Analyzes general ambivalences about time, place, and the individual, and specific attitudes about religion, economics, sex roles, urban growth, etc. A bibliography is included, pp. 181–213, listing 160 utopias from 1888–1900 and secondary works with full annotations that cite related writings.

See also **32.37.**

Literature of the sea

29.78 **Albion, Robert G.   Naval and maritime history: an annotated bibliography.** 4th ed., rev. Mystic, Conn.: Munson Institute of American Maritime History, 1972.

A source book with more than 5,000 entries. Useful for sections on reference works, merchantmen and warships, captains and crews, navies, and whaling.

29.79 **Skallerup, Harry R.   Books afloat and ashore: a history of books, libraries, and reading among seamen during the age of sail.** Hamden, Conn.: Archon Books, 1974.

29.80 **Smith, Myron J., Jr., and Robert C. Weller, eds.   Sea fiction guide.** Metuchen, N.J.: Scarecrow, 1976.

Seven brief introductory essays, followed by a selective listing of 2,525 English and American titles with an index of pseudonyms and joint authors.

29.81 **Chapelle, Howard I.   The history of the American sailing navy: the ships and their development.** New York: Norton, 1949.

The standard work.

29.82 **Kemp, Peter.   The Oxford companion to ships and the sea.** London: Oxford Univ. Pr., 1976.

International in scope, with expected British emphasis. Useful for biographical entries and definitions of nautical terms. On sailor language, see also *The Visual Encyclopedia of Nautical Terms Under Sail,* by Bathe W. Basil, Alan Villiers, et al., New York: Crown, 1978; and W. A. McEwen and A. H. Lewis, *Encyclopedia of Nautical Knowledge,* Cambridge, Md.: Cornell Maritime Press, 1953.

29.83 **Lovette, Leland P.   Naval customs, traditions, and usage.** Annapolis, Md.: Naval Institute Pr., 1934. 5th ed. Published under the title Naval Ceremonies, Customs, and Traditions. 1980.

29.84 **Stackpole, Edouard A.   The sea-hunters: the New England whalemen during two centuries, 1635–1835.** Philadelphia: J. P. Lippincott, 1953.

The authoritative history; includes an account of the *Essex* disaster.

29.85 **Auden, W. H.   The enchafèd flood; or, the romantic iconography of the sea.** New York: Random House, 1950.

An often brilliant exposition of romantic sea (life-giving), stone, and desert imagery with particular references to *Moby-Dick.*

29.86 **Lewis, Charles Lee.   Books of the sea: an introduction to nautical literature.** Annapolis, Md.: Naval Institute Pr., 1943.

Contains separate, largely uncritical, chapters on American sea fiction, poetry, and drama with suggested reading lists.

29.87 **Miller, Pamela A.   And the whale is ours: creative writing of American whalemen.** Boston: D. R. Godine, 1979.

Excerpts from whaling logs and journals; published in association with the Kendall Whaling Museum of Sharon, Mass.

29.88 **Philbrick, Thomas. James Fenimore Cooper and the development of American sea fiction.** Cambridge, Mass.: Harvard Univ. Pr., 1961.
Critical analyses of Cooper's sea stories and works of maritime novelists before 1850.

29.89 **Santraud, Jeanne-Marie. La Mer et le roman américain dans la première moitié du dix neuvième siecle.** Paris: Didier, 1972.

29.90 **Selincourt, Aubrey de, ed. The book of the sea.** London: Eyre & Spottiswoode, 1961.
A collection of literary pieces related to the sea; contrasts the romantic view of the sea with that of the classical Greeks and Romans.

29.91 **Solley, George C., and Eric Steinbaugh, eds. Moods of the sea: masterworks of sea poetry.** Annapolis, Md.: Naval Institute Pr., 1981.
Contains ninety-four American selections, a third of them written by 20th-century poets.

29.92 **Vincent, Howard P. The trying-out of *Moby-Dick*.** Boston: Houghton Mifflin, 1949.
An outstanding example of the way in which source materials are assimilated creatively into a novel—in this case, whaling literature in the creation of *Moby-Dick*. A recent edition, Kent, Ohio: Kent State Univ. Pr., 1980, restored the illustrations deleted from the original in an edition issued at Carbondale: Southern Illinois Univ. Pr., 1965.

29.93 **Colcord, Joanna C. Songs of American sailormen.** New York: Bramhall House, 1938. New ed. New York: Oak Publ., 1964.
The original edition of this collection appeared in 1924 under the title of *Roll and Go: Songs of American Sailormen;* the 1938 edition is revised and enlarged from that version. This is a useful introduction. See also Horace Beck, *Folklore and the Sea,* Middletown, Conn.: Wesleyan Univ. Pr., 1973, which is a rich store of information that includes a selection of songs and comments on them; variations of the songs in Colcord may be found in a collection by Frederick Pease Harlow, *Chanteying Aboard American Ships,* Barre, Mass.: Barre Gazette, 1962.

29.94 **Huntington, Gale, ed. Songs the whalemen sang.** Barre, Mass: Barre Publ., 1964. 2d ed. New York: Dover Publ., 1970.
Texts and tunes of songs with illustrations of whalemen's journals and scrimshaw. See also Burl Ives, *Sea Songs of Sailing, Whaling, and Fishing,* New York: Ballantine Books, 1956.

29.95 **Stein, Roger B. Seascape and the American imagination.** New York: C. N. Potter/Crown Publ., 1975.
Cultural background of American marine painters; beautifully illustrated and especially useful in relation to Poe, Cooper, Melville, and other American authors of the early and mid-19th century who depicted verbal seascapes. Published in association with the Whitney Museum of American Art.

See also **27.43.**

30. *Literary regionalism and selected studies of American regional literature*

30.1   **American guide series.** 1937–1949.

Travel guidebooks for each of the states, a number of larger cities, etc., containing materials originally compiled by the WPA. Various publishers have sponsored them, and a number have been more recently reprinted; the original editions have been reprinted by Somerset Press, St. Clair Shores, Mich. Many of these volumes in their introductory matter contain brief sketches of the literary and other artistic contributions of the localities or states.

30.2   **Bernard, Harry. Le Roman régionaliste aux États-Unis, 1913–1940.** Montreal: Fides, 1949.

A largely descriptive account.

30.3   **Burke, John G., ed.   Regional perspectives: an examination of America's literary heritage.** Chicago: American Library Assoc., 1973.

Creative writers supply long essays on their native regions, personal in tone. The bibliography appended helps to update previous studies.

30.4   **Gohdes, Clarence.   Literature and theater of the states and regions of the U.S.A.: an historical bibliography.** Durham, N.C.: Duke Univ. Pr., 1967.

Under the names of the fifty states, the dependencies, and principal regions, this volume lists monographs, anthologies, pamphlets, chapters of books, and periodical articles that provide materials for the study of the local belles lettres and theater, from earliest times to 1965. (A few more recent items have been included.) In the appendix appear lists of works on regionalism, especially in its literary aspects, and on "the western."

30.5   **Jensen, Merrill, ed. Regionalism in America.**   Madison: Univ. of Wisconsin Pr., 1951. Foreword by Felix Frankfurter.

Proceedings of a 1949 symposium on American regionalism; includes Benjamin T. Spencer, "Regionalism in American Literature," pp. 219–260.

30.6   **McMurtrie, Douglas C.   "Locating the printed source materials for United States history: with a bibliography of lists of regional imprints."** Mississippi Valley Historical Review, 31 (1944), 369–406.

The WPA sponsored an American Imprints Inventory—listings of the imprints of various states, etc. McMurtrie records these listings to 1943.

30.7   **Milton, John R., ed.   The writer's sense of place.** Special issue of South Dakota Review, 13 (1975).

American writers discuss the importance of place-awareness in their work; includes statements by Farrell, Manfred, Caldwell, Stegner, Eastlake, Wilbur, and others.

30.8   **Myerson, Joel, ed.   Antebellum writers in New York and the South.** Detroit: Gale Research Co., 1979.
Vol. 3 of the *Dictionary of Literary Biography.*

30.9   **Tuan, Yi-Fu.   Topophilia: a study of environmental perception, attitudes, and values.** Englewood Cliffs, N.J.: Prentice-Hall, 1974.
Considers the influence of environmental perceptions upon artistic expressions, including literature; an excellent study for students of literary regionalism.

See also **3.7, 10.42, 19.52, 20.14, 23.22, 26.46, 33.20, 34.2, 34.10.** *For additional items on specific regions beyond those listed immediately below, consult the subject index of this Guide.*

The Northeast

30.10   **ATQ: a journal of New England writers.**   Kingston, R.I.: Univ. of Rhode Island Pr., 1969–.
Formerly *American Transcendental Quarterly;* focuses on the authors and culture of New England.

30.11   **Nagel, James, and Richard Astro, eds.   American literature: the New England heritage.** New York: Garland, 1981.
A collection of papers read at a 1980 conference in which the topics ranged from colonial literature, through various literary coteries and individual writers of the 19th century, to black and women authors of the 20th century, with New England at the emanating center.

30.12   **New England quarterly.**   Brunswick, Me.: Bowdoin College, 1928–.
Articles related to New England life and literature. (Many items on New England literature of the colonial period appear in section 27 of this *Guide.*)

30.13   **Westbrook, Perry D.   The New England town in fact and fiction.** East Brunswick, N.J.: Fairleigh Dickinson Univ. Pr., 1982.
Examines "ideas *about* the towns" and discusses the persistent myth of New England town life as a panacea for social ills; includes commentary on such authors as Dwight, Emerson, and Jewett.

The Midwest

30.14   **Nemanic, Gerald C., ed.   A bibliographical guide to midwestern literature.** Iowa City: Univ. of Iowa Pr., 1981.
Arranged under two major headings and appendixes, this *Guide* comprises nine topical bibliographies on Midwestern literary and folk culture; bibliographical listings on more than 120 authors.

30.15   **Dondore, Dorothy Anne.   The prairie and the making of middle America: four centuries of description.** Cedar Rapids, Iowa: Torch Press, 1926.
History of literature of the Middle West; includes a dated but extensive

and still useful gathering of bibliographical notes. See also Duffey, 28.16, and Kramer, 28.27, on Chicago writers.

30.16   **Faulkner, Virginia, and Frederick C. Luebke, eds.   Vision and refuge: essays on the literature of the Great Plains.** Lincoln: Univ. of Nebraska Pr., 1982.
Eight essays on a variety of subjects such as Scandinavian immigrants, Chicanos, F. J. Turner, and Willa Cather.

30.17   **Flanagan, John T., ed.   America is west: an anthology of middlewestern life and literature.** Minneapolis: Univ. of Minnesota Pr., 1945.
Contains biographical notes.

30.18   **Hansen, Harry.   Midwest portraits: a book of memories and friendships.** New York: Harcourt-Brace, 1923.
Sandburg, Anderson, Herrick, Masters, et al.; a personal account and appreciation.

30.19   **Meyer, Roy W.   The middle western farm novel in the twentieth century.** Lincoln: Univ. of Nebraska Pr., 1965.
Contains also a background chapter on "The Farm in Nineteenth Century Fiction."

30.20   **Midamerica: the yearbook of the Society for the Study of Midwestern Literature.**   East Lansing: Michigan State Univ. Pr., 1973–.
The 1975 number began publishing an annual bibliography of studies in the field, in 1983 edited by David D. Anderson.

30.21   **Rusk, Ralph L. The literature of the middle western frontier.** 2 vols. New York: Columbia Univ. Pr., 1925.
The standard history and bibliography, to 1840; vol. 2 is chiefly bibliographical, pp. 42–363.

The South

30.22   **Bain, Robert, et al., eds.   Southern writers: a biographical dictionary.** Baton Rouge: Louisiana State Univ. Pr., 1979.

30.23   **Emerson, O. B., and Marion C. Michael, eds.   Southern literary culture: a bibliography of master's and doctor's theses.** Rev. ed. University: Univ. of Alabama Pr., 1979.
Supplement compiled by Jack D. Wages and William L. Andrews and published as a special issue of *Mississippi Quarterly,* 32 (1978–1979).

30.24   **Harwell, Richard B.   Confederate belles-lettres, a bibliography and a finding list of the fiction, poetry, songsters, and miscellaneous literature published in the Confederate States of America.** Hattiesburg, Miss.: The Book Farm, 1941.
This limited original printing of only 195 copies has been reissued by University Microfilms, Ann Arbor, Mich., 1972; and by the Gordon Press, N.Y., 1976.

30.25 **Rubin, Louis D., Jr., ed.** **A bibliographical guide to the study of southern literature.** Baton Rouge: Louisiana State Univ. Pr., 1969.

A valuable bibliography, compiled by numerous scholars. The first section is devoted to general topics; the second consists of checklists of the works of 134 authors, from John Smith to Walker Percy. An appendix includes notes on 68 additional colonial authors.

30.26 **Wages, Jack D., ed.** **Seventy-four writers of the colonial South.** Boston: G. K. Hall, 1979.

An annotated bibliography of secondary material.

30.27 **Williams, Jerry T., ed.** **Southern literature, 1968–1975: a checklist of scholarship.** Boston: G. K. Hall, 1978.

Compiled by the Committee on Bibliography of the Society for the Study of Southern Literature. Conflates the first eight annual bibliographies from the spring issues of *Mississippi Quarterly*. Supplements *A Bibliographical Guide to the Study of Southern Literature*, ed. Rubin, 30.25. Includes some items not in the original *Mississippi Quarterly* checklists. Alphabetized within four chronological sections. Name index included.

30.28 **Holman, C. Hugh.** **The immoderate past: the southern writer and history.** Athens: Univ. of Georgia Pr., 1977.

30.29 **Holman, C. Hugh.** **The roots of southern writing: essays on the literature of the American South.** Athens: Univ. of Georgia Pr., 1972.

30.30 **Hubbell, Jay B.** **The South in American literature, 1607–1900.** Durham, N.C.: Duke Univ. Pr., 1954.

Covers not only the southern authors but also other writers who treated the region. Replaces all preceding studies in thoroughness, especially for the period to the Civil War. Its extensive bibliography is filled with valuable comment.

30.31 **Jones, Anne Goodwyn.** **Tomorrow is another day: the woman writer in the South, 1859–1936.** Baton Rouge: Louisiana State Univ. Pr., 1982.

A study of seven southern women novelists, major (Chopin and Glasgow) and minor (Mary Johnston, Grace King, Margaret Mitchell, et al.).

30.32 **McIlwaine, Shields.** **The southern poor-white from lubberland to tobacco road.** Norman: Univ. of Oklahoma Pr., 1939.

The social history of the poor whites and their treatment in literature of various periods. See also Cook, 30.49.

30.33 **MacKethan, Lucinda H.** **The dream of Arcady: place and time in southern literature.** Baton Rouge: Louisiana State Univ. Pr., 1980.

Traces the pastoral theme in southern writing from Lanier to Walker Percy.

30.34 **Roller, David C., and Robert W. Twyman, eds.** **Encyclopedia of southern history.** Baton Rouge: Louisiana State Univ. Pr., 1979.

Includes many entries on southern literature and culture.

30.35 **Rubin, Louis D., Jr., ed.** **The American South: portrait of a culture.** Baton Rouge: Louisiana State Univ. Pr., 1980.

Twenty-two essays on southern literature and culture, originally prepared for publication by the U.S. International Communications Agency.

30.36 **Rubin, Louis D., Jr., ed. The literary South.** New York: Wiley, 1979.
A substantial anthology compiled by one of the foremost southern literary scholars; covers the literature from the colonial period to date.

30.37 **Rubin, Louis D., Jr., and C. Hugh Holman, eds. Southern literary study.** Chapel Hill: Univ. of North Carolina Pr., 1975.
Conference papers from a gathering of scholars at the Univ. of North Carolina, Nov. 30 to Dec. 2, 1972, during which problems in the general area were discussed and new subjects for investigation were proposed.

30.38 **Rubin, Louis D., Jr. William Elliott shoots a bear: essays on the southern literary imagination.** Baton Rouge: Louisiana State Univ. Pr., 1975.
A selection of occasional essays on individual authors address the same question: "Why do southern writers write the way they do?" What particulars of the South have affected their work and made it distinctive?

30.39 **Skaggs, Merrill M. The folk of southern fiction.** Athens: Univ. of Georgia Pr., 1972.
The ordinary, plain southerner as treated in the work of authors from the time of A. B. Longstreet to that of Eudora Welty. The heaviest weight is on the later 19th century and the early decades of the 20th.

30.40 **Young, Thomas Daniel. The past in the present: a thematic study of modern southern fiction.** Baton Rouge: Louisiana State Univ. Pr., 1981.
Changing southern values explored through chapters on 20th-century writers, including Faulkner, Warren, and Welty.

30.41 **Southern literary journal.** Chapel Hill: Univ. of North Carolina Pr., 1968–.
Semiannual, with essays on the literature and culture of the region and review-essays covering current books in the field. (Beginning in 1969, the spring issue of *Mississippi Quarterly* includes an annual checklist of scholarship dealing with southern literature.)

30.42 **Southern studies.** Natchitoches: Northwestern State Univ. of Louisiana Pr., 1961–.
An interdisciplinary journal of the South; issued quarterly.

30.43 **Gaines, Francis Pendleton. The southern plantation: a study in the development and the accuracy of a tradition.** New York: Columbia Univ. Pr., 1924.
Old South plantation life as treated in literature.

30.44 **Library of southern literature.** 17 vols. Atlanta, Ga.: Martin and Hoyt Co., 1909–1923.
An extensive amateurish anthology of selections from numerous authors. Vol. 15 is devoted solely to biographical sketches of the writers; very inaccurate.

30.45 **Ridgely, J[oseph] V. Nineteenth-century southern literature.** Lexington: Univ. Pr. of Kentucky, 1980.

Shows the tendency of 19th-century southern authors to fictionalize their history and mythologize their present.

30.46 **Watson, Charles S. Antebellum Charleston dramatists.** University: Univ. of Alabama Pr., 1976.

The most important southern city for theater was Charleston, and W. G. Simms was its outstanding playwright. Watson shows the movement from nationalism to sectionalism as the Civil War drew near.

30.47 **Bradbury, John M. The Fugitives: a critical account.** Chapel Hill: Univ. of North Carolina Pr., 1958.

Attempts "to set the Fugitive group as a whole in its proper historical place" and to indicate the nature of the literary work of each member—especially Ransom, Tate, and Warren. See also Louise Cowan, *The Fugitive Group: A Literary History,* Baton Rouge: Louisiana State Univ. Pr., 1959; Rob R. Purdy, ed., *Fugitives' Reunion: Conversations at Vanderbilt,* Nashville, Tenn.: Vanderbilt Univ. Pr., 1959; and John L. Stewart, *The Burden of Time,* Princeton, N.J.: Princeton Univ. Pr., 1965.

30.48 **Bradbury, John M. Renaissance in the South: a critical history of the literature, 1920–1960.** Chapel Hill: Univ. of North Carolina Pr., 1963.

30.49 **Cook, Sylvia Jenkins. From tobacco road to route 66: the southern poor white in fiction.** Chapel Hill: Univ. of North Carolina Pr., 1976.

Covers the period from the 1930s on; see also McIlwaine, 30.32.

30.50 **King, Richard H. A southern renaissance: the cultural awakening of the American South, 1930–1955.** New York: Oxford Univ. Pr., 1980.

Treats literature of the modern South from an essentially "social-science perspective."

30.51 **Rubin, Louis D., Jr., and Robert D. Jacobs, eds. Southern renascence: the literature of the modern South.** Baltimore, Md.: Johns Hopkins Univ. Pr., 1953.

Collects articles by divers hands on a variety of 20th-century writers of the region.

30.52 **Rubin, Louis D., Jr., and Robert D. Jacobs, eds. South: modern southern literature in its cultural setting.** Garden City, N.Y.: Doubleday, 1961.

Essays on various authors and themes, followed by a valuable checklist on thirty-six writers, compiled by James B. Meriwether.

See also **34.22.**

The West

30.53 **Erisman, Fred, and Richard W. Etulain, eds. Fifty western writers: a bio-bibliographical sourcebook.** Westport, Conn.: Greenwood Pr., 1982.

Only a few 19th-century authors keep this "representative" selection of western writers from dealing entirely with 20th-century work, but the selection itself is excellent nonetheless, and the bio-bibliographies have been prepared by prominent scholars.

30.54 Etulain, Richard W.   "The American literary West and its interpreters: the rise of a new historiography." Pacific Historical Review, 45 (1976), 311–348.
A comprehensive account of the different approaches to western literature that have been taken by literary historians.

30.55 Etulain, Richard W.   A bibliographical guide to the study of western American literature. Lincoln: Univ. of Nebraska Pr., 1982.
Over 5,000 unannotated items on more than 350 authors entirely or in part associated with the American West. Bibliographies, general studies, and special topics (e.g., "Popular Western Literature," "Western Film," "The Chicano in Western Literature") are treated separately. Includes an author index. Supersedes the compiler's earlier bibliography, *Western American Literature,* Vermillion, S.D.: Dakota Press, 1972.

30.56 Marovitz, Sanford E.   "Myth and realism in recent criticism of the American literary West." Journal of American Studies, 15 (1981), 95–114.
A review-essay that focuses on criticism of the past fifteen years with references to important earlier studies. Emphasis is on the elusive definition of "realism" as that term is applied in critical discussions of American western literature.

30.57 Vinson, James, and D. L. Kirkpatrick, eds.   Twentieth-century western writers. Pref. C. L. Sonnichsen. Detroit: Gale Research Co., 1982.
Bio-bibliographies of more than 300 American western authors, mostly of fiction, with informative critical essays for each; up-to-date checklists of primary and secondary material; pseudonyms also accounted for in overall alphabetical compilation. Popular "westerns" are emphasized.

30.58 Etulain, Richard W., ed.   The American literary West. Manhattan, Kans.: Sunflower Univ. Pr., 1980.
Originally published as a special issue of *Journal of the American West,* 19 (1980), this volume comprises a collection of essays with accompanying photographs on major authors and periods of western literary history.

30.59 Etulain, Richard W., and Michael T. Marsden, eds.   The popular western: essays toward a definition. Bowling Green, Ohio: Bowling Green Univ. Popular Pr., 1974.
Ten essays, half on specific authors and the others on general topics, vary considerably in length and constitute an introduction to the genre. A short unannotated bibliography by Michael D. Gibson appears on pp. 101–06.

30.60 Folsom, James K.   The American western novel. New Haven, Conn.: College and University Pr., 1966.
A discriminating critical history of the western novel from Cooper through Guthrie and Richter; an excellent starting point.

30.61 Gurian, Jay.   Western American writing: tradition and promise. Deland, Fla.: Everett/Edwards, 1975.
A concise but exceptionally worthwhile and honest look at the field of western American letters.

30.62 **Haslam, Gerald W., ed.** **Western writing.** Albuquerque: Univ. of New Mexico Pr., 1974.

Reprints selected essays on literary and historical productions. "The Regional Approach to Literature," by George R. Stewart, is especially rewarding. See also the interviews with various contemporary writers conducted by John R. Milton for *The South Dakota Review* (1964), reprinted in J. Golden Taylor, *The Literature of the American West,* Boston: Houghton Mifflin, 1971, an excellent anthology.

30.63 **Lee, Robert E.** **From West to East: studies in the literature of the American West.** Urbana: Univ. of Illinois Pr., 1966.

Essays on Lewis and Clark, Timothy Flint and James Hall, Irving and Parkman, Clemens, Cather, and De Voto. The criterion of realism is applied to their writings.

30.64 **Lewis, Merrill, and L. L. Lee, eds.** **The westering experience in American literature: bicentennial essays.** Bellingham: Bureau for Faculty Research, Western Washington Univ. Pr., 1977.

A good collection of essays on general and specific frontier and western topics written by several critics, including Max Westbrook and Don D. Walker.

30.65 **Milton, John R.** **The novel of the American West.** Lincoln: Univ. of Nebraska Pr., 1980.

Controversial on some of its major points, this is nevertheless the best general study of the western novel to date.

30.66 **Western American literature.** Logan: Utah State Univ., 1966–.

Quarterly journal of the Western Literature Assoc.; runs a bibliography and announcements of research in progress in the February issue. *The South Dakota Review,* Vermillion: Univ. of South Dakota/Dakota Pr., 1963–, also provides worthwhile criticism of the American literary West.

30.67 **Western writers series.** Ed. Wayne Chatterton and James H. Maguire. Boise, Ida.: Boise State Univ. Pr., 1972–.

Pamphlets containing information and bibliographies dealing with both older authors like Bret Harte, Mary H. Foote, and Owen Wister and contemporaries like Vardis Fisher, Jack Schaefer, and Frederick Manfred. The tenth number is devoted to *Plains Indians Autobiographies,* 31.95.

30.68 **Davidson, Levett J., and Prudence Bostwick, eds.** **The literature of the Rocky Mountain West, 1803–1903.** Caldwell, Ida.: Caxton Printers Ltd., 1939.

An anthology with a bibliography.

30.69 **West, Ray B., Jr.** **Writing in the Rocky Mountains.** Lincoln: Univ. of Nebraska Pr., 1947.

Essays on various authors of the section, with a slight bibliography by Nellie Cliff.

30.70 **Anderson, John Q., et al., eds.** **Southwestern American literature: bibliography.** Chicago: Swallow Pr., 1980.

Topical, thematic, and author bibliographies are listed; especially useful on minor writers.

30.71 **Dobie, J. Frank.** **Guide to life and literature of the Southwest.** Rev. ed. Dallas, Tex.: Southern Methodist Univ. Pr., 1952.

A bibliography with valuable critical comment by an author and scholar who knew the region intimately.

30.72 **Major, Mabel, et al.** **Southwest heritage: a literary history with bibliography.** Albuquerque: Univ. of New Mexico Pr., 1938. 3d ed. 1972.

See also Kenneth Kurtz, *Literature of the American Southwest: A Selective Bibliography,* Los Angeles, Calif.: Occidental College, 1956, an interesting though inaccurate "reading list of a thousand books which express the American Southwest"; Edwin J. Gaston, Jr., *The Early Novel of the Southwest,* Albuquerque: Univ. of New Mexico Pr., 1961; and "Southwest Writers Series," pamphlets on various authors of the region, Austin, Tex.: Steck-Vaughn Co., 1967–1970.

30.73 **Powell, Lawrence C.** **Heart of the Southwest: a selective bibliography of novels, stories, and tales laid in Arizona and New Mexico & adjacent lands.** Los Angeles, Calif.: Dawson's Book Shop/Plantin Pr., 1955.

See also Powell's essays on the creative writers in *Southwest Classics,* Los Angeles, Calif.: W. Ritchie Pr., 1974.

30.74 **Baird, Newton D., and Robert Greenwood.** **An annotated bibliography of California fiction, 1664–1970.** Georgetown, Calif.: Talisman Literary Research, 1971.

Novels and short stories of all sorts except juveniles are listed.

30.75 **Hinkel, Edgar J., ed.** **Bibliography of California fiction, poetry, drama. Criticism of California literature, a digest and bibliography. Biographies of California authors and indexes of California literature.** 3 vols. Oakland, Calif.: Alameda County Library, 1938.

Mimeographed material gathered by a WPA project.

30.76 **Starr, Kevin.** **Americans and the California dream, 1850–1915.** New York: Oxford Univ. Pr., 1973.

Views and attitudes constituent in the generation and effect of "the California dream" as revealed through discussions of major cultural and literary figures associated with California over a period of sixty-five years.

30.77 **Walker, Franklin D.** **A literary history of southern California.** Berkeley: Univ. of California Pr., 1950.

Here, as elsewhere, Walker approaches the literature chiefly from a biographical and cultural-historical perspective rather than a critical one.

30.78 **Walker, Franklin D.** **San Francisco's literary frontier.** New York: Knopf, 1939.

The period covered is 1848–1875, with emphasis upon the 1860s.

30.79 **Walker, Franklin D.** **The seacoast of Bohemia: an account of early Carmel.** San Francisco: Book Club of California, 1966. New and enl. ed. Santa Barbara, Calif.: Peregrine Smith, 1973.

The best history of early Carmel as a literary oasis.

30.80   **Wilson, Edmund. The boys in the backroom: notes on California novelists.** San Francisco, Calif.: The Colt Press, 1941.
Includes comments on Cain, O'Hara, Saroyan, Steinbeck, et al.

30.81   **[Coleman, Rufus A., ed.] Northwest books.** 2d ed. Lincoln: Univ. of Nebraska Pr., 1949.
Cooperative descriptive lists of works by authors of the region and works on it. One of the lists classifies titles according to the state or area treated. Includes reviews and biographical data. The supplement includes "over 1,000 reviews of over 600 books with biographical data."

30.82   **Wright, Frances V. Who's who among Pacific Northwest authors.** 2d ed. [Missoula, Mont.:] Pacific Northwest Library Assoc., 1969.
Bio-bibliographical information on selected contemporary authors of Idaho, Montana, Oregon, and Washington.

See also **32.151, 34.16, 34.21–22.**

31. *Racial and other minorities*

31.1   **Baker, Houston A., Jr. Three American literatures: essays in Chicano, Native-American, and Asian-American literature for teachers of American literature.** New York: Modern Language Assoc., 1982.
Includes overviews as well as analyses of specific literary works following an introduction by Walter J. Ong.

31.2   **Fisher, Dexter, ed. The third woman: minority women writers of the United States.** Boston: Houghton Mifflin, 1980.
A representative selection of essays and autobiographies as well as fiction and poetry, this volume is intended as a textbook and includes appendixes with study questions and projects.

31.3   **Lowenfels, Walter, ed. From the belly of the shark, a new anthology of Native Americans: poems by Chicanos, Eskimos, Hawaiians, Indians, Puerto Ricans in the U.S.A. with related poems by others.** New York: Random House/Vintage Books, 1973.

31.4   **MELUS: the journal of the Society for the Study of the Multi-ethnic Literature of the United States.** Los Angeles: Univ. of Southern California Pr., 1975–.
Published quarterly; each issue has a specific focus. Topics include the literary treatment of oppression, ethnic alienation, nontraditional genres, and ethnic women writers. Also see Robert J. Di Pietro and Edward Ifkovic, eds., *Ethnic Perspectives in American Literature: Selected Essays on the European Contribution,* New York: Modern Language Assoc., 1983, which

comprises essays on the major writers, themes, and periods associated with European ethnic groups in the U.S.; the literature is examined from historical, sociological, and linguistic perspectives.

31.5 **Mohr, Eugene V. The Nuyorican experience: literature of the Puerto Rican minority.** Westport, Conn.: Greenwood Pr., 1982.
Focuses on 20th-century writing by Puerto Ricans in New York.

31.6 **Scheick, William J. The half-blood: a cultural symbol in 19th-century American fiction.** Lexington: Univ. Pr. of Kentucky, 1979.
A study of American ambivalence and fear as apparent in attitudes toward figures of mixed races in the fiction.

31.7 **Takaki, Ronald T. Iron cages: race and culture in 19th-century America.** New York: Knopf, 1979.
Traces subjugation of minorities and discloses relationship of problems among the diverse minority groups.

31.8 **Thernstrom, Stephan, ed. Harvard encyclopedia of American ethnic groups.** Cambridge, Mass.: Harvard Univ. Pr., 1980.
A compendium of information on the ethnic diversity of the population of the U.S. Includes 106 entries on more than 1,000 pages devoted to groups and to the continuing discussion on ethnic diversity vs. assimilation through Americanization.

See also **8.19, 8.21, 30.16, 32.6, 32.188, 34.20.**

Black

31.9 **Arata, Esther S., and Nicholas J. Rotoli. Black American playwrights, 1800 to the present: a bibliography.** Metuchen, N.J.: Scarecrow Pr., 1976. 2d ed. **More black American playwrights: a bibliography.** 1978.
Lists 530 playwrights, their work, and criticism; also includes 1,550 play titles.

31.10 **Chapman, Dorothy H. Index to black poetry.** Boston: G. K. Hall, 1974.
An index of poetry on black subjects but not limited to black poets.

31.11 **Deodene, Frank, and William P. French. Black American poetry since 1944: a preliminary checklist.** Chatham, N.J.: Chatham Booksellers, 1971.
An effort to update Porter, 31.22.

31.12 **Fisher, Mary L. The Negro in America: a bibliography.** 2d ed. Cambridge, Mass.: Harvard Univ. Pr., 1970.
The first edition was compiled by Elizabeth W. Miller. Contains sections on folklore and literature.

31.13 **Hatch, James V., and Omanii Abdullah. Black playwrights, 1823–1977: an annotated bibliography of plays.** New York: R. R. Bowker, 1977.

Excellent source for drama information on black playwrights; includes very brief plot summaries.

31.14 **Houston, Helen Ruth. The Afro-American novel, 1965–1975: a descriptive bibliography of primary and secondary materials.** New York: Whitston Publ. Co., 1977.

An annotated bibliography covering a productive decade; provides comprehensive coverage on the novels of fifty-six authors.

31.15 **Inge, M. Thomas, et al., eds. Black American writers: bibliographical essays.** 2 vols. New York: St. Martin's Pr., 1978.

Vol. 1 includes six essays by various hands covering black writers through Langston Hughes. Four essays in vol. 2 deal with Wright, Ellison, Baldwin, and Baraka.

31.16 **Matthews, Geraldine, et al., comps. Black American writers, 1773–1949.** Boston: G. K. Hall, 1975.

Lists over 1,600 authors in various fields but needs to be supplemented by other sources.

31.17 **McPherson, James M., et al. Blacks in America: bibliographical essays.** New York: Doubleday, 1971.

The various essays are organized both thematically and chronologically and range from poor to good. Listings on literature and art, pp. 14–17, are followed by a substantial roster of "current and recent" periodicals that deal with "black life" and race relations.

31.18 **The Negro in print: bibliographic survey.** Washington, D.C.: Negro Bibliographic and Research Center, 1965–1971. Microfilm. Ann Arbor, Mich.: University Microfilms, [n.d.].

Issued bimonthly except for the final year when one number was dropped.

31.19 **No crystal stair: a bibliography of black literature, 1971.** 10th ed. New York: New York Public Library, 1971.

A pamphlet, formerly entitled *The Negro in the United States,* which lists about 500 titles published since 1965, along with certain sturdier works from prior years.

31.20 **Olsson, Martin. A selected bibliography of black literature: the Harlem Renaissance.** Exeter, England: Univ. of Exeter, American Arts Documentation Center, 1973.

Provides for the European public audiovisual materials for American studies.

31.21 **Perry, Margaret. The Harlem Renaissance: an annotated bibliography and commentary.** New York: Garland, 1981.

Over 700 entries covering all phases and aspects of the Harlem Renaissance, from about 1919 to 1934.

31.22 **Porter, Dorothy B. North American Negro poets, a bibliographical checklist of their writings, 1760–1944.** Hattiesburg, Miss.: The Book Farm, 1945.

Originally published in *Papers of the Bibliographical Society of America,*

39 (1945), 192–268. See also Deodene and French, 31.11, for an updated listing.

31.23 **Rush, Theresa Gunnels, et al., eds.   Black American writers past and present: a biographical and bibliographical dictionary.** 2 vols. Metuchen, N.J.: Scarecrow Pr., 1975.
Includes many minor writers, with publication lists.

31.24 **Schomburg, Arthur Alfonso.   A bibliographical checklist of American Negro poetry.** New York: C. F. Heartman, 1916. 9 vols. Boston: G. K. Hall, 1962. Supplement. 2 vols. 1967. 2d supplement. 4 vols. 1972.
The Schomburg Collection, in the N.Y. Public Library, is one of the major black collections.

31.25 **Shockely, Ann Allen, and Sue Chandler, eds.   Living black American authors: a biographical directory.** New York: R. R. Bowker, 1973.
Helpful chiefly for minor figures.

31.26 **Whiteman, Maxwell.   A century of fiction by American Negroes, 1853–1952: a descriptive bibliography.** Philadelphia: [n.p.], 1955. Repr. Philadelphia: A. Saifer, 1968, 1974.
A short item of only sixty-eight pages but useful enough to warrant reprinting twice.

31.27 **Whitlow, Roger.   Black American literature: a critical history with a 1,520-title bibliography of works written by and about black Americans.** Chicago: Nelson-Hall, 1973. Rev. ed. 1976.
To the serious student the bibliography is often more useful than the text.

31.28 **Baker, Houston A., Jr.   Long black song: essays in black American literature.** Charlottesville: Univ. Pr. of Virginia, 1972.
The thesis of this work is that the major elements of black culture today spring from the oral tradition of days of yore. Special attention is afforded Walker, Douglass, Washington, Du Bois, and Wright.

31.29 **Bell, Roseann P., Betty J. Parker, and Beverly Guy Sheftall.   Sturdy black bridges.** Garden City, N.Y.: Doubleday/Anchor Pr., 1979.
A collection of essays and interviews that analyze black women in American, African, and Caribbean literatures; includes bibliographies.

31.30 **Bigsby, C. W. E.   The second black renaissance: essays in black literature.** Westport, Conn.: Greenwood Pr., 1980.
An exploration of the conflict of values as presented by contemporary black authors, private and personal as opposed to public and popular conflict, moral as opposed to material.

31.31 **Black American literature forum.**   Terre Haute: Indiana State Univ. Pr., 1967–.
Issued quarterly; until 1976, entitled *Negro American Literature Forum*.

31.32 **Boitani, Piero.   Prosatori negri americani del novecento.** Rome: Edizioni di Storia e Letteratura, 1973.
Picking up from B. Washington and Du Bois, with separate chapters on Wright, Ellison, Baldwin, and the Harlem Renaissance; briefer treatment is afforded Malcolm X, Jones, Cleaver, and Jackson.

31.33 **Butcher, Margaret Just. The Negro in American culture.** New York: Knopf, 1956. 2d ed. 1972.
Surveys contribution to the arts.

31.34 **Davis, Arthur P. From the dark tower: Afro-American writers, 1900–1960.** Washington, D.C.: Howard Univ. Pr., 1974.
Arranged in two main sections; the first deals with the "New Negro Renaissance," 1900–1940; the second with "In the Mainstream," 1940–1960. Davis sees the mainstream of American literature as holding the only viable future for black American writers. With a helpful bibliography, pp. 230–89, this volume provides a guide and reference to 20th-century Afro-American literature to 1960.

31.35 **Levine, Lawrence W. Black culture and black consciousness: Afro-American folk thought from slavery to freedom.** New York: Oxford Univ. Pr., 1977.
A full and acute treatment of the subject, including the role of religion, from the antebellum period to the present.

31.36 **Loggins, Vernon. The Negro author: his development in America.** New York: Columbia Univ. Pr., 1931.
A basic survey ending its coverage about 1900.

31.37 **Nelson, John H. The Negro character in American literature.** Lawrence: Univ. of Kansas, Dept. of Journalism Pr., 1926.

31.38 **O'Brien, John, ed. Interviews with black authors.** New York: Liveright, 1973.
Reprints conversations with Bontemps, Ellison, Reed, Williams, Wright, and other authors. Chiefly from *Studies in Black Literature,* Fredericksburg, Va.: Mary Washington College, 1970– .

31.39 **Young, James O. Black writers of the thirties.** Baton Rouge: Louisiana State Univ. Pr., 1973.
Writers of all sorts are meant; the result is more emphasis on social science and less on belles lettres. There is, however, a chapter on poets, with chief consideration, naturally, of their political, economic, and sociological ideas.

31.40 **Anderson, Jervis. This was Harlem: a cultural portrait, 1900–1950.** New York: Farrar, Straus, Giroux, 1982.
A history of the Harlem Renaissance; traces the movement to its roots in antebellum America and extends the account to show its influence on black (and white) culture in the 1930s and 1940s.

31.41 **Bontemps, Arna, ed. The Harlem Renaissance remembered.** New York: Dodd, Mead, 1972.
A collection of poor to middling essays by various hands.

31.42 **Huggins, Nathan Irvin. Harlem Renaissance.** New York: Oxford Univ. Pr., 1971.
Examines the search for identity and heritage, and the racial awareness and assumptions of the creative people in Harlem during the 1920s.

31.43　**Lewis, David Levering. When Harlem was in vogue.** New York: Knopf, 1981.
　　Focuses on the Harlem Renaissance of the 1920s and several of the major figures who promoted it, including James Weldon Johnson and Alain Locke, among others. Offers a sound analysis of the climactic years of the "New Negro."

31.44　**Singh, Amritjit. The novels of the Harlem Renaissance: twelve black writers, 1923–1933.** University Park: Pennsylvania State Univ. Pr., 1976.
　　A study of the major fiction of the predominant writers, including Bontemps, Du Bois, Cullen, Toomer, McKay, and six others.

31.45　**Bone, Robert A. The Negro novel in America.** New Haven, Conn.: Yale Univ. Pr., 1958. Rev. ed. 1965.
　　Attempts to "measure the contribution of the Negro novelist to American letters" since 1853. See also Carl M. Hughes [pseud.], *The Negro Novelist: A Discussion of the Writings of American Negro Novelists, 1940–1950,* New York: Citadel Pr., 1953.

31.46　**Gayle, Addison, Jr. The way of the New World: the black novel in America.** Garden City, N.Y.: Anchor Books, 1972, 1976.
　　A general historical survey from the beginnings to the present.

31.47　**Bell, Bernard W. The folk roots of Afro-American poetry.** Detroit: Broadside Pr., 1974.
　　Shows the great importance of folklore in black poetry.

31.48　**Redding, J. Saunders. To make a poet black.** Chapel Hill: Univ. of North Carolina Pr., 1939.
　　Critical survey of black poets, from the 18th century to the 1930s.

31.49　**Wagner, Jean. Les Poètes nègres des États-Unis: le sentiment racial et religieux dans la poésie de P. L. Dunbar à L. Hughes (1890–1940).** Paris: Librairie Istra, 1963.
　　Treats the religious and racial sentiment but goes wider in its excellent bibliography. A translation by Kenneth Douglas has been published as *Black Poets of the United States: From Paul Laurence Dunbar to Langston Hughes,* Urbana: Univ. of Illinois Pr., 1973, with an updated bibliography.

31.50　**Stetson, Erlene, ed. Black sister: poetry by black American women, 1746–1980.** Bloomington: Indiana Univ. Pr., 1981.
　　Includes selections from more than fifty poets, from Lucy Terry through writers of the present.

31.51　**Abramson, Doris E. Negro playwrights in the American theatre, 1925–1959.** New York: Columbia Univ. Pr., 1969.
　　The social context is kept in mind. In an introductory chapter W. W. Brown and Joseph Cotter are briefly discussed, and certain works of the 1960s are touched upon in an epilogue.

31.52　**Hill, Errol, ed. Theater of black Americans.** 2 vols. Englewood Cliffs, N.J.: Prentice-Hall, 1980.
　　A collection of essays by assorted scholars on black drama.

31.53 Isaacs, Edith J. R. **The Negro in the American theatre.** New York: Theatre Arts, 1947.
Six of the eight chapters deal with the period 1917–1946.

31.54 Barksdale, Richard, and Keneth Kinnamon, eds. **Black writers of America.** New York: Macmillan, 1972.
An anthology which ranges from the 18th century to date in its selections and offers unusually well-chosen bibliographical aids, useful both to beginning and advanced students. Folklore is given a section by itself.

31.55 Gloster, Hugh M. **Negro voices in American fiction.** Chapel Hill: Univ. of North Carolina Pr., 1948.

31.56 Gross, Seymour L., and John Edward Hardy, eds. **Images of the Negro in American literature.** Chicago: Univ. of Chicago Pr., 1966.
Contains reprints plus a valuable introduction and an excellent checklist of critical and scholarly studies.

See also 7.11, 10.57–61, 11.30, 11.34, 12.25, 13.6, 13.20, 15.44–45, 19.2, 19.28, 19.43, 19.51, 23.16, 26.15, 30.11, 31.9, 32.50, 34.9.

Jewish

31.57 Bryer, Jackson R. **"Contemporary American-Jewish literature: a selected checklist of criticism."** In Contemporary American-Jewish Literature: Critical Essays. Ed. Irving Malin. Bloomington: Indiana Univ. Pr., 1973.
A handy selection with a section on general studies, both books and articles, and another on individual writers, including Bellow, Fiedler, Friedman, Howe, Kazin, Mailer, Malamud, Roth, Schwartz, Shapiro, Singer, Trilling, and Wallant.

31.58 Chyet, Stanley F. **"American Jewish literary productivity: a selected bicentennial bibliography."** Studies in Bibliography and Booklore, 2 (Winter 1975–1976), 5–24.
Annotated bibliography of anthologies, bibliographies, criticism, drama, fiction, and poetry.

31.59 Coleman, Edward D. **The Jew in English drama: an annotated bibliography.** Rev. ed. New York: New York Public Library and Ktav Publishing House, 1970.
The revision includes a contribution by Edgar Rosenberg, "The Jew in Western Drama: An Essay and a Checklist" (1968). *English* drama refers to drama in English rather than to drama of the British Isles only.

31.60 Nadel, Ira Bruce. **Jewish writers of North America: a guide to information sources.** Detroit: Gale Research Co., 1981.
Excellent resource, superseding previous listings and covering 118 writers; includes general and specific references; Yiddish appendix.

31.61 Alter, Robert. **Defenses of the imagination: Jewish writers and modern historical crises.** Philadelphia: Jewish Publ. Soc. of America, 1977.

Comprises fifteen critical essays. See also Alter's *After the Tradition: Essays on Modern Jewish Writing,* New York: Dutton, 1969.

31.62 **Cohen, Sarah Blacher. "The Jewish literary comediennes."** Comic Relief: Humor in Contemporary American Literature. Ed. Sarah Blacher Cohen. Urbana: Univ. of Illinois Pr., 1978. Pp. 172–186.
Focuses on Gail Parent, Erica Jong, and Cynthia Ozick.

31.63 **Fiedler, Leslie. The Jew in the American novel.** New York: Herzl Press, 1959. 2d ed. 1966.
A perceptive but very brief discussion of the Jew in American fiction.

31.64 **Gittleman, Sol. From shtetl to suburbia: the family in Jewish literary imagination.** Boston: Beacon Press, 1978.
Concise treatment with a good bibliography.

31.65 **Guttmann, Allen. The Jewish writer in America: assimilation and the crisis of identity.** New York: Oxford Univ. Pr., 1971.
A quick history and a spotlighting of a few selected novelists and poets who represent aspects of the struggle among American Jews between total acceptance of American cultural values and retention of traditional Judaic ones.

31.66 **Harap, Louis. The image of the Jew in American literature: from early Republic to mass immigration.** Philadelphia: Jewish Publ. Soc. of America, 1974. 2d ed. 1978.
A thoughtful and extensive coverage of major and minor writers in the context of American literary and cultural history. This is a principal reference for American-Jewish literary history from the end of the 18th century through the early 20th and the fiction of Abraham Cahan. The profuse endnotes may be used as bibliographical aids.

31.67 **Jewish book annual.** New York: Jewish Book Council of the National Jewish Welfare Board, 1942–.
Edited now by Jacob Kabakoff. Text in English, Hebrew, and Yiddish. Includes bibliographies and annotated checklists of current books of Jewish interest as well as articles on books and people associated with them as scholars, authors, illustrators, etc. Cumulative indexes to vols. 1–25, 1967; vols. 26–40, 1982.

31.68 **Knopp, Josephine Zadovsky. The trial of Judaism in contemporary Jewish writing.** Urbana: Univ. of Illinois Pr., 1975.
The thesis, which supports and defines the Jewish novel as a genre, is more convincing in itself than the limited selection of fiction with which the author attempts to develop it. She deals with ethical dimensions in selected works of Bellow, Malamud, Singer, and Wiesel.

31.69 **Liptzin, Sol. The Jew in American literature.** New York: Bloch, 1966.
The "image" of the Jew as well as his role as author, from colonial times to the present. See also Harap, 31.66.

31.70 **Malin, Irving. Jews and Americans.** Carbondale: Southern Illinois Univ. Pr., 1965.

Chiefly concerned with Shapiro, Schwartz, Rosenfeld, Fiedler, Bellow, Malamud, and Roth, who are viewed as involved with traditional concepts of the Jewish experience. See also Alter, 31.61.

31.71 **Mersand, Joseph. Traditions in American literature: a study of Jewish characters and authors.** New York: The Modern Chapbooks, 1932.
Incomplete account of Jewish authors in 20th-century U.S. (Many earlier works in Yiddish, German, and French are listed in the bibliography of vol. 4 of *The Cambridge History of American Literature*.) Although dated and far from complete, it still provides a useful survey with a valuable appendix, listing many now obscure authors with the titles of their works.

31.72 **Sandrow, Nahma. Vagabond stars: a world history of the Yiddish theatre.** New York: Harper & Row, 1977.
A study of the past hundred years, including chapters on notable individual figures. For a history that relates the Yiddish theater to current European theater movements, see David S. Lifson, *The Yiddish Theatre in America,* New York: Thomas Yoseloff, 1965.

31.73 **Studies in American Jewish literature.** Binghamton: State Univ. of New York Pr., 1975–.
Devoted to fiction, drama, and poetry in English that deal with "Jews in the American experience." Edited by Daniel Walden, *SAJL* became an annual in 1981.

31.74 **Wisse, Ruth R. The schlemiel as modern hero.** Chicago: Univ. of Chicago Pr., 1971.
An intensive study, based on a comprehensive reading of primary materials, of works and authors from Mendele to the moderns; shows a good command of Yiddish backgrounds.

31.75 **Chapman, Abraham, ed. Jewish-American literature: an anthology of fiction, poetry, autobiography, and criticism.** New York: New American Library, 1974.
An excellent introduction precedes more than seventy selections drawn from both famous and little-known works, with accompanying notes; the selection of criticism is especially good. See also Theodore L. Gross, ed., *The Literature of American Jews,* New York: Free Press, 1973, which anthologizes forty authors.

31.76 **Howe, Irving, ed. Jewish-American stories.** New York: New American Library, 1977.
A collection of short fiction by twenty-six American Jewish authors; shows the continuity of Jewish experience and the writings about it. Includes a valuable introduction.

31.77 **Walden, Daniel, ed. On being Jewish: American Jewish writers from Cahan to Bellow.** Greenwich, Conn.: Fawcett Publ., 1974.
A judicious selection of the best literature, divided chronologically; especially strong in the interwar era.

See also **10.14, 11.24, 33.81.**

Native American

31.78   **Brumble, H. David, III.   An annotated bibliography of American Indian and Eskimo autobiographies.** Lincoln: Univ. of Nebraska Pr., 1981.
First-person accounts only, though many are "as-told-to" narratives actually written by collaborators, and others are merely claimed to be autobiographies. Supplemented in *Western American Literature,* 17 (1982), 243–260, by Brumble.

31.79   **Evans, Edward, et al.   Bibliography of language arts materials for Native North Americans.** 3 vols. Los Angeles: American Indian Studies Center, Univ. of California at Los Angeles, 1977–1979.
Listing by tribe of materials in native languages or bilingual formats, as well as books in English dealing with native languages. Many of the books are published by tribal presses. Marginal notations indicate the grade level for which the publications are intended. Covers the period 1890–1976.

31.80   **Freeman, John E.   A guide to manuscripts relating to the American Indian in the library of the American Philosophical Society.** Philadelphia: American Philosophical Soc. Pr., 1965, 1966.
Valuable bibliography with detailed annotations that cite many unpublished documents and manuscripts by and about Indians; literary as well as political and ethnographic subjects.

31.81   **Gill, George A.   A reference resource guide of the American Indian.** Tempe: Arizona State Univ. Pr., 1974.
Listings, divided by subject, include publications, presses, and agencies.

31.82   **Hirschfelder, Arlene B.   American Indian authors: a representative bibliography.** New York: Assoc. on American Indian Affairs, 1973.
Includes a tribal index in the front providing an easy overview of authors' names and tribal backgrounds; arranged alphabetically and well annotated, this is one of the most useful bibliographies available. See also the bibliography in Barry T. Klein and Daniel Icolari, *Reference Encyclopedia of the American Indian,* 3d ed., 2 vols., Rye, N.Y.: Todd Publ., 1978; especially vol. 2, which is a who's who of Native Americans, many of whom are authors.

31.83   **Jacobson, Angeline.   Contemporary Native American literature: a selected and partially annotated bibliography.** Metuchen, N.J.: Scarecrow Pr., 1977.
Includes over 2,000 entries but occasionally overlooks entire books by Indian authors while extensively listing citations for individual poems.

31.84   **Littlefield, Daniel F., Jr., and James W. Parins, eds.   A bibliography of Native American writers, 1772–1924.** Metuchen, N.J.: Scarecrow Pr., 1981.
Includes literary and nonliterary works in English by Native Americans, excluding Canada.

31.85   **Mallery, Garrick.   Picture-writing of the American Indian.** Washington, D.C.: Bureau of American Ethnology, 1893. Repr. 2 vols. Foreword by J. W. Powell. New York: Dover, 1972.

A classic that discusses various kinds of native written literatures, including winter counts, Midewiwin scrolls, rock writing, etc. Mallery was one of the first scholars to acknowledge pictographic works as literature.

31.86 **Marken, Jack. The American Indian: language and literature.** Arlington Heights, Ill.: AHM Pr., 1978.

A Goldentree bibliography with some emphasis on works by Indian authors; especially useful for autobiography.

31.87 **Stensland, Anna L. Literature by and about the American Indian: an annotated bibliography for junior and senior high school students.** Urbana, Ill.: National Council of Teachers of English, 1973. 2d ed. 1979.

The annotations are particularly detailed, often with quotations from Indian reviewers; there are study guides, appendixes on sources of additional materials, publishers, authors, and basic books for children. Includes useful biographical sketches of native authors. Entries are divided according to genre, but poetry is excluded. Nevertheless, this is one of the most useful resources available for teachers.

31.88 **Vasquez, Sue Ann. Educational materials by and about the American Indian.** Concord, Calif.: The Project, 1977.

A comprehensive bibliography chiefly for use in primary and secondary schools, compiled for the American Indian Education Project, Mt. Diablo School District. Especially valuable for the ratings by Indian critics of materials selected for classroom use. See also Paula Gunn Allen, ed., *Studies in American Indian Literature: Critical Essays and Course Designs,* New York: Modern Language Assoc., 1983.

31.89 **Chapman, Abraham, ed. Literature of the American Indians: views and interpretations. . . .** New York: New American Library, 1975.

A widely diversified collection of material with editorial notes. Possibly the best single source for essays on Indian literature, spanning over 100 years. Faces up to controversial issues and presents both sides.

31.90 **Collier, John. The Indians of America.** New York: Norton, 1947.

A history of the "death hunt" against Indian society from 1492 to the 1940s and discussion of the life-affirming aspects of Indian belief. Recent editions are "slightly abridged."

31.91 **Day, A. Grove. The sky clears: poetry of the American Indians.** Lincoln: Univ. of Nebraska Pr., 1951.

A scholarly view on context and styles of Native American poetry, with examples, but no attempt has been made to ensure accurate translations. Contemporary work is not included.

31.92 **Jones, Louis Thomas. Aboriginal American oratory: the tradition of eloquence among the Indians of the United States.** Los Angeles, Calif.: Southwest Museum, 1965.

A scholarly treatment and anthology of oratory as a form of literature that has been especially important to Native North Americans.

31.93 **Keiser, Albert. The Indian in American literature.** New York: Oxford Univ. Pr., 1933.

A pioneering study with insights still worth considering, though it has been largely outdated by more recent scholarship.

31.94 **Larson, Charles R. American Indian fiction.** Albuquerque: Univ. of New Mexico Pr., 1978.
A critical discussion of fiction written by Indian authors.

31.95 **O'Brien, Lynne Woods. Plains Indian autobiographies.** Western Writers Series, No. 10. Boise, Idaho: Boise State Coll., 1973.
Provides a scholarly look at the genre of autobiography in Plains Indian culture as a tradition of long standing that began with coup stories and winter counts and culminated with published as-told-to autobiographies in English.

31.96 **Dodge, Robert K., and Joseph McCullough, eds. Voices from Wah'-kon-tah: contemporary poetry of Native Americans.** Foreword by Vine Deloria, Jr. New York: International Publ., 1974. 2d ed. 1976.
This anthology contains the early work of thirty-four poets.

31.97 **Evers, Lawrence, ed. The south corner of time: Hopi, Navajo, Papago, Yaqui tribal literature.** Tucson, Ariz.: Suntracks Pr., 1980.
Each tribal section is edited by a scholar from that tribe and followed by a discussion of other works by authors from that tribe with excellent bibliographical references. The anthology contains examples of traditional literature in a contemporary context as well as thoroughly contemporary works.

31.98 **Hobson, Geary, ed. The remembered earth: an anthology of contemporary Native American literature.** Albuquerque, N. M.: Red Earth Pr., 1979.
Possibly the nearest to a definitive anthology of Native American authors in print; contains the work of virtually every serious Indian writer in the U.S.; sixty-eight writers are represented, though James Welch and Gerald Vizenor are omitted. The divisions are based on regions east to west, and each section is introduced by one of its writers. The editor, a Cherokee, provides a valuable general introduction. Fiction, poetry, and essays are included, as well as drawings and photographs by Indian artists.

31.99 **Katz, Jane B., ed. I am the fire of time: the voices of Native American women.** New York: E. P. Dutton, 1977.
An anthology comprising various kinds of writing by Indian women authors pertaining to their work in the arts, visual as well as literary.

31.100 **Levitas, Gloria B., ed. American Indian prose and poetry: we wait in darkness.** New York: G. P. Putnam's Sons, 1974.
An anthology in which the contemporary section is the smallest, containing the work of nineteen poets. Three bibliographies are included, one of them on works by Indian authors.

31.101 **Milton, John, ed. The American Indian speaks: poetry, fiction, art, music, religion.** Vermillion: Dakota Press, Univ. of South Dakota, 1969.
A pioneering anthology that includes thirty-four creative writers along with visual artists and anthropologists, all Indian. See also Milton's *American Indian II,* 1971, and *Four Indian Poets,* 1974, same publisher.

31.102 **Sanders, Thomas, and Walter Peek, eds. Literature of the American Indian.** Beverly Hills, Calif.: Glencoe Pr., 1973. Abridged ed. 1976.

An anthology of Native American writings in translation with elaborate introductions to the sections. Generally weak in contemporary work.

31.103 **Witt, Shirley Hill, and Stan Steiner, eds. The way: an anthology of American Indian literature.** New York: Knopf/Random House/Vintage, 1972.

A useful introduction is followed by sections divided according to time periods and general subject matter (e.g., education, law, ritual, etc.). The works are expressive though not necessarily literary. Some poetry is included.

See also **8.18, 10.53–56, 31.1, 31.3, 31.6.**

Chicano

31.104 **Cabello-Argandoña, Roberto. The Chicana: a comprehensive bibliographic study.** Los Angeles: Bibliographic Research and Collection Development Unit, Univ. of California, 1976.

Lists books on folk culture, sex roles, literature, and other topics in relation to Chicanas.

31.105 **Ordoñez, Elizabeth. "Chicana literature and related sources: a selected and annotated bibliography."** The Bilingual Review (La Revista bilingüe), 7 (1980), 143–164.

31.106 **El Grito: journal of contemporary Mexican American thought.** Berkeley, Calif.: Quinto Sol Publ., 1967–1974.

A bilingual quarterly devoted to contemporary Mexican-American thought. For more recent materials, see *Grito del Sol: A Chicano Quarterly,* Berkeley, Calif.: Tontatiuh-Quinto Sol International, 1976–.

31.107 **Pettit, Arthur G. Images of the Mexican American in fiction and film.** College Station: Texas A & M Univ. Pr., 1980.

31.108 **Rocard, Marcienne. Les Fils du soleil: la minorité mexicaine à travers la littérature des Etats-Unis.** Paris: Maisonneuve, 1980.

Explores the problem of double identity among the Chicanos and the manner in which it is reflected in fiction.

31.109 **Simmen, Edward, ed. The Chicano: from caricature to self-portrait.** New York: New American Library, 1971.

A collection of short fiction by writers from the late 19th century to 1970; not all of the authors are Mexican-American.

31.110 **Bruce-Novoa, [Juan D.]. Chicano poetry: a response to chaos.** Austin: Univ. of Texas Pr., 1982.

A critical-historical study. See also Bruce-Novoa's *Chicano Authors: Inquiry by Interview,* same publ., 1980, for a series of illuminating discussions with Chicano authors following an informative introduction.

See also **32.151, 33.72.**

32. *Relations with other countries*

32.1 **Aldridge, A. Owen. Early American literature: a comparatist perspective.** Princeton, N.J.: Princeton Univ. Pr., 1982.
Universal influences in the creation and development of American literature.

32.2 **Books abroad.** Norman: Univ. of Oklahoma Pr., 1927–1976.
A quarterly especially devoted to foreign literature: articles, reviews, lists of periodical articles. After vol. 50, continued by *World Literature Today,* 35.44.

32.3 **Denny, Margaret, and William H. Gilman, eds. The American writer and the European tradition.** Minneapolis: Univ. of Minnesota Pr., 1950.
A symposium covering the colonial period to the present. Two of the twelve essays deal with the impact of American literature in Europe; the others, with the reverse.

32.4 **Kirby, David. America's hive of honey; or, foreign influences on American fiction through Henry James: essays & bibliographies.** Metuchen, N.J.: Scarecrow Pr., 1980.
An annotated compilation arranged according to the influence of specific foreign authors and broad literary periods.

32.5 **Koht, Halvdan. The American spirit in Europe: a survey of transatlantic influences.** Philadelphia: Univ. of Pennsylvania Pr., 1949.
A "preliminary survey," containing sections on a variety of matters, including literature. See also Skard, 8.11.

32.6 **Wang, L. Ling-chi. "Asian American studies."** American Quarterly, 33 (1981), 339–354.
A general résumé of work in the field, with emphasis on the past decade.

See also **8.28, 10.28–35, 29.9, 35.23.**

England

32.7 **The American writer in England: an exhibition arranged in honor of the sesquicentennial of the University of Virginia.** Charlottesville: Univ. Pr. of Virginia, 1969.
An extensive exhibition catalog with an introduction by C. Waller Barrett, the noted collector of literary Americana.

32.8 **Barnes, James J. Authors, publishers, and politicians: the quest for an Anglo-American copyright agreement, 1815–1854.** Columbus: Ohio State Univ. Pr., 1974.

32.9 **Boyd, Alice Katherine. The interchange of plays between London and New York, 1910–1939.** New York: King's Crown Pr., 1948.
Valuable chiefly for statistics.

32.10 **Brussel, Isidore R.** **Anglo-American first editions.** 2 vols. New York: R. R. Bowker, 1935–1936.

Part I, "East to West [1826–1900]," describes first editions of English authors whose books were published in the U.S. prior to appearing in England. Part II, "West to East [1786–1930]," similarly treats books by Americans first published in England.

32.11 **Cairns, William B.** **British criticisms of American writings, 1783–1815.** Madison: Univ. of Wisconsin Pr., 1918. Rev. ed. 1922.

The revision takes the account through 1833.

32.12 **Coffin, Tristram P.** **The British traditional ballad in North America.** Philadelphia: American Folklore Soc., 1950. Rev. ed. 1963.

A critical inventory of Child ballads transported to the New World. Bibliography, pp. 173–182. Supplement added by Roger de V. Renwick, Austin: Univ. of Texas Pr., 1977.

32.13 **Conrad, Peter.** **Imagining America.** New York: New York Univ. Pr., 1980.

British writers on America; very controversial in the U.S. but the only modern book of its kind.

32.14 **Dickason, David H.** **The daring young men: the story of the American Pre-Raphaelites.** Bloomington: Indiana Univ. Pr., 1953.

32.15 **Enkvist, Nils E.** **American humour in England before Mark Twain.** Åbo, Finland: Åbo Akademi, 1953.

32.16 **Gohdes, Clarence.** **American literature in nineteenth-century England.** New York: Columbia Univ. Pr., 1944.

Begins where Cairns, 32.11, leaves off and contains chapters on the book trade, periodicals, humor, the vogue of Longfellow, and critics and influences. An appendix lists representative articles on American literature that appeared in British periodicals, 1833–1901.

32.17 **Green, Martin.** **Transatlantic patterns: cultural comparisons with America.** New York: Basic Books, 1977.

A collection of miscellaneous short chapters, most of which have been separately published before, dealing with British or American literature or both jointly.

32.18 **Lease, Benjamin.** **Anglo-American encounters: England and the rise of American literature.** Cambridge, England: Cambridge Univ. Pr., 1981.

The British connections of ten American authors, Irving to Whitman.

32.19 **LeClair, Robert Charles.** **Three American travellers in England: James Russell Lowell, Henry Adams, Henry James.** Philadelphia: Univ. of Pennsylvania Pr., 1945.

32.20 **Mesick, Jane E.** **The English traveller in America, 1785–1835.** New York: Columbia Univ. Pr., 1922.

With Rapson, 32.24, covers the area. See also Conrad, 32.13.

32.21 **Mowat, R. B.** **Americans in England.** London: George G. Harrap Co., 1900.

Somewhat old-fashioned but covers background well; best used in conjunction with Lease, 32.18.

32.22 **Pachter, Marc, and Frances Wein, eds. Abroad in America: visitors to the new nation, 1776–1914.** Reading, Mass.: Addison-Wesley Publ. Co., 1976.

A bicentennial item with chapters on Frances Trollope, Harriet Martineau, Fanny Kemble, Dickens, Yeats, Wells, et al.

32.23 **Raleigh, John H. Matthew Arnold and American culture.** Berkeley: Univ. of California Pr., 1957.

32.24 **Rapson, Richard L. Britons view America: travel commentary, 1860–1935.** Seattle: Univ. of Washington Pr., 1971.

Supersedes all other books to date on the subject; bibliography, pp. 213–65.

32.25 **Sowder, William J. Emerson's impact on the British Isles and Canada.** Charlottesville: Univ. Pr. of Virginia, 1966.

32.26 **Spender, Stephen. Love-hate relations: English and American sensibilities.** New York: Random House, 1974.

A somewhat uneven personal view of the conflicting attitudes held by selected British and American authors toward each other's culture and their own.

32.27 **Spiller, Robert E. The American in England during the first half century of independence.** New York: Holt, 1926.

Includes Irving, Cooper, N. P. Willis, and other authors.

32.28 **Stanley, William T. Broadway in the West End: an index of reviews of American theatre in London, 1950–1975.** Westport, Conn.: Greenwood Pr., 1978.

32.29 **Stein, Roger B. John Ruskin and aesthetic thought in America, 1840–1900.** Cambridge, Mass.: Harvard Univ. Pr., 1967.

Ruskin's impact on American aesthetic and critical ideas. Also see Dickason, 32.14.

32.30 **Ward, William S. "American authors and British reviewers, 1798–1826: a bibliography."** American Literature, 49 (1977), 1–21.

Includes over 450 reviews and articles; the most popular subjects were the works of Irving and Cooper.

32.31 **Weintraub, Stanley. The London Yankees: portraits of American writers and artists in England, 1894–1914.** New York: Harcourt Brace Jovanovich, 1979.

Gossipy biography on Clemens, Harte, James, Eliot, and others, showing the extensive or limited effect of England on each.

32.32 **Dunn, Esther Cloudman. Shakespeare in America.** New York: Macmillan, 1939.

A comprehensive history which includes a substantial chapter on Shakespearean performances on the frontier and another on the reactions of major 19th-century American writers to his works.

32.33 **Shattuck, Charles H. Shakespeare on the American stage: from the Hallams to Edwin Booth.** Washington, D.C.: The Folger Shakespeare Library, 1976.

A superb detailed text enhanced with beautiful illustrations.

32.34 **Sherzer, Jane. "American editions of Shakespeare: 1753–1866."** PMLA, 23 (1907), 633–696.

An old but still excellent account of the American editions; this essay is complemented but not superseded by Westfall, 32.35.

32.35 **Westfall, Alfred Van Rensselaer. American Shakespeare criticism, 1607–1865.** New York: H. W. Wilson, 1939.

A scholarly account of the criticism and the American editions.

See also **31.20, 34.4.**

France

32.36 **Alexander, Jean, ed. Affidavits of genius: Edgar Allan Poe and the French critics.** Port Washington, N.Y.: Kennikat Pr., 1971.

Essays on Poe by fifteen French poets or critics appear in translation with a long introduction which touches on his influence on the Symbolists.

32.37 **Allain, Mathé, ed. France and North America: utopias and utopians.** Lafayette: Univ. of Southwestern Louisiana Pr., 1978.

Proceedings of the Third Symposium of French-American Studies, on the French Utopian Impulse in American Life, March 4–5, 1974. (The first Proceedings, *Over Three Hundred Years of Dialogue,* were published in 1973; the second, *The Revolutionary Experience,* in 1974.)

32.38 **Ansermoz-Dubois, Félix. L'Interprétation française de la littérature américaine d'entre deux guerres (1919–1933): essai de bibliographie.** Lausanne: La Concorde, 1944.

Published dissertation from the Univ. of Lausanne with the dates listed as 1919–1939.

32.39 **Arnavon, Cyrille. Les Lettres américaines devant la critique francaise (1887–1917).** Paris: Les Belles Lettres, 1951.

32.40 **Austin, James C. American humor in France: two centuries of French criticism of the comic spirit in American literature.** Ames: Iowa State Univ. Pr., 1978.

A survey of French attitudes toward American humorists with references also to comic elements in more serious writers. A concluding chapter, "American Humor and the French Psyche," was added by Daniel Royot. The bibliography is substantial.

32.41 **Baker, Vaughn, and Amos E. Simpson, eds. France and North America: l'entre deux guerres, the state of democracy.** Lafayette: Univ. of Southwestern Louisiana Pr., 1980.

Proceedings of the Fourth Symposium of French-American Studies, April 7–11, 1975. See also Allain, 32.37, for earlier items in the series.

32.42 **[Balcou, Jean, ed.] L'Amérique des lumières (Partie Littéraire du Colloque du Bicentenaire de l'Indépendance Américaine).** Geneva and Paris: Droz, 1977.
Essays on America and the Enlightenment.

32.43 **Béranger, Jean, ed.   Le Facteur religieux en Amérique du Nord.** Bordeaux: Maison des Sciences Humaines d'Aquitaine, 1980.
Essays with a religious focus on specific topics in American literature from Edwards and Crèvecoeur to Bellow.

32.44 **Blumenthal, Henry.   American and French culture, 1800–1900: interchanges in art, science, literature, and society.** Baton Rouge: Louisiana State Univ. Pr., 1975.
Deals only in part with interchanges in literature but constitutes nevertheless a useful and comprehensive history of cultural relations.

32.45 **Bowe, Forrest, comp., and Mary F. Daniels, ed.   French literature in early American translation: a bibliographical survey of books and pamphlets printed in the United States from 1668 through 1820.** Reference Library of the Humanities. Vol. 77. New York: Garland, 1979.

32.46 **Braun, Sidney D., and Seymour Lainoff.   Transatlantic mirrors: essays in Franco-American literary relations.** Boston: Twayne/G. K. Hall, 1978.
Selections from French writers on America and American writers on France; includes a bibliography.

32.47 **Dommergues, Pierre, ed.   Les U.S.A. à la recherche de leur identité: recontres avec 40 écrivains américains.** Paris: B. Grasset, 1967.
The authors interviewed run from Albee and Algren to Updike and T. Williams, and the topics covered are often of considerable interest. By way of conclusion there is a section on the intellectual in the 1960s and a glossary of black language. In the terminal Fiches d'Identité, translations of the authors' works into French are mentioned.

32.48 **Durand, Régis, ed.   Le Discours de la violence dans la culture américaine.** Lille: Presses Universitaires de Lille, 1979.
Violence is the thematic key to this perceptive and generally excellent collection of essays by French scholars.

32.49 **Erkkila, Betsy.   Walt Whitman among the French: poet and myth.** Princeton, N.J.: Princeton Univ. Pr., 1980.
A useful though occasionally overstated study of Whitman's likely French sources and his influence in turn on the French authors who followed him.

32.50 **Fabre, Michel, ed.   Regards sur la littérature noire américaine/French approaches to black American literature.** Paris: Publications de la Sorbonne Nouvelle, 1980.
Includes articles on the fiction of Toomer, Wright, and various broad topics as well as a general essay by the editor on the title subject.

32.51 **Falb, Lewis.   American drama in Paris, 1945–1970: a study of its critical reception.** Chapel Hill: Univ. of North Carolina Pr., 1972.

32.52   **Fauchereau, Serge. Paris–New York: échanges littéraires au vingtiéme siécle.** Paris: Centre . . . George Pompidou, 1977.
Based on an exposition of public library holdings at the Pompidou Center, June 9, 1977–September 12, 1977; includes bibliographical materials.

32.53   **The French-American review.** Fort Worth, Tex.: Texas Christian Univ. Pr., 1976–.
A semiannual journal devoted to French-American intellectual, political, and literary relations; essay-reviews on current books, translations of significant French texts, and occasional annotated bibliographies are among the materials published.

32.54   **Jaffe, Adrian H. Bibliography of French literature in American magazines in the 18th century.** East Lansing: Michigan State Coll. Pr., 1951.

32.55   **Jeune, Simon. De F. T. Graindorge à A. O. Barnabooth: les types américains dans le roman et le theâtre français, 1861–1917.** Paris: Didier, 1963.
Traces the history of American types from the Revolution to World War I as reflected in French novels and plays; a substantial study.

32.56   **Jones, Howard Mumford. America and French culture, 1750–1848.** Chapel Hill: Univ. of North Carolina Pr., 1927.

32.57   **Lehan, Richard. A dangerous crossing: French literary existentialism and the modern American novel.** Carbondale: Southern Illinois Univ. Pr., 1973.

32.58   **Mandé, Philippe. Écrivain U.S.A.: écrivain U.R.S.S.** Paris: Téqui, 1952.
Contains a list of works in French on various aspects of the U.S. including (pp. 100–102) literature.

32.59   **Mantz, Harold E. French criticism of American literature before 1850.** New York: Columbia Univ. Pr., 1917.

32.60   **Mason, Hamilton. French theatre in New York: a list of plays, 1899–1939.** New York: Columbia Univ. Pr., 1940.

32.61   **McGee, Sidney L. La Littérature américaine dans la "Revue des Deux Mondes" (1831–1900).** Montpellier: Imprimerie de la Manufacture de la Charité, 1927.

32.62   **Rabinovitz, Albert. New York University index to early American periodical literature, 1728–1870: no. 5, French fiction.** New York: William Frederick Pr., 1943.
A bibliography of articles and reviews concerned with French fiction and published in American periodicals.

32.63   **Salvan, Albert J. Zola aux États-Unis.** Providence, R.I.: Brown Univ. Pr., 1943.

32.64   **Schoenberger, Harold W. American adaptations of French plays on the New York and Philadelphia stages from 1790–1833.** Philadelphia: Univ. of Pennsylvania Pr., 1924.

A sequel, taking the adaptations from 1834 to the Civil War, was published in 1930.

32.65 **Smith, Thelma M., and Ward L. Miner. Transatlantic migration: the contemporary American novel in France.** Durham, N.C.: Duke Univ. Pr., 1955.

More statistical than critical; the first half is general and the last half comprises short chapters on a few individual American authors, including Hemingway, Faulkner, Steinbeck. A useful checklist of French criticism and translations of American authors precedes the index.

32.66 **Spurlin, Paul M. Rousseau in America, 1760–1809.** University: Univ. of Alabama Pr., 1969.

A carefully researched and detailed study.

32.67 **Strauss, David. Menace in the West: the rise of French anti-Americanism in modern times.** Westport, Conn.: Greenwood Pr., 1978.

32.68 **Taupin, René. L'Influence du symbolisme francais sur la poésie américaine de 1910 à 1930.** Paris: H. Champion, 1929.

32.69 **Waldo, Lewis P. The French drama in America in the eighteenth century and its influence on the American drama of that period, 1701–1800.** Baltimore, Md.: Johns Hopkins Univ. Pr., 1942.

32.70 **Wickes, George. Americans in Paris.** Garden City, N.Y.: Doubleday, 1969.

Popular sketches of the Parisian days (1903–1939) of Stein, Cummings, Virgil Thomson, Man Ray, Hemingway, and Henry Miller. See also Virgil Thomson's *Virgil Thomson*, New York: Alfred A. Knopf, 1966, for valuable references to American authors in Europe during this period and especially for his portrait of Gertrude Stein.

See also **17.43, 28.18, 28.29, 29.89, 31.49.**

Germany

32.71 **American-German review.** Philadelphia, Pa.: Carl Shurz Assoc., 1934–1970.

April–May issues contain annual bibliography of Americana Germanica of all sorts, including literature; originally issued quarterly, it became a bimonthly in 1939.

32.72 **Baruch, Gertrud, ed. Hauptwerke der amerikanischen Literatur: Einsteldarstellungen und Interpretationen.** Intro. Edgar Lohner. Munich: Kindler, 1975.

A critical survey of major works with an historical introduction.

32.73 **Bauland, Peter. The hooded eagle: modern German drama on the New York stage.** Syracuse, N.Y.: Syracuse Univ. Pr., 1968.

Covers the period 1894–1967.

32.74 **Bauschinger, Sigrid, Horst Denkler, and Wilfried Malsch, eds. Amerika in der deutschen Literatur. Neue Welt—Nordamerika—USA.** Stuttgart: Reclam, 1975.

32.75 **Borchers, Hans, and Klaus Vowe, eds. Die zarte Pflanze Demokratie: Amerikanische Re-education in Deutschland im Spiegel Ausgewählter politischer und literarischer Zeitschriften (1945–1949).** Tübingen: Narr, 1979.

An account of the use of American literature to aid in the development of democracy in post–World War II Germany; includes source materials and articles from contemporary German magazines with American links; the introduction is substantial.

32.76 **Bridgwater, Patrick. Nietzsche in Anglosaxony: a study of Nietzsche's impact on English and American literature.** Leicester, England: Leicester Univ. Pr., 1972.

A compact account of the subject. London, Dreiser, J. G. Fletcher, O'Neill, and Stevens are given more extended treatment than Huneker, Mencken, et al.

32.77 **Brumm, Ursula. Geschichte und Wildnis in amerikanischen Literatur.** Berlin: Schmidt, 1980.

American literary prose is regarded from an American studies approach with a broadly conceived notion of the wilderness as the thematic center in this comprehensive and perceptive study.

32.78 **Bungert, Hans. Die amerikanische Short Story.** Darmstadt: Wissenschaftliche Buchgesellschaft, 1972.

An anthology of remarks on the theory and nature of the short story by American novelists or critics and German scholars.

32.79 **Dippel, Horst, ed. Americana Germanica, 1770–1800: Bibliographie deutscher Amerikaliteratur.** Stuttgart: J. B. Metzler, 1976.

A substantial compilation of some 214 pages.

32.80 **Durzak, Manfred. Das Amerika-Bild in der deutschen Gegenwartsliteratur. Historische Voraussetzungen und aktuelle Beispiele.** Stuttgart, etc.: Kohlhammer, 1979.

32.81 **Frenz, Horst, and H. J. Lang, eds. Nordamerikanische Literatur im deutschen Sprachraum seit 1945.** Munich: Winkler, 1973.

Covers the reception of American literature by German-speaking Europe.

32.82 **Galinsky, Hans. Amerikanisch-deutsche Sprach- und Literaturbeziehungen: Systematische Übersicht und Forschungsbericht, 1945–70.** Frankfurt: Athenäum, 1972.

An overview of German-American linguistic and literary relations during the years indicated.

32.83 **Galinsky, Hans. Wegbereiter moderner amerikanischer Lyrik.** Heidelberg: Carl Winter, 1968.

Contains material dealing with the reception of E. Dickinson and W. C. Williams in Germany.

32.84 **Gehring, Hansjörg. Amerikanische Literaturpolitik in Deutschland, 1945–1953. Ein Aspekt des Re-Education-Programms.** Stuttgart: Deutsche Verlags-Anstalt, 1976.

See also Borchers and Vowe, 32.75, for additional material on this subject, and Hoenisch et al., 32.85.

32.85   Hoenisch, Michael, et al., eds. U.S.A. und Deutschland: Amerikanische Kulturpolitik, 1942–1949. Bibliographie—Materialien—Dokumente. Berlin: John F. Kennedy Institute, 1980.

Part bibliography, part reprints of selected documents and other relevant materials, and part printed interviews (held long after the period under consideration), this volume supplements the more restrictive work of Borchers and Vowe, 32.75, and of Gehring, 32.84.

32.86   Jantz, Harold S. "Amerika im deutschen Dichten und Denken." In Deutsche Philologie im Aufriss. Ed. Wolfgang Stammler. Berlin: E. Schmidt, 1957. III, 146–205.

A quick survey covering the subject from earliest times to the present, with selected bibliography.

32.87   JEGP [Journal of English and Germanic philology.]   Urbana: Univ. of Illinois Pr., 1897– .

July issues contain a special bibliography on Anglo-German and American-German literary relations. Published as *JEGP* since 1959.

32.88   Kaes, Anton. Expressionismus in Amerika. Rezeption und Innovation. Tübingen: Max Niemeyer, 1975.

A study of the American response to German expressionism in drama; bibliography, pp. 150–62.

32.89   Klein, Karl Kurt. Literaturgeschichte des Deutschtums im Ausland. Hildesheim: Georg Olms Verlag, 1979.

A substantial account of German literature written outside of Germany. The 1979 edition is a reprint of the original, published in Leipzig: Bibliographisches Inst., 1939; it includes an updated bibliography (1945–1978) by Alexander Ritter, pp. 475–555.

32.90   Kopp, W. Lamarr. German literature in the United States, 1945–1960. Chapel Hill: Univ. of North Carolina Pr., 1967.

A list of translations and a selected bibliography are appended. This work constitutes the third volume of Shelley et al., 32.107.

32.91   Leuchs, Fritz A. H. The early German theatre in New York, 1840–1872. New York: Columbia Univ. Pr., 1928.

32.92   Locher, Kaspar T. German histories of American literature: a chronological and critical description . . . 1800–1950. Chicago: Univ. of Chicago Pr., 1955.

Printed on microcards.

32.93   Long, Orie W. Literary pioneers: early American explorers of European culture. Cambridge, Mass.: Harvard Univ. Pr., 1935.

Ticknor, Everett, Bancroft, Longfellow, Motley, et al., as students in Germany.

32.94   Marjasch, Sonja. Der amerikanische Bestseller: sein Wesen und seine Verbreitung unter besonderer Berücksichtigung der Schweiz. Bern: A Francke, 1946.

Incidentally revelatory; an appended bibliography lists certain editions of works of Hervey Allen, Louis Bromfield, Margaret Mitchell, Kenneth Roberts, et al., published in England, France, Italy, and Germany.

32.95 **Möhl, Gertrud. Die Aufnahme amerkanischer Literatur in der deutschsprachigen Schweiz während der Jahre 1945–1950.** Zurich: Juris-Verlag, 1961.
See also Mönnig, 32.96.

32.96 **Mönnig, Richard. Amerika und England im deutschen, österreichischen und schweizerischen Schriftum der Jahre 1945–1949: eine Bibliographie.** Stuttgart: W. Kohlhammer, 1951.
Lists British and American works translated into German.

32.97 **Morgan, Bayard Q. A critical bibliography of German literature in English translation.** 2 vols. New York: Scarecrow Press, 1965.
Covers the period 1481–1927 in the first volume (a reprint of a work published in 1938) and 1928–1955 in the second. First published in 1922 as *A Bibliography of German Literature in English Translation;* the 1938 edition was a major revision. Many of the translations listed are of American origin. See also 32.108.

32.98 **Mummendey, Richard. Belles lettres of the United States of America in German translations: a bibliography.** Charlottesville: Bibliographical Soc. of the Univ. of Virginia, 1961.
Originally published in Bonn, this useful book lists only works brought out in separate volumes—no periodical articles or collections. Covers the period from Franklin's day to 1957.

32.99 **Nirenberg, Morton. The reception of American literature in German periodicals, 1820–1850.** Heidelberg: Carl Winter, 1970.

32.100 **Paulsen, Wolfgang, ed. Die U.S.A. und Deutschland: Wechselseitige Spiegelungen in der Literatur der Gegenwart.** Bern and Munich: Francke, 1976.
Papers from a colloquium sponsored by the Dept. of German at the Univ. of Massachusetts; translated into German.

32.101 **Pochmann, Henry A. German culture in America: philosophical and literary influences, 1600–1900.** Madison: Univ. of Wisconsin Pr., 1957.
The most extensive treatment of the influence of German philosophy and literature in the U.S.

32.102 **Pochmann, Henry A., and Arthur R. Schultz. Bibliography of German culture in America to 1940.** Madison: Univ. of Wisconsin Pr., 1953. Rev. ed. 1982.
Supplemented since 1941 by annual bibliographies in 32.71 and 32.87.

32.103 **Price, Lawrence M. The reception of United States literature in Germany.** Chapel Hill: Univ. of North Carolina Pr., 1966.
A compact survey from the colonial period to the days of Thornton Wilder and Tennessee Williams, followed by a forty-page list of bibliographies and surveys.

32.104 Ritter, Alexander, ed.   **Deutschlands literarisches Amerikabild. Neuere Forschungen zur Amerikarezeption der deutschen Literatur.** Hildesheim: G. Olms, 1977.

Provides a modern American view of German literature; includes a bibliography, pp. 565–610.

32.105 Schirmer, Gustav.   **Die Schweiz im Spiegel der englischen und amerikanischen Literatur bis 1848.** Zurich and Leipzig: Orell Füssli Verlag, 1929.

The Swiss as represented in British and American literature to 1848.

32.106 Schmitt-Kaufhold,   Angelika.   **Nordamerikanische   Literatur   im deutschen Sprachraum nach 1945. Positionen der Kritik und Kriterien der Urteilsbildung.** Frankfurt: P. Lang, 1977.

North American literature in German-speaking areas since 1945.

32.107 Shelley, Philip A., et al.   **Anglo-German and American-German crosscurrents.** 2 vols. Chapel Hill: Univ. of North Carolina Pr., 1957–1962.

German literature as sources for Simms, Lanier, Howells, et al. See also 32.90.

32.108 Smith, Murray F.   **A selected bibliography of German literature in English translation, 1956–1960.** Metuchen, N.J.: Scarecrow Press, 1972.

A supplement to Morgan, 32.97.

32.109 Springer, Anne M.   **The American novel in Germany: a study of the critical reception of eight American novelists between the two world wars.** Hamburg: Cram, De Gruyter, 1960.

The novelists are London, Sinclair, Lewis, Dreiser, Dos Passos, Hemingway, Faulkner, and Wolfe.

32.110 Thomas, J. Wesley.   **Amerikanische Dichter und die deutsche Literatur.** Goslar: Volksbücherei-Verlag, 1950.

A brief survey of the entire range of literary influences from Germany on authors from the time of Cotton Mather to O'Neill.

32.111 Timpe, Eugene F.   **American literature in German, 1861–1872.** Chapel Hill: Univ. of North Carolina Pr., 1964.

32.112 Zuther, Gerhard H. W.   **Eine Bibliographie der Aufnahme amerikanischer Literatur in deutschen Zeitschriften, 1945–1960.** Munich: Dissertationsdruck Franz Frank, 1965.

See also **8.29, 17.51, 21.27–28, 21.30, 25.8, 28.11, 28.35, 33.5, 33.84.**

Italy

32.113 Amfitheatrof, Erik.   **The enchanted ground: Americans in Italy, 1760–1980.** Boston: Little, Brown, 1980.

A well-written, beautifully illustrated account of Americans in Italy. The author calls it a "social history" that instructs as well as entertains, but it is not meant to be a scholarly study, and American authors constitute only a small part of the total subject matter.

32.114 Battilana, Marilla. Il tranello diabolico. Venice: Neri Pozza, 1978.
An intelligent, appreciative discussion of the relation between the visual and literary arts as manifest in numerous American writers from the Puritans (who saw it as "the devil's trap"—hence the title—) through Henry James.

32.115 Brooks, Van Wyck. The dream of Arcadia: American writers and artists in Italy, 1760–1915. New York: Dutton, 1958.
Includes short chapters on major and minor figures from Irving to Wharton and B. Berenson; reflective, discursive, somewhat impressionistic, and very readable—but not a scholarly account.

32.116 Centro di Studi Americani. Repertorio bibliografico della letteratura americana in Italia. 3 vols. Rome: Edizioni di Storia e Letteratura, 1966.
The first vol., 1945–1949, was compiled by Robert Perrault; the remaining two, 1950–1954 and 1955–1959, were compiled by Alessandre Pinto Surdi.

32.117 Friederich, Werner P. Dante's fame abroad, 1350–1850. Chapel Hill: Univ. of North Carolina Pr., 1950.
Contains a section on the U.S. See also V. Branca and E. Caccia, *Dante nel Mondo,* Florence: Olschki, 1965; and William DeSua, *Dante into English,* Chapel Hill: Univ. of North Carolina Pr., 1964.

32.118 Heiney, Donald. America in modern Italian literature. New Brunswick, N.J.: Rutgers Univ. Pr., 1964.
The myth of America as reflected through 20th-century Italian writing from about 1930.

32.119 Italia e Stati Uniti nell' eta del risorgimento e della guerra civile. Florence: La Nuova Italia, 1969.
Several of the essays from the Symposium on American Studies, Florence, May 27–29, 1966, deal with literary and cultural relations.

32.120 Italian Americana. Buffalo: State Univ. of New York at Buffalo, 1974–.
A cultural and historical review published semiannually and devoted to the Italian experience in the New World.

32.121 Italica. New York: State Univ. of New York at Stony Brook, 1924–.
Contains a quarterly bibliography of Italian Studies in the U.S., including those dealing with literature, and since 1976 a separate rubric for Italian-American Studies. Cumulative fifty-year index (1924–1973) appears in the winter issue, 1975. Official journal of the American Assoc. of Teachers of Italian.

32.122 La Piana, Angelina. La cultura americana e l'Italia. Torino: G. Einaudi, 1938.

32.123 Lombardo , Agostino, ed. "Italian criticism of American literature: an anthology." Sewanee Review, 68 (1960), 353–515.
A special issue in which various Italians or Italian-Americans contribute essays on a variety of authors or topics. None of the essays appeared previously in English. Although not all of the essays are equal in quality, on the whole this is a useful and important collection of critical views. Among the

authors given special attention are Poe, Melville, Dickinson, Hemingway, and O'Neill.

32.124 Pavese, Cesare.   American literature: essays and opinions. Trans. Edwin Fussell. Berkeley: Univ. of California Pr., 1970.

A selection from Pavese's criticisms that supplies a good example of the impact of American authors on the Italian literary world between 1930 and 1950.

32.125 Peragallo, Olga.   Italian-American authors and their contribution to American literature. New York: S. F. Vanni, 1949.

Includes bibliographies.

32.126 Prezzolini, Giuseppe.   Come gli Americani scoprinono l'Italia (1750–1850). Milano: Fratelli Treves, 1933.

32.127 Shields, N[ancy] C.   Italian translations in America. New York: Columbia Univ., 1931.

Items arranged chronologically by date of publication. See also Vincent Luciana, "Modern Italian Fiction in America, 1929–1954: An Annotated Bibliography of Translations," *Bulletin of the New York Public Library,* 60 (1956), 12–34; and Joseph G. Fucilla, "Italian Literature," in *The Literature of the World in English Translation,* ed. George B. Parks and Ruth Z. Temple, New York: Frederick Ungar Publ. Co., 1970, III, 47–169.

32.128 Zolla, Elémire, ed.   L'esotismo nella letteratura anglo-americana. Florence: La Nuova Italia, 1978–1979.

Four impressive essays on the influence of the Far East on American literature of the 19th and 20th centuries.

See also **8.34, 31.32.**

Japan

32.129 American literature in the 1940's.   Annual Report, 1975, of the Tokyo Chapter of the American Literature Society of Japan. Tokyo: Tokyo Chapter of the ALSJ, 1976.

See also *American Literature in the 1950's,* same publ., 1977. With the exception of a single essay on Hawthorne in the first volume, the criticism pertains to American literature of the specified decades. These collections testify to the importance of observing American literature from the point of view of discriminating and perceptive Japanese critics during the past few decades.

32.130 Ando, Masaru, et al., eds.   A bibliographical survey of literature on the study of foreign literature. Vol. 1. English and American literature, 1965–1974: a general survey of literature in the 20th century. Tokyo: Nichigai Assoc., 1977.

A bibliography of Japanese criticism of British and American literature; it includes 15,200 items, and the text is in Japanese.

32.131 **Bibliography on American history, politics, economy, and literature: books and articles published in Japan, 1975–1979.** Comp. The American Studies Bibliography Committee. Tokyo: Univ. of Tokyo Pr., 1982. ["Literature."] Pp. 173–284.

An extensive but incomplete compilation of 311 pages; arranged by general subjects and individual authors; includes author index. In Japanese except for selected names and titles.

32.132 **Fukuda, Naomi. A bibliography of translations: American literary works into Japanese, 1868–1967.** Tokyo: Hara Shobo, 1968.

Text in Japanese.

32.133 **Fukuda, Rikutaro, ed. Amerika Joryusakka Gunzo [American Literary Women].** Kyoto: Shinshindo, 1980.

Bio-bibliographies with brief critical commentary on thirty American women authors from Bradstreet to the present.

32.134 **Kenkyusha yearbook of English.** Tokyo: Kenkyusha, 1960–.

Provides a considerable amount of diverse information relevant to the past year's study of English and American literature, including lists of articles written by individual scholars, names and addresses of English associations and English departments throughout Japan.

32.135 **Miner, Earl R. The Japanese tradition in British and American literature.** Princeton, N.J.: Princeton Univ. Pr., 1958.

See also Judith Bloomingdale, "Haiku: An Annotated Checklist," *Papers of the Bibliographical Society of America,* 56 (1962), 488–94, a list on, and history of, the reception of haiku in the U.S. since 1911.

32.136 **Ohasi, Kenzaburo. Shosetsue No Tameni: Amerika-teki Sozoryoku To Konnichi No Bungaku [For the novel: the American imagination and contemporary literature].** Tokyo: Kenkyusha, 1978.

A collection of Ohasi's essays and other writings, some of which have been previously published, with an emphasis on the form and place of the novel in American literature.

32.137 **The rising generation/Eigo Seinen.** Tokyo: Kenkyusha, 1898–.

A Japanese monthly dealing with English and American literature. Includes sections for "Books from Abroad" and "Newly Published Books" (reviews), which cover Japanese translations of foreign books on American literature and American studies as well as Japanese books in the same fields. Text in Japanese and English.

32.138 **Sakamoto, Masayuki. Amerika Bungaku O Do Yomitoruka: Bungakushi No Kochiku O Mezashite [Interpretations of American literature: toward the construction of literary history].** Tokyo: Chukyoshuppan, 1978.

A collection of articles published earlier with an emphasis on the method and value of comparative studies.

32.139 **Sugiki, Takashi. "A checklist of Japanese journals in English and American literature."** Bulletin of the New York Public Library, 65 (1961), 185–199.

Useful for research in older scholarship; though many new journals have appeared in the past quarter century, the earlier items are often worth consulting for historical perspective.

32.140 **Studies in American literature.** Kyoto: American Literature Soc. of Japan, 1964–.

The journal of the ALSJ. The 1978 issue includes a checklist of criticism on American literature published in Japan during the preceding fifteen years. From 1981 includes reviews and an "Annotated Checklist of American Literature [in Japan]." Text generally in Japanese with occasional English articles. (Each of many geographical areas of Japan has its own American Literature Society, which usually issues its own journal, e.g., Chu-shikoku, Kyushu, Tokyo, etc.)

32.141 **Studies in English literature.** Tokyo: English Literature Soc. of Japan, 1919–.

Journal of the ELSJ; issues two Japanese and one English number annually. Includes American literature as well as British. The issue in English contains "Synopses of the Articles Published in the Japanese Number[s]." Cumulative indexes for vols. 1–42, 1967; vols. 43–47, 1972.

See also **17.28, 32.128.**

Latin America

32.142 **Chapman, Arnold. The Spanish American reception of United States fiction, 1920–1940.** Berkeley and Los Angeles: Univ. of Calif. Pr., 1966.

Reviews and interprets the reception of thirteen fiction writers, including Harte, Clemens, L. Alcott, London, Lewis, Faulkner, Dreiser, and Pearl Buck.

32.143 **Cobb, Martha. Harlem, Haiti, and Havana: a comparative critical study of Langston Hughes, Jacques Romain, and Nicolás Guillén.** Washington, D.C.: Three Continents Pr., 1979.

32.144 **El Grito: journal of contemporary Mexican American thought.** Berkeley, Calif.: Quinto Sol Publ., 1967–1974.

A bilingual quarterly. See 31.106 for an updated sequel.

32.145 **Englekirk, John Eugene. A Literatura Norteamericana no Brasil.** Mexico: [n.p.], 1950.

A bibliography of literary and nonliterary works translated and published in Brazil.

32.146 **Gunn, Drewey Wayne. Mexico in American and British letters: a bibliography of fiction and travel books.** Metuchen, N.J.: Scarecrow Pr., 1974.

A companion to the same author's *American and British Writers in Mexico, 1556–1973*, Austin: Univ. of Texas Pr., 1974.

32.147 **Johnson, John J. Latin America in caricature.** Austin: Univ. of Texas Pr., 1980.

Documents more than 100 years of hemispheric relations, a visual record of U.S. attitudes toward Latin America through political cartoons collected from leading U.S. periodicals from the 1860s to the present.

32.148 **Onís, José de. The United States as seen by Spanish American writers, 1776–1890.** New York: The Hispanic Institute of the United States, 1952.

32.149 **Reid, John T. Spanish America's images of the United States, 1790–1960.** Gainesville: University Presses of Florida, 1977.
Surveys Spanish-American views of North American customs, politics, society, and individual character; discusses the impact of North American movies, television, textbook publication, and student exchange on image formation.

32.150 **Roberts, John Storm. The Latin tinge: the impact of Latin American music on the United States.** New York: Oxford Univ. Pr., 1979.

32.151 **Robinson, Cecil. Mexico and the Hispanic Southwest in American literature.** Tucson: Univ. of Arizona Pr., 1977.
Revised from *With the Ears of Strangers: The Mexican in American Literature,* same publ., 1963. Presents the 19th-century image of Mexico and the Southwest as projected through such figures as traders, explorers, and soldiers; also shows attitudes towards Mexico and the borderlands in modern American literature. Exploring the implications of double identity among Chicanos in fiction is 31.108.

See also **31.104–110.**

Eastern Europe, including the USSR

32.152 **Kunzová, Hela, and Hava Rybáková. American literature in Czechoslavakia, 1945–1965.** Trans. Roberta F. Samsourová. Ed. Jīrina Tumová. Prague: Czechoslovak P.E.N., 1966.
A bibliography of the postwar decades.

32.153 **Brüning, Eberhard. "Amerikanische Dramen an den Bühnen der Deutschen Demokratischen Republik und Berlins von 1945–1955."** Zeitschrift für Anglistik und Amerikanistik, 4 (1979), 246–59.

32.154 **Brüning, Eberhard. "U.S.-amerikanische Literatur in der D.D.R. seit 1965."** Zeitschrift für Anglistik und Amerikanistik, 4 (1980), 293–319.

32.155 **Brüning, Eberhard, Klaus Köhler, and Bernhard Scheller. Studien zum amerikanischen Drama nach dem zweiten Weltkreig.** Berlin: Rütten & Loening, 1977.

32.156 **Freitag, Christian, et al., eds. Bibliographie amerikanistischer Veröffentlichungen in der D.D.R. bis 1968.** In Materialien, 5. Berlin: John F. Kennedy Inst., 1976.
A bibliography of research on American literature, linguistics, and culture to 1968; with essays by Freitag, Michael Hoenisch, et al.

32.157 Angol Filologiai Tanulmanyok/Hungarian studies in English. Debrecen, Hungary: Kossuth Lajos Tudomanyegyetem (Angol Tanszek, Nagyerdei Korut), 1962–.

Issued irregularly; text in English; many issues include information on Hungarian translations of American literature.

32.158 Gergely, Emro J.   Hungarian drama in New York: American adaptations, 1908–1940. Philadelphia: Univ. of Pennsylvania Pr., 1947.

A study of the adaptation and production of fifty-three Hungarian plays in New York between 1908 and 1940. Includes a bibliography and play list, pp. 172–85, and a chronology of New York productions, pp. 186–90.

32.159 Marinovich, Sarolta.   "Hungarian essays on American literature (1945–1977)." Acta Litteraria Academiae Scientiarum Hungaricae, 20 (1978), 179–186.

Lists introductions and postscripts to Hungarian translations of American authors.

32.160 Vadon, Lehel, and Garbriella Zsuffa.   "Bibliography of Hungarian writings on English literature, 1961–1965." Hungarian Studies in English, 3 (1967), 123–146.

Includes criticism on American literature.

32.161 Zöld, Magdolna.   "American *Belles Lettres* in Hungarian translation, 1962–1970." Hungarian Studies in English, 9 (1975), 33–57.

A bibliographical essay that continues Anna Katona's bibliographical article covering 1945–1961 and another article dealing with Hungarian writings, chiefly articles, on English and American literature, 1957–1960, both in *Hungarian Studies in English,* I (1963)—see 32.157.

32.162 Coleman, Marion M.   Polish literature in English translation: a bibliography. Cheshire, Conn.: Cherry Hill Books, 1963.

A considerable number of the translations listed are of American origin.

32.163 Grabczak-Ryszka, Elzbieta.   "American studies in the institutes of English at Polish universities." Zeitschrift für Anglistik und Amerikanistik, 4 (1979), 346–59.

32.164 Kieniewicz, Teresa.   Recepcja literatury amerykanskiej w Polsce w dwudziestoleciu miedzywojennym [The reception of American literature in Poland between the world wars]. Warsaw: Wydawnictwa Universytetu Warszawskiego, 1977.

The first part soundly discusses the Polish reception of American literature between the wars. The second part constitutes a bibliography of translations arranged chronologically from 1918 to 1939; also lists Polish criticism of American literature.

32.165 Lyra, Franciszek.   "Grounds for connections: the pattern of Polish-American literary relations." Shifting Currents in Polish-American Relations. Ed. Wallace Farnham. Polish-American Studies, I (1976), 89–111.

A sound topical study by one of the foremost Americanists in Poland. A forthcoming item by the same author is his "Bibliography of Polish Translations and Criticism of American Literature," which covers the period from about 1750 to 1975. It attempts to document all translations, but criticism is treated selectively. The bibliography was completed under the auspices of the Neophilological Committee of the Polish Academy of Sciences.

32.166 **Maciuszko, Jerzy J. The Polish short story in English: a guide and critical bibliography.** Detroit: Wayne State Univ. Pr., 1968.
Includes much American material. Each story itemized is summarized in the annotation and accompanied by a brief sketch of the author.

32.167 **Polish-American studies.** Chicago: Polish-American Historical Assoc., 1944– .
A semiannual journal devoted to Polish-American life and history with some literary materials. Text is usually in English and only occasionally in Polish.

32.168 **Szkup, Jerzy. Recepcja prozy amerikanskiej w Polsce Ludowej w latach, 1945–1965 [The reception of American prose in the People's Republic of Poland in the years 1945–1965].** Warsaw: University of Warsaw, Institute for English Studies, 1972.
Comprises a descriptive section, pp. 3–112, and a bibliographical one, pp. 113–85, but includes no Polish criticism.

32.169 **Taborski, Boleslaw. Polish plays in English translation: a bibliography.** New York: Polish Institute of Arts and Sciences in America, 1968.
Supplemented revision of original published in *Polish Review,* 9, no. 3 (1964), and 12, no. 1 (1967). Contains a considerable amount of American data, including material on performances of the plays. A competent and informative listing.

32.170 **20th century American literature: a Soviet view.** Trans. Ronald Vroon. Pref. Y. Kovalev. Moscow: Progress Publ., 1976.
Contains thirty-three articles by twenty-one Soviet scholars on American literature. Includes a list of American writers whose work has been translated into one or another of the many languages in the U.S.S.R. (1960–1974). Published in commemoration of the U.S. bicentennial.

32.171 **Brown, Deming B. Soviet attitudes toward American writing.** Princeton, N.J.: Princeton Univ. Pr., 1962.
A comprehensive and thorough survey, in which Dos Passos, Sinclair, London, O. Henry, Lewis, Dreiser, Fast, and Hemingway are afforded more extended discussion.

32.172 **Brown, Glenora W., and Deming B. Brown. A guide to Soviet Russian translations of American literature.** New York: King's Crown Pr., Columbia Univ., 1954.
Based on incomplete sources.

32.173 **Gettmann, Royal A. Turgenev in England and America.** Urbana: Univ. of Illinois Pr., 1941.

32.174 **Libman, Valentina A. Amerikanskaia literatura v russkikh perevodakh i kritike: Bibliografiia, 1776–1975 [American literature in Russian translations and criticism: bibliography, 1776–1975].** Moscow: Nauka, 1977.

The most extensive bibliography in its field. Works on separate periods and topics are followed by those on 234 American authors of the more than 700 whose writings have been translated into Russian. Covers writers from Franklin and Jefferson to the present, but excludes Bellamy, Lewis, O. Henry, Clemens, and, prior to 1966 studies, London. Updates 32.175.

32.175 **Libman, Valentina A., comp.** **Russian studies of American literature: a bibliography.** Trans. Robert V. Allen. Ed. Clarence Gohdes. Chapel Hill: Univ. of North Carolina Pr., 1969.

Still the most thorough compilation of this material in English (see 32.174 for a newer listing that has not yet been translated). Works on separate periods and topics are followed by works on 148 American authors. Criticism and scholarship are covered from 18th-century productions on Franklin and Jefferson to 1963 comment on Updike, Tennessee Williams, et al.

32.176 **Mulyarchik, Aleksandr S.** **Poslevoenniye amerikanskie romanisty [Postwar American novelists].** Moscow: "Khudozh. Lit-Ra.," 1980.

Representative Soviet study of postwar American literature. Several authors are discussed from the perspective of critical realism as the best standard of evaluation. Lacks in-depth analysis and discussion of postmodernist authors.

32.177 **Proffer, Carl R., ed. and trans.** **Soviet criticism of American literature in the sixties: an anthology.** Ann Arbor, Mich.: Ardis, 1972.

Illustrates the nature of socialist realism as applied to American fiction; each essay deals with an individual novelist or novel.

32.178 **Zasurski, Yasen N., ed.** **Literatura SSHA XX veka. Opyt tipologicheskogo issledovaniia. (Avtorskáiaya pozytsiia, konflikt, geroi.) [Literature of the U.S.A. of the 20th century: an attempt at typological analysis. The position of the writer, conflict, hero.]** Moscow: Nauka, 1978.

Contains nine studies by seven Soviet scholars on themes indicated in the subtitle.

See also **8.35.**

General foreign

32.179 **North, William Robert.** **Chinese themes in American verse.** Philadelphia: [Univ. of Pennsylvania,] 1937.

Excluded are the drama and translations as well as poetry written after 1900.

32.180 **Pritchard, John Paul.** **Return to the fountains: some classical sources of American criticsm.** Durham, N.C.: Duke Univ. Pr., 1942.

Influence of Aristotle and Horace on fifteen writers, chiefly of the 19th century. For classical influence, see also Gummere, 27.15.

32.181 **Larrabee, Stephen A.** **Hellas observed: the American experience of Greece, 1775–1865.** New York: New York Univ. Pr., 1957.

Shows the strong emotional involvement of America with Greece during the first century of independence and the effect of that involvement in the development of philhellenism in the U.S.

32.182 **Raizis, Marios Byron, and Alexander Papas. American poets and the Greek Revolution, 1821–1828: a study in Byronic philhellenism.** Thessaloniki: Inst. of Balkan Studies, [1971].

Substantial quotations from the poems accompany the historical backgrounds to document the considerable interest of 19th-century American poets in the Greek revolution.

32.183 **Narasimhaiah, C. D. Asian response to American literature.** New York: Barnes and Noble, 1972.

An anthology of studies of American authors in which are scattered a few essays on the "Asian influence" and on the response to American poetry, drama, fiction, and criticism in Malaysia, Ceylon, the Philippines, and elsewhere. To be used with caution.

32.184 **Riepe, Dale M. The philosophy of India and its impact on American thought.** Springfield, Ill.: Thomas, 1970.

Chiefly concerned with philosophers of the present century, but contains material on Emerson, Thoreau, Santayana, and other literary figures.

32.185 **Anderson, Carl L. The Swedish acceptance of American literature.** Philadelphia: Univ. of Pennsylvania Pr., 1957.

Centers on fiction, especially that of Sinclair Lewis, from World War I to 1930. An appendix lists Swedish translations of American fiction 1916–1945. See also Stephen E. Whicher, "Swedish Knowledge of American Literature: A Supplementary Bibliography," *Journal of English and Germanic Philology,* 58 (1959), 666–71.

32.186 **Durham, Philip, and Tauno F. Mustanoja. American fiction in Finland: an essay and bibliography.** Helsinki: Société neophilologique, 1960.

32.187 **Scandinavian studies.** Lawrence, Kans.: Allen Press, 1911–.

The issues for May contain an annual bibliography of books, articles, and reviews dealing with Scandinavian languages and literature published in the U.S. or Canada. See also the series, *Americana Norvegica: Norwegian Contributions to American Studies,* ed. Sigmund Skard, Oslo and Philadelphia: Univ. of Oslo and Univ. of Pennsylvania Pr., 1966–.

32.188 **Skårdal, Dorothy Burton. The divided heart: Scandinavian immigrant experience through literary sources.** Pref. Oscar Handlin. Lincoln: Univ. of Nebraska Pr., 1974.

32.189 **White, George Leroy, Jr. Scandinavian themes in America fiction.** Philadelphia: Univ. of Pennsylvania Pr., 1937.

32.190 **Ferguson, J. Delancey. American literature in Spain.** New York: Columbia Univ. Pr., 1916.

32.191 **Williams, Stanley T. The Spanish background of American literature.** 2 vols. New Haven, Conn.: Yale Univ. Pr., 1955.

Influence of Spain and Spanish literature on the 19th century in particular.

See also **8.30, 17.32, 32.128, 33.83.**

33. *The American language*

33.1   **Baron, Dennis E.   Grammar and good taste: reforming the American language.** New Haven, Conn.: Yale Univ. Pr., 1982.
A history of largely futile attempts to "reform" American English over the past two and a half centuries.

33.2   **Carroll, John B.   The study of language: a survey of linguistics and related disciplines in America.** Cambridge, Mass.: Harvard Univ. Pr., 1953.
Relationship of linguistic studies with science, psychology, etc.

33.3   **Forgue, Guy J.   La Langue des Américains.** Paris: Aubier-Montaigne, 1972.
Lively, independent complement to Mencken, 33.15.

33.4   **Fries, Charles C.   American English grammar: the grammatical structure of present-day American English with special reference to social difference or class dialects.** New York: Appleton-Century Co., 1940.
A landmark study.

33.5   **Galinsky, Hans.   Die Sprache des Amerikaners: eine Einführung in die Hauptunterschiede zwischen amerikanischem und britischem Englisch der Gegenwart.** 2 vols. Heidelberg: F. H. Kerle, 1951–1952.
See also Galinsky's *Sprache und Sprachkunstwerk in Amerika: Studien und Interpretationen*, Heidelberg: Quelle & Meyer, 1961.

33.6   **Gates, J. Edward.   "A bibliography on general and English lexicography."** In Lexicography in English. Ed. Raven I. McDavid, Jr., and Audrey R. Duckert. Annals of the New York Academy of Sciences. Vol. 211. New York: New York Academy of Sciences, 1973. Pp. 320–37.

33.7   **Journal of English linguistics.**   Bellingham, Wash.: Western Washington Univ. Pr., 1966–.
A standard work.

33.8   **Krapp, George P.   The English language in America.** 2 vols. New York: The Century Co., 1925.
Still highly regarded, this study was published originally for the Modern Language Assoc.

33.9   **Kurath, Hans.   Studies in area linguistics.** Bloomington: Indiana Univ. Pr., 1972.
"The whole gamut of problems encountered in area linguistics and the techniques used in handling them are presented in the first 5 chapters of the book with reference to American English." Bibliography, pp. 186–202.

33.10   **Marckwardt, Albert H.   American English.** New York: Oxford Univ. Pr., 1958. 2d ed. Rev. by J. L. Dillard. 1980.
A brief, elementary, but clearheaded synthesis of previous investigations calculated to illustrate the "close interaction of linguistic and cultural factors in the growth of American English." The first edition is still important.

33.11 **Marckwardt, Albert H., ed.** **Linguistics in school programs.** National Society for the Study of Education Yearbook 1969. Pt. 2. Chicago: Univ. of Chicago Pr., 1970.

Useful background for surveys of American English.

33.12 **Mathews, Mitford M., ed.** **The beginnings of American English.** Chicago: Univ. of Chicago Pr., 1931.

33.13 **McConnell, Ruth E.** **Our own voice: Canadian English and how it is studied.** Toronto: Gage, 1978. Textbook ed. 1979.

Perhaps the best book for an introductory course in American English; according to Raven I. McDavid, Jr., "there is nothing as good—or as useful at showing comparisons—published in the U.S.A."

33.14 **McDavid, Raven I., Jr.** **"American English: a bibliographic essay."** American Studies International, 17 (1979), 3–45.

A substantial résumé of recent scholarship in the field.

33.15 **Mencken, H[enry] L.** **The American language.** 4th ed. New York: Alfred A. Knopf, 1936.

Originally published in 1919 as *A Preliminary Inquiry into the Development of English in the United States,* Mencken's study must now be used with two supplements, which appeared in 1945 and 1948. It is a popular account, useful because of its extensive coverage. A judiciously abridged edition, edited by Raven I. McDavid, Jr., and David W. Maurer, with annotations and new material, was published by Knopf in one volume in 1963.

33.16 **Murphy, James, ed. The rhetorical tradition and modern writing.** New York: Modern Language Assoc., 1982.

A collection of essays generally calling for better integration between the teaching of writing and literature.

33.17 **Pyles, Thomas.** **Words and ways of American English.** New York: Random House, 1952.

Excellent but no longer in print.

33.18 **Sebeok, Thomas A., et al., eds.** **Current trends in linguistics X: Linguistics in North America.** The Hague: Mouton, 1973.

See also **26.34, 33.66.**

Dictionaries

33.19 **Adams, Ramon F.** **Western words: a dictionary of the American West.** Rev. ed. Norman: Univ. of Oklahoma Pr., 1968.

Provincialisms of the cattleman's West; limited but useful coverage for students of western dialect, literature, and lore. Colorful but somewhat amateurish because of the compiler's apparently inadequate linguistic knowledge and unsound methodology. See Atwood, 33.61.

33.20 **Cassidy, Frederic G.** **Dictionary of American regional English.** Cambridge, Mass.: Harvard Univ. Pr., [1984; projected date].

An introductory study of American regional speech is also being prepared by Raven I. McDavid, Jr., for publication by Oxford Univ. Pr., probably in 1984.

33.21 **Cassidy, Frederic G., and Robert LePage. Dictionary of Jamaican English.** Cambridge, England: Cambridge Univ. Pr., 1967.
Important for study of the speech of American blacks.

33.22 **Craigie, William A., and James R. Hulbert, eds. A dictionary of American English on historical principles.** 4 vols. Chicago: Univ. of Chicago Pr., 1938–1944.

33.23 **Farmer, John S. Americanisms old and new.** London: Thomas Poulter and Sons, 1889. Micro. ed. East Lansing: Michigan State Univ. Library, 1980.
A dictionary of American words, phrases, and usage; includes the U.S., Canada, the West Indies, etc.

33.24 **Harder, Kelsie B., ed. Illustrated dictionary of place names, United States and Canada.** New York: Van Nostrand Reinhold Co., 1976.

33.25 **Mathews, Mitford M., ed. A Dictionary of Americanisms on historical principles.** 2 vols. Chicago: Univ. of Chicago Pr., 1951.
See also 33.22.

33.26 **Partridge, Eric. A dictionary of slang and unconventional English.** 7th ed. 2 vols. in 1. New York: Macmillan, 1970.
Not always trustworthy but still the best available. Vol. 1 is the dictionary; vol. 2 is a supplement. See also Harold Wentworth and Stuart Berg Flexner, comps. and eds., *Dictionary of American Slang,* 2d supplemented ed., New York: Thomas Y. Crowell, 1975, which includes a selected bibliography to 1957, pp. 655–69, updated to 1973, pp. 764–66.

33.27 **Sledd, James H., and Wilma R. Ebbitt. Dictionaries and THAT dictionary: a casebook on the aims of lexicographers and the targets of reviewers.** Chicago: Scott, Foresman, 1962.
The best discussion of the controversy over Webster's *Third New International*; see 33.31.

33.28 **Sperber, Hans, and Travis Trittschuh. Dictionary of American political terms.** Detroit: Wayne State Univ. Pr., 1962.

33.29 **Taylor, Archer, and Bartlett J. Whiting. A dictionary of American proverbs and proverbial phrases, 1820–1880.** Cambridge, Mass.: Harvard Univ. Pr., 1958.
This compilation has been augmented by Whiting's *Early American Proverbs and Phrases,* same publ., 1977, which covers the prior period from the early settlement to 1820.

33.30 **Thornton, Richard. An American glossary: being an attempt to illustrate certain Americanisms upon historical principles.** 3 vols. London: Francis & Co., 1912, 1931–1939.
The third volume was published in installments in *Dialect Notes* during the 1930s. This is the best lexicon of American English before Cassidy's *Dictionary of American Regional English,* 33.20, projected for 1984.

33.31 **Webster's new international dictionary.** Springfield, Mass.: G. & C. Merriam, 1909. 2d ed. 1934.

Webster's *Third New International Dictionary,* same publ., 1961, bears a new title; it is still controversial, but it is the last general English dictionary published that has such extensive coverage.

33.32 **Wentworth, Harold.   American dialect dictionary.** New York: Thomas Y. Crowell, 1944.

In addition to section 4 passim of this Guide, see **33.6, 33.35–37, 33.40–41, 33.44, 33.87–88, 34.14, 35.15.**

Usage

33.33 **American speech: a quarterly of linguistic usage.** University: Univ. of Alabama Pr., 1925–.

Publishes articles, reviews, and the chief current bibliography of works in its field; journal of the American Dialect Society.

33.34 **Copperud, Roy H.   American usage: the concensus.** New York: Van Nostrand Reinhold Co., 1970.

33.35 **Creswell, Thomas J.   Usage in dictionaries and dictionaries of usage.** Publ. of the American Dialect Soc. 63–64. University: Univ. of Alabama Pr., 1970.

33.36 **Evans, Bergen, and Cornelia Evans.   A dictionary of contemporary American usage.** New York: Random House, 1957.

A popular compilation that is highly idiosyncratic and dated in spots. The best usage work is still 33.38.

33.37 **Hamp, Eric P.   A glossary of American technical linguistic usage, 1925–1950.** Utrecht: Spectrum, 1957. 3d ed. 1966.

33.38 **Krapp, George Philip.   A comprehensive guide to good English.** Chicago: Rand, McNally, 1927.

Still the most accurate and sensitive work of its kind, especially in recognizing the diversity of American educated usage.

33.39 **Kucern, Henry, and W. Nelson Francis.   Computational analysis of present day American English.** Providence, R.I.: Brown Univ. Pr., 1967.

33.40 **Maurer, David W.   Language of the underworld.** Ed. Allan W. Futrell and Charles B. Wordell. Lexington: Univ. Pr. of Kentucky, 1981.

A collection drawn from more than 200 of Maurer's publications with commentaries and word lists updated. Among Maurer's important earlier volumes are: *The Big Con,* Indianapolis, Ind.: Bobbs-Merrill, 1941; 2d ed., New York: New American Library, 1962; *Narcotics and Narcotic Addiction,* Springfield, Ill: Charles C. Thomas, 1954; 4th ed., 1973; *Whiz Mob,* New Haven, Conn.: College and University Pr., 1964 (originally published by PADS, 1955 and 1959); and *The American Confidence Man,* Springfield, Ill.: Charles C. Thomas, 1974.

33.41 **Pickering, John. Vocabulary, or collection of words and phrases which have been supposed to be peculiar to the United States of America.** Boston: Cummings and Hilliard, 1816.

This is the first serious study of Americanisms; preceded by an essay on "the present state" of the language.

See also **5.1.**

Pronunciation

33.42 **Bronstein, Arthur J. The pronunciation of American English: an introduction to phonetics.** New York: Appleton-Century-Crofts, 1960.
Includes bibliographies.

33.43 **Kenyon, John Samuel. American pronunciation: a textbook of phonetics for students of English.** Ann Arbor, Mich.: G. Wahr Publ. Co., 1924. 10th ed. 1950.

33.44 **Kenyon, John Samuel, and Thomas Albert Knott, eds. A pronouncing dictionary of American English.** Springfield, Mass.: G. & C. Merriam Co., 1944.
The only American analogue to the British work of Daniel Jones.

33.45 **Kurath, Hans. "A bibliography of American pronunciation, 1888–1928."** Language, 5 (1929), 115–62.
Includes a discography.

33.46 **Thomas, Charles Kenneth. An introduction to the phonetics of American English.** New York: Ronald Press Co., 1947. 2d ed. 1958.

See also **33.51, 33.67.**

Linguistic geography

33.47 **Allen, Harold B. The linguistic atlas of the upper Midwest.** 3 vols. Minneapolis: Univ. of Minnesota Pr., 1973–1976.
Essentially interpretive works.

33.48 **Atwood, E. Bagby. A survey of verb forms in the eastern United States.** Ann Arbor: Univ. of Michigan Pr., 1953.

33.49 **Kurath, Hans, et al. Handbook of the linguistic geography of New England.** Providence, R.I.: Brown Univ. Pr., 1939. 2d ed. New York: AMS, 1973.

33.50 **Kurath, Hans, et al. Linguistic atlas of New England.** 3 vols. in 6. Providence, R.I.: Brown Univ. Pr., 1939–1943.

Provides evidence of the actual usage of selected Americans in selected communities on selected items of grammar, pronunciation, and vocabulary. Atlases for other regions are either already in print or in preparation. See Raymond K. O'Cain's review in 33.57.

33.51 **Kurath, Hans, and Raven I. McDavid, Jr.   The pronunciation of English in the United States.** Ann Arbor: Univ. of Michigan Pr., 1961.
Analyzes regional and social features of pronunciation of 157 "cultural speakers," Maine to Florida.

33.52 **Kurath, Hans.   A word geography of the eastern United States.** Ann Arbor: Univ. of Michigan Pr., 1949.
Based on material collected for a linguistic atlas of the eastern U.S. begun in 1931 and sponsored by the American Council of Learned Societies.

33.53 **Marckwardt, Albert H., et al.   Linguistic atlas of the north-central states.** Chicago: Univ. of Chicago Libraries, 1976–.
Field records published in microfilm in Chicago Manuscripts in Cultural Anthropology (Series XXXVIII, Nos. 200–208).

33.54 **McDavid, Raven I., Jr., et al.   Linguistic atlas of the middle and south Atlantic states.** Chicago: Univ. of Chicago Pr., 1980–.
Field records published in microfilm in Chicago Manuscripts on Cultural Anthropology (Series LXVII, nos. 360–).

33.55 **McDavid, Virginia.   "Verb forms in the north central states and upper Midwest."** Diss. Univ. of Minnesota, 1956.

33.56 **McMillan, James B.   Annotated bibliography of southern American English.** Coral Gables, Fla.: Univ. of Miami Pr., 1971.
Contents range from about 1870 to date and cover a heterogeneous assortment of sources.

33.57 **O'Cain, Raymond K.   "'Linguistic atlas of New England': a review article."** American Speech, 54 (1979), 243–78.
A substantial, detailed, and highly laudatory review article of 33.49 and 33.50.

33.58 **RLS: regional language studies.** St. Johns, Nfld.: Univ. of Newfoundland Pr., 1968–.
Valuable because of its significant bibliographical articles and because Newfoundland speech both provides evidence on early modern English background of other varieties of North American English (black and white) and relates to various significant American subcultures that have enriched our language, from cod-fishing to rum-running.

33.59 **Reed, David, and Allan Metcalf.   Linguistic atlas of the Pacific Coast.** Microfilm. Berkeley: Bancroft Library of the Univ. of California, 1979.
Microfilm publication of field records.

33.60 **Van Riper, W. R., et al.   Linguistic atlas of Oklahoma.** Chicago: Univ. of Chicago Libraries, [forthcoming].
When published in microfilm, this will become part of the Chicago Manuscripts in Cultural Anthropology series. It includes excellent interviewing techniques in the field work; especially good on syntax.

See also **33.74–75.**

Dialect

33.61 **Atwood, E. Bagby.** **The regional vocabulary of Texas.** Austin: Univ. of Texas Pr., 1962.
Considerably more useful than 33.19.

33.62 **Brasch, Walter M.** **Black English and the mass media.** Amherst: Univ. of Massachusetts Pr., 1981.
A study of the manner in which the mass media have affected the development of black English and reflected it in its various stages.

33.63 **Brasch, Walter M., and Ila Wales Brasch.** **A comprehensive annotated bibliography of American black English.** Baton Rouge: Louisiana State Univ. Pr., 1974.
A substantial and generally well-edited compilation. See the review by John T. Algeo, in *American Speech*, 49 (1974), 142–46.

33.64 **Dialect notes.** New Haven, Conn.: American Dialect Society, 1890–1939.
Predecessor of 33.73. The six volumes have been reprinted by the Univ. of Alabama Pr., 1965.

33.65 **Dillard, Joey L.** **Black English.** New York: Random House, 1972.
Perhaps as important as the book itself is the review by Sarah G. D'Eloia, "Issues in the Analysis of Non-standard Negro English," *Journal of English Linguistics*, 7 (1973), 87–106.

33.66 **Francis, W. Nelson.** **The structure of American English.** New York: Ronald Press, 1958.
Contains a chapter on American dialects by Raven I. McDavid, Jr., which is a handy survey-interpretation of the dialect field. See also McDavid's article "Sense and Nonsense about American Dialects," *PMLA*, 81 (1966), 7–17, which has a bibliography.

33.67 **Frank, Yakira H.** **"The speech of New York City."** Diss. Univ. of Michigan, 1948.
Other studies of urban language in the U.S. include Allan F. Hubbell, *The Pronunciation of English in New York City: Consonants and Vowels*, New York: King's Crown Pr., 1950; William Labov, *The Social Stratification of English in New York City*, Washington, D.C.: Center for Applied Linguistics, 1966; *Language in the Inner City: Studies in the Black English Vernacular*, Philadelphia: Univ of Pennsylvania Pr., 1972; and *Sociolinguistic Patterns*, same publ. and date; Lee A. Pederson, *The Pronunciation of English in Metropolitan Chicago*, University: Univ. of Alabama Pr., 1965; and Roger W. Shuy, et al., *Field Techniques in Our Urban Language Study*, Washington, D.C.: Center for Applied Linguistics, 1968.

33.68 **Ives, Sumner.** **"A theory of literary dialect."** Tulane Studies in English, 2 (1950), 137–182.
A classic, fundamental article often considered indispensable to those who would evaluate dialect literature.

33.69 **McDavid, Raven I., Jr.** **"American English dialects."** In The Structure of American English. By W. N. Francis. New York: The Ronald Press, 1958. Chapter 9.

33.70 McDavid, Raven I., Jr. **Dialects in culture: essays in general dialectology.** Ed. William A. Kretzschmar, Jr., University: Univ. of Alabama Pr., 1979.

33.71 McDavid, Raven I., Jr. **Varieties of American English.** Ed. Anavar S. Dil. Stanford, Calif.: Stanford Univ. Pr., 1980.

33.72 Metcalf, Allan A. **Chicano English.** Arlington, Va.: Center for Applied Linguistics, 1979.

33.73 PADS [Publications of the American Dialect Society]. Nos. 1–. University: Univ. of Alabama Pr., 1944–.
A series of monographs such as "The Argot of the Racetrack" (no. 16), "Bilingualism in the Americas: A Bibliography and Research Guide" (no. 26), and "The Phonology of the Uncle Remus Stories" (no. 22).

33.74 Pederson, Lee, et al., eds. **A manual for dialect research in the southern states.** Atlanta: Georgia State Univ. Pr., 1972. 2d ed. University: Univ. of Alabama Pr., 1974.
A manual for field workers. An introduction gives a brief history of "Dialectology." This volume is now out of print, and the data have been revised and reinterpreted in Pederson's *Linguistic Atlas of the Gulf States,* Athens: Univ. of Georgia Pr., 1981–. An *Introduction and Guide to the Microfiche Collection* concerning this material was prepared by Vicki L. Smith and Jean Hoornstra and published at Ann Arbor, Mich.: University Microfilms International, 1981.

33.75 Reed, Carroll E. **Dialects of American English.** Amherst: Univ. of Massachusetts Pr., 1967. Rev. ed. 1977.

33.76 Reinecke, John E. **Language and dialect in Hawaii: a sociolinguistic history to 1935.** Ed. Stanley M. Tsuzaki. Honolulu: Univ of Hawaii Pr., 1969.
Breaks ground for the study of both the Creole and the colonial English dialect now rapidly fading from the islands.

33.77 Shuy, Roger. **Discovering American dialects.** Champaign, Ill.: National Council of Teachers of English, 1967.

33.78 Turner, Lorenzo D. **Africanisms in the Gullah dialect.** Chicago: Univ. of Chicago Pr., 1949.
The first serious study of Gullah by a scholar with modern linguistic training.

33.79 Williamson, Juanita V., and Virginia M. Burke, eds. **A various language: perspectives on American dialects.** New York: Holt, Rinehart, and Winston, 1971.
An anthology of scholarly articles concerned with the history and scope of dialect studies. An appendix lists a selection of dissertations on the subject.

33.80 Wood, Gordon R. **Vocabulary change: a study of variation in regional words in eight of the southern states.** Carbondale: Southern Illinois Univ. Pr., 1971.
Based on a list of words collected in Alabama, Arkansas, Florida, Georgia, Louisiana, Mississippi, Oklahoma, and Tennessee.

See also **26.5, 33.32.**

Bilingualism

33.81 **Fishman, Joshua A. Yiddish in America: socio-linguistic description and analysis.** Indiana Univ. Research Center in Anthropology, Folklore, and Linguistics Publ. 36. International Journal of American Linguistics, 31, No. 2, Part 2 (1965).

33.82 **Haugen, Einar. Bilingualism in the Americas: a bibliography and research guide.** Publication of the American Dialect Society No. 26. University: Univ. of Alabama Pr., 1956.

This fundamental study has been updated in Haugen's "Bilingualism Language Contact and Immigrant Languages in the United States: A Research Report, 1956–1970," in Sebeok, Marckwardt, et al., *Current Trends in Linguistics: Linguistic Trends in North America,* vol. 10, The Hague: Mouton, 1973.

33.83 **Haugen, Einar. The Norwegian language in America.** 2 vols. Philadelphia: Univ. of Pennsylvania Pr., 1953. 2d ed. 2 vols. in 1. 1969.

33.84 **Viereck, Wolfgang. "German dialects in the United States and Canada and problems of German-English contact . . . : a bibliography."** Orbis. [Publ. in Louvain.] 16 (1967), 549–68.

Amplifies Haugen, 1956 et seq., 33.83. See also Viereck's supplement in *Orbis,* 17 (1968). (Because German-speaking people were present in many areas and strata of American society, a study of "double dialect geography" with reference to German is helpful in sorting out American regional speech.) See also Glenn Gilbert, *Linguistic Atlas of Texas German,* Austin: Univ. of Texas Pr., 1972; and Carroll A. Reed and Lester W. Seifert, *A Linguistic Atlas of Pennsylvania German,* Marburg an der Lahn: Becker, 1954.

See also 33.72–73.

Names

33.85 **Sealock, Richard B., and Pauline A. Seely. Bibliography of place name literature: United States and Canada.** 3d ed. Chicago: American Library Assoc., 1982.

Supplements appear as needed in *Names: Journal of the American Name Society,* Pottsdam: State Univ. of New York, 1953–, a journal which deals with personal names and names of characters in literary works; not confined to the U.S.

33.86 **Shankle, George E. American nicknames, their origin and significance.** New York: H. W. Wilson, 1937. 2d ed. 1955.

33.87 **Smith, Elsdon C. New dictionary of American family names.** New York: Harper and Row, 1972.

A semipopular compilation originally published in 1956 under the title *Dictionary of American Family Names.*

33.88 Stewart, George R. **American place-names: a concise and selective dictionary for the continental United States of America.** New York: Oxford Univ. Pr., 1970.

A useful work of sound scholarship; includes a bibliography.

33.89 Stewart, George R. **Names on the land: a historical account of place-naming in the United States.** 4th ed. San Francisco, Calif.: Lexicos, 1982.

Emphasis is put on the process whereby places were named. The 4th ed. is a reprint of the 3d (Boston: Houghton Mifflin, 1967) but includes a new introduction and a bibliography of Stewart's works.

See also **33.24.**

34. *Folklore*

34.1 Flanagan, Cathleen C., and John T. Flanagan. **American folklore: a bibliography, 1950–1974.** Metuchen, N.J.: Scarecrow Pr., 1977.

Over 3,000 entries predominantly on North American folklore with some attention to Mexico and the Caribbean islands.

34.2 Haywood, Charles. **A bibliography of North American folklore and folksong.** New York: Greenberg, 1951. 2d ed. 2 vols. New York: Dover, 1961.

Indexed by state, region, race, occupation, etc. The bibliographies of local sources are immensely useful to students of the literature of the various states and regions. Incomplete in certain areas, such as Afro-American lore, and occasionally unreliable.

34.3 **Internationale volkskundliche Bibliographie [International folklore bibliography].** Bonn: R. H. Habelt, 1939/41–.

Issued irregularly 1939–1954; biennially 1955–. Sponsored by the International Commission on Folklore under the French name, Commission Internationale des Arts et de Traditions Populaires, to 1971, and afterwards Société Internationale d'Ethnologie et de Folklore. This is the most complete serial bibliography, though often a few years late in its recording. More current and almost as complete is the *MLA International Bibliography* though there are many areas in it to consult besides the special section on comparative literature.

34.4 Abrahams, Roger, and George Foss, eds. **Anglo-American folksong style.** Englewood Cliffs, N.J.: Prentice-Hall, 1968.

Textbook introducing analysis and interpretation of the words and music of American folksongs. See also 29.93 and 29.94.

34.5 Baughman, Ernest W. **Type and motif-index of the folktales of England and North America.** The Hague: Mouton, 1966.

Includes 13,083 variants of types and motifs, most of them American.

34.6 **Botkin, Benjamin A., ed. A treasury of American folklore: stories, ballads, and traditions of the people.** New York: Crown, 1944.

An anthology similar to those which Botkin has edited on both city and regional folklore. See also the field-collected texts in Dorson, *Buying the Wind,* 34.10, which are more scholarly and offer more authentic texts than Botkin.

34.7 **Brunvand, Jan Harold. The study of American folklore: an introduction.** New York: W. W. Norton, 1968. 2d ed. 1978.

An elementary but useful textbook that surveys the genres, using American examples; provides good introduction to current theory and methods; thorough, discursive notes guide further research.

34.8 **Dorson, Richard M. American folklore.** Chicago: Univ. of Chicago Pr., 1959. Rev. ed. 1977.

The chief general survey from colonial times to the present. Dorson's *American Folklore and the American Historian,* same publ., 1971, theorizes on differing uses of oral and printed sources. See also *Handbook of American Folklore,* Bloomington: Indiana Univ. Pr., 1983, edited by Dorson, which includes his preface and sixty-eight essays by folklorists on a wide range of methodologies and subjects.

34.9 **Dorson, Richard M. American Negro folktales.** Greenwich, Conn.: Fawcett Publ., 1967.

A combination of field-collected texts and annotations that provide comparative remarks and index numbers for types of motifs and tales. An invaluable selection of materials which serves as an introduction to collections and analyses of Afro-American folklore in many genres is found in *Mother Wit from the Laughing Barrel,* ed. Alan Dundes, Englewood Cliffs, N.J.: Prentice-Hall, 1973. See also 34.23.

34.10 **Dorson, Richard M. Buying the wind: regional folklore in the United States.** Chicago: Univ. of Chicago Pr., 1964.

An exemplary presentation of field-collected texts in a variety of genres, with scholarly annotations. See also Greenway, 34.16, and Botkin, 34.6.

34.11 **Dorson, Richard M. Land of the millrats.** Cambridge, Mass.: Harvard Univ. Pr., 1981.

A study of urban American folklore.

34.12 **Edmonson, Munro S. LORE: an introduction to the science of folklore and literature.** New York: Holt, Rinehart, and Winston, 1971.

A consideration of "the primitive field from which literary patterns are derived"; emphasis is placed on analogical systems of thought and connotative meaning.

34.13 **Folk music: a selection of folk songs, ballads, dances, instrumental pieces, and folk tales of the United States and Latin America: catalog of phonograph records.** Rev. ed. Washington, D.C.: Library of Congress, 1964.

Compiled under the auspices of the Archive of American Folk Song, Library of Congress, which is the chief repository of American songs and ballads. Lists 166 disks with 1,240 titles representative of the more than 16,000 records in the Archive of American Folk Song (now Folk Culture). A more recent and shorter catalog was issued (1978?) under the title *Folk Recordings Selected from the Archive of Folk Song.*

34.14 Funk and Wagnalls standard dictionary of folklore, mythology and legend. Ed. Maria Leach. 2 vols. New York: Funk and Wagnalls, 1949–1950. Reissued "with minor corrections." 1972.

Includes 8,000 entries on motifs, tales, genres, countries, regions, peoples, etc.; surveys articles by specialists. See also *Folklore Research around the World: A North American Point of View,* ed. Richard M. Dorson, Bloomington: Indiana Univ. Pr., 1961, also published as vol. 74, no. 294 (Oct.–Dec. 1961) of *Journal of American Folk-Lore.*

34.15 Glassie, Henry. Patterns in the material folk culture of the eastern United States. Philadelphia: Univ. of Pennsylvania Pr., 1968.

Indispensable, though the extensive bibliography is rapidly becoming out of date.

34.16 Greenway, John, ed. Folklore of the great West. Palo Alto, Calif.: American West Publ. Co., 1969.

Selections from the *Journal of American Folk-Lore* with commentary by Greenway. The best single-volume sampling of western American folklore. See also B. A. Botkin, ed., *A Treasury of Western Folklore,* New York: Crown, 1951.

34.17 Journal of American folk-lore. Washington, D.C.: American Folklore Soc., 1888– .

Prior to 1964 supplements, appearing in April, contained a bibliography of international folklore. An analytical index covering the contents of this journal appeared in 1958, by Tristram P. Coffin.

34.18 Laws, G. Malcolm, Jr. Native American balladry: a descriptive study and a bibliographical syllabus. Philadelphia: American Folklore Soc., 1950. Rev. ed. 1964.

A broad study of autochthonous American balladry according to origin, subject matter, distribution, and variations in form, narrative method, and historical accuracy. Laws distinguishes "native American" ballads from imported ones, but those which he discusses are not American Indian songs or poems. A very useful bibliographical syllabus, pp. 114–243, offers references to recordings and scholarship on individual ballads, and a general bibliography appears on pp. 267–270 (page nos. refer to first ed.).

34.19 Paredes, Americo, and Richard Bauman, eds. Toward new perspectives in folklore. Austin: Univ. of Texas Pr., 1972.

Important essays covering current theories and methods related to issues such as defining folklore, genres, contextual studies, style, and performance.

34.20 Puckett, Newbell Niles, comp. Popular beliefs and superstitions: a compendium of American folklore. Ed. Wayland D. Hand et al. Boston: Twayne/G. K. Hall, 1981.

Comprises about 36,000 entries on many aspects of life from 87 ethnic groups.

34.21 Rosenberg, Bruce A.   The code of the West. Bloomington: Indiana Univ. Pr., 1982.
Traces popular western legends to their origins and discusses their significance in relation to American culture as a whole.

34.22 Southern folklore quarterly. Gainesville: Univ. of Florida Pr., 1937–.
March issues contain annual bibliographies, covering principally North and South America. (Other folklore journals of the U.S. include *New York Folklore Quarterly* and *Western Folklore*. Texas Folklore Society Publications is a series of volumes. Indiana University publishes a *Journal of the Folklore Institute* as well as a monograph series.)

34.23 Thompson, Stith.   Motif-index of folk-literature. 6 vols. Bloomington: [Indiana Univ. Pr.,] 1932–1936. 2d rev. ed. 1976.
Classifies "narrative elements" in folk tales, ballads, myths, etc. See also 34.9.

34.24 Toelken, Barre.   The dynamics of folklore. Boston: Houghton Mifflin, 1979.
Complements Brunvand, 34.7, and organizes its material around principles current since that introductory study was originally published in 1968.

See also **15.46–47, 24.19, 26.6, 31.12, 31.35, 31.47, 31.54, 34.12.**

35. *Comparative and general literature*

35.1 Baldensperger, Fernand, and Werner P. Friederich.   Bibliography of comparative literature. Chapel Hill: Univ. of North Carolina Pr., 1950.
The most comprehensive bibliography of its subject. American literature as a source of influence is treated on pp. 668–81. Supplements enlarging or bringing this work nearer to date appear annually in *Yearbook of Comparative and General Literature*, same publ., 1952–1960, and Bloomington: Indiana Univ. Pr., 1961–. See also the appropriate sections of the annual *MLA International Bibliography*, 20.2.

35.2 Conover, Helen F.   Current national bibliographies. Washington, D.C.: Library of Congress, 1955.
Lists works which record the current output of books and periodicals in various individual countries, from Algeria to Yugoslavia.

35.3 Elkins, A. C., Jr., and L. J. Forstner, eds.   The Romantic movement bibliography, 1936–1970. Foreword by David V. Erdman. Ann Arbor, Mich.: Pierian Press, 1973.
A master cumulation from *ELH, Philological Quarterly,* and *English Language Notes*.

35.4 **Meyers Handbuch über die Literatur.** Mannheim: Bibliographische Institut, 1964. 2d ed. 1970.
Bio-bibliographical sketches of authors from various countries, including the U.S.

35.5 **Pownall, David E. Articles on twentieth century literature: an annotated bibliography, 1954 to 1970.** 7 vols. Milwood, N.Y.: Kraus-Thomson Organization, 1973–1980.
Cumulates "Current Bibliography" from the journal *Twentieth Century Literature* and adds material from other sources. American literature is only a part of the coverage.

35.6 **Von Wilpert, Gero. Lexikon der Weltliteratur.** 2d ed. 2 vols. Stuttgart: A. Kröner, 1975.
A bio-bibliographical handbook with about 9,000 articles listed. Includes more than 300 entries on American literature. Originally published in 1950, edited by Heinz Kindermann and Margarete Dietrich.

35.7 **Wortman, William A. A guide to serial bibliographies for modern literatures.** New York: Modern Language Assoc., 1982.
A guide to current bibliographies in literature and related nonliterary fields.

35.8 **American Comparative Literature Association newsletter.** Binghamton, N.Y.: State Univ. of New York, 1972–.

35.9 **Arcadia. Zeitschrift für vergleichende Literaturwissenschaft.** Berlin: Walter de Gruyter und Co., 1966–.
Issued three times a year. Text chiefly in German but occasionally in English, French, Spanish, and Italian.

35.10 **Block, Haskell M. Nouvelles tendances en littérature comparée.** Paris: A.-G. Nizet, 1970.
Papers from a conference held at the universities of Lund, Uppsala, and Utrecht.

35.11 **Cassell's encyclopaedia of world literature.** Rev. ed. 3 vols. New York: Morrow, 1973.
Vol. 1 includes histories and general articles; vols. 2 and 3 are biographical.

35.12 **Clements, Robert J. Comparative literature as academic discipline: a statement of principles, praxis, standards.** New York: Modern Language Assoc., 1978.
A comprehensive exposition of comparative literature as an academic discipline with reference to procedures and expectations for a department.

35.13 **Comparative literature.** Eugene: Univ. of Oregon Pr., 1949–.
The earliest American journal in its field; "issued occasionally."

35.14 **Comparative literature studies.** Urbana: Univ. of Illinois Pr., 1963–.
Has a special interest in European literary relations with both South and North America; issued quarterly.

35.15 **Dizionario biographico degli autori di tutti i tempi [formerly Dizionario letterario Bompiani].** Milan: V. Bompiani, 1970.

Very extensive and elaborately illustrated dictionary of world literature. General terms, like *expressionism* and *symbolism,* are defined; important works are outlined; a limited group of literary characters are sketched; and a considerable number of authors are provided with biographical accounts. Works synopsized are alphabetized according to the Italian translations of their titles. A French adaptation is available in the following: *Dictionnaire des oeuvres de tous les temps et tous les pays,* 5 vols., Paris: S.E.D.E., 1952–1968; *Dictionnaire des personnages littéraires et dramatiques de tous les temps et de tous les pays,* Paris: S.E.D.E., 1960.

35.16 **Eppelsheimer, Hanns W. Handbuch der Weltliteratur.** 3d ed. Frankfurt a.M.: V. Klostermann, 1960.

Covers beginnings through the 18th century; then surveys various national literatures for the 19th century and 20th century separately.

35.17 **Escarpit, Robert. Sociologie de la littérature.** Paris: Presses Universitaires de France, 1958. 6th ed. 1978.

35.18 **Etiemble, René. The crisis of comparative literature.** Trans. Georges Joyaux and Herbert Weisinger. East Lansing: Michigan State Univ., 1966.

An important statement about the methodology of comparative literature, this study was originally published in Paris as *Comparaison n'est pas raison: la crise de la littérature* in 1963. It is one of numerous responses to M. Guyard's controversial *La Littérature comparée,* 35.28.

35.19 **Fleischmann, Wolfgang Bernard. Encyclopedia of world literature in the 20th century.** 3 vols. New York: Ungar Publ. Co., 1967–1971.

A translation and expansion of a standard German work. Includes bibliographies. A 4th volume, 1975, ed. F. Ungar and L. Mainiero, includes a supplement and index.

35.20 **Frauwallner, Erich, et al. Die Weltliteratur.** 3 vols. Vienna: Brüder Hollinek, 1951–1954. Supplement. 1968.

Encyclopedia covering earliest times to 1951; articles on national literatures, literary forms, eminent authors; alphabetically arranged. The bibliographies sometimes help pick up stray works on American authors published in Europe, especially in Austria.

35.21 **Frenzel, Elisabeth. Stoff- und Motivgeschichte.** Berlin: E. Schmidt, 1966. 2d ed. 1974.

Contains a good bibliography.

35.22 **Friederich, Werner P. The challenge of comparative literature and other addresses.** Ed. William J. DeSua. Chapel Hill: Univ. of North Carolina Pr., 1970.

Essays on programmatic and methodological concerns as well as literary problems from an historical—*geistesgeschichte*—viewpoint, all by Friederich.

35.23 **Friederich, Werner P., ed. Comparative literature: proceedings of the Second Congress of the International Comparative Literature Association.** 2 vols. Chapel Hill: Univ. of North Carolina Pr., 1959.

Vol. 2 contains many papers concerned with European-American literary relations.

35.24　**Friederich, Werner P., and David Henry Malone. Outline of comparative literature from Dante Alighieri to Eugene O'Neill.** Chapel Hill: Univ. of North Carolina Pr., 1954.
An elementary but neat outline, with emphasis on literary influence.

35.25　**Gassner, John, and Edward Quinn, eds. The reader's encyclopedia of world drama.** New York: Crowell, 1969.
Almost a hundred scholars, chiefly Americans, contributed to this volume. The longer articles are supplied with bibliographies.

35.26　**Gifford, Henry. Comparative literature.** New York: Humanities Pr., 1969.
A description of the character and purposes of comparative literary studies in broad terms. The author is concerned with translations and with the "Transatlantic character of modern literary experience."

35.27　**Guillén, Claudio. Literature as system: essays toward the theory of literary history.** Princeton, N.J.: Princeton Univ. Pr., 1971.
Essays by a distinguished comparatist on a structuralist approach to literary study.

35.28　**Guyard, Marius-François. La Littérature comparée.** Paris: Presses Universitaires de France, 1951. 6th rev. ed. 1978.
A controversial approach to the methodology of comparative literature that has evoked many varying responses.

35.29　**Highet, Gilbert. The classical tradition: Greek and Roman influences on western literature.** New York: Oxford Univ. Pr., 1949. Rev. ed. 1967.

35.30　**Index Translationum . . . : International bibliography of translation.** Paris: Institute International de Cooperation Intellectuelle, 1933–.
Cooperating nations report translations of books to UNESCO, which periodically issues this list. The record is incomplete.

35.31　**Jeune, Simon. Littérature generale et littérature comparée: essai d'orientation.** Paris: Lettres Modernes, 1968.

35.32　**Jost, François. Essais de littérature comparée.** Vol. I. Helvetica. Fribourg, Switz.: Editions Universitaires, 1964. Vol. 2. Europeana. First Series. Fribourg and Urbana: Editions Universitaires and Univ. of Illinois Pr., 1968.
Four essays representing literary criticism as an international enterprise.

35.33　**Jost, François. Introduction to comparative literature.** Indianapolis, Ind.: Pegasus, 1974.
Includes a bibliography, pp. 305–310.

35.34　**Levin, Harry. Refractions: essays in comparative literature.** New York: Oxford Univ. Pr., 1966.

35.35　**McGraw-Hill encyclopedia of world drama: an international reference work.** 4 vols. New York: McGraw-Hill, 1972.

Chiefly biographical sketches of about 900 authors of plays. A "complete" chronology of scripts is provided for 300 deemed "major."

35.36 **Nichols, Stephen G., and Richard B. Vowles, eds. Comparatists at work: studies in comparative literature.** Waltham, Mass.: Blaisdell, 1968.

An anthology of essays which attempts to demonstrate the nature of the discipline by showing how comparatists work. Essays are concerned with literary-critical methodology, the role of literature in the history of ideas, and the interaction of literature and the arts.

35.37 **Olbrich, Wilhelm, ed. Der Romanführer.** Stuttgart: Hiersemann, 1950– 1971.

Digests of novels and stories; first volumes cover Germany, in particular, and various other European countries. North America, up to 1900, enters in vol. 7.

35.38 **Prawer, S[iegbert] S. Comparative literary studies: an introduction.** New York: Barnes and Noble, 1973.

A defense of comparative literature that shows its significant work "on the detail as well as the overall contours of the literary map." A good review of the field, its problems, and its methodology, especially for beginning students.

35.39 **Revue de littérature comparée.** Paris: Didier Erudition, 1921–1940, 1947–.

Each issue through January–March 1960 contains a bibliography of its subject, including latterly a special section on North American influences. The text is in various languages.

35.40 **Rhein, Phillip H., and Hans Joachim Schulz, eds. Comparative literature: the early years.** Chapel Hill: Univ. of North Carolina Pr., 1973.

A collection of essays by writers from Goethe to Croce exemplifying methods of comparing literatures from different times and places.

35.41 **Tamkang review: comparative studies between Chinese and foreign literatures.** Taipei, Taiwan: Tamkang Coll. of Arts and Sciences, 1970–.

Text in English. Issued semiannually. See also *Tamkang Journal*, same publ., 1958–; issued annually.

35.42 **Wakeman, John, ed. World authors 1950–1970.** New York: H. W. Wilson, 1975.

A companion volume to Kunitz and Haycraft, 11.21. Almost a thousand authors are added, "most of whom came into prominence between 1950 and 1970." About half of the sketches are supplied by the authors themselves. Americans continue to preponderate.

35.43 **Weisstein, Ulrich. Comparative literature and literary theory: survey and introduction.** Trans. William Riggan. Bloomington: Indiana Univ. Pr., 1973.

Originally published in German as *Einführung in die vergleichende Literaturwissenschaft,* Stuttgart: Kohlhammer, 1968. An excellent survey of methodology and history; "the first systematically conceived and historically as well as theoretically oriented survey of the field." Comparative literature is interpreted as a specialized branch of literary history and theory which lacks a methodology of its own.

35.44 **World literature today [formerly Books abroad].** Norman: Univ. of Oklahoma Pr., 1927–.

Issued quarterly; formerly *Books Abroad*. See 32.2.

35.45 **Wrenn, C. L.** **The idea of comparative literature.** Cambridge, England: [Modern Humanities Research Assoc.,] 1968.

A basic statement about the nature of comparative literature as an academic discipline. The author excludes from his definition studies "emphasizing independent trends" and stresses linguistic knowledge.

35.46 **Yearbook of comparative and general literature.** Bloomington: Indiana Univ. Pr., 1952–.

Published from 1952–1960 by the Univ. of North Carolina Pr.

See also **2.1, 2.26, 19.34, 22.44–46, 27.15, 29.43–56, 29.95, 32.1, 32.3–5, 32.44, 34.3, 34.23.**

Appendix: Principal biographies of *135* American authors

Although only one study is listed for most of the following authors, in certain instances we have provided two. This has been done either where a recent biographer with access to new information about the subject has added significantly to our knowledge of the life without altogether superseding the major earlier biography, or where the two most important biographical studies may be contemporary but complementary rather than redundant. Where no significant full-length biography exists for an author, we have listed the best available general bio-critical study to serve as a convenient starting point for researchers.

Adams, Henry. Samuels, Ernest. *The Young Henry Adams*. Cambridge, Mass.: Harvard Univ. Pr., 1948. *Henry Adams: The Middle Years*. Same publ., 1958. *Henry Adams: The Major Phase*. Same publ., 1964.

Aiken, Conrad. Hoffman, Frederick J. *Conrad Aiken*. New York: Twayne, 1962.

Alcott, Amos Bronson. Shepard, Odell. *Pedlar's Progress: The Life of Bronson Alcott*. Boston: Little, Brown, 1937.

Alcott, Louisa May. Stern, Madeleine B. *Louisa May Alcott*. Norman: Univ. of Oklahoma Pr., 1950.

Allen, James Lane. Knight, Grant C. *James Lane Allen and the Genteel Tradition*. Chapel Hill: Univ. of North Carolina Pr., 1935.

Anderson, Sherwood. Howe, Irving. *Sherwood Anderson*. New York: William Sloane Assoc., 1951.

Barlow, Joel. Woodress, James L. *A Yankee's Odyssey: The Life of Joel Barlow*. Philadelphia, Pa.: Lippincott, 1958.

Bellamy, Edward. Bowman, Sylvia E. *The Year 2000: A Critical Biography of Edward Bellamy*. New York: Bookman Assoc., 1958.

Benét, Stephen Vincent. Fenton, Charles A. *Stephen Vincent Benét: The Life and Times of an American Man of Letters, 1898–1943*. New Haven, Conn.: Yale Univ. Pr., 1958.

Berryman, John. Haffenden, John. *The Life of John Berryman*. Boston: Routledge & Kegan Paul, 1982.

Bierce, Ambrose. Fatout, Paul. *Ambrose Bierce: The Devil's Lexicographer*. Norman: Univ. of Oklahoma Pr., 1951.

Bird, Robert Montgomery. Foust, Clement E. *The Life and Dramatic Works of Robert Montgomery Bird*. New York: Knickerbocker Pr., 1919.

Boker, George Henry. Bradley, Edward Sculley. *George Henry Boker: Poet and Patriot*. Philadelphia: Univ. of Pennsylvania Pr., 1927.

Brackenridge, Hugh Henry. Newlin, Claude Milton. *The Life and Writings of Hugh Henry Brackenridge*. Princeton, N.J.: Princeton Univ. Pr., 1932.

Bradford, William. Smith, Bradford. *Bradford of Plymouth.* Philadelphia, Pa.: Lippincott, 1951.

Bradstreet, Anne. White, Elizabeth W. *Anne Bradstreet: "The Tenth Muse."* New York: Oxford Univ. Pr., 1971.

Brown, Charles Brockden. Clark, David Lee. *Charles Brockden Brown: Pioneer Voice of America.* Durham, N.C.: Duke Univ. Pr., 1952.

Bryant, William Cullen. Brown, Charles H. *William Cullen Bryant: A Biography.* New York: Charles Scribner's Sons, 1971.

Buck, Pearl. Harris, Theodore F. *Pearl S. Buck: A Biography.* 2 vols. New York: John Day, 1969–1971.

Byrd, William. Marambaud, Pierre. *William Byrd of Westover, 1674–1744.* Charlottesville: Univ. Pr. of Virginia, 1971.

Cable, George Washington. Turner, Arlin. *George W. Cable: A Biography.* Durham, N.C.: Duke Univ. Pr., 1956.

Cahan, Abraham. Pollock, Theodore Marvin. "The Solitary Clarinetist: A Critical Biography of Abraham Cahan, 1860–1917." Diss. Columbia Univ. 1959.

Cather, Willa. Woodress, James. *Willa Cather: Her Life and Art.* New York: Pegasus, 1970.

Chesnutt, Charles W. Heermance, J. Noel. *Charles W. Chesnutt: America's First Great Black Novelist.* Hamden, Conn.: Archon, 1974.

Chopin, Kate. Seyersted, Per. *Kate Chopin: A Critical Biography.* Baton Rouge: Louisiana State Univ. Pr., 1969.

Clark, Walter Van Tilburg. Westbrook, Max. *Walter Van Tilburg Clark.* New York: Twayne, 1969.

Clemens, Samuel Langhorne. Ferguson, DeLancey. *Mark Twain: Man and Legend.* Indianapolis, Ind.: Bobbs-Merrill, 1943. And: Paine, Albert Bigelow. *Mark Twain: A Biography.* 3 vols. New York: Harper & Brothers, 1912.

Cooper, James Fenimore. Grossman, James F. *James Fenimore Cooper.* New York: William Sloane Assoc., 1949.

Cotton, John. Ziff, Larzer. *The Career of John Cotton: Puritanism and the American Experience.* Princeton, N.J.: Princeton Univ. Pr., 1962.

Crane, Hart. Unterecker, John. *Voyager: A Life of Hart Crane.* New York: Farrar, Straus & Giroux, 1969.

Crane, Stephen. Stallman, R[obert] W[ooster]. *Stephen Crane: A Biography.* New York: G. Braziller, 1968.

Crèvecoeur, Hector St. Jean de. Crèvecoeur, Robert de. *Saint John de Crèvecoeur: Sa vie et ses ouvrages (1735–1813).* Paris: Librairie des Bibliophiles, 1883. And: Mitchell, Julia Post. *St. John de Crèvecoeur.* New York: Columbia Univ. Pr., 1916.

Cummings, E. E. Kennedy, Richard S. *Dreams in the Mirror: A Biography of E. E. Cummings.* New York: Liveright, 1980.

Dana, Richard Henry, Jr. Shapiro, Samuel. *Richard Henry Dana, Jr.: 1815–1882.* East Lansing: Michigan State Univ. Pr., 1961.

De Forest, John William. Light, James F. *John William De Forest.* New York: Twayne, 1965.

Dickinson, Emily. Sewall, Richard B. *The Life of Emily Dickinson.* 2 vols. New York: Farrar, Straus & Giroux, 1974.

Doolittle, Hilda. Robinson, Janice S. *H.D.: The Life and Work of an American Poet.* Boston: Houghton Mifflin, 1982.

Dos Passos, John. Ludington, Townsend. *John Dos Passos: A Twentieth Century Odyssey.* New York: E. P. Dutton, 1980.

Douglass, Frederick C. Huggins, Nathan I. *Slave and Citizen: The Life of Frederick Douglass.* Boston: Little, Brown, 1980.

Dreiser, Theodore. Swanberg, W. A. *Dreiser.* New York: Charles Scribner's Sons, 1965.

Dwight, Timothy. Silverman, Kenneth. *Timothy Dwight.* New York: Twayne, 1969.

Edwards, Jonathan. Winslow, Ola E. *Jonathan Edwards, 1703–1758: A Biography.* New York: Macmillan, 1940.

Eliot, T. S. Spender, Stephen. *T. S. Eliot.* New York: Viking, 1975, 1976.

Emerson, Ralph Waldo. Allen, Gay Wilson. *Waldo Emerson: A Biography.* New York: Viking, 1981. And: Rusk, Ralph L. *The Life of Ralph Waldo Emerson.* New York: Charles Scribner's Sons, 1949.

Farrell, James T. Branch, Edgar M. *James T. Farrell.* New York: Twayne, 1971.

Faulkner, William. Blotner, Joseph. *Faulkner: A Biography.* 2 vols. New York: Random House, 1974.

Fitzgerald, F. Scott. Bruccoli, Matthew J. *Some Sort of Epic Grandeur: The Life of F. Scott Fitzgerald with a Genealogical Afterword by Scottie Fitzgerald Smith.* New York: Harcourt, Brace, Jovanovich, 1981.

Franklin, Benjamin. Clark, Ronald W. *Benjamin Franklin: A Biography.* New York: Random House, 1983. And: Van Doren, Carl. *Benjamin Franklin.* New York: Viking, 1938.

Frederic, Harold. O'Donnell, Thomas F., and Hoyt C. Franchere. *Harold Frederic.* New York: Twayne, 1961.

Freeman, Mary E. Wilkins. Foster, Edward. *Mary E. Wilkins Freeman.* New York: Hendricks House, 1956.

Freneau, Philip. Axelrad, Jacob. *Philip Freneau: Champion of Democracy.* Austin: Univ. of Texas Pr., 1967. And: Leary, Lewis. *That Rascal Freneau: A Study in Literary Failure.* New Brunswick, N.J.: Rutgers Univ. Pr., 1941.

Frost, Robert. Thompson, Lawrance. *Robert Frost.* 3 vols. New York: Holt, Rinehart and Winston, 1966–1976.

Fuller, Henry Blake. Bowron, Bernard R., Jr. *Henry B. Fuller of Chicago: The Ordeal of a Genteel Realist in Ungenteel America.* Westport, Conn.: Greenwood Pr., 1974.

Fuller, Margaret. Blanchard, Paula. *Margaret Fuller: From Transcendentalism to Revolution.* New York: Delacorte Press and Seymour Lawrence, 1978. And: Wade, Mason. *Margaret Fuller: Whetstone of Genius.* New York: Viking, 1940.

Garland, Hamlin. Holloway, Jean. *Hamlin Garland: A Biography.* Austin: Univ. of Texas Pr., 1960.

Glasgow, Ellen. Godbold, E. Stanly, Jr. *Ellen Glasgow and the Woman Within.* Baton Rouge: Louisiana State Univ. Pr., 1972.

H.D. See **Doolittle, Hilda.**

Harris, Joel Chandler. Cousins, Paul M. *Joel Chandler Harris: A Biography.* Baton Rouge: Louisiana State Univ. Pr., 1968.

Harte, Francis Bret. Stewart, George R., Jr. *Bret Harte: Argonaut and Exile.* Boston and N.Y.: Houghton Mifflin, 1931.

Hawthorne, Nathaniel. Mellow, James R. *Nathaniel Hawthorne in His Times.*

Boston: Houghton Mifflin, 1980. And: Turner, Arlin. *Nathaniel Hawthorne: A Biography*. New York: Oxford Univ. Pr., 1980.

Hearn, Lafcadio. Stevenson, Elisabeth. *Lafcadio Hearn*. New York: Macmillan, 1961.

Hemingway, Ernest. Baker, Carlos H. *Ernest Hemingway: A Life Story*. New York: Charles Scribner's Sons, 1969.

Henry, O. See **Porter, William Sydney.**

Holmes, Oliver Wendell. Tilton, Eleanor M. *Amiable Autocrat: A Biography of Dr. Oliver Wendell Holmes*. New York: Henry H. Schuman, 1947.

Howe, Edgar Watson. Pickett, Calder M. *Ed Howe: Country Town Philosopher*. Lawrence: Univ. Pr. of Kansas, 1968, 1969.

Howells, William Dean. Cady, Edwin H. *The Road to Realism: The Early Years, 1837–1885, of William Dean Howells*. Syracuse, N.Y.: Syracuse Univ. Pr., 1956. *The Realist at War: The Mature Years, 1885–1920, of William Dean Howells*. Same publ., 1958.

Hughes, Langston. Dickinson, Donald C. *A Bio-bibliography of Langston Hughes, 1902–1967*. Preface by Arna Bontemps. 2d ed., rev. Hamden, Conn.: Archon, 1972.

Irving, Washington. Williams, Stanley T. *The Life of Washington Irving*. 2 vols. New York: Oxford Univ. Pr., 1935.

James, Henry. Edel, Leon. *Henry James*. 5 vols. Philadelphia, Pa.: Lippincott, 1953–1972.

Jeffers, Robinson. Carpenter, Frederic I. *Robinson Jeffers*. New York: Twayne, 1962.

Jewett, Sarah Orne. Frost, John E. *Sarah Orne Jewett*. Kittery Point, Me.: Gundalow Club, 1960.

Kennedy, John Pendleton. Bohner, Charles H. *John Pendleton Kennedy: Gentleman from Baltimore*. Baltimore, Md.: Johns Hopkins Univ. Pr., 1961.

Kerouac, Jack. McNally, Dennis. *Desolate Angel: Jack Kerouac, the Beat Generation, and America*. New York: Random House, 1979.

Lanier, Sidney. Stark, Aubrey Harrison. *Sidney Lanier: A Biographical and Critical Study*. Chapel Hill: Univ. of North Carolina Pr., 1933.

Lardner, Ring. Elder, Donald. *Ring Lardner: A Biography*. Garden City, N.Y.: Doubleday, 1956.

Lewis, Sinclair. Schorer, Mark. *Sinclair Lewis: An American Life*. New York: McGraw-Hill, 1961.

Lindsay, Nicholas Vachel. Ruggles, Eleanor. *The West-Going Heart: A Life of Vachel Lindsay*. New York: Norton, 1959.

London, Jack. Sinclair, Andrew. *Jack: A Biography of Jack London*. New York: Harper and Row, 1977.

Longfellow, Henry Wadsworth. Longfellow, Samuel. *Life of Henry Wadsworth Longfellow*. 3 vols. Boston: Houghton Mifflin, 1891. And: Wagenknecht, Edward. *Henry Wadsworth Longfellow: Portrait of an American Humanist*. New York: Oxford Univ. Pr., 1966.

Lowell, Amy. Damon, S. Foster. *Amy Lowell: A Chronicle*. Boston and N.Y.: Houghton Mifflin, 1935.

Lowell, James Russell. Duberman, Martin. *James Russell Lowell*. Boston: Houghton Mifflin, 1966. And: Scudder, Horace Elisha. *James Russell Lowell: A Biography*. 2 vols. Boston and N.Y.: Houghton Mifflin, 1901.

Lowell, Robert. Hamilton, Ian. *Robert Lowell: A Biography*. New York: Random House, 1982.

McCullers, Carson. Carr, Virginia Spencer. *The Lonely Hunter: A Biography of Carson McCullers*. Garden City, N.Y.: Doubleday, 1975.

Marquand, John. Bell, Millicent. *Marquand: An American Life*. Boston: Little, Brown, 1979.

Mather, Cotton. Silverman, Kenneth. *The Life and Times of Cotton Mather*. New York: Harper & Row, 1984.

Melville, Herman. Howard, Leon. *Herman Melville: A Biography*. Berkeley: Univ. of California Pr., 1951. And: Leyda, Jay. *The Melville Log: A Documentary Life of Herman Melville, 1819–1891*. 2 vols. New York: Harcourt, Brace, 1951. Supplement. 1969.

Mencken, H. L. Bode, Carl. *Mencken*. Carbondale and Edwardsville: Southern Illniois Univ. Pr., 1969.

Millay, Edna St. Vincent. Gould, Jean. *The Poet and Her Book: A Biography of Edna St. Vincent Millay*. New York: Dodd, Mead, 1969.

Miller, Henry, Martin, Jay. *Always Merry and Bright: The Life of Henry Miller, An Unauthorized Biography*. Santa Barbara, Calif.: Capra Pr., 1978.

Norris, Frank. Walker, Franklin D. *Frank Norris: A Biography*. Garden City, N.Y.: Doubleday, Doran, 1932.

O'Connor, Flannery. Walters, Dorothy. *Flannery O'Connor*. Boston: Twayne, 1973.

O'Hara, John. MacShane, Frank. *The Life of John O'Hara*. New York: Dutton, 1980.

O'Neill, Eugene. Sheaffer, Louis. *O'Neill*. 2 vols. Boston: Little, Brown, 1968, 1973.

Page, Thomas Nelson. Page, Rosewell. *Thomas Nelson Page: A Memoir of a Virginia Gentleman*. New York: Charles Scribner's Sons, 1923.

Paine, Thomas. Hawke, David Freeman. *Paine*. New York: Harper and Row, 1975.

Parker, Theodore. Commager, Henry Steele. *Theodore Parker*. Boston: Little, Brown, 1936.

Parkman, Francis. Wade, Mason. *Francis Parkman: Heroic Historian*. New York: Viking, 1942.

Patchen, Kenneth. Smith, Larry B. *Kenneth Patchen*. Boston: Twayne, 1978.

Paulding, James Kirke. Herold, Amos L. *James Kirke Paulding: Versatile American*. New York: Columbia Univ. Pr., 1926.

Poe, Edgar Allan. Quinn, Arthur Hobson. *Edgar Allan Poe: A Critical Biography*. New York: Appleton-Century, 1941.

Porter, Katherine Anne. Givner, Joan. *Katherine Anne Porter: A Life*. New York: Simon and Schuster, 1982.

Porter, William Sydney. Langford, Gerald. *Alias O. Henry: A Biography of William Sidney Porter*. New York: Macmillan, 1957.

Pound, Ezra. Heymann, C. David. *Ezra Pound, The Last Rower: A Political Profile*. New York: Viking, 1976. And: Norman, Charles. *Ezra Pound*. New York: Macmillan, 1960.

Ransom, John Crowe. Young, Thomas Daniel. *Gentleman in a Dustcoat: A Biography of John Crowe Ransom*. Baton Rouge: Louisiana State Univ. Pr., 1976.

Remington, Frederic. Samuels, Peggy, and Harold Samuels. *Frederic Remington: A Biography*. Garden City, N.Y.: Doubleday, 1982.

Robinson, Edwin Arlington. Hagedorn, Hermann. *Edwin Arlington Robinson: A Biography*. New York: Macmillan, 1938.

Roethke, Theodore. Seager, Allan. *The Glass House: The Life of Theodore Roethke*. New York: McGraw-Hill, 1968.

Sandburg, Carl. Callahan, North. *Carl Sandburg, Lincoln of Our Literature: A Biography*. New York: New York Univ. Pr., 1970.

Sewall, Samuel. Winslow, Ola E. *Samuel Sewall of Boston*. New York: Macmillan, 1964.

Simms, William Gilmore. Trent, William P. *William Gilmore Simms*. Boston: Houghton Mifflin, 1892.

Sinclair, Upton, Harris, Leon. *Upton Sinclair: American Rebel*. New York: Crowell, 1975.

Smith, John. Barbour, Philip L. *The Three Worlds of Captain John Smith*. Boston: Houghton Mifflin, 1964.

Stein, Gertrude. Brinnin, John Malcolm. *The Third Rose: Gertrude Stein and Her World*. Boston: Little, Brown, 1959. And: Mellow, James R. *Charmed Circle: Gertrude Stein & Company*. New York: Praeger, 1974.

Steinbeck, John. Benson, Jackson J. *The True Adventures of John Steinbeck, Writer*. New York: Viking, 1984.

Stevens, Wallace. Morse, Samuel French. *Wallace Stevens: Poetry as Life*. New York: Pegasus, 1970.

Stowe, Harriet Beecher. Wilson, Forrest. *Crusader in Crinoline: The Life of Harriet Beecher Stowe*. Philadelphia, Pa.: Lippincott, 1941.

Tarkington, Booth. Woodress, James. *Booth Tarkington: Gentleman from Indiana*. Philadelphia, Pa.: Lippincott, 1955.

Tate, Allen. Squires, Radcliffe. *Allen Tate: A Literary Biography*. New York: Pegasus, 1971.

Taylor, Bayard. Beatty, Richmond Croom. *Bayard Taylor: Laureate of the Gilded Age*. Norman: Univ. of Oklahoma Pr., 1936.

Taylor, Edward. Grabo, Norman S. *Edward Taylor*. New York: Twayne, 1961, 1967.

Thoreau, Henry David. Harding, Walter. *The Days of Henry Thoreau*. New York: Knopf, 1965.

Toomer, Jean. Benson, Brian Joseph, and Mabel Mayle Dillard. *Jean Toomer*. Boston: Twayne, 1980.

Tourgée, Albion W. Olsen, Otto H. *Carpetbagger's Crusade: The Life of Albion Winegar Tourgée*. Baltimore, Md.: Johns Hopkins Univ. Pr., 1965.

Trumbull, John. Cowie, Alexander. *John Trumbull: Connecticut Wit*. Chapel Hill: Univ. of North Carolina Pr., 1936.

Twain, Mark. See **Clemens, Samuel Langhorne.**

Tyler, Royall. Tanselle, G. Thomas. *Royall Tyler*. Cambridge, Mass.: Harvard Univ. Pr., 1967.

Very, Jones. Bartlett, William Irving. *Jones Very: Emerson's "Brave Saint."* Durham, N.C.: Duke Univ. Pr., 1942. And: Gittleman, Edwin. *Jones Very: The Effective Years, 1833–1840*. New York: Columbia Univ. Pr., 1967.

West, Nathanael. Martin, Jay. *Nathanael West: The Art of His Life*. New York: Farrar, Straus & Giroux, 1970.

Wharton, Edith.   Lewis, R. W. B. *Edith Wharton: A Biography*. New York: Harper & Row, 1975.

Wheatley, Phillis.   Graham, Shirley. *The Story of Phillis Wheatley*. New York: J. Messner, 1949.

Whitman, Walt.   Allen, Gay Wilson. *The Solitary Singer: A Critical Biography of Walt Whitman*. Rev. ed. New York: New York Univ. Pr., 1967.

Whittier, John Greenleaf.   Pickard, Samuel T. *Life and Letters of John Greenleaf Whittier*. 2 vols. Boston and N.Y.: Houghton Mifflin, 1894.   And: Pollard, John A. *John Greenleaf Whittier: Friend of Man*. Boston: Houghton Mifflin, 1949.

Wilder, Thornton.   Harrison, Gilbert A. *The Enthusiast: A Life of Thornton Wilder*. New York: Ticknor & Fields, 1983.

Williams, William Carlos.   Mariani, Paul. *William Carlos Williams: A New World Naked*. New York: McGraw-Hill, 1981.

Wilson, Edmund.   Paul, Sherman. *Edmund Wilson: A Study of Literary Vocation in Our Time*. Urbana: Univ. of Illinois Pr., 1965.

Winthrop, John.   Morgan, Edmund S. *The Puritan Dilemma: The Story of John Winthrop*. Boston: Little, Brown, 1958.

Wolfe, Thomas.   Nowell, Elizabeth. *Thomas Wolfe: A Biography*. Garden City, N.Y.: Doubleday, 1960.

Wright, Richard.   Fabre, Michel. *The Unfinished Quest of Richard Wright*. Trans. Isabel Barzun. New York: William Morrow, 1973.

Index of subjects

Abrams, M. H., 25.19
Abstracts: American history, 2.11, 9.25; American literature, 7.1; dissertation, 1.15; historical, 2.11, 9.6, 9.9; methodology of, 3.20; services available, 3.20; women's studies, 19.5, 19.12
Adam as symbol of America, 15.13, 15.27
Adams, Henry, 32.19, App.
Adams, John, 20.32
Adventure stories, 8.39
Advertising, 13.3
Aesthetics, 25.4, 25.17, 25.36
Aesthetic thought, 32.29
Afro-Americans. *See* Blacks
Agee, James, 24.64
Agrarianism, 15.48, 28.17
Aiken, Conrad, App.
Albee, Edward, 23.45
Alcott, Amos Bronson, 17.32, App.
Alcott, Louisa May, App.
Algren, Nelson, 24.70
Alienation, 28.17
Allen, James Lane, App.
Almanacs, 26.35–36
American civilization. *See* American studies
American English. *See* English language in U.S.
American Guide series, 30.1
American history: abstracts of, 2.11, 9.25; archives of, 9.18; articles abstracted, 2.11; articles on, 9.19–20; atlases and maps, 9.13, 9.15; bibliographies of, 9.1, 9.19–20, 9.26, 9.36; Civil War, 10.8, 15.22, 21.1; colonial, 14.2, 15.9, 27.1, 27.7–8, 27.37, 27.43–44; cultural, 2.18, 9.11, 9.20, 9.31, 9.44, 10.7, 10.40, 10.45, 19.14, 19.18; dissertations on, 9.6, 9.9; encyclopedias of, 9.12, 30.34; general tools for study, 2.14, 9.8, 9.11, 9.13–14, 9.17, 9.30, 9.44–45; historians of, 9.34–35, 9.37, 9.42, 9.48, 9.50, 9.52; historiography of, 2.13, 3.7, 3.12, 9.21–22, 9.33, 9.38–41, 9.43, 9.49–52; journals concerning, 9.25–29; manuscript

collections of, 9.2; maps of, 9.15; Revolutionary War, 27.26, 27.30, 27.36; social studies in, 2.21, 2.25, 9.27, 9.52, 10.5, 10.10, 10.16, 15.23, 15.28, 15.48; societies, 9.5, 9.7, 9.23–24, 9.50; special studies in, 9.3–4, 9.10, 9.46, 10.1–61; statistics, 9.16; of 20th century, 28.6–7. *See also* History
American imprints, 6.4, 6.6–10, 6.12–15, 6.17–20, 14.1–2, 14.25, 30.6
Americanisms, 33.20, 33.23, 33.25, 33.30, 33.32, 33.41. *See also* Linguistics; Speeches and oratory; Writing
American studies, 8.2, 8.5, 9.14–16, 8.23, 8.31; abroad, 8.1, 8.4, 8.7, 8.11, 8.24, 8.29–30, 8.32, 8.34–35, 8.52; methodology of, 8.5–6, 8.8, 8.12–13, 8.25; periodicals concerning, 8.26–35; sources for study of, 6.8, 6.15, 8.3–4, 8.8, 8.10, 8.19, 8.25, 8.33. *See also* Popular culture
American thought, 15.1–8, 15.16, 15.19, 15.23, 15.30, 15.32–33, 17.6; colonial, 15.9–10
American Writers series, 20.5
Anarchism, 12.24
Anderson, Sherwood, 20.9, 24.67, 24.70, 28.36, App.
Annuals, literary, 26.33–34
Anonyms, 3.16–17
Anti-Americanism, 32.67
Antislavery in literature, 29.34
Antinomianism, 18.37
Archetypal criticism, 25.21, 25.26
Architecture, 4.21, 9.11, 10.7, 23.78, 23.100
Archives, guides to, 1.14, 9.18, 19.1, 19.6, 20.3; use of, 3.5
Area linguistics. *See* Linguistic atlases; Linguistic geography
Aristotle, 32.180
Art, 1.2, 9.11, 10.7, 16.31; and literature, 2.26, 29.44–48
Articles, indexes to, 1.19
Asia, literary relations with, 32.6, 32.183

Comparative literature (*cont.*)
of, 35.1–3, 35.5–7, 35.21; biography in, 35.4, 35.6, 35.42; classical influences on, 35.29; dictionaries of, 35.15; encyclopedias on, 35.11, 35.19–20, 35.25, 35.35; handbooks of, 35.6, 35.16; history of, 35.40; methodology of, 2.1 2.26, 35.12, 35.18, 35.22, 35.28, 35.36, 35.38, 35.45; periodicals, 35.7–9, 35.13–14, 35.39, 35.44, 35.46; terms used in, 35.15; theory of, 35.27, 35.43; yearbooks on, 35.46

Computers: bibliographies on, 3.42; and collation, 3.38; and concordances, 3.30; essays on, 3.31–32; and historical research, 3.40; and the humanities, 1.32, 3.34–35; and linguistic research, 3.41. *See also* Cliometrics

Comstockery, 15.41

Concordance making, 3.30

Confederate states imprints, 30.24. *See also* Civil War; South

Confidence men: in literature, 29.24; language of, 33.40

Connecticut Wits, 27.17

Consciousness, history of, 16.12

Conservatism, 10.26, 15.40, 15.42

Constitution of U.S., 10.25, 27.26, 27.36

Cooper, James Fenimore, 18.52, 20.32, 21.10, 24.52, 27.20, 29.47, 29.88, 32.30, App.

Copyediting, 5.7, 14.6. *See also* Editing

Copyright, 5.13, 32.8

Cotter, Joseph, 31.51

Cotton, John, App.

Cozzens, James Gould, 22.24

Crane, Hart, 20.9, 20.32, 22.22, 22.45, 26.15, App.

Crane, Ronald, 25.19

Crane, Stephen, 24.41, 24.68, App.

Creativity, 16.31

Crèvecoeur, Hector St. Jean de, App.

Crime fiction, 29.18. *See also* Detective stories; Mystery stories; Suspense fiction

Critical realism, 17.25

Critical terms, 4.10, 4.18, 25.35. *See also* Literary terms

Criticism, 25.5–9, 25.13–24, 25.26–31, 25.34–35, 25.37, 25.45–49; aesthetics of, 25.4, 25.17, 25.36; bibliography on, 25.2–3, 25.36, 25.48, 29.43; deconstructionist, 25.22; European influence on, 25.3, 25.17; existentialism and, 25.26; formalism and, 25.29; historical studies of, 25.28, 25.32, 25.36, 25.44;

interdisciplinary, 25.1, 29.43; methodology of, 25.24, 25.26; and morality, 25.27, 25.31; and mythology, 25.38–43; New, 25.26, 25.33; New Humanist, 25.15; in New York, 25.12; and phenomenology, 25.26; pluralist, 25.19; poetic, 25.25; poststructuralist, 25.26; southern, 25.10; structuralist, 25.26; terms used in, 4.10, 4.18, 25.35

Critics' Circle Awards, 23.4

Cullen, Countee, 31.44

Cummings, E. E., 22.22, 28.15, 32.70, App.

Czechoslovakia, American literature in, 32.152

Daly, Augustin, 23.61

Dana, Richard Henry, Jr., App.

Dance, 4.21

Dante Alighieri, 32.117, 35.24

Darwinism, 24.47, 29.46, 29.50. *See also* Evolution; Science and technology

Data bases: in the humanities, 1.32

Data centers, 1.40

Dates: dictionary of, 1.24; in U.S. history, 9.3

De Voto, Bernard, 30.63

Debs, Eugene V., 12.24

Deconstructionism, 25.22

De Forrest, John William, App.

deMan, Paul, 25.26

Deism, 18.22

Democratic idealism, 15.26, 29.19

Depression, Great, 15.36, 23.64

Destiny, national, 15.19

Detective stories, 8.42, 8.44, 8.48–49, 8.52, 8.54, 29.18. *See also* Crime fiction; Mystery stories; Suspense fiction

Determinism, 29.37. *See also* Naturalism

Dewey, John, 17.6, 17.8, 17.13, 17.21

Dialects, 33.32, 33.66, 33.68–71, 33.75, 33.77, 33.79; black, 33.62–65, 33.78; Chicano, 33.72; German, 33.84; Hawaiian, 33.76; of New York City, 33.67; periodicals on, 33.73; southern, 33.80; western, 33.61, 33.80; Yiddish, 33.81

Diaries, 11.39–40, 19.56, 27.43–44. *See also* Autobiographies

Dickinson, Emily, 16.20, 20.32, 32.83, 32.123, App.

Dictionaries: American English, 33.31; bibliographies of, 1.41; compilation of, 3.30, 3.41, 33.6, 33.27; drama, 4.6; on historical principles, 33.22; literary terms,

Minorities. *See specific groups by name*
Minstrel shows, 23.99, 26.15
Mission, American idea of, 15.19
Missionaries, 18.16
Moby-Dick, 29.85, 29.92. *See also* Melville, Herman
Modernism in fiction, 24.78, 28.25
Moore, Marianne, 22.22, 22.27, 28.25
Morality, 15.27, 15.29, 25.27, 25.31
Motion pictures. *See* Film
Muckraking movement, 10.21, 12.26
Music: colonial, 27.30; ethnic, 8.19; influence of on literature, 2.29; influence of on poetry, 22.44, 22.46; musical comedy, 23.75, 23.93; popular, 23.75, 23.93; resources for study of, 8.19; terms used in, 4.21
Mystery stories, 8.39, 8.42, 29.18. *See also* Crime fiction; Detective stories; Suspense fiction
Myth, 34.14; Adamic, 15.13, 15.27, 29.32; American, 26.6; and symbolism, 16.9, 16.12; classical, 32.180, 35.29; heroic, 21.20; in vaudeville, 23.57; pastoral idea and, 15.15, 30.33; relations with literary study, 2.29, 25.1–2, 25.38–43; western, 30.56

Names: of persons, 11.22, 33.86–87; of places, 33.24, 33.85, 33.88–89
Nationalism, 10.32; in literature, 10.45, 29.28
Native Americans, 8.18, 8.22, 10.11, 10.56, 15.46; anthologies by and about, 31.3, 31.10, 31.91–92, 31.94–103; as authors and subjects, 31.1, 31.3, 31.82–84, 31.86; autobiographies of, 31.78, 31.86, 31.94; bibliography of, 10.55, 31.79, 31.81–84, 31.86; criticism by and about, 31.89, 31.93; culture of, 31.90, 31.95, 31.101; educational materials on, 31.87–88; Eskimo, 31.3; European religious influence on, 18.16; Hawaiian, 31.3, 33.76; literature of, 31.85, 31.94–95, 31.97–101; manuscripts by and about, 31.80; oratory of, 31.92; pictography of, 31.85; poetry of, 31.91, 31.96, 31.98, 31.100–103; as symbol, 10.53; women, 19.4, 31.99
Nativism, 10.32, 18.38
Natural history: essays on, 26.32
Naturalism, 15.12; in literature, 21.32, 21.39, 24.41, 24.62, 28.17, 29.36–39; scientific, 15.26. *See also* Determinism

Nature: in literature, 29.7, 29.11
Nautical terms, 29.82. *See also* Sea, literature of the
Naval literature. *See* Sea, literature of the
Neoclassicism, 21.12
New Criticism, 2.31, 25.26, 25.33, 28.17
New England. *See* Northeast
New England renaissance. *See* Transcendentalism
New Humanism, 25.14–15
New Left, 15.37. *See also* Communism; Left wing; Marxism; Radicalism
New Journalism, 24.94–95
New Netherland, literary culture in, 27.29
New Realism, 17.26
New York, 21.24; and criticism, 25.12; dialects of, 33.67; guide to studies on, 8.3, 30.8; newspapers, 13.12–13. *See also* Drama and theater
New York Daily Tribune, 13.13
New York Times, 11.2, 13.12
Newspapers, 3.5, 13.3; bibliography of, 13.5–7, 13.16; black, 13.6, 13.20; circulation of, 13.25; colonial, 13.25, 14.12; columnists for, 13.15; content of, 13.15; directories of, 13.1, 13.8, 13.17; frontier, 13.22; German-American, 13.2; history of, 13.5; indexes of, 13.4, 13.10, 13.12–13, 13.18; on microfilm, 13.14; syndicates of, 13.26; union lists of, 13.9, 13.11, 13.14. *See also* Journalism
Nietzsche, Friedrich Wilhelm, 32.76
Nonfiction novels, 24.94–95
Norris, Frank, 20.32, 24.41, 24.68, App.
Northeast, 30.10–13; linguistic geography of, 33.48–52, 33.57–58
Northwest: linguistic geography of, 33.59; literature of, 30.81–82. *See also* California; West
Norwegian language in America, 33.83
Novels. *See* Fiction

Oates, Joyce Carol, 24.58
Obituaries, 11.1–2
O'Connor, Flannery, 24.64, 24.77, App.
O'Hara, John, App.
Olson, Charles, 22.31
O'Neill, Eugene, 20.9, 23.45, 28.36, 32.123, 35.24, App.
Optimism, 29.6
Oral history, 3.6, 8.21, 9.10, 31.28
Oratory. *See* Speeches and oratory
Organizations, directories to, 1.19
Ozick, Cynthia, 31.62

Pacific Northwest. *See* Northwest; West

Page, Thomas Nelson, App.

Paine, Thomas, 17.6, App.

Painting and drawing: colonial, 27.30; landscape, 29.44–47; seascape, 29.95; terms used in, 4.21

Pamphlets, 1.37

Paperback books, 14.6, 14.20, 28.14

Papermaking, 14.32

Parent, Gail, 31.62

Paris Review: interviews in, 28.37

Parker, Theodore, App.

Parkman, Francis, 30.63, App.

Parodies, 26.8

Pastoral ideal, 15.15, 30.33

Patchen, Kenneth, App.

Paulding, James Kirke, App.

Peirce, Charles Sanders, 17.5, 17.7, 17.13, 17.21

Pennsylvania, early Quaker culture in, 27.33. *See also* Philadelphia

Percy, Walker, 28.21, 30.33

Periodicals: bibliography of, 12.1–3, 12.5, 12.8, 12.21, 20.15, 20.22, 20.26–27; black, 12.25; on drama and theater, 7.6, 23.30, 23.34, 23.36, 23.54, 23.60; history of, 12.1–2, 12.6, 12.16–19; indexes of, 7.5, 7.7–11, 7.13–14, 7.16, 12.4; radical, 12.24; science fiction, 29.59–60, 29.62, 29.65, 29.71; Transcendentalism, 12.16; union lists of, 12.9; women's, 19.8, 19.12–13. *See also* Little Magazines; Magazines; Newspapers; Serials

Pessimism. *See* Naturalism

Phenomenology, 2.22, 25.26

Philadelphia, 8.17; in fiction, 24.45; magazines of, 12.13; theater of, 23.72, 23.86, 23.96, 32.64

Philosophy, 17.2–3, 17.7, 17.10–11, 17.17; of American literature, 17.15, 17.25; of authors, 17.6–7; bibliographies of, 17.1, 17.16, 17.20; directories concerning, 17.16; of historical studies, 17.2, 17.4–6, 17.8–9, 17.12–14, 17.16–19, 17.21–26; and religion, 17.20. *See also* Transcendentalism

Phonetics, 33.42–46

Photoduplication, 3.26–28

Phrenology, 16.2

Pictorial histories, 9.36, 9.46

Picture books, 26.42

Plays. *See* Drama and theater

Pluralism, 25.19, 25.26

Poe, Edgar Allan, 16.20, 20.43, 21.10,

22.16, 24.52, 29.10, 29.32, 32.36, 32.123, App.

Poetry, 22.9, 22.12–17, 22.35, 22.43, 22.46; analytical studies of, 2.23, 4.15, 16.21; and music, 22.44, 22.46; and painting, 29.45; and religion, 18.51; and science, 22.45; anthologies of, 22.2, 22.19; Beat, 22.21; bibliographies on, 22.2, 22.25; black, 31.10–11, 31.39, 31.47–50; Chicano, 31.110; colonial, 22.4, 22.7, 27.39–42; critical theory of, 25.25; dictionaries of terms in, 4.9, 4.13; directories concerning, 22.1; dramatic, 23.39; explication of, 22.28; free verse, 22.38; handbooks to, 4.9, 4.13, 22.30; imagist, 22.20, 22.24; indexes to, 22.3, 22.8; literary histories of, 21.47, 22.10; Native American, 31.91, 31.96, 31.98, 31.100–103; prosody of, 22.6, 22.42; recordings of, 22.5; sea, 29.91; visionary, 22.11; terms used in, 4.9, 4.13; Transcendentalist, 17.33; of 20th century, 22.18–30, 22.32–34, 22.36–41, 22.43, 22.45, 28.11, 28.15, 28.30, 28.34; women's, 19.33, 19.42, 19.51, 19.53, 19.61, 22.26

Poland, literary relations with, 32.162–169

Political ideas, 10.16, 10.24, 15.6, 15.17–18, 15.24, 27.14, 29.29; of Whigs, 15.11

Political parties, 10.20, 10.24, 10.27

Political terms, 33.28

Popular culture, 8.31, 8.36–54, 29.27, 30.55. *See also* American studies

Porter, Katherine Anne, App.

Porter, William Sydney, 32.171, App.

Porter, William T., 26.20

Portraits, dictionary of, 9.4

Postmodernism, 29.53

Poststructuralism, 25.26

Pound, Ezra, 20.9, 22.22, 22.27, App.

Pragmatism, 15.12, 17.5, 17.21, 17.23

Preaching: in early New England, 18.32, 27.22

Pre-Raphaelites: American, 32.14

Printing, 3.2, 14.1, 14.31, 20.28; history of, 14.2, 14.13, 14.15, 14.17–18, 14.23, 14.28–29, 14.31; mechanics of, 14.10

Prison literature, 29.12

Private collections, 3.5

Prizes and awards, 5.5, 21.5. *See also* Critics' Circle Awards; Pulitzer Prizes

Progressive Era, 10.19, 10.26, 10.39

Proofreading, 5.7, 5.10

Prosody, 22.6, 22.42

Index of authors, editors, and compilers

Baron, Dennis E., 33.1
Baron, Salo W., 18.50
Barrett, C. Waller, 32.7
Barricelli, Jean-Pierre, 25.1
Barron, Neil, 29.69
Bartlett, William Irving, App. (Very)
Baruch, Gertrude, 32.72
Barzun, Jacques, 3.12
Basil, Bathe W., 29.82
Baskerville, Barnet, 26.22
Basler, Roy Prentice, 8.10, 29.2
Batchelder, Eleanor, 19.30
Battilana, Marilla, 32.114
Batty, Linda, 23.101
Bauer, Andrew, 3.15
Baughman, Ernest W., 34.5
Bauland, Peter, 32.73
Baum, Paull F., 4.9
Bauman, Richard, 34.19
Baumbach, Jonathan, 24.55
Baumol, William J., 23.43
Baushinger, Sigrid, 32.74
Baym, Max I., 25.4
Baym, Nina, 19.41
Beach, Joseph Warren, 24.56
Beach, Mark, 10.38
Beard, Charles A., 15.1
Beard, Mary R., 15.1
Beatty, Richmond Croom, App. (B. Taylor)
Beck, Horace, 29.93
Beckson, Karl, 4.3
Beers, Henry Putney, 9.1
Beitzinger, A. J., 15.17
Beja, Morris, 23.108, 24.57
Bell, Bernard W., 31.47
Bell, Michael Davitt, 29.3
Bell, Millicent, App. (Marquand)
Bell, Roseann P., 31.29
Bellamy, Joe David, 24.58
Benét, William Rose, 11.8
Benson, Brian Joseph, App. (Toomer)
Benson, Jackson J., App. (Steinbeck)
Bentley, Eric, 23.48
Béranger, Jean, 32.43
Bercovitch, Sacvan, 15.18, 18.30, 27.2–3
Bergstrom, Len V., 19.31
Berkhofer, Robert F., Jr., 2.4, 10.53
Bernard, Harry, 30.2
Bernard, Jessie, 10.1
Bernard, Luther L., 10.1
Bernhardt, William F., 22.3
Bernstein, Theodore M., 5.1
Berry, G. G., 2.17
Berthoff, Rowland, 15.28

Berthoff, Warner, 21.5, 28.8
Besterman, Theodore, 1.7
Biblowitz, Iris, 19.37
Bickman, Martin, 16.20
Bier, Jesse, 26.2
Bigsby, C. W. E., 31.30
Billias, George A., 9.30
Billington, Ray Allen, 9.2, 10.15, 10.50–51, 18.38
Binkley, Wilfred T., 10.20
Blair, Walter, 26.3–6
Blake, Fay M., 24.15
Blanchard, Paula, App. (M. Fuller)
Blanck, Jacob, 20.7, 20.17, 26.40
Blasing, Mutlu Konuk, 11.33
Blassingame, John, 10.58
Blau, Joseph L., 18.49–50
Block, Haskell M., 35.10
Bloom, Harold, 16.21
Bloomingdale, Judith, 32.135
Blotner, Joseph, 24.59, App. (Faulkner)
Bluestone, George, 23.109
Blum, Eleanor, 13.3
Blumenthal, Henry, 32.44
Blumenthal, Joseph, 14.13
Bode, Carl, 8.37, 10.36, 29.4, App. (Mencken)
Boehm, Eric, H., 9.25
Bogan, Louise, 22.18
Bogard, Travis, 23.90
Bogardus, Ralph F., 28.9
Bohner, Charles H., App. (Kennedy)
Boitani, Piero, 31.32
Boller, Paul F., Jr., 17.6, 17.30
Bone, Robert A., 31.45
Bonin, Jane F., 23.4
Bontemps, Arna, 31.41
Boorstin, Daniel J., 9.31–32
Booth, Wayne, 25.19
Borchers, Hans, 32.75
Borges, Jorge Luis, 21.6
Boring, Edwin G., 16.1, 16.7–8
Bostwick, Prudence, 30.68
Botkin, Benjamin A., 34.6, 34.16
Bowden, Henry Ward, 18.16
Bowe, Forrest, 32.45
Bowen, Catherine D., 3.10
Bowen, William G., 23.43
Bowers, David F., 10.28
Bowers, Fredson, 2.5, 3.1
Bowles, Edmund A., 3.31
Bowman, Sylvia E., App. (Bellamy)
Bowman, Walter Parker, 4.6
Bowron, Bernard R., Jr., App. (H. Fuller)

Wentworth, Harold, 33.26, 33.32
Werkmeister, William H., 17.25
West, Dorothy H., 23.13
West, Ray B., Jr., 24.92, 30.69
Westbrook, Arlen Runzler, 19.63
Westbrook, Max, 30.64, App. (Clark)
Westbrook, Perry D., 19.63, 30.13
Westfall, Alfred Van Rensselaer, 32.35
Wetherill, Peter M., 2.32
Whicher, George F., 21.40
Whicher, Stephen E., 32.185
Whipple, T. K., 28.36
White, Barbara Anne, 19.36
White, Carl M., 1.39
White, Elizabeth W., App. (Bradstreet)
White, George Leroy, Jr., 32.189
White, Morton G., 15.32, 17.26
Whitehill, Walter M., 9.24
Whiteman, Maxwell, 31.26
Whiting, Bartlett J., 33.29
Whitlow, Roger, 31.27
Wickes, George, 32.70
Wiebe, Robert H., 10.19
Wiener, Philip P., 25.36
Wiesel, Elie, 10.14
Wilbur, Earl M., 18.45
Wilbur, Richard, 30.7
Williams, Jerry T., 30.27
Williams, Kenny J., 26.18, 28.16
Williams, Neville, 1.24
Williams, Stanley T., 32.191, App. (Irving)
Williams, William Appleman, 15.38
Williamson, Jane, 19.10
Williamson, Juanita, 33.79
Wilmes, Douglas M., 27.38
Wilmeth, Don B., 8.53, 23.41
Wilson, Arthur Herman, 23.96
Wilson, Douglas L., 25.15
Wilson, Edmund, 21.48–49, 30.80
Wilson, Forrest, App. (Stowe)
Wilson, Garff B., 23.97–98
Wilson, Harold S., 12.26
Wilson, John F., 18.9, 18.14
Wimsatt, William K., Jr., 25.18, 25.37
Wing, Donald G., 6.19–20
Winks, Robin W., 8.54, 9.34
Winn, James Anderson, 22.46
Winner, Viola Hopkins, 24.29
Winslow, Ola E., App. (Edwards, Sewall)
Wisbey, R. A., 3.41
Wise, Gene, 8.16, 9.51

Wish, Harvey, 9.52, 15.33
Wisse, Ruth, 31.74
Witt, Shirley Hill, 31.103
Wittenberg, Philip, 5.13
Wittington, Jennifer, 22.5
Wittke, Carl F., 10.35, 23.99
Wolf, Martin L., 4.21
Wood, Gordon R., 33.80
Wood, Gordon S., 27.36
Wood, James Playsted, 12.27
Woodbridge, I. Riley, 17.18–19
Woodress, James, 20.40–43, 24.10, App.
  (Barlow, Cather, Tarkington)
Woodward, C. Vann, 10.49
Wordell, Charles B., 33.40
Wortman, William A., 20.44, 35.7
Wrenn, C. L., 35.45
Wright, Andrew, 20.1
Wright, Austin M., 24.93
Wright, Conrad, 18.46–47
Wright, Frances V., 30.82
Wright, John Kirtland, 9.13
Wright, Louis B., 27.37
Wright, Lyle H., 24.14
Wroth, Lawrence C., 14.17, 14.29
Wyld, Lionel D., 8.25
Wynar, Bohdan S., 1.3
Wynkoop, Sally, 1.22

Yannella, Donald J., 27.38
Yates, Norris W., 26.19–20
Youden, W. W., 3.42
Young, Harold C., 1.40
Young, James O., 31.39
Young, Margaret L., 1.40
Young, Thomas Daniel, 30.40, App.
  (Ransom)
Young, William C., 23.42, 23.100
Yule, G. Udny, 2.33

Zabel, Morton D., 25.3
Zasurski, Yasen N., 32.178
Zaturenska, Marya, 22.23
Zaunmüller, Wolfram, 1.41
Zechlin, Egmont, 8.1
Ziff, Larzer, 21.50, App. (Cotton)
Zöld, Magdolna, 32.161
Zolla, Elémire, 32.128
Zsuffa, Garbriella, 32.160
Zulauf, Sander W., 22.8
Zuther, Gerhard H. W., 32.112